# PROSE MODELS

## CANADIAN, AMERICAN, AND BRITISH ESSAYS FOR COMPOSITION

### GERALD LEVIN
*University of Akron*

### GERALD LYNCH
*University of Ottawa*

### DAVID RAMPTON
*University of Ottawa*

Harcourt Brace Jovanovich, Canada
Toronto  Orlando  San Diego  London  Sydney

Copyright © 1989
Harcourt Brace Jovanovich Canada Inc.

**Canadian Cataloguing in Publication Data**

Levin, Gerald, 1929–
Prose models

Includes index.
ISBN 0-7747-3123-0

1. College readers.     2. English language — Rhetoric.
I. Rampton, David, 1950–   .    II. Lynch, Gerald,
1953–   .   III. Title.

PE1417.L48 1989     808'.0427     C88-094661-X

Publisher: David Dimmell
Acquisitions Editor: Heather McWhinney
Developmental Editor: Donna Adams
Publishing Services Manager: Karen Eakin
Editorial Co-ordinator: Liz Radojkovic
Editorial Assistant: Graeme Whitley
Copy Editor: June Trusty
Cover and Interior Design: Michael Landgraff
Typesetting and Assembly: Vellum Print & Graphic Services Inc.
**Printing and Binding**: Metrolitho Inc.

Printed in Canada

2 3 4 5     93 92 91 90

# PREFACE

This first Canadian edition of *Prose Models* is based on Gerald Levin's seventh American edition, with Canadian material replacing approximately half the original essays. In our selection of new material we have followed the original editor's practice regarding sampling of writers and disciplines, variety of models, and introductions to each section. Our edition, like Levin's, presents examples of writing from various disciplines: literature, science, history, autobiography, and journalism.

As in previous editions, this Canadian edition of *Prose Models* contains numerous models for composition and detailed discussion of the sentence, the paragraph, and the essay. The book gives a thorough presentation of the personal, the expository, and the persuasive essay, and introduces inductive and deductive reasoning through interesting and accessible essays.

The present edition contains the following elements:

• An explanatory note to the student discussing the relationship between reading and writing and the general uses of the book.

• Introductions to each part relating the topics to the student's own writing.

• Earlier editions included separate sections on the paragraph and the essay. These have been conflated and streamlined, though within each section there is a rough progression from shorter to longer pieces.

• Part 1, "Methods of Organization," focusses attention immediately on the coherence of the whole essay.

• Part 2, "Methods of Development," comprises the traditional rhetorical modes.

• Part 3, "Matters of Style," deals with tone, figurative language, and faulty diction. Three essays in which writers discuss their craft and a section on writing effective sentences conclude this section.

Each essay contains a headnote that usually provides a few details about the author and information about the essay or the context of an excerpt. Questions and suggestions for writing follow all selections except the supplementary essays on writing.

In an essay on composition, Mark Twain refers to the "model-chamber" in the head of the writer — a store of effective sentences gathered from many kinds of reading. As important as such models are, the student writer should also be reminded of Stephen Leacock's dictum: "Writing is thinking." These statements express the philosophy of this book. Student writers need to understand the methods of prose composition, and must learn to think clearly. But these methods alone cannot teach the skills developed in the composition course. Students must see these methods in practice. Although discussion of the writing process and exercises in invention enhance writing skills, analysis and discussion of a wide selection of readings are essential.

In choosing the selections, we have looked not only for instructive models but also for interesting and challenging readings. Many of the readings are similar in theme though different in approach and treatment. For example, the essays of Sir John A. Macdonald, Hugh MacLennan, and Margaret Atwood attempt to explore and define various aspects of Canadian political and social life. Eric Nicol, Harry Bruce, and Erika Ritter provide examples of a lighter, more colloquial approach to their subjects. Norman Mailer and Norman Cousins on boxing, Stephen Leacock, Eric Sevareid, and John Kenneth Galbraith on small-town life, even E.B. White and Cam Stirling on "elevator travel" — all offer different perspectives and opportunities for comparison and contrast.

The following Canadian writers are new to *Prose Models*: Barbara Amiel, Margaret Atwood, Debra Black, Bob Blackburn, Harry J. Boyle, Harry Bruce, June Callwood, Danielle Crittenden, Robertson Davies, William Deverell, Terence Dickinson, T.C. (Tommy) Douglas, Ken Dryden, John Ferguson, Allan Fotheringham, Northrop Frye, Robert Fulford, John Kenneth Galbraith, George Galt, George Grant, Roderick Haig-Brown, Michael Ignatieff, Martin Kitchen, Joy Kogawa, Michele Landsberg, Margaret Laurence, Stephen Leacock, Charles Long, Sir John A. Macdonald, Hugh MacLennan, Fredelle Maynard, Robert McGhee, Alice Munro, Eric Nicol, Mordecai Richler, Erika Ritter, Gary L. Saunders, Arthur Schafer, Walter Stewart, Cam Stirling, David Suzuki, Charles Taylor, Guy Vanderhaeghe, and Richard B. Wright. The following American and British writers are also new to this edition: Martin Amis, Wendell Berry, Joan Didion, Thomas Henry Huxley, Sir James Jeans, Desmond Morris, Alexander Petrunkevitch, Gloria Steinem, and Barbara Tuchman.

We owe an enormous debt of gratitude to Gerald Levin. We would also like to thank Heather McWhinney, our editor at Harcourt Brace Jovanovich, Canada for her enthusiasm and helpful suggestions; Liz Radojkovic, editorial co-ordinator; June Trusty, copy editor; the reviewers selected by HBJ: Joanne Buckley (University of Western Ontario), Nan Johnson (University of British Columbia), Marianne Micros (University of Guelph), Tom G. Middlebro' (Carleton University), and Karen C. Ogden (University of Manitoba); Julie Sévigny Roy and our colleagues in the Department of English at the University of Ottawa for their advice and encouragement; and our families for their sacrifice of the time — much of it vacation time — that we spent away from them while working on *Prose Models*.

# TO THE STUDENT: HOW TO USE THIS BOOK

The readings in this book are examples of effective writing by Canadian, American, and British authors. They show how various writers have chosen to organize and build their sentences, paragraphs, and essays. They do not, however, represent every kind of effective writing, nor are they "models" in the sense that they represent the best and only ways to write essays. Rather, they constitute a repertory of choices available to you in practising and refining your own writing skills.

Although the reading, study, and discussion of paragraphs and essays are not the whole process of writing, they are indispensable, for you learn to write as you learn to speak — by reading and listening to the words of others. Thus, in drafting and revising your own essays, you will have many opportunities to return to your reading and perhaps discover new ways to build and develop your ideas.

The lists of vocabulary words contain unfamiliar words as well as many that you use every day. These familiar words are singled out because the author of the reading uses them in a special or unusual way. Often you will recognize the general meaning of a word, but you will need your dictionary to discover a subtler meaning that the author has in mind. In preparing these essays for class discussion, you will gain the most from the reading if you keep a dictionary at hand and check the meanings of these words and others about which you are doubtful.

The readings in this book have been selected to help you draw on your personal experiences and observations in writing your own essays. You will discover that many of the selections connect in theme or point of view. The expository and argumentative essays — many dealing with important issues in our time — offer an opportunity for you to work out your own ideas and to bring your experience to bear on the issue.

In your reading, you probably have noticed that a particular writer often writes similar types of sentences, favours certain expressions or ways of phrasing ideas, or builds paragraphs and essays in the same way. The word *style* describes this recurrent quality in a writer. Though still connected for many people with what is "correct" or proper in writing (style for the eighteenth-century writer Jonathan Swift was "proper words in proper places"), style refers commonly to the individual choices in diction and sentence construction as well as organization. It is in this sense that people refer to a "Hemingway style" in fiction or a "Woody Allen style" in the movies.

However, probably much of what we describe as style in speaking and writing is not a matter of choice at all. One writer may favour long, heavily co-ordinated sentences, as in the speech of a non-stop talker. Another person, used to speaking in clipped sentences, may write in very short sentences or very short paragraphs. Your writing is governed strongly by habits that develop as you grow up. Habits of speech strongly influence how you write, though written communication requires more attention to such matters as sentence structure, punctuation, and the organization of the whole essay.

You do have control, then, over your writing. Though you will continue to speak and write in ways natural to you, you can make your writing more expressive and effective. The more writing you do, the more aware you will become of your own habitual choices. As your awareness increases, you will have the opportunity to experiment with new ways of writing — as college and university give you the opportunity to think about new ideas in new ways. The discovery and mastery of your own style of writing and thinking is one important purpose of this book.

# PUBLISHER'S NOTE TO INSTRUCTORS AND STUDENTS

This textbook is a key component of your course. If you are the instructor of this course, you undoubtedly considered a number of texts carefully before choosing this as the one that will work best for your students and you. The authors and publishers of this book spent considerable time and money to ensure its high quality, and we appreciate your recognition of this effort and accomplishment.

If you are a student, we are confident that this text will help you to meet the objectives of your course. You will also find it helpful after the course is finished, as a valuable addition to your personal library. So hold on to it.

As well, please do not forget that photocopying copyright work means the authors lose royalties that are rightfully theirs. This loss will discourage them from writing another edition of this text or other books, because doing so will simply not be worth their time and effort. If this happens, we all lose — students, instructors, authors, and publishers.

We want to hear what you think about this book, so please be sure to send us the stamped reply card that has been inserted at the end of the text. This will help us to continue publishing high-quality books for your courses.

# CONTENTS

## PART 2: METHODS OF DEVELOPMENT    81

### Description    83

### Narration    96

### Example    110

## Classification and Division   124

## Analogy   143

## Comparison and Contrast   156

## Definition   173

## Writers on Writing    314

## Writing Effective Sentences    323

# THEMATIC TABLE OF CONTENTS

## SCIENCE

## LANGUAGE

## POPULAR CULTURE

## CITY LIFE

## TECHNOLOGY AND CULTURE

# PART 1

## METHODS OF ORGANIZATION

# INTRODUCTION: METHODS OF ORGANIZATION

An essay can be defined as the explication of a thesis. Whether the essay argues in support of or against some proposition, explains the steps of some difficult process, or simply displays the humour of the writer on some whimsical subject, every essay contains a thesis; and that thesis is the essay's *raison d'être*, its purpose, its justification, which is to say, the justification for the writer's decision to write and consequently to make his demands upon the reader's time. The thesis of an essay may be stated forthrightly in its opening sentence, deployed as the concluding statement of the introductory paragraph, concealed until the end of the essay, or left implied. Student writers may do a great deal of thinking and planning before they begin to write and so be able to summarize their essay's central concerns in a thesis statement, or they may not discover the thesis of their essay until they have begun to write or until they finish the first draft of their essay. Different writers employ different methods. What is of prime importance is that the writer have something to say — an idea — and that the essay have a thesis which the reader can point to or infer and paraphrase. When the writer has a thesis and a first draft, then begins the next important task: revising and organizing the material to display the thesis to greatest advantage.

"Organization" refers both to the way in which the writer arranges his ideas and arguments in support of his thesis, and to the way in which the essay's structure facilitates the retention of those ideas and arguments. In this first part of the book, "Thesis and Unity" comes first because having a subject to explain or an argument to make, and developing it in paragraphs that cohere around a central idea, is the *sine qua non* of good writing. In "Order of Ideas" we explore the different ways in which such ideas and paragraphs can be organized within the essay itself. Devices used to create effective introductions, conclusions, and smooth transitions are dealt with in the third section, "Beginnings, Middles, and Endings."

# THESIS AND UNITY

The thesis of an essay is its central or controlling idea, the proposition or chief argument — the point of the essay. The topic sentence of a paragraph may be either a full or a partial statement of the controlling idea: the thesis is always a full statement of it.

Where the thesis appears depends largely on the audience. If we believe that the audience requires no introduction to the thesis — no background or explanation of the issue or important terms — we may state it in the first sentence. Many newspaper editorials begin with a statement of the thesis — a practice consistent with that of putting the important information in the opening sentences of a news story. Most essayists, by contrast, prefer to build to the thesis — stating it partially or fully in the introductory paragraphs, in company with an explanation of important terms and the issues to be discussed. William Zinsser gives such an explanation in the opening paragraph of "Simplicity":

> Clutter is the disease of American writing. We are a society strangling in unnecessary words, circular constructions, pompous frills and meaningless jargon. — William Zinsser, "Simplicity"

In the opening sentence of his second paragraph, Zinsser expands this statement to cover the specific concern of the essay — the importance of simplicity in writing:

> Who can understand the viscous language of everyday American commerce and enterprise . . .? — Zinsser, "Simplicity"

In later paragraphs he restates his thesis as he presents various evidence in support of it:

> But the secret of good writing is to strip every sentence to its cleanest components.
> Thinking clearly is a conscious act that the writer must force upon himself . . .
> Keep thinking and rewriting until you say what you want to say. — Zinsser, "Simplicity"

Zinsser introduces his thesis early in his essay and restates it throughout. If the thesis needs extensive background and discussion to be understood — or perhaps is so controversial that we will win our audience only by building to it slowly — we could put it at the end of the essay. In some essays we might not want to state the thesis at all, but rather let the reader draw conclusions from the details or facts we provide. In this case the thesis is said to be *implied*.

In reading an essay, we depend on the opening sentence of each paragraph to direct us from one idea to the next. As in the following paragraph from Margaret Atwood's essay on the Canadian North, the opening sentence (italicized here) sometimes directs us through a topic sentence or statement of the central idea:

> *Where is the north, exactly?* It's not only a place but a direction, and as such its location is relative: to the Mexicans, the United States is the north, to Americans, Toronto is, even though it's on roughly the same latitude as Boston . . . — Margaret Atwood, "True North"

Not all opening sentences state the central idea fully. Some state only the subject or topic of the paragraph — occasionally through a single word, as in this paragraph by Eric Sevareid:

> *Consolidation.* The nearby hamlets of Sawyer and Logan and Voltaire had their own separate banks and papers and schools in my days of dusty buggies and Model Ts marooned

in the snowdrifts. Now these hamlets are dying . . . — Eric Sevareid, "Velva, North Dakota" [italics added]

The subject or topic might also be introduced through a question that the remainder of the paragraph answers:

> *But now I must ask myself: Are they nearer to one another?* And the answer is no; yet I am certain that this is good. The shrinking of time and distance has made contrast and relief available to their daily lives. They do not know one another quite so well because they are not so much obliged to. . . . — Sevareid, "Velva, North Dakota" [italics added]

In paragraphs that open with a statement of the subject or topic, the central or topic idea may follow immediately, as in the paragraph just cited. In other paragraphs, details and explanatory statements may build to the central idea. Paragraphs of this latter sort sometimes generate suspense or a sense of climax, for the reader must wait for the central statement to gain the full impact of the paragraph. The paragraph is said to have an implied topic sentence when the details alone make the point; the central idea or generalization remains unstated.

The topic sentence is important in unifying the paragraph. A unified paragraph not only develops one idea at a time but also makes each idea and detail relevant to the topic idea. In a unified paragraph, the reader immediately sees the relation of ideas and details. A disunified paragraph, by contrast, seems disconnected, its ideas and details introduced without transition or apparent reason.

Most paragraphs develop one impression or idea fully, as a unit; the paragraphs presented and discussed in this section are of this type. Other paragraphs are transitional, as in this linking paragraph that asks questions to be answered in the remainder of the essay:

> So where in September, amid such common concerns, does the anxious writer, sitting perplexed under his September ash tree, turn in order to glimpse the magic bird of Christmas? For surely a thing so perennial can never be wholly absent at any season — appearances and feelings to the contrary? — Gary L. Saunders, "September Christmas"

Many paragraphs also serve as summaries, sometimes pinpointing the central impression, idea, or thesis of the essay:

> Canada today faces no Fort Sumter or *blitzkrieg*, but unless we soon make up our minds about our future relations with the United States, we will drift or be pushed into such a position that our nation will become a mere territorial expression of American aspirations — as Scotland is a territorial expression of England. — Hugh MacLennan, "Scotland's Fate, Canada's Lesson"

The following examples illustrate ways in which well-developed paragraphs and essays can be organized.

## EDWIN WAY TEALE

*Edwin Way Teale (1899–1980) wrote much about nature in numerous articles and books and was also a distinguished photographer. His discussion of country superstitions appears in his book,* Wandering Through Winter, *for which Teale received the Pulitzer Prize in 1965. The book is one in a series describing the seasons of the year in North*

*America. In his paragraph here, Teale develops a single idea through a series of unusual examples.*

## COUNTRY SUPERSTITIONS

[1]In the folklore of the country, numerous superstitions relate to winter weather. [2]Back-country farmers examine their corn husks — the thicker the husk, the colder the winter. [3]They watch the acorn crop — the more acorns, the more severe the season. [4]They observe where white-faced hornets place their paper nests — the higher they are, the deeper will be the snow. [5]They examine the size and shape and color of the spleens of butchered hogs for clues to the severity of the season. [6]They keep track of the blooming of dogwood in the spring — the more abundant the blooms, the more bitter the cold in January. [7]When chipmunks carry their tails high and squirrels have heavier fur and mice come into country houses early in the fall, the superstitious gird themselves for a long, hard winter. [8]Without any scientific basis, a wider-than-usual black band on a woolly-bear caterpillar is accepted as a sign that winter will arrive early and stay late. [9]Even the way a cat sits beside the stove carries its message to the credulous. [10]According to a belief once widely held in the Ozarks, a cat sitting with its tail to the fire indicates very cold weather is on the way.

**1**

## VOCABULARY

a. *paragraph 1:* spleen, superstitious, gird, credulous

## QUESTIONS

1. How do sentences 2 through 10 illustrate the topic sentence of the paragraph?

2. How does Teale remind us of his topic idea in later sentences?

3. What do these illustrations tell us about country life?

## WRITING ASSIGNMENTS

1. Describe a series of superstitions related to another season or to a particular acitivity. Build your paragraph to a conclusion about these superstitions.

2. Use one of the following statements, or a similar statement of your own, as the topic sentence of a paragraph. Develop it through a series of illustrations:

   a) Winter or summer, sports make special demands on participants or spectators.

   b) Riding the subway (or a similar activity) requires special skills.

   c) People have different driving habits.

# JOY KOGAWA

Joy Kogawa *was born in 1935 in Vancouver. She finished high school in Alberta and studied music and theology in Toronto. Her publications include four volumes of poetry, a children's book,* Naomi's Road, *and the novel* Obasan, *which has won a number of awards.*

# THE OLD HOUSE

1    The house is indeed old, as she is also old. Every home-made piece of furniture, each pot holder and paper doily is a link in her lifeline. She has preserved in shelves, in cupboards, under beds — a box of marbles, half-filled colouring books, a red, white and blue rubber ball. The items are endless. Every short stub pencil, every cornflakes box stuffed with paper bags and old letters is of her ordering. They rest in the corners like parts of her body, hair cells, skin tissues, tiny specks of memory. This house is now her blood and bones.

# VOCABULARY

a.  *paragraph 1:* doily, lifeline

# QUESTIONS

1. Kogawa builds to her central idea instead of starting the paragraph with it. How does the opening topic sentence introduce the subject and prepare the reader for the details that follow?

2. How do the details develop the central idea, stated in the final sentence?

3. Did Kogawa need to state the central idea, or could she have depended on the details to state it implicitly?

4. How is the paragraph appropriate as an illustration of the importance of ancestors and their sense of place?

# WRITING ASSIGNMENTS

1. Use Kogawa's paragraph as a model for a description of someone's bedroom. Describe the room for someone who has not seen it — building through a series of details to the central idea as Kogawa does.

2. Write a second paragraph describing a room from the point of view of a person seeing it for the first time. Let your details develop an idea; do not state it explicitly. Your details should be vivid enough and well enough organized to make the idea clear to your reader.

# GARY L. SAUNDERS

Gary L. Saunders *was born in Newfoundland in 1935. He received a degree in forestry from the University of New Brunswick in 1959 and a degree in fine arts from Mount Allison in 1965. He has published environmental guides, children's books, a memoir, and more than fifty essays in regional and national magazines. He writes that "September Christmas" was the result of "my frustration with trying to write a traditional Christmas piece — my seventh in as many years — for a traditional regional magazine while the world seemed to be falling about our ears."*

# SEPTEMBER CHRISTMAS

I write these words sitting outdoors in the morning sun at an old picnic table under an ash tree that is in full, slightly shopworn, leaf. I am supposed to be writing a Christmas piece. But as it is only the eighth of September, Christmas is far from my mind.     1

One of the quirks of magazine writing and publishing is that monthly magazines like this must work two or three months ahead — longer with special issues. For a writer this is ordinarily no problem. It's perfectly possible to put together in March a convincing piece on summer gardening, or to bang out a story on deer hunting between cold beers at the beach in August. But Christmas, unlike broccoli culture or deer stalking, is no ordinary thing.     2

And, as luck would have it, I seem to have picked a poor day and place. This particular September day seems laden with distractions. The sky, for instance. Seldom have I seen it wear such a shade of peacock blue. And it is remarkable, I think, how very white are the high cirrus streamers hung across its vault. For that matter it is remarkable how very golden is my golden retriever as he worries the bumblebees mumbling over their late summer shopping among the balsam blossoms. And the crabapples — it seems I have never seen the little scarlet Dolgos burn so bright.     3

Another distraction that follows naturally on these observations is the distraction of every country place — country chores. It has been well said that a garden is a job forever. I see that the onions need their spears bent down and their shoulders uncovered, to build bigger bulbs. I note too that the raspberry canes are whispering among themselves that I've been slow to prune this year, despite a good crop. Before I know it the Netted Gems will need digging, and after that the strawberries will want tucking in. And soon the firewood will have to be put under cover.     4

I would have been smarter to have stayed indoors at my desk, where I've things arranged so that the only window faces *away* from chores. Looking out, I can see only the lane, a bit of my neighbor's pasture, and a big sugar maple. Actually the maple has a serious crack that opens and closes in high winds. But that doesn't disturb me any more because I've already taken precautions, with cables and turnbuckles, to prevent its coming apart.     5

A further distraction, internal but never far below the surface, is the matter of the doings of the several offspring of my spouse and me, living their separate lives away from home this Monday, while their father is on vacation writing this, and their mother is on the telephone building community. The three youngest are at their desks in local schools, too busy coping with new teachers, new classmates and new topics to muse on Christmas. In southern Manitoba the eldest is probably squinting across miles of rippling blond grain from the cab of a dusty red combine, while a thousand miles westward his brother is     6 settling into university life again. And their sister is this very week travelling from Montreal to Togo, West Africa, following a dream. Will she think about Christmas at thirty-three degrees Celsius in the shade? Will the three offspring get home for the holidays this winter, or will this be our first Yuletide without them?

7    Below that level of consciousness are everyday concerns (too numerous and too mundane to bear repeating, except that they too conspire to crowd out thoughts of Christmas Future). Ironically, among them are the irritations of early Christmas advertising, portents of the onslaught to come. Already *National Geographic* has offered me "the perfect planner for you, your family, your friends." The fact is, we are already planning as hard as we can, and would prefer to leave Christmas unplanned — if we dared. And a book company advises me to "get a head start on your holiday preparations . . ." A head start? What is this, a race? Most folks I know are already running as fast as they can just to stay in one place. They certainly don't need head-starters out in front taunting them. That's why I always send my Christmas cards *after* Christmas.

8    So where in September, amid such common concerns, does the anxious writer, sitting perplexed under his September ash tree, turn in order to glimpse the magic bird of Christmas? For surely a thing so perennial can never be wholly absent at any season — appearances and feelings to the contrary? Like the grass it must surely have deep roots, roots deeper in the human heart than the memory of turkey and tinsel, deeper even than sentimental songs and a fat man in a red and white suit.

9    One wouldn't expect to find such magic in the media, especially not of late. One of the oppressive features of this September has been the blizzard of bad news — not just the steady rain from Africa and the Middle East, but now the gunning down of worshippers in an Istanbul synagogue, the brutal Pan Am hijacking massacre in Karachi, the Soviet cruise ship disaster, the Lake Nyos gas cloud that snuffed out hundreds of human and animal lives in Cameroon, the devastating drought in the American Southeast, two horrific jet crashes, and many more such calamities. These are dark and wintry times on Planet Earth.

10    And yet when humankind — Christians, Moslems, Jews and Hindus alike — celebrate our festivals of light and life, is it pure coincidence that we do it at the very season of the darkest day and the longest night, at the very time when, in the northern hemisphere at least, every summer songbird has fled and every garden blossom is a shrivelled husk? The words of American poet Emily Dickinson come to mind:

> Hope is the thing with feathers
> That perches in the soul,
> And sings the tune without the words . . .

11    One thinks of weary Second World War soldiers downing their rifles to clamber from their bloody trenches at that mystical season to hug the enemy for an interlude between the shouting of the guns.

12    Well, if blood and hurt make the best soil for this green thing called the Christmas spirit, then this year of Our Lord 1986 will not lack for blessing. We can be thankful that life in Canada is not so calamitous. If anything, our Christmas is in danger of suffocating under sheer largesse of material wealth. But we have our moments. Last year, on the afternoon of the Eve, I met a friend who hadn't had time to fetch a tree for his family. "Why not come right now and cut one on my woodlot?" I said. So we spent a pleasant hour tramping the woods and chatting until we saw the Right Tree.

13    In the mail a few days after Christmas came six poems he had written, including one which said in part:

The first morning
Of a rising joy
A shining roundness in the soul . . .
The glorious sun of eternal life.

Between my friend and Emily I think they have just about said it.

## VOCABULARY

a. *paragraph   3:* Dolgos

b. *paragraph   4:* Netted Gems

c. *paragraph   5:* turnbuckles

d. *paragraph 12:* largesse

## QUESTIONS

1. Where does Saunders state his thesis? Could he have better placed his thesis statement?

2. What details establish the writer's physical setting? Why does he feel it important to do that at the outset?

3. How do Saunders's "internal distractions" compare? In what order does he evoke them?

4. How do the lines quoted in paragraph 10 answer the message of the catalogue of horrors rehearsed in paragraph 9?

5. Do you believe that Saunders achieves the purpose intended in his account of writing in September an essay on Christmas? What other purposes might the same inventory of objects serve?

## WRITING ASSIGNMENT

Write a description of the objects and slogans associated with another holiday, perhaps Thanksgiving or Hallowe'en. Let your point of view and tone emerge through your details. Be as specific as you can in describing these objects and slogans.

## ROBERT MCGHEE

Robert McGhee *was born in 1941 and received his* B.A. *in Anthropology from the University of Toronto. He later completed his* Ph.D. *in Archeology at the University of Calgary. Dr. McGhee is now an archeologist with the Canadian Museum of Civilization, specializing in the Arctic. He first became interested in the Norse discovery of Canada when he found Norse artifacts in prehistoric Inuit villages. The following essay examines the Norse influence in northern Canada.*

# THE VIKINGS

1   The year 1837, a year of rebellion in the colonies of Upper and Lower Canada, saw the publication in Copenhagen of a book, *Antiquitates Americanae*, in which the Danish professor, Carl Christian Rafn, argued that two obscure Icelandic sagas provided evidence that Norse explorers had discovered North America 500 years before Columbus. Earlier scholars had proposed the same idea, but Rafn's publication was the first to find a large and interested audience. Translated into English and French, it quickly led to a hunt for Viking antiquities in North America. The search has continued for the past 150 years, intriguing historians, literary scholars, archeologists and laymen alike.

2   As in most scholarly hunts, this one turned up many false trails and unearthed much evidence that was mistaken or misunderstood. Most learned pursuits are carried out within the insulated confines of an academic discipline. The subject of the medieval Norse in North America, however, was largely played up in the press, where any discovery or claim of discovery roused keen public enthusiasm.

3   Several generations of Canadians and Americans have, in fact, been fascinated by Viking exploration in the New World, and hundreds of books and articles have been written, some of them by crackpots and confidence artists. Since the historical and literary data is so limited — two legendary stories and a few vague references in other ancient texts — archeology has been the main field of contention. A stone windmill built by a 17th-Century governor of Rhode Island has long been misinterpreted as a "Viking tower." In 1898, a stone slab with a message carved in the ancient Scandinavian runic alphabet was found by a Swedish immigrant farmer in Minnesota. The inscription was immediately denounced as a forgery, a view reinforced by 50 years of research. Nevertheless, the message, telling of a Viking expedition to Minnesota, survived in the public imagination; the Minnesota Vikings, a team in the National Football League, is an example.

4   Fake runic inscriptions, and similar pieces of phony or misjudged clues, have been reported from Maine to Oklahoma and Paraguay. The major Canadian contribution to this panoply of fraud has been the "Beardmore find" — an iron sword, axe and portions of a shield said to have been found in 1930 by a prospector in northwestern Ontario. The objects, recognized as genuine Viking-age Scandinavian weapons, were purchased by the Royal Ontario Museum. Unfortunately, these same weapons had been seen in the prospector's home long before the "discovery." It seems he had received them from a young Norwegian immigrant whose father was a collector of such material.

5   A generation ago, the scholarly search for New World Vikings appeared to be at an impasse. Few professionals were willing to join the hunt or risk their reputations by association with the mounting accumulation of deceit and exaggeration. No genuine archeological artifacts had been found in more than a century of searching. The few literary and historical records seemed to be mined out; all useful information in the Norse sagas had long ago been recognized, leaving only quibbles over the meanings of unclear terms and vague geographical descriptions. By the mid-20th Century we knew little more than Professor Rafn did in 1837.

6   The last 30 years, however, have produced a new wave of archeological discovery which has validated the literary documentation and brought new respect to the search for Vikings. Almost all of these new finds have been in Canada, suggesting that the medieval Norse did indeed reach the eastern shores of Canada, and that they may have visited the area over several centuries.

7   Christian Europe first became painfully aware of their heathen Scandinavian neighbours to the north in AD 793, when ship-borne raiders sacked the monastery at Lindisfarne in

northeastern England. During the following century, isolated Viking raids gradually developed into Norse armies that seized and occupied large areas of western Europe. In the east, Norse adventurers explored and traded as far as the Black Sea and Constantinople. But by the late 9th Century things had begun to go badly for the Norse, with military defeats in Europe and, at home, the attempt of King Harald Fairhair to unify Norway by suppressing the powers of local chiefs.

For many of these chiefs, the best solution to their problems lay in moving to another place. The most attractive land then lay in the almost uninhabited islands of the North Atlantic. For decades the Norse had occupied Ireland, living and intermarrying with the local people. Here they must have learned of the islands discovered by Irish monks, who for centuries had taken to the sea in their skin-covered *curraghs* (light, bowl-shaped boats) seeking solitude and an absence of temptation far from the haunts of men. These pious men had established small monastic communities on the Shetlands, Orkneys and Faroes, and by AD 800 were occupying Iceland during at least the summer months. Their isolation on these islands was not to last for long, as Norse settlers followed in their wake. When the Norse reached Iceland about AD 860, they recounted finding communities of monks who "went away" leaving religious books and other equipment that showed them to have been Irish. **8**

During the "settlement period" of Iceland, between about AD 870 and 930, immigrants flocked to the island. By the end of the period, the population was estimated to be 30,000 people. All of the useful land had now been taken, and adventurers or those who could not get along with their neighbours began to look elsewhere. **9**

Eric the Red's exploration of Greenland about AD 980 arose from such circumstances, and the immigrants who followed him to establish colonies on the southwestern coast of the island soon swelled the population to an estimated 3,000 people. For the next four centuries ships from Greenland, Iceland and northern Europe crossed and recrossed the North Atlantic, bringing immigrants, taking people on visits to the Old Country, and especially carrying the trade in ivory and furs on which the Greenland colonies depended for a livelihood. **10**

The Greenland settlements were only 800 kilometres from the Labrador coast of North America, and less than 500 kilometres, a little over two days' sailing, from Baffin Island. The Norse were excellent seamen with ships capable of extended ocean voyaging, yet they had only the most primitive methods of navigation, and ships could often survive storms only by running before them for days. The accounts of the period tell many stories of ships being storm-driven far from their intended course, and in such a situation it was inevitable that North America would be discovered by ships travelling between Greenland and Europe. **11**

This is exactly what happened, probably within a year or so of the founding of the Greenland settlements. According to *The Greenlanders' Saga*, the first sighting was by Bjarni Herjölfsson, who was blown far off course on his first voyage from Iceland to visit his family in Greenland. **12**

Bjarni's discoveries were followed a few years later, probably around AD 1000, by Leif Ericsson (son of Eric the Red), who visited and named three countries: Helluland, a rocky and barren land, probably Baffin Island; Markland, a low forested coast, almost certainly Labrador; and Vinland, where there was good grazing and timber, and where they even claim to have found the grapes for which Leif named the country. After wintering and exploring, Leif and his crew loaded a cargo of grapes and timber and sailed for Greenland. **13**

Leif's reports led to four voyages to Vinland over the next several years. The largest was led by an Icelander named Thorfinn Karlsefni who intended to settle a colony in Vinland, and whose son, Snorri, was reported to be the first European child born in the New World. During their three years in Vinland, Karlsefni's people explored and traded with **14** the indigenous people for furs. Eventually, however, their relations with the natives turned hostile and two battles ensued. Probably as a result of this opposition, the Norse abandoned their colony and sailed home.

15   A number of authentic artifacts of Norse origin have come from the remains of villages occupied by ancestral Inuit in Arctic Canada. The widespread distribution of smelted iron, copper and bronze in Canadian arctic Inuit sites suggests that metal, even in small fragments, was a valuable trade commodity to the early Inuit, and was widely distributed through their trade routes. The Vinland sagas indicate that the Norse were willing to trade with the Skraelings, and it seems likely that trade with Inuit would have been beneficial too. The Greenland colonies depended on trade with Europe for many of their requirements — grain, metal, timber and luxury goods, such as bishop's vestments. In addition, after 1261, they were required to pay fines and annual tribute to the Norwegian king, as well as tithes and crusade taxes to the Roman church. This tribute was paid in the materials of the country: walrus hides, polar bear skins (on at least one occasion a live polar bear), but primarily ivory from walrus tusks.

16   Walrus almost certainly did not occur in southwestern Greenland in the relatively warm period when the colonies were occupied. Thus, the Norse hunters had to travel 400 kilometres north of the settlements to the area known as the *Nordrsetur*, the northern hunting grounds. Such hunts must have put great pressure on the Norse economy, depriving the colonies of manpower needed for farming, fishing and hunting for food. Yet the importance of European trade was such that the Nordrsetur hunt was an integral part of the Greenlandic Norse way of life. The early Inuit who had occupied Arctic Canada and northwestern Greenland by about AD 1100 had quantities of ivory, as can be seen from the archeological remains of their settlements. If they were willing to trade ivory for small scraps of metal and worn-out tools, as were their descendants of the 17th and 18th centuries, it would seem to have been profitable for the Norse to exploit this trade.

17   Is there any evidence that such trade did occur? Two finds from early Inuit villages in the eastern Arctic provide some hints. The first, from northwestern Ellesmere Island, is a hinged bar of bronze, unearthed by archeologist Patricia Sutherland. This is the beam of a folding balance similar to those used by Norse traders for weighing coins and other small objects. This characteristic trader's artifact, the only one known west of Iceland, was found in an Inuit village 2,000 kilometres from the Greenlandic Norse colonies.

18   The second object, obtained from a 13th-Century village on the south coast of Baffin Island, suggests the actual presence of Norsemen in Arctic Canada at the time. This is a small wooden figurine carved in typically Inuit style with flat, featureless face and stumpy arms, but dressed, untypically, in a long robe with what appears to be a cross on the chest. The clothing is consistent with European apparel of the period. The most plausible explanation is that the figurine was made locally by someone who had seen a Norse Greenlander, perhaps on Baffin Island or in Labrador.

19   Baffin Island, of course, was known to the Norse, and the Norse may have coasted it for some 300 years on their voyages to the forests of Markland. Occasional landings may well have been made, and with them contact with the Inuit occupants of the region. A sporadic, opportunistic trading relationship could then have been established, one that served as a basis for relationships between the Norse Greenlanders and the Inuit, who eventually began to move into southwestern Greenland.

20   This relationship must have been considerably more intensive than that with the peoples encountered in voyages along the fringes of Arctic Canada, and also much more intensive and complex than that suggested by Norse historical records. Recent archeological work has shown that the Inuit advance along the west Greenland coast occurred considerably earlier than had been generally thought. Radiocarbon dates indicate that by the

14th Century the Inuit had settled the outer coastal regions of southwestern Greenland, in the same areas where Norse farms were established in the inner fiords. For the next one or two centuries, substantial populations of Norse and Inuit lived in this region, and it seems inevitable that, despite the animosity of which the historical records speak, they must have worked out some means of sharing the country and its resources.

The Norse Greenland colonies died out about the time that John Cabot, Portuguese navigator Gaspar Cortereal and Jacques Cartier were reestablishing contact between Europe and the eastern coast of Canada. Their decline was probably not due to hostilities with the Inuit, but rather the result of a deteriorating climate, combined with a rapid decline in the value of their commercial products as furs and ivory began to reach Europe through the growth of Hanseatic League trade with the East and Portuguese exploration in Africa. Abandoned by their Norse king and by the Pope in Rome, neither of whom any longer bothered to send ships to Greenland, and increasingly harassed by European pirates, the Norse colonies were the victims of economic forces, not of Inuit attacks. **21**

It was a sad end to a heroic venture, one that had lasted almost 500 years and which resulted in the European discovery of what is now Canada. Here, for the first time in their westward expansion, the Norse came upon regions that were already populated by an unknown people who outnumbered the exploring and colonizing parties carried by the small Norse ships, and who had weapons that were almost as efficient as those of the Norse at killing men in small-scale skirmishes. In such a situation, the extended exploration and colonization of a continent was unthinkable. The Norse appear to have been content to make occasional visits to the northeastern coasts of Canada over a period of several centuries, probably cutting timber from the Labrador forests and warily trading with the natives of the country. **22**

Those who have pictured a "Norse America," in which redoubtable Vikings wandered across the continent, settling at will, raising stone towers and carving runic inscriptions, have chosen to ignore the presence of the natives of North America. The author of *The Greenlanders' Saga* probably gives a more accurate picture of Norse abilities to colonize the newly discovered lands. He places the first meeting between New and Old World peoples in Labrador where Thorvald Ericsson's party met and fought with the Skraelings, and where Thorvald received a fatal wound. The dying Thorvald is reported to have drawn the arrow from his stomach and remarked, "There is fat around my belly! We have won a fine and fruitful country, but will hardly be allowed to enjoy it." **23**

# VOCABULARY

a. *paragraph 3:* contention, runic

b. *paragraph 14:* indigenous

c. *paragraph 15:* tithes

d. *paragraph 18:* figurine, apparel, plausible

e. *paragraph 19:* sporadic, opportunistic

f. *paragraph 20:* intensive, Radiocarbon, fiords, animosity

g. *paragraph 22:* skirmishes, warily

h. *paragraph 23:* redoubtable

## QUESTIONS

1. McGhee's essay employs a narrative strategy; that is, he tells the story of the Vikings. Does this narrative have a thesis? Does he state it or does the thesis emerge as the essay proceeds?

2. Besides narrative, what other strategies does the writer use to give unity to his account of the Viking explorations?

3. Discuss the use of specific examples. How do they help McGhee prove his contentions?

4. How are transitions made through the twenty-three short paragraphs?

## WRITING ASSIGNMENTS

1. McGhee compares the keen popular interest in the Vikings with the cooler, more scientific approach of the archeologists. Consider other phenomena — dinosaurs, astrology, UFOs — towards which there is a similar contrast of attitudes. Cite examples from the popular press on the one hand, science textbooks on the other.

2. Consult a similar essay in magazines such as the *Canadian Geographic* or *National Geographic*. Write a short summary of its thesis and show how the author uses evidence to support his claims.

## GEORGE GALT

George Galt *was born in 1948 and educated at Sir George Williams University, where he received his B.A. in Economics in 1970. A full-time freelance writer and editor, he has published two books and more than a hundred essays and articles on literary subjects, Canadian history, travel, and architecture. The relation between Canada's past and its monuments is the subject of the following essay on Louisburg.*

## MAKING HISTORY

1   In the 1930s, while [Prime Minister Mackenzie] King was attending to his fake ruins, a senator from Nova Scotia, J.S. McLennan, lobbied in Ottawa for support for his own pet piece of historic real estate, the authentic ruins at Louisbourg, Nova Scotia, which had been declared a national historic site in 1928. McLennan succeeded in extracting modest sums from the government for excavations and the construction of a small museum. But it was a faltering local economy, rather than reverence for the past, that actually determined Louisbourg's fate. In 1960 a royal commission investigating unemployment in the coal-mining industry recommended the reconstruction of the fortress as a temporary make-work project and permanent tourist attraction, and in 1961 the Diefenbaker government provided money for it.

2   Thus began a curious chapter in the preservation of our material history. Some fifty buildings have been built on the ruins. As far as anyone knows, they are nearly identical to those constructed by the French 240 years ago. Today Louisbourg stands as a symbol of our national puzzlement over what history is truly Canadian and how to possess it.

Over its twenty years of reconstruction, Louisbourg cost far more than any other historic site in Canada (its replacement value is now estimated at about $100-million), and it commands a much higher annual budget than any other federal site. Unlike Mackenzie King's ruins, the fortress played a real and dramatic role in Canadian history. Some historians argue that Louisbourg had to fall before Quebec could be safely taken. But its connection to contemporary Canada is tenuous. The fortress was culturally and administratively separate from New France, and during its forty-five-year life it remained on the far edge of Quebec history. The Loyalist and Scottish immigrants whose descendants now populate Cape Breton did not begin to arrive until after the fortress was demolished in 1760. For them Louisbourg was no more than a rocky sheep pasture. As the architect of the reconstruction remarked before leaving the finished project in 1983, "Nobody has any heritage from Louisbourg, nobody at all. [In that sense] it's meaningless." **3**

Why, then, is Louisbourg our flagship historic site? Partly because it was a military installation. The historic sites and monuments board was dominated in its formative years by a retired brigadier general and amateur historian, E.A. Cruikshank, the chairman. He was disposed to favour military sites, and the board quickly came to express the same bias. It was an easy way of reaching consensus on the most troublesome questions then facing students of Canada's past. How should the country's national history be defined? Which events transcended local implications and took on Canadian importance? **4**

In one way or another such questions continued to bedevil intellectuals until a century after Confederation. For my generation, born after the Second World War, the refrain was: what makes us distinct as a people? What is the national character? General Cruikshank's board needed answers, not philosophical debate. Military structures were attractive because national defence was by definition a national achievement. Besides, military buildings were available without charge to the federal treasury. Property was simply transferred from the department of defence to the low-budget parks bureaucracy. Obsolete forts were rechristened historic sites. **5**

Canada has now declared more than 1,000 national historic sites. You can see them by the road, the older ones marked by a stone cairn holding a metal plate embossed with commemorative script. The newer markers, metal plaques on poles, have raised gold lettering on a dark red background. About ten per cent of these sites have been developed into historic parks, and it is through them that Parks Canada tries to interpret our national history. Nearly half of them are forts, fortifications, or battlefields. **6**

A recreated French colonial town in anglophone Cape Breton, Louisbourg clearly embodies at least one national trait — the baffling ambiguity of our past. What's the meaning of its history, French settlement or British conquest? No-one at Louisbourg has any stake in that question; it can be answered either way. Removed from the formative currents of Canadian history, Louisbourg celebrates neither official language group, or both. It's an ideal monument: it offends no school of Canadian history. **7**

In other parts of the country, our historic ambiguities have been more controversial, and often the controversies have been exacerbated by an imported view of history. The three countries to which Canada has the strongest ties — France, Great Britain, and the United States — cherish grand monuments that express national mythologies. The Louvre and the Arc de Triomphe in Paris, Buckingham Palace and Westminster in London, the Lincoln Memorial and the White House in Washington are unifying totems of a common past. Canadians may yearn for similar shrines, but our history departs radically from the experiences of our mother countries and our neighbour. **8**

Some Canadians claim Province House — the legislature in Charlottetown where delegates from four provinces met in 1864 to discuss Confederation — as our great architectural emblem of nation-making. We may take pride in the peaceful compromise of **9**

Confederation, but it was a cautious step towards unity and independence, not a brash break with an oppressive past. Compared to the Boston Tea Party or the storming of the Bastille, the meetings and debates that led to Canada's union were hardly high drama. Through the reverse telescope of history, Confederation seems less a momentous thunderclap than a sensible pact negotiated by prudent burghers. It's not surprising that Province House has ignited no eternal flame in the Canadian imagination.

10      Our history has unfolded without revolution or civil war. Except for the Plains of Abraham, violent acts of national consolidation and liberation — the great turning points of European and American history — are foreign to us. The European tradition of monuments, to some degree adopted by the Americans, has been to focus on these violent pivots of history. Great military leaders, such as Nelson and Napoleon, are enshrined in great monuments.

11      In Canada war as a metaphor for history translates badly. General Cruikshank and his board were pursuing this metaphor at Batoche, Saskatchewan, when they commemorated the North-West Rebellion as a victory for the infant nation over seditious malcontents. People with British loyalties wanted to believe in Batoche as a civilizing event, a continuation of the imperial march westward, a historic victory of right over wrong. That interpretation did not stick, and Batoche remained a sore point among the Métis and their sympathizers in Quebec for generations.

12      The battle of Batoche, fought in 1885, sits at the crossroads of Canada's primal inner conflicts: French against English, native against white, east against west. No wonder it's been troublesome for Parks Canada. The first plaque, mounted on a cairn in 1924, celebrated the militia units that had, under Major General Middleton, "ended the Rebellion." The inscription was denounced locally and in Quebec as an insult. In 1947 an altered text dropped the word "rebellion," but the message of defeat remained. Two years ago a third plaque was mounted to mollify a century of Métis resentment. The last line of the script now reads: "The resistance failed but the battle did not mean the end of the community of Batoche." The historic event itself, originally commemorated as one of the great battles of nation-making, is now also interpreted as an eastern land-grab.

13      Not everyone agrees with this interpretation. Yet the success of the surviving Métis — having their heritage remembered on a site where, so British loyalists like to think, the Métis civilization had been put to rout — mocks the great-battlefield theory. And it illustrates the difficulty we have in fitting Canadian history, not yet remote and mythologized, into our borrowed vision of historic sites.

14      In the 1870s, when Mackenzie King was born, two of every three Canadians were of British descent. During his lifetime the make-up of the population changed radically, but King held to the view that Canada should maintain a close, though not submissive, affinity for the United Kingdom and its heritage. For years the historic sites and monuments board reinforced a narrow, conservative view of Canada's identity. In the 1920s and 1930s, the board rejected proposals to commemorate sites associated with the rebellions of 1837. Most board members still regarded people such as William Lyon Mackenzie as criminals. Quebec members who suggested recognition of events in their province were often snubbed. A Quebec member sneered in turn at a request in 1945 that the site of the first synagogue in Canada be celebrated with a marker. "I am not particularly interested," came the cold reply, "in the commemoration of Jewish activities." The same member, asked to comment on the proposed recognition of the first black American immigrants to Vancouver Island, wrote, "I do not think the immigration of negroes is a fact to rejoice upon."

15      More than one board member may have held racist views. Mackenzie King himself was anti-Semitic. The more recent ethnic groups were considered marginal to the national

culture, and for most of this century commemorations of historic figures neither British nor French in origin were rare. Only in 1982 did the board finally recognize a group as important as any in stitching the country together: the Chinese who built the CPR through British Columbia. There had earlier been a few markers at native sites, but many had only fuelled native grievances. A plaque erected in Saskatchewan in the 1920s so enraged the Cree with its one-sided record of the skirmish at Cut Knife ("On 2nd May, 1885, Lt. Col. W.D. Otter led 325 troops . . .") that they wrote "LIE" on it in red paint. The replacement acknowledges that "the surprise attack failed."

In 1951 the Massey commission on the arts and sciences reported that a preponderance of military buildings was skewing the presentation of our past. Still, Parks Canada continued to develop old forts. One of the most recent, Fort Chambly near Montreal, was reopened to the public only a few years ago. Imitating the British, we have also saved a number of notable residences — the houses of prime ministers and exceptional men such as Alexander Graham Bell.    **16**

Some of this has been amazingly casual. An Ottawa story has John Diefenbaker in Kingston in 1959 coming across an old Italianate house for sale. He was told the building had once been occupied by Sir John A. Macdonald. Back in Ottawa Diefenbaker impressed his strong views on the parks branch, and Bellevue House was eventually acquired and restored by the government.    **17**

We have preserved several old fur trading posts, three prehistoric sites (including an Indian hilltop stronghold at Kitwanga, B.C.), and one Viking site (at L'Anse aux Meadows, Newfoundland). But our aboriginal history, our labour history, our industrial history, the history of groups other than British or French? All go virtually unrecognized.    **18**

The way we select our historic parks may finally be changing. One of the newest sites is the W.R. Motherwell homestead in Saskatchewan, intended to commemorate early western agriculture. Motherwell was a leader in developing scientific farming, and was federal minister of agriculture in the 1920s. His house, garden, and barn, painstakingly restored, constitute the only national historic park devoted to the industry that occupied the vast majority of settlers in this country.    **19**

Even at that site, however, you see familiar biases. Motherwell was not among the hundreds of thousands of prairie farmers who emigrated from Eastern Europe, building sod huts and, later, synagogues and onion-domed churches. He came instead from prosperous WASP Ontario, and built a dwelling of cut fieldstone, like the houses in his home town, Perth. In spite of some distinct prairie features, the Motherwell site pays homage to the old British-Canadian establishment, and venerates the closest approximation on the open prairie to a stately home.    **20**

My grandmother was saddened in the 1950s when the Winnipeg mansion her merchant husband had built in 1912 was demolished by a developer. The house had historic resonance that went beyond our family heritage. My grandparents had once held a long-remembered dance for Edward, Prince of Wales, in their ballroom. The opulent dwelling, and a few others like it, symbolized the apogee of Winnipeg's economic boom. But converting it into a historic monument would not have been very instructive. It would have been one more museum showing how the upper bourgeoisie lived in its golden age before 1929.    **21**

Far more illuminating has been the conservation of the warehouses built by Winnipeg businessmen of my grandfather's generation. The old warehouse district contains a concentration of finely crafted industrial architecture unique in Canada. Here you sense the Winnipeg that burgeoned between 1880 and 1920, and deduce the role it played as broker to the new West. The preservation of the city's old exchange district adjacent to its modern    **22** downtown is partly a happy accident — Winnipeg was largely overlooked in the re-development frenzy that hit other Canadian cities in the 1960s and 1970s — but this living conjunction of past and present can also be planned and encouraged.

23        At Louisbourg, a pretend town that conveys a compelling period atmosphere, I was struck by two things. First, you can't help but be impressed by its architectural and museological excellence. Some federal sites developed before 1960, such as the Sir Wilfrid Laurier house in St-Lin, Quebec, were based on dubious historical data. At Louis-bourg, the archaeological and archival research conducted for the reconstruction set new standards for Parks Canada. But the second impression was more lasting: Canadians are inept at incorporating their material past into the present.

24        Look across the harbour from the rebuilt fortress at Louisbourg and you see a stretch of shoreline, empty except for a small Catholic cemetery. The gravestones bear the names of Kennedys and Popes, families that trace their history on this shore back through two centuries. The graveyard once belonged to a place called West Louisbourg, or Old Town. At the reconstructed forge I found a man named Kennedy dressed as a blacksmith, ham-mering out period hardware in view of the tourists. Thirty years ago he lived across the water in Old Town. "We used to play cowboys and Indians in the ruins here," he said. "My father's house was low on the hill over there. A little farther up was my grandfather's house, and a little further up from that my great-grandfather's."

25        These layers of cultural encrustation are the real stuff of history. Yet when the govern-ment began to develop Louisbourg as a historic monument most of the planners, and the residents themselves, were persuaded that Old Town would only detract from the romantic fantasy of a French colonial fortress. The community was dispersed, and its houses, school, and church were levelled.

## VOCABULARY

a. *paragraph   3:* tenuous

b. *paragraph   4:* transcended

c. *paragraph   7:* ambiguity

d. *paragraph   8:* exacerbated, totems

e. *paragraph   9:* momentous

f. *paragraph 10:* consolidation

g. *paragraph 13:* mythologized

h. *paragraph 14:* snubbed

i. *paragraph 16:* preponderance, skewing

j. *paragraph 21:* opulent, apogee, bourgeoisie

k. *paragraph 23:* museological

l. *paragraph 25:* encrustation

# QUESTIONS

1. Why does Galt speak of "national puzzlement" in his thesis statement (paragraph 2)? Does the essay explain this phrase?

2. Galt's essay begins and ends with the fortress at Louisbourg. What else does he discuss? Why?

3. In paragraph 8 Galt uses the phrase "historic ambiguities." Does he explain what he means? How?

4. Galt states in paragraph 11: "In Canada war as a metaphor for history translates badly." What examples does he use to illustrate this point?

5. Compare the views of Canada that Galt discusses with those expressed in Margaret Atwood's "True North."

# WRITING ASSIGNMENT

Reread the last sentence of paragraph 23. How valid is Galt's claim? Make reference to historical sites you have visited — Upper Canada Village, Fort Huronia, Fort Langley, for example.

# ERIC SEVAREID

*Born in 1912 in Velva, North Dakota,* Eric Sevareid *graduated from the University of Minnesota in 1935 and immediately began his career as a journalist with the* Minneapolis Journal. *He later reported for the Paris edition of* The New York Herald Tribune. *In 1939 Sevareid began his long association with the Columbia Broadcasting Company as a war correspondent in Europe. From 1964 to 1977 he delivered his commentary on the* CBS Evening News. *His numerous books include* Small Sounds in the Night *(1956) and an autobiography,* Not So Wild a Dream *(1976). In "Velva, North Dakota" Sevareid builds through a careful presentation of detail to increasingly broad truths about the world of his youth and human nature generally.*

# VELVA, NORTH DAKOTA

My home town has changed in these thirty years of the American story. It is changing now, will go on changing as America changes. Its biography, I suspect, would read much the same as that of all other home towns. Depression and war and prosperity have all left their marks; modern science, modern tastes, manners, philosophies, fears and ambitions have touched my town as indelibly as they have touched New York or Panama City.

Sights have changed: there is a new precision about street and home, a clearing away of chicken yards, cow barns, pigeon-crested cupolas, weed lots and coulees, the dim and secret adult-free rendezvous of boys. An intricate metal "jungle gym" is a common back-yard sight, the sack swing uncommon. There are wide expanses of clear windows, designed to let in the parlor light, fewer ornamental windows of colored glass designed to keep it out. Attic and screen porch are slowly vanishing and lovely shades of pastel are painted upon new houses, tints that once would have embarrassed farmer and merchant alike.

3    Sounds have changed; I heard not once the clopping of a horse's hoof, nor the mourn of a coyote. I heard instead the shriek of brakes, the heavy throbbing of the once-a-day Braniff airliner into Minot, the shattering sirens born of war, the honk of a diesel locomotive which surely cannot call to faraway places the heart of a wakeful boy like the old steam whistle in the night. You can walk down the streets of my town now and hear from open windows the intimate voices of the Washington commentators in casual converse on the great affairs of state; but you cannot hear on Sunday morning the singing in Norwegian of the Lutheran hymns; the old country seems now part of a world left long behind and the old-country accents grow fainter in the speech of my Velva neighbors.

4    The people have not changed, but the *kinds* of people have changed: there is no longer an official, certified town drunk, no longer a "Crazy John," spitting his worst epithet, "rotten chicken legs," as you hurriedly passed him by. People so sick are now sent to places of proper care. No longer is there an official town joker, like the druggist Mac-Knight, who would spot a customer in the front of the store, have him called to the phone, then slip to the phone behind the prescription case, and imitate the man's wife to perfection with orders to bring home more bread and sausage and Cream of Wheat. No longer anyone like the early attorney, J.L. Lee, who sent fabulous dispatches to that fabulous tabloid, the *Chicago Blade*, such as his story of the wild man captured on the prairie and chained to the wall in the drugstore basement. (This, surely, was Velva's first notoriety; inquiries came from anthropologists all over the world.)

5    No, the "characters" are vanishing in Velva, just as they are vanishing in our cities, in business, in politics. The "well-rounded, socially integrated" personality that the progressive schoolteachers are so obsessed with is increasing rapidly, and I am not at all sure that this is good. Maybe we need more personalities with knobs and handles and rugged lumps of individuality. They may not make life more smooth; more interesting they surely make it.

6    They eat differently in Velva now; there are frozen fruits and sea food and exotic delicacies we only read about in novels in those meat-and-potato days. They dress differently. The hard white collars of the businessmen are gone with the shiny alpaca coats. There are comfortable tweeds now, and casual blazers with a touch in their colors of California, which seems so close in time and distance.

7    It is distance and time that have changed the most and worked the deepest changes in Velva's life. The telephone, the car, the smooth highway, radio and television are consolidating the entities of our country. The county seat of Towner now seems no closer than the state capital of Bismarck; the voices and concerns of Presidents, French premiers and Moroccan pashas are no farther away than the portable radio on Aunt Jessey's kitchen table. The national news magazines are stacked each week in Harold Anderson's drugstore beside the new soda fountain, and the excellent *Minot Daily News* smells hot from the press each afternoon.

8    Consolidation. The nearby hamlets of Sawyer and Logan and Voltaire had their own separate banks and papers and schools in my days of dusty buggies and Model Ts marooned in the snowdrifts. Now these hamlets are dying. A bright yellow bus takes the Voltaire kids to Velva each day for high school. Velva has grown — from 800 to 1,300 — because the miners from the Truax coal mine can commute to their labors each morning and the nearby farmers can live in town if they choose. Minot has tripled in size to 30,000. Once the "Magic City" was a distant and splendid Baghdad, visited on special occasions long prepared for. Now it is a twenty-five minute commuter's jump away. So P.W. Miller

and Jay Louis Monicken run their business in Minot but live on in their old family homes in Velva. So Ray Michelson's two girls on his farm to the west drive up each morning to their jobs as maids in Minot homes. Aunt Jessey said, "Why, Saturday night I counted sixty-five cars just between here and Sawyer, all going up to the show in Minot."

The hills are prison battlements no longer; the prairies no heart-sinking barrier, but a 　**9** passageway free as the swelling ocean, inviting you to sail home and away at your whim and your leisure. (John and Helen made an easy little jaunt of 700 miles that week-end to see their eldest daughter in Wyoming.)

Consolidation. Art Kumm's bank serves a big region now; its assets are $2,000,000 to 　**10** $3,000,000 instead of the $200,000 or $300,000 in my father's day. Eighteen farms near Velva are under three ownerships now. They calculate in sections; "acres" is an almost forgotten term. Aunt Jessey owns a couple of farms, and she knows they are much better run. "It's no longer all take out and no put in," she said. "Folks strip farm now; they know all about fertilizers. They care for it and they'll hand on the land in good shape." The farmers gripe about their cash income, and not without reason at the moment, but they will admit that life is good compared with those days of drought and foreclosure, manure banked against the house for warmth, the hand pump frozen at 30 below and the fitful kerosene lamp on the kitchen table. Electrification has done much of this, eased back-breaking chores that made their wives old as parchment at forty, brought life and music and the sound of human voices into their parlors at night.

And light upon the prairie. "From the hilltop," said Aunt Jessey, "the farms look like 　**11** stars at night."

Many politicians deplore the passing of the old family-size farm, but I am not so sure. I 　**12** saw around Velva a release from what was like slavery to the tyrannical soil, release from the ignorance that darkens the soul and from the loneliness that corrodes it. In this generation my Velva friends have rejoined the general American society that their pioneering fathers left behind when they first made the barren trek in the days of the wheat rush. As I sit here in Washington writing this, I can feel their nearness. I never felt it before save in my dreams.

But now I must ask myself: Are they nearer to one another? And the answer is no; yet I 　**13** am certain that this is good. The shrinking of time and distance has made contrast and relief available to their daily lives. They do not know one another quite so well because they are not so much obliged to. I know that democracy rests upon social discipline, which in turn rests upon personal discipline; passions checked, hard words withheld, civic tasks accepted, work well done, accountings honestly rendered. The old-fashioned small town was this discipline in its starkest, most primitive form; without this discipline the small town would have blown itself apart.

For personal and social neuroses festered under this hard scab of conformity. There 　**14** was no place to go, no place to let off steam; few dared to voice unorthodox ideas, read strange books, admire esoteric art or publicly write or speak of their dreams and their soul's longings. The world was not "too much with us," the world was too little with us and we were too much with one another.

The door to the world stands open now, inviting them to leave anytime they wish. It is 　**15** the simple fact of the open door that makes all the difference; with its opening the stale air rushed out. So, of course, the people themselves do not have to leave, because, as the stale air went out, the fresh air came in.

Human nature is everywhere the same. He who is not forced to help his neighbor for 　**16** his own existence will not only give him help, but his true good will as well. Minot and its hospital are now close at hand, but the people of Velva put their purses together, built their own clinic and homes for the two young doctors they persuaded to come and live among them. Velva has no organized charity, but when a farmer falls ill, his neighbors get in his crop; if a townsman has a financial catastrophe his personal friends raise a fund to help him out. When Bill's wife, Ethel, lay dying so long in the Minot hospital and nurses were not available, Helen and others took their turns driving up there just to sit with her so she would know in her gathering dark that friends were at hand.

17      It is personal freedom that makes us better persons, and they are freer in Velva now. There is no real freedom without privacy, and a resident of my home town can be a private person much more than he could before. People are able to draw at least a little apart from one another. In drawing apart, they gave their best human instincts room for expansion.

## VOCABULARY

a. *paragraph  1:* indelibly

b. *paragraph  4:* certified, epithet, tabloid, notoriety, anthropologists

c. *paragraph  5:* progressive

d. *paragraph  6:* alpaca, blazers

e. *paragraph  7:* pashas

f. *paragraph  8:* consolidation, commute

g. *paragraph  9:* battlements, whim, jaunt

h. *paragraph 10:* foreclosure

i. *paragraph 12:* deplore, corrodes, trek

j. *paragraph 13:* starkest

k. *paragraph 14:* neuroses, scab, unorthodox, esoteric

## QUESTIONS

1. Where does Sevareid indicate his attitude toward his home town? What is his thesis?

2. How does the selection of detail in the whole essay support the dominating impression Sevareid creates of the town in his opening paragraph? Is any of this detail unrelated to this impression?

3. What is the tone of the comment on the story of the wild man, and how is the comment related to the thesis?

4. How does Sevareid emphasize the causes of the change in life in Velva? Does he indicate a main cause?

5. What does Sevareid mean by the statement in paragraph 13, "without this discipline the small town would have blown itself apart"?

6. Sevareid points up a series of paradoxes toward the end. What are these, and what do they contribute to the tone of the conclusion?

## WRITING ASSIGNMENTS

1. Analyse how Eric Sevareid introduces his thesis and keeps it before the reader. Then discuss another way he might have organized the essay.

2. Describe the changes that have occurred in the neighbourhood in which you grew up and discuss the reasons for these.

## FREDELLE BRUSER MAYNARD

*Fredelle Bruser Maynard is a Canadian journalist and writer on child development. Her book includes* Guiding Your Child to a More Creative Life *and two memoirs,* Raisins and Almonds *and* Tree of Life. *In this account of the Canadian Readers of her youth, taken from* Raisins and Almonds, *she movingly re-creates and comments on an era that has vanished.*

## THE WINDLESS WORLD

I remember the dog. He was a Spitz, I think, or a mongrel with a Spitzy tail, and he    1 balanced on his hind legs on the cover of the Canadian Primer. There was an old woman, too — I learned afterward that she was Mother Goose — contained, like the dog, within a sharp black circle. The angle of the old lady's scarf, blown forward with stiffly outthrust fringe, suggested wind, but the world of the figures was windless. The blackish, olive-tinted sky seemed absolutely serene; the meadow flowers, each separate on its tuft of careful grass, were still and perfect as the matching flowers on Mother Goose's gown. What was she saying, her pointing finger outlined against the sculptured scarf? Surely nothing so insipid as "Bow-wow-wow, whose dog art thou?" Momentous as an Egyptian hieroglyph on the door of an unopened tomb, the picture haunted me through all the hours in prairie schoolrooms. It mingled with the smell of chalk dust and eraser crumbs, of crude ink splashed into inkwells by unsteady jug-bearers, of apples and pencil shavings and gum. Perhaps it was only when I left the Canadian Readers, in grade six, that I knew for sure the message frozen on those parted lips. The voice of the reader was the voice of the Union Jack: Be Brave (red); Be Pure (white); Be True Blue.

Every autumn, after Labor Day, we got a new book. What a moment that was, the crisp    2 stacks of readers lined up at the head of each row as we sat in the approved position, eyes front, hands folded, waiting for the signal: "Take one and pass them back." The sour green binding looked unpromising enough. After Books I and II, with their cover pictures, the Nelson Publishing Company made no further concessions to frivolity. Books III, IV, and V presented a uniform front, a Canadian coat of arms with the lion, the unicorn, and the fought-for crown poised above a shaky maple leaf spray. *A mari usque ad mare*, the banner read. From sea to sea, from September to September, the contents of those books were imprinted on the minds of young Canadians. In the small towns where I lived, there was little competition from other influences. We had no library, no magazine stands (or comic books); the radio was dominated by sopranos and the phonograph required cranking. So I read the readers. All through the years, I have remembered the thrilling stories of Horatius and Robin Hood. Fragments of verses, memorized long ago for the school inspector's visit, have blown about the borders of adult consciousness. "Let me live in a house by the side of the road / And be a friend to man." "Those behind cried 'Forward!' and those before cried 'Back!'" Were the Canadian Readers so rich as in retrospect they seemed? I often wondered. And then, in the musty basement of a Winnipeg bookstore, I found them — a full glorious set. Books I to V. Magic casements opening on the foam by faery seas — or windows on a petrified forest? I could scarcely wait to know.

3    I have gone all through the Canadian Readers now, starting with "Tom Tinker had a dog" and ending with Kipling's *Recessional*. A strange journey. A journey in search of myself, perhaps, but even more in search of the attitudes which molded my generation, and of a long since vanished world. It is easy to criticize the readers. What an extraordinary list of authors, for example: there is no Milton, no Shakespeare except for a snippet from *Julius Caesar* and a scene from *As You Like It*. There is not one song from Blake or Burns or Water de la Mare. Longfellow, however, is most plentifully represented; so is James Whitcomb Riley. Much of the material is anonymous — for reasons which to the mature judgment seem clear. Imperialists abound. Kipling, Edward Shirley, Sir Henry Newbolt, Canon F.G. Scott blow their bugles mightily.

> Children of the Empire, you are brothers all;
> Childen of the Empire, answer to the call;
> Let your voices mingle, lift your heads and sing;
> "God save dear old Britain, and God save Britain's king."

And behind them — a formidable array — march battalions of female poets with resonant triple names: Hannah Flagg Gould, Agnes Maule Machar, Julia Augusta Schwarz. Looking now at "The Crocus's Song" and "Christmas" ("Every mile is as warm as a smile, / And every hour is a song") I can understand why I thought, as a child, that poetry must be easy to write.

4    Illustrations for the Canadian Readers include a good deal of amateurish line drawing, dark blurred photographs, and acres of third-rate academy painting. Sometimes the pictures bear directly on the text, sometimes they are just vaguely related in feeling, as when "Dog of Flanders," about a boy and his dog, is introduced by the painting of a girl and her sheep. Landscape studies predominate, but it is a landscape startlingly irrelevant to the experience of the audience. Apart from some amusing "oriental" scenes, the world of the readers is English: indoors, nannies and beautifully groomed children at teatime; outdoors, a fairyland of stone walls and hawthorns where blackbirds sing from the blooming apple boughs. To the child who rode to school on horseback, past sloughs and wheatfields and elevators, the visions of Rosa Bonheur must have been outlandish as Aladdin.

5    In addition to being remote, the world of the readers is limited. An adult today is struck by a peculiarly English class consciousness. For example, the account of a rogue named Greene, who led the mutiny against Henry Hudson, begins with a raised-monocle observation to the effect that "this Greene was of respectable connections." Not surprisingly, it's a man's world. The few women celebrated are those who prove themselves in war the equal of men — Boadicea, Laura Secord, Florence Nightingale, Edith Cavell. (There is one essay called "A Pioneer Woman," but the achievements of its heroine are a sad anticlimax. "Mrs. Lajimodière was not, of course, expected to carry a load or to use a paddle, but the journey from Montreal to Pembina must have been one of great hardship to

her. She had often to pass the whole day seated on the bottom of the canoe." We are not told whether she carried a parasol.) Even more serious is the indifference, through all five volumes, to people of other lands. There is the British Empire, and beyond that a wasteland inhabited by funny little people like Oogly the Eskimo and Ning Ting "away over in an eastern country called China." Japan is a place where "there isn't a sofa or chair," where one eats without a fork and rides in neat little rickshaws. You will find "in Japan that your horse is a man." Not surprising, I guess, to a child who, in the phonetic tables accompanying Book I, is given the series "nap, rap, gap, *Jap*." There are Indians in these stories, but not the Sioux or Cree of any Canadian's real experience. Gorgeously outfitted in buckskin, they sit under giant oaks whispering their secrets to squirrels. They have never seen a reservation, and they have no embarrassing Problems.

Perhaps it is unfair to protest, in material for the primary grades, the absence of any scholarly or scientific spirit. Still, it does seem that the borders between real and fanciful might have been more clearly defined. In grade three the student learns how umbrellas were invented (an elf, threatened with a soaking, uproots a toadstool) and how James Watt discovered the principle of steam. He passes, without change in style or tone, from Robinson Crusoe to Lord Nelson. (I suspect that most little readers found Crusoe the more credible of the two.) Imaginary events are "proved" by the real existence of places named. Allan-a-Dale's marriage? "To this day you can still see the ruins of the great abbey in which it took place." The Pied Piper? "If you go to Hamelin, the people will show you the hill and the river." *Quod erat demonstrandum.*\* Even historical material is presented with a curious indifference to fact. Florence Nightingale is described as having personally cared for 10,000 sick. We are told how Sir Philip Sidney looked when he offered a dying soldier his last cup of water — but not the name of the "great battle" just fought. Did the teachers of the 1920s fill in the blanks, supply the necessary correctives? Perhaps some did. But in the one-room schools of my acquaintance the teacher, often fresh out of Normal School, was glad if she had time to hear us recite. Anything else was extra and impossible.    6

In order that our chubby childhood might be secure from temptation, the readers lectured us continually. "Teach us to bear the yoke in youth" was the burden of the inappropriately named "Children's Song." "Teach us to rule ourselves alway, / Controlled and cleanly night and day." Goodness was a full-time job, *that* was clear. How we marveled at the story of David Livingstone, a perfect lad even before Africa beckoned. "When he swept the room for his mother, there was no leaving of dust in dark corners where it might not be noticed, no dusting round in circles and not underneath." At ten, this paragon earned his own living at a cotton mill: up at five, then fourteen hours at the loom, a Latin grammar (bought with his first earnings) propped at eye level. "It might have been supposed," ran the text, "that after fourteen hours at the factory, David would have been glad to rest or play when he got home at night." But no. Home from work, he hurried off to night school; home from night school, he pored over his books until Mother blew out the candle. Of course, "whenever there was a Missionary Meeting held within walking distance he was always there." At the looms, too, joining threads, "he began to weave his plan of service for his Master." And from all the grueling routine he emerged fresh as a sprig of Scots heather. "Whenever a holiday came round he showed what a splendid out-of-door boy he was as well."    7

Few of us could have hoped to emulate this noble life — for one thing, cotton mills were scarce on the Canadian prairies — but we were given plenty of help. Poems, stories,    8

*"Which was to be proved."

biographies — all uplifted. There were tongues in the trees, books in the running brooks, sermons in stones, and Good in everything. Literally. What does the crocus say, deep in the snow?

> I will peer up with my bright little head
> I will peer up with my bright little head.

giving us a lesson to borrow, that

> Patient today, through its gloomiest hour
> We come out the brighter tomorrow.

Willows demonstrate helpfulness; rabbits, the rewards of unselfishness. Sunbeams discover that "in seeking the pleasures / Of others [we've] filled to the full [our] own measure." Hens are punctual; bees, naturally, industrious; horses know how important it is to "Do your best wherever you are, and keep up your good name." . . . Over and over again, we are reminded that though intelligence and tender feeling are goods, there is one Good greater far. With the anonymous singer of Book IV, we cheerfully learn to say,

> Head, you may think; Heart, you may feel;
> But, Hand you shall work alway.

I can smile, now, at the naïve moralizing of the Canadian Readers. It did no harm; perhaps many children profited. But one aspect, one direction, of the material still seems to me pernicious, unforgivable: the exaltation of empire and the glorification of war. Through the whole five volumes, only two selections suggest in any way the virtues of peace. One is about a statue of Christ erected in the Andes, the other a rather pallid account of the League of Nations. Drowning out these faint whispers, the drums of war beat loud. This is a world where little boys dream of battle. "I will try to be very good," says Jackanapes, son of a father killed at Waterloo. "But I should like to be a soldier." His grandfather's old heart swells with pride. "You shall, my boy, you shall." A tale of powder-monkeys, for the third grade, describes the thrill of children on warships "going about [their] work amid the smoke and thunder of the guns, and seeing men struck down beside them by the fire of the enemy." A bit dangerous, of course, "but it was a fine training for the boys." Some of them even become admirals, and in this world making admiral is a big thing. Columbus was an admiral. So was Sir Cloudesley Shovell and Grenville and Raleigh and Drake.

> Admirals, all, for England's sake . . .
> They left us a kingdom none can take,
> The realm of the circling sea.

If the kingdom must be won with human lives, that is a pity, certainly. But the true Briton sees these things *sub specie deternitatis.**

> Though our only reward be the thrust of a sword
> And a bullet in heart or brain,
> What matters one gone, if the flag float on,
> And Britain be Lord of the Main!

---

*"In their proper perspective."

Four years after the close of the First World War, schoolchildren are invited to admire a battle for the Yser Canal, "an inferno of destruction and death." Shells burst, flames cloud the moon, and the great guns roar. "It was glorious," writes the author. "It was terrible. It was inspiring." Poet Laureate John Masefield describes the battle of Gallipoli in terms which emphasize, ultimately, its dreadful brilliance. Within hours, he speculates of a departing troop ship, one tenth of the men "would have looked their last on the sun, and be a part of foreign earth or dumb things that the tides push." One third would be "mangled, blinded, or broken, lamed, made imbecile, or disfigured"; the rest would suffer agonies in the trenches. Still the little readers are reminded "these things were but the end they asked, the reward they had come for, the unseen cross upon the breast. All that they felt was a gladness of exultation that their young courage was to be used. They went like kings in a pageant to the imminent death."

One can smile, now, at the Canadian Readers. Naïve, jingoistic, unscholarly, sentimental, moralistic — they were all these. And yet the fact remains that they were also memorable and moving. Few children of this generation will cherish their memories of Dick and Jane. But who could forget Jack Cornwall, the hero of the Battle of Jutland, or Madeleine, the heroine of Verchères? What are Spot and Puff compared with Bruin, the Canadian bear who terrorized a lumber camp, and gentle Patrasche, who pulled a milk cart for love? The world of the readers was a world of heroes. And in the end it didn't much matter, I think, that these heroes were dedicated to purposes which a modern finds questionable — the invincibility of the British fleet, or the glories of empire. What mattered greatly, to all of us who succumbed to its spell, was the vision of men committed to a principle beyond self. I think of Grace Darling, rowing out to a shipwreck through furious seas; of plucky little Pierre, who stole through the German lines to bring news that would save his village; of Captain Scott's last journey, and the dying Oates, who walked out into the blizzard to relieve others of responsibility for his care. In the end, the British Empire became a kind of metaphor — for honor, dignity, unselfishness, and courage. In today's schoolbooks, the captains and the kings depart — and what is left is the kid next door. **9**

Along with the sense of the heroic the readers communicated something equally valuable, a sense of the importance of the individual. Every man *mattered*. Any man might become great. Little Antonio, who carved a lion out of butter for a rich man's table, becomes a famous sculptor; honest Michael, an ordinary Dutch sailor, risks death rather than betray his master and rises "step by step till he became an admiral." Whatever stone you cast into the waters carried reverberations to distant shores. John Cornwall, mortally wounded but still manning a gun, wins "a renown that can never fade so long as men reverence . . . Duty and Honor." The story of Grace Darling's brave deed "was told all over Europe and America. High and low, rich and poor, united to sing her praises and extol her bravery." It is not true, I see now, that Alan McLeod, V.C., "left behind an undying story and an immortal name." (Who *was* Alan McLeod?) But I am glad that I grew up believing in such a possibility. **10**

The vision of the Canadian Readers was limited; it focused almost exclusively on a Protestant, Anglo-Saxon ideal. But it was always a moral vision. Open a modern school anthology and you will be struck with its efficient treatment of man as a social being: here is the real world of real children working, playing, or, as the psychologists would say, interacting. Open the Canadian Readers and you will find an often passionate concentration on what makes a man a *man*. This is true from the very beginning. Consider, for example, the First Reader story of "The Little Blue Egg." A boy, a decent chap really, takes just one peep at the nest, and then — they are so pretty — just one egg. The bird will surely not miss it. But at night, the egg safely hidden, he cannot sleep. How- **11** ever deep he huddles into the bedclothes he hears at the window a voice louder than any bird: BRING BACK MY LITTLE BLUE EGG. Compare this with an episode from a modern grade one reader.

> Sally found a big white egg.
> "I will take this," she said.
> "It looks like a ball."

Her brother sets her straight.

> "You funny girl," laughed Dick.
> "I cannot play ball with that egg.
> You must take it to Grandmother."
> Away Sally ran to the house.

Sally has learned, I suppose, a useful lesson. An egg is an egg is not a ball. But it's a far cry from the deep moral shudder communicated by that long-ago tale of the fatal blue egg.

12    Instead of the familiar — in vocabulary, situation, and scene — the Canadian Readers confronted us constantly with the unfamiliar, the strange. It was not a bad idea. "Sleep, baby, sleep!" runs a poem in the primer. "The large stars are the sheep; / The little stars are the lambs, I guess, / The bright moon is the shepherdess. / Sleep, baby, sleep." Any first-grade teacher knows that "shepherdess" is a hard word for six-year-olds — but how nice that we heard it so young. As for the unfamiliar scenery presented in the Academy paintings; we had all seen enough tractors, and one mile of prairie is much like another. The images of orchards and castle walls were not baffling but liberating; they gave us room to grow.

13    A final observation about the Canadian Readers. Theirs was a world of extraordinary security and joy. The pages shine with birds and stars and flowers. . . . Above all, it was a solid, comfortable, ordered universe, where evil was always vanquished and right enthroned.

> Truth shall conquer at the last,
> For round and round we run,
> And ever the right comes uppermost,
> And ever is justice done.

And what was truth? It was not various and shifting, but a standard clear to rational man. "Teach us," we sang in "Land of Our Birth," "The Truth whereby the Nations live." *The Truth*, in capital letters — single, absolute, in all times and places infallible. Perhaps it is this sense which, in the end, makes the intellectual landscape of the readers remote as the Land of Oz. Chicken Little sets out, in the primer, to tell the king the sky was falling, but we knew it was only a leaf. For this was indeed the windless world.

14    How could we have guessed the sky would ever fall?

# VOCABULARY

a. *paragraph 1:* insipid, momentous

b. *paragraph 3:* imperialists

c. *paragraph 6:* correctives

d. *paragraph 7:* paragon

e. *paragraph 8:* emulate, pernicious, exaltation, powder-monkeys

f. *paragraph 9:* jingoistic, invincibility, metaphor

## QUESTIONS

1. What point or thesis is Maynard developing through the description of the Canadian Readers? Does she state the point directly or leave the reader to infer it?

2. What aspect of the books does she emphasize? What details best reveal this emphasis?

3. What is the tone of the narrative? Does Maynard dramatize her experience as a student through heightened characterization of the figures and events in the Readers?

4. What do you think is Maynard's purpose in writing — to inform the reader of the facts, to come to terms with her own past, to explain a formative influence on Canadian culture, or some other reason?

5. What criticisms of the Readers does she offer? How does she qualify her criticisms?

## WRITING ASSIGNMENTS

1. Give an account of how a similar experience in elementary or high school affected your own life. Let your details make your point, and emphasize those that develop it most.

2. What effects do today's television and movies have on children's development? Be specific in discussing the attitudes and values these media inculcate: do not merely name them or describe them in general terms.

## DEBRA BLACK

*Debra Black has a B.A. from the University of Toronto and a degree in journalism from Carleton University. She has worked in a number of capacities in newspapers and television and is now a freelance journalist. Her work has been published in a score of prominent national magazines and newspapers. In this essay she reports on the latest findings in scientists' attempts to understand the process of ageing.*

## THE ETERNAL QUEST

With electrodes pasted to his chest and a clamp squeezed tightly over his nose, 70-year-old Clare Brawn steps gingerly onto a treadmill inside a sterile, yellow laboratory at London's University of Western Ontario. Pushing an apparatus that resembles a vacuum hose into his mouth, the retired psychologist gives the thumbs-up signal to a nearby researcher and waits for the machine to start moving. As the speed increases, the platform tilts slightly, and Brawn begins walking uphill. For the next 20 minutes, while he strides forward effortlessly, scientists map his heartbeat and the exchange of oxygen and carbon dioxide in his lungs. One of 200 participants in a longitudinal study tracking the physiology of ageing, Brawn is an anomaly among his peers: he routinely jogs three miles (5 km) in less than 30 minutes and has neither visible wrinkles nor sagging skin. Indeed, the only outward signs of his many years of living are his silver-grey hair and white moustache.

2   The same fall morning, in a dimly lit room across the tree-lined campus, 90-year-old Melvin Cravetz sits on a bench with wires trailing from one of his legs and smiles as a graduate student shoots a mild current of electricity through the extremity. "Nah, it doesn't hurt," he says as his calf muscle involuntarily flexes. The former railroad foreman, who retired and went on to work full-time as a gardener until the age of 84, has, not surprisingly, the physical responses of a much younger man. Researchers are performing a battery of tests on him to try to find out why, but to Cravetz, there is no mystery: "I don't drink, I don't smoke — gave that up in 1924 — and I walk a mile every day."

3   Although plain to Cravetz, to the scientists in London, Ontario, and to the scores of others across the continent studying how the body ages, the reasons that some people remain healthy and active much longer than others are far from simple. And their quest for the answers is becoming increasingly urgent. Populations around the world are growing old fast: in Canada, for example, studies estimate that by the year 2031, nearly 24 percent of Canadians — more than seven million men and women — will be over the age of 65, compared with 9.7 percent in 1981. If they can discover exactly how humans grow old, the researchers say, they should be able to intervene in the process and enable the elderly to live more active and productive lives, free of the chronic degenerative diseases that now strike most senior citizens.

4   Their task is not an easy one. At the Gerontology Research Center in Baltimore, Maryland, where some 300 staff members will spend almost $22.5 million this year pursuing the molecular and cellular changes that occur in humans over time, a long-term study suggests that heredity dictates the rate of physical deterioration in individuals. The ongoing 25-year-old investigation, which is following approximately 1 000 Americans between the ages of 20 and 96, has shown that the body changes most commonly associated with old age — grey or thinning hair, diminished vision and hearing, wrinkled and sagging skin, poor memory and shrinking height and mass — can begin as early as age 30. However, the Baltimore researchers have also documented cases of 90-year-olds, with internal organs that functioned as though they were 60 years younger.

## DEATH HORMONE

5   In spite of the striking individual variations in the ageing process, the Ponce de Leóns of the 1980s are confident that they are finally closing in on the most fundamental of biological secrets. By the 21st century, they predict, North Americans will live well beyond their current average life spans. Some suggest the norm will be between 110 and 120 years; others are betting even that can be extended.

6   There are two broad theories concerning what triggers a human's inevitable decline to death. The first is the wear-and-tear hypothesis that suggests the body eventually succumbs to the environmental insults of life. The second is the notion that we all have an internal clock which is genetically programmed to run down. Supporters of the wear-and-tear theory maintain that the very practice of breathing causes us to age because inhaled oxygen produces toxic by-products called free radicals, which roam the body tearing at cells and attacking their DNA. While the body produces antioxidants to combat the free radicals, low levels of damage still occur and build over time. Advocates of the internal-clock theory believe that individual cells are told to stop dividing and thus eventually to die by, for example, hormones produced by the brain or by their own genes. One premise

holds that at puberty, the pituitary gland releases a death hormone which then begins to choreograph the gradual ageing process.

Since there is no consensus among the small but growing army of longevity researchers on why humans fall prey to the ravages of time, there is no agreement on how to forestall the effects of many years of living. "No one is going to hand you a pill that will allow you to live to be 200," says Michael Rose, an associate professor of biology at Halifax's Dalhousie University, whose own research with fruit flies has convinced him that some form of genetic engineering will ultimately prolong life. Yet other researchers anticipate there will be pills — elixirs that will supplement the body's stores of such antioxidants as vitamin E and uric acid; boost its immune system; alter its hormone levels; or increase its supply of enzymes to repair damage to the cells and their genes.    **7**

According to Rose, a 31-year-old avowed Darwinist whose meticulous office displays both a poster and a biography of the famous naturalist, ageing is a consequence of evolution. Humans have survived, he says, because natural selection favours healthy, youthful reproduction over longevity. Thus senescence, or the physical deterioration associated with ageing, has been built into human genes over time.    **8**

For the past 10 years, Rose has been attempting to prove that hypothesis, which was first postulated in the 1940s. And he has achieved some success: by reversing the normal forces of natural selection, he has lengthened the life span of fruit flies by 30 to 50 percent. Moreover, he and graduate student Ted Hutchinson have discovered that over the course of the study, several of the flies' genes have changed. The finding has led them to conclude that more than one gene is responsible for either triggering or postponing the ageing process. If that is true in the fruit fly, says Rose, it is probably true in humans.    **9**

As the song *Across the Universe* reverberates through the stereo system in his sunny laboratory, Rose removes a small cage of the tiny, red-eyed flies from a row of incubators and explains his experiment. Essentially, he says, by forcing generations of fruit flies to breed late in life, he has actually reprogrammed their genes to allow them to live longer. To do that, he discarded all the eggs the insects laid until they were just about to die. "They were like hard-core Yuppies, living in their wonderful pastel apartments with everything spotless. They had no kids to mess things up; they were just getting old together." The flies' final attempts at reproduction were not thwarted, however, and when their offspring matured, the entire process was repeated. After 15 generations, the flies' genes had changed.    **10**

The point is, says Rose, natural selection "doesn't give a damn" about what happens to flies, or humans, after reproduction ceases. There are several theories, however, on how we fall apart. One submits that when we reach about 40, our genes begin to mutate and go awry. It suggests that the older individual is a genetic garbage can where anything bad can and will happen. Another hypothesis proposes that there is a trade-off between the early and late stages of development. Because genes are working to enhance early reproduction, not longevity, they may have a good effect during youth and a debilitating impact later. "Let's say," says Rose, "there's a gene in a 50-year-old man that causes him to keel over from a heart attack because he is 250 beefy pounds." The same gene may years before have made the man physically strong and handsome so he could attract women and reproduce. "This would have increased his evolutionary fitness. It doesn't matter if he drops dead at 50."    **11**

By manipulating the same forces of natural selection, Rose created a strain of flies with genes that push for longevity, rather than early reproduction. His results suggest, he says, that decades from now, it may be possible through gene-transfer operations to endow human beings with the same propensity. But first, researchers have to isolate the genes that control life span and understand how they work.    **12**

## AGEING TRIGGERS

13    Determining the involvement of genes in the ageing process is the goal of Calvin Harley, a molecular biologist at McMaster University in Hamilton, Ontario. The 34-year-old marathon runner is examining a process called terminal differentiation — the final stage of the growth of cells when they have finished developing and stop dividing. Harley, who has earned an international reputation as a leading longevity researcher, theorizes that the genes and proteins which tell cells to stop growing are fundamentally linked to ageing. Like Rose, he believes that when cells stop dividing, there are both good and bad effects for the body: the initial advantage to the tissue or organ can later in life prove harmful; for example, when brain cells do not regenerate following a stroke.

14    American scientist Leonard Hayflick was the first to demonstrate in 1961 that most human cells are mortal, dividing some 60 times over a period of years before they die. Two photographs of young and old cells on Harley's office wall graphically illustrate that transience. The first looks like a smooth-flowing waterway; the second, like a dried-up riverbed. "If you look at these, you can become fairly convinced there is a dramatic change in the cell because of age," says Harley. By following cells through the progression, he hopes to discover which genes switch on or off and which proteins are produced to cause the cell to stop dividing.

15    Harley and graduate student Michael Tyers have already made some inroads in the search. They have discovered that when special leukemia cells with the ability to cease replicating do stop dividing, they always contain a decreased level of a protein produced by a gene called "myc." (The myc gene is part of the DNA structure in all cells.) Furthermore, they have found that when activated myc genes are added to the same leukemia cells in a petri dish, the cells begin replicating again. "The fact that cells which have been genetically altered are able to pick up and start dividing again has important implications in terms of our long-term understanding of ageing," says Harley. If the same results can be produced in normal cells, it may one day be possible through gene-transfer operations, probably at the embryonic stage, to instil in the human body the ability to regenerate damaged or destroyed cells. That, in turn, could mean many additional years of life.

16    While Harley and others search for ageing triggers inside cells, biochemist Vincent Cristofalo and his colleagues at the University of Pennsylvania are looking at how the inside substances respond to factors outside the cells. The researchers have found, for example, that as cells age, they lose their ability to respond to certain growth factors. They speculate that something has happened to the cells' receptors to prevent the growth messages from being received and internalized. "It's like the music played on a stereo," says Cristofalo. "The sound you hear is modulated not merely by the 'on-off' switch but by where the volume, treble and bass are set as well." The team's most exciting discovery, however, is that there are proteins in cell membranes which can revive old cells, causing them to begin dividing again.

17    More evidence for the notion of an internal clock that controls ageing has been uncovered by Eugenia Wang, a cell biologist at New York's Rockefeller University, who will move to Montreal later this year to direct a special ageing research division at the Lady Davis Medical Research Centre. Wang has discovered a protein called statin in old cells, which she says may be an indicator of a family of genes that regulate the final stages of a cell's life.

18    Researchers are also pursuing a new twist to an old idea. The belief that diet affects longevity has been accepted in scientific circles since 1935, when studies by Clive McKay of Cornell University first demonstrated that cutting back on calories extends the life spans of animals. But why that occurs has remained a mystery. Montreal biologist Hildegard

Enesco, who chairs the biological division of the Canadian Association on Gerontology and is a professor at Concordia University, suggests that dietary changes may alter the levels of either hormones or free radicals in the body. Enesco has discovered that rotifers, microscopic invertebrates usually found in marshy areas and streams, live 20 percent longer when their diets are restricted. Their life spans are also extended, says Enesco, when they are fed vitamin E or another antioxidant called thiazolidine-4-carboxylic acid (TCA). Natural scavengers of free radicals, the antioxidants act as mops, soaking up high levels of the toxic molecules before they can wreak havoc on cells.

John Carlson, a University of Waterloo biologist, has also shown that a low-calorie **19** diet, supplements of vitamin E and light restriction all extend the life spans of rotifers. Furthermore, he has demonstrated that raising the temperature of rotifers tends to shorten their lives, possibly because the heat increases their metabolic reactions, stepping up the production of free radicals.

If changes in hormone levels are the cause of ageing, speculates Enesco, it could be **20** that the controversial hypothesis first suggested by American biochemist Donner Denckla — that the pituitary gland releases a death hormone at puberty — is true. Indeed, experiments by longevity scientists demonstrated that removing the pituitary gland of animals extended their lives. But Enesco believes that hormones released by other parts of the brain, including the thymus — the master gland of the immune system — also contribute to the ageing process.

The view that the thymus is central to ageing is supported by the research findings of **21** Allan Goldstein, a biochemist at George Washington University. He has discovered that the thymus — the first gland in the body to atrophy, beginning to shrink at puberty — produces hormones called thymosins, which act on the body in two ways. First, they boost the immune system by activating white blood cells called T-cells that kill foreign organisms. Second, they prompt the release of other hormones in the brain. Thus, as the production of thymosins decreases with age, the immune system becomes less able to ward off disease, and the body's hormone levels change, which in turn causes general deterioration. Goldstein says it may one day be possible to turn back the ageing clock in the brain simply by increasing body levels of thymosin.

The link between hormones and ageing is also the subject of an investigation by James **22** Nelson and Lêda Felicio, a husband-and-wife team at Montreal's McGill University. Both endocrinologists, they believe that there is no one cause of ageing but, rather, that cells in different parts of the body age at different rates for different reasons. The resulting changes, they speculate, combine in intricate and complex ways to produce an increased vulnerability to death. "You can't talk about a single pacemaker of ageing even in a single physiological system," says Nelson, who is affiliated with the newly formed McGill Centre for Studies in Age and Aging. The changes in one system promote changes in other systems, he believes, ultimately causing "a cascade of effects" that characterizes ageing.

Nelson and Felicio's studies illustrate, for example, an interrelationship among the **23** brain, the hormones it releases into the bloodstream and the ageing of the female reproductive system. By transplanting a young ovary into an old mouse, the researchers doubled its reproductive life span. However, they also discovered that chronic exposure to ovarian hormones in mice accelerates ageing of the hypothalamus, the part of the brain that controls reproduction. Thus ironically, it appears, the very hormones necessary for the functioning of the reproductive system ultimately contribute to its demise.

At Queen's University at Kingston, Ontario, immunologist Miron Szewchuk has dis- **24** covered that ageing mice, when confronted with a foreign agent, produce two sets of antibodies. As the first begins to fight the invader, the second — called autoantibodies — starts shutting down the cells that manufacture the defenders, in effect switching off the immune system. When the same old mice receive injections of immune cells extracted from genetically identical younger mice, however, they do not make the autoantibodies and are able to kill invading organisms. Similar research by other scientists has shown that immune-cell transplants enable old mice not only to remain healthy but to live up to two-thirds longer.

25    While the discoveries made so far by longevity researchers may eventually help to quell the ravages of time in humans, they have not yet unlocked the mystery of ageing, says Nelson, who proposes that a team effort is necessary to find the ultimate key. "We need to study the disruption of communication between the body's cells and tissues during ageing — what's happening between the brain and the ovary, the brain and the adrenal gland, the brain and the pituitary." Enesco agrees: "We know fragments. We know something about cell-division potential. That's a piece of the puzzle. But to tie everything together, we'll have to look at basic genetic programmes, at the influence of free radicals, at how hormones affect the body, how proteins interact . . . there are no ultimate answers right now."

26    While it waits for the definitive breakthrough, a segment of today's generation has turned to interim measures such as diet restriction, exercise and supplements of antioxidants. However, the jury is out on these. Some researchers suggest that exercise is important in warding off mortality; others believe, as did the Victorians, that vigorous exercise may in fact decrease longevity because it increases oxygen intake and, therefore, the production of free radicals. Moreover, say the detractors, unsupervised exercise can cause health problems in imprudent novices. Some scientists also scoff at vitamin E supplements and low-calorie diets, pointing out that humans are a very different species from a mouse or a rotifer.

27    For now, most longevity researchers agree, the best route to living a longer life remains the tried-and-true one: practise moderation. "Don't eat too much," recommends Sam Goldstein, a former Winnipeg internist who is now head of the division of gerontology at the University of Arkansas. "Exercise. Get plenty of rest. Keep cool and calm. Avoid tension. Don't smoke. It sounds clichéd, but all the old adages apply."

28    Although the fountain of youth remains elusive, it does not seem to matter to Clare Brawn as he warms up on the University of Western Ontario's outdoor track on a chilly fall morning. As he and his running partner, Bloss Doupé, a 71-year-old former civil servant, prepare to begin their 14 laps — both dressed in shorts and t-shirts that read "It's Hard to be Humble" — Brawn remarks that longevity perhaps is not as important as feeling good. "And I feel good after a run," he says with a grin as he sprints onto the frosty track.

## VOCABULARY

a. *paragraph   1:* longitudinal, physiology

b. *paragraph   3:* degenerative

c. *paragraph   6:* antioxidants, choreograph

d. *paragraph   7:* consensus

e. *paragraph  16:* internalized, modulated

f. *paragraph  18:* scavengers

# QUESTIONS

1. Why does Black delay the two theories of ageing until paragraph 6? Why does she begin with two examples and a common-sense theory of ageing?

2. How does Black organize her material? Make an outline that shows the different parts of the essay.

3. Summarize in a sentence the main idea of each paragraph. Do the sentences, when put together, make a coherent argument?

4. Notice that the researchers generalize carefully from clearly identified evidence. How does Black suggest to the reader the relative importance of the various kinds of evidence presented — that is, the weight they should be prepared to give it?

5. For whom is this essay written? How much scientific knowledge is the reader assumed to have?

6. Why does Black twice allude to Ponce de León and his fountain of youth? How hopeful is her conclusion? Does she suggest that medical research and scientific knowledge generally have limits?

# WRITING ASSIGNMENTS

1. Discuss the common-sense advice for prolonging life that comes at the conclusion of the essay. What other suggestions can you add to the list? What kind of evidence can you provide for these claims?

2. Choose a field in which scientists are working for a breakthrough — cancer research, AIDS, Alzheimer's disease — and summarize the current state of the research.

# ORDER OF IDEAS

An author may develop the main or central idea of a paragraph through a series of subordinate ideas. Consider the opening sentences of Teale's paragraph on country superstitions. The first sentence is the main idea; the second sentence, a subordinate idea that develops it through illustration:

> In the folklore of the country, numerous superstitions relate to winter weather.
>> Back-country farmers examine their corn husks —
>>> the thicker the husk, the colder the winter. — Edwin Way Teale, "Country Superstitions"

We have indented to show the levels of subordination in these sentences. Notice that the third sentence has the same importance as the second in developing the main idea:

> They watch the acorn crop —
>> the more acorns, the more severe the season. — Teale, "Country Superstitions"

Of course, in writing paragraphs you do not indent in this way to show the relative importance of your ideas. But you do in writing essays: the break for a new paragraph — through an indentation — tells the reader that you are introducing a new idea or topic. Within the paragraph you need ways of substituting for the indentations shown above. One of these ways is the use of parallel phrasing to show that ideas have the same importance:

> They watch the acorn crop. . . .
> They observe. . . .
> They examine. . . .
> — Teale, "Country Superstitions"

We will consider later in this section other devices that show the relative importance of ideas — among them transitional words and phrases (for example, the phrase *of equal importance*).

In longer paragraphs, the main idea may be distinguished by repeating or restating it at the end. We will see in the next section that the beginning and ending are usually the most emphatic parts of sentences because of their prominence. The same is true of paragraphs and essays.

A unified paragraph develops one idea at a time and makes each idea relevant to the topic idea. You will keep a paragraph unified if, as you write, you consider the order in which you want to present your ideas and details. This order is sometimes determined by the subject of the paragraph and sometimes by the audience you have in mind — and sometimes by both. For example, in describing parallel parking for people learning to drive, you usually will present each step as it occurs. But in describing the same process to driving instructors, you might present these steps in the order of their difficulty, to single out those steps needing most practice.

An account of a process, or a narrative, is usually chronological. A description of a scene is generally spatial in organization — the details are presented as the eye sees them, moving from one part of what is seen to another. The details or ideas can also be ordered in other ways. For example, you can write them

- from the easy to the difficult, as in the paragraph written for driving instructors

- from the less to the more important

- from the less to the more interesting or exciting

- from the general to the specific — for example, from the theory of combustion to the details of the process

- from the specific to the general — for example, from simple effects of gravity, like falling off a bike, to a definition or comment on these effects

A paragraph may combine two or more orders of ideas. For instance, a paragraph written for driving instructors may move from the easy to the difficult steps of parallel parking, and at the same time from the less to the more important or even interesting.

The same is true of the order of ideas in an essay. Both the nature of the essay and the nature of the audience influence the choices you make. An essay describing a process requires the usual step-by-step presentation. If the audience is already familiar with the general process, you may refer briefly to the familiar steps and then focus on the more difficult ones. In a persuasive essay, you may introduce your thesis at the beginning if your audience will understand it without explanation; if the thesis requires explanation or is controversial, you may decide to build to it through explanatory details and ideas.

The essay of personal experience can follow a freer course than a formal essay of ideas. In her book *Pilgrim at Tinker Creek*, Annie Dillard divides an essay on winter into sections, each dealing with experiences and reflections suggested by the subject. Here are the sentences that introduce the opening sections:

> It is the first of February, and everyone is talking about starlings.
> It is winter proper; the cold weather, such as it is, has come to stay.
> Some weather's coming; you can taste on the sides of your tongue a quince tang in the air.
> This is the sort of stuff I read all winter. — Annie Dillard, *Pilgrim at Tinker Creek*

An expository essay, one that explains, analyses, or clarifies, will show the logical relationship of ideas, as these sentences from Arthur Schafer's essay on modern morals illustrate:

> The most profoundly important innovation of Western liberal society has been to put the marketplace at the centre of all social transactions.
> Or so the theory would have it.
> Neo-conservatives such as U.S. President Ronald Reagan and British Prime Minister Margaret Thatcher lament the collapse of traditional social values: family, work, patriotism, restraint.
> Ironically, it is the very marketplace morality at whose shrine the neo-conservatives worship that produces the social disintegration they lament.
> As long as only a minority is motivated by ruthless self-interest, social bonds can remain largely intact. — Arthur Schafer, "Morals in the Rat Race"

The ordering of ideas can reveal a characteristic way of thinking — one that we find in other essays of the same writer. Other essays of Annie Dillard, for instance, reveal the same organization that helps her to express the feelings and thoughts of the moment. Even expository and argumentative essays may reveal an organization of ideas characteristic of the writer — perhaps a tendency to build to the thesis instead of introducing it early in the essay.

As we saw in the last section, the thesis is the most important idea in an essay. When an essay builds to its thesis through a series of subordinate ideas and details, we sense a rising importance of ideas in it, even perhaps a sense of climax. It is crucial that we sense the relative importance of these ideas and details. An essay in which all of these seem to have the same weight would be extremely hard to read.

We can sense this relative importance of ideas even in the topic sentences, as in these sentences that open the first seven paragraphs of Sevareid's essay on Velva, North Dakota. The different indentations show the relative weight of each idea:

> My home town has changed in these thirty years . . .
>> Sights have changed . . .
>> Sounds have changed . . .
>> The people have not changed, but the *kinds* of people have changed . . .
>>> No, the "characters" are vanishing in Velva. . . .
>> They eat differently in Velva now . . .
> It is distance and time that have changed the most and worked the deepest changes in Velva's life. . . . — Sevareid, "Velva, North Dakota"

Sevareid builds to his thesis through a series of increasingly broad generalizations. Here are the opening sentences of the last six paragraphs:

>> Many politicians deplore the passing of the old family-size farm, but I am not so sure. . . .
>> But now I must ask myself: Are they nearer to one another? . . .
>> For personal and social neuroses festered under this hard scab of conformity. . . .
>> The door to the world stands open now. . . .
> Human nature is everywhere the same. . . .
> It is personal freedom that makes us better persons, and they are freer in Velva now [*thesis*].
> — Sevareid, "Velva, North Dakota"

Sevareid's sentences show that we do not always need formal transitions to tell us which ideas are main and which are subordinate. The clear logical relationship of Sevareid's ideas shows their relative importance. But as in the paragraph, formal transitions are sometimes needed. Having a sense of the relative importance of our ideas and details is important as we write.

## ALICE MUNRO

*Born in Wingham, Ontario, in 1931,* Alice Munro *has become one of Canadian literature's most perceptive recorders of small-town life. Her first collection of short stories,* Dance of the Happy Shades, *was published in 1968, and it is in the genre of the short story that she has continued to excel. Three-time winner of the Governor General's Award for fiction, she writes about the lives of adolescent girls, lonely middle-aged women, and the elderly. The meticulous clarity of the detail recorded to recreate those lives makes for a photographic realism of compelling vividness and a sensitivity of emotional nuance that is to be found in few contemporary writers. In the following passage from "Walker Brothers Cowboy," a young girl goes for a walk with her father and contrasts the way they perceive the world they share.*

## WALKER BROTHERS COWBOY

1   After supper my father says, "Want to go down and see if the Lake's still there?" We leave my mother sewing under the dining-room light, making clothes for me against the opening

of school. She has ripped up for this purpose an old suit and an old plaid wool dress of hers, and she has to cut and match very cleverly and also make me stand and turn for endless fittings, sweaty, itching from the hot wool, ungrateful. We leave my brother in bed in the little screened porch at the end of the front verandah, and sometimes he kneels on his bed and presses his face against the screen and calls mournfully, "Bring me an ice cream cone!" but I call back, "You will be asleep," and do not even turn my head.

Then my father and I walk gradually down a long, shabby sort of street, with Silverwoods Ice Cream signs standing on the sidewalk, outside tiny, lighted stores. This is in Tuppertown, an old town on Lake Huron, an old grain port. The street is shaded, in some places, by maple trees whose roots have cracked and heaved the sidewalk and spread out like crocodiles into the bare yards. People are sitting out, men in shirt-sleeves and undershirts and women in aprons — not people we know but if anybody looks ready to nod and say, "Warm night," my father will nod too and say something the same. Children are still playing. I don't know them either because my mother keeps my brother and me in our own yard, saying he is too young to leave it and I have to mind him. I am not so sad to watch their evening games because the games themselves are ragged, dissolving. Children, of their own will, draw apart, separate into islands of two or one under the heavy trees, occupying themselves in such solitary ways as I do all day, planting pebbles in the dirt or writing in it with a stick.    2

Presently we leave these yards and houses behind, we pass a factory with boarded-up windows, a lumberyard whose high wooden gates are locked for the night. Then the town falls away in a defeated jumble of sheds and small junkyards, the sidewalk gives up and we are walking on a sandy path with burdocks, plantains, humble nameless weeds all around. We enter a vacant lot, a kind of park really, for it is kept clear of junk and there is one bench with a slat missing on the back, a place to sit and look at the water. Which is generally grey in the evening, under a lightly overcast sky, no sunsets, the horizon dim. A very quiet, washing noise on the stones of the beach. Further along, towards the main part of town, there is a stretch of sand, a water slide, floats bobbing around the safe swimming area, a life guard's rickety throne. Also a long dark green building, like a roofed verandah, called the Pavilion, full of farmers and their wives, in stiff good clothes, on Sundays. That is the part of the town we used to know when we lived at Dungannon and came here three or four times a summer, to the Lake. That, and the docks where we would go and look at the grain boats, ancient, rusty, wallowing, making us wonder how they got past the breakwater let alone to Fort William.    3

Tramps hang around the docks and occasionally on these evenings wander up the dwindling beach and climb the shifting, precarious path boys have made, hanging onto dry bushes, and say something to my father which, being frightened of tramps, I am too alarmed to catch. My father says he is a bit hard up himself. "I'll roll you a cigarette if it's any use to you," he says, and he shakes tobacco out carefully on one of the thin butterfly papers, flicks it with his tongue, seals it and hands it to the tramp who takes it and walks away. My father also rolls and lights and smokes one cigarette of his own.    4

He tells me how the Great Lakes came to be. All where Lake Huron is now, he says, used to be flat land, a wide flat plain. Then came the ice, creeping down from the north, pushing down into the low places. Like *that* — and he shows me his hand with his spread fingers pressing the rock-hard ground where we are sitting. His fingers make hardly any impression at all and he says, "Well, the old ice cap had a lot more power behind it than this hand has." And then the ice went back, shrank back towards the North Pole where it came from, and left its fingers of ice in the deep places it had gouged, and ice turned to lakes and there they were today. They were *new*, as time went. I try to see that plain before me, dinosaurs walking on it, but I am not able even to imagine the shore of the Lake when    5 the Indians were there, before Tuppertown. The tiny share we have of time appalls me, though my father seems to regard it with tranquillity. Even my father, who sometimes seems to me to have been at home in the world as long as it has lasted, has really lived on this earth only a little longer than I have, in terms of all the time there has been to live in. He has not known a time, any more than I, when automobiles and electric lights did not at least exist. He was not alive when this century started. I will be barely alive — old, old — when it ends. I do not like to think of it. I wish the Lake to be always just a lake, with the safe-swimming floats marking it, and the breakwater and the lights of Tuppertown.

## VOCABULARY

a. *paragraph 3:* burdocks, plantains, wallowing

b. *paragraph 5:* tranquility

## QUESTIONS

1. Munro orders her description chronologically and spatially. Which parts does she present chronologically — in the order of time — and which parts does she present spatially?

2. What is the main idea of paragraph 5? How are subordinate ideas distinguished from the main idea?

3. What overall impression do you get of Tuppertown? Does Munro state the impression directly, or does she let it emerge from the details? Which details contribute most to this impression?

4. Does Munro present each feature of the story and her experiences one at a time, without repetition, or does she return to earlier features or details?

## WRITING ASSIGNMENTS

1. Describe a neighbourhood you remember from childhood. Decide on a dominant impression and choose details that develop it. Then decide on an order of details appropriate to your purpose. Remember that, although your reader has not seen the neighbourhood, you need not give all of its details to develop an impression of it.

2. Munro states in paragraph 5: "The tiny share we have of time appalls me, though my father seems to regard it with tranquillity." Write a description of an institution like a government office or a schoolroom to show how your feelings and attitude determine what you notice and consider important.

## JOHN KENNETH GALBRAITH

John Kenneth Galbraith *is the author of dozens of books on economic theory and practice and has an international reputation as a teacher and scholar. He was born in Elgin*

*County, Ontario in 1908, educated at the Ontario Agricultural College, and received a* Ph.D. *in agricultural economics from the University of California at Berkeley. He was an economic adviser to every democratic candidate for the American presidency from Franklin Roosevelt to Lyndon Johnson, and was U.S. ambassador to India from 1961 to 1963. A liberal intellectual, Galbraith has outlined his alternative concept of capitalism in such influential books as* American Capitalism *(1952),* The Affluent Society *(1958), and* The New Industrial State *(1968). The passage that follows is taken from* The Scotch *(1964), Galbraith's entertaining account of his boyhood in southern Ontario.*

## THE URBAN LIFE

If one went east on Hogg Street for a little under three miles to where it met the Southwold     1
Townline, he came to our nearest market center, Iona Station. Here the railroads, the
Canada Southern become the double-tracked Michigan Central, then the New York Central and paralleled by the single line of the Pere Marquette (since the Chesapeake and
Ohio), came in at an angle across the countryside and also crossed the Townline. It was
this intersection of roads and railroads which had made the place. In earlier years, life had
centered on another community two miles nearer the Lake, Iona by name, but the railroads had missed it, and it had gone into decline. Iona Station had risen in its place.

It was a pleasant community with a sound basic plan. At one side of town, where Hogg     2
Street met the Townline, and a little apart from both the commercial and industrial areas,
was the religious and cultural center. North along the principal street, one came first to the
residential section and then the main shopping center with the service industries conven-
iently close. After that came the railroads, the railroad stations, stockyards, another small
residential area, another shopping center and a small manufacturing establishment. A
good half mile north of town, intelligently remote from all urban influences, was the
school. Maples shaded the mercantile, manufacturing and residential areas alike; people
walked not on harsh aslphalt but on grass. No activity or function of the town intruded
itself on any other save that, of a night, people might be momentarily aroused by a passing
train. No one resented this for, potentially at least, the railroads provided as fine a system
of communications as that of any community in the world. Were one to step on a train,
one could proceed westward without changing cars to Windsor, Detroit and Chicago. A
single change would bring him to San Francisco, and the gateway to the Orient. To the
east, he could go with equal convenience to Niagara Falls, Buffalo, Syracuse, Albany and
New York City. With a single change from train to ship, he could be on to Liverpool,
Southampton or Glasgow.

Unfortunately, the trains did not stop. Largely for this reason, Iona Station, the diver-     3
sity of its economic life notwithstanding, was very small — in my time not more than
twenty-five souls. The cultural center comprised a white brick church and a small frame
hall used for box socials, an occasional political meeting and, in later and morally more
relaxed times, an infrequent dance. (The Scotch were divided on dancing, Highland dancing apart. An older and sterner generation held it to be wicked and likely to divert attention from serious labor. But the moderate majority now approved of it in moderation.) The
church served a very small congregation, and its architect had solved a difficult problem in
an interesting way. No matter how small it is, a church must have a certain minimum
height — there must be headroom for the people and religious dignity requires a certain
altitude. Since the building needed to accommodate only a handful of people, he had reduced its length until it slightly resembled a small pancake stood on edge. By the time of
this study, the church was served only by an itinerant divine. The residential section con-

sisted of four or five frame houses all in need of paint. John Dundas, a very good black-smith, provided a universal repair service all by himself. The Pere Marquette station stood empty, a monument to unrealized commercial hopes, and one day the company loaded it on a flatcar and carried it away. The stockyards were also in decline. The store to the north of the tracks was financially insecure, and after one fire had been put out by the neighbors it was carried away by a second. Manufacturing was in the hands of an aged harness-maker whose enterprise was also sadly athwart the march of technology. One could still buy a ticket on the mail and accommodation trains at the Michigan Central Station, and the stationmaster was a man of consequence.

## VOCABULARY

a. *paragraph 2:* mercantile

b. *paragraph 3:* box socials, itinerant, athwart

## QUESTIONS

1. How do the opening topic sentences of paragraphs 1 and 2 suggest a focus and organi-zation of the details?

2. How does Galbraith manage the transition between paragraphs 2 and 3?

3. Is paragraph 3 unified in the sense that it develops only one idea?

## WRITING ASSIGNMENT

Write two or more paragraphs of your own that open with a dominant impression of a scene and then develop this impression through details. You might describe a view from a window in your house or dormitory or a walk through your neighbourhood or your campus.

## CHARLES TAYLOR

Charles Taylor, *born in 1935, is the author of* Six Journeys: A Canadian Pattern. *He has also written two books on Asia. He is a past chairman of The Writers' Union of Canada and was a journalist for many years, serving as bureau chief for the* Toronto Globe and Mail *in Hong Kong, Peking, Nairobi, and London.* Radical Tories, *from which this ex-cerpt is taken, is Taylor's personal exploration of the tradition of radical toryism in Canada. Taylor's journey begins with the suggestion that "Creighton rehabilitated Macdonald and reasserted the conservative tradition as our dominant historical force."*

## DONALD CREIGHTON

1    During his last two decades, Donald Creighton lived with his wife Luella in a red brick farmhouse in the village of Brooklin, about thirty miles east of Toronto along the old

Highway Seven. In anticipation of his retirement from the University of Toronto, Canada's foremost historian had sought his roots on a nineteenth century street in the heartland of rural Ontario. It is a short street with other red-and-white brick homes and a towering Methodist church at the end: a mid-Victorian street of lilac bushes and tidy gardens suggesting yeoman squires, comfortable families, simple pleasures and un-challenged verities. If Princess Street seems prim and puritanical today, there is also a touch of elegance — restrained elegance — to those stolid dwellings. Neither rustic nor city-slick, it is a street where gentlefolk have always lived, where manners have always counted, and where peace and order still prevail.

I drove to Brooklin on three occasions during Creighton's last year. (He died in his sleep on the night of December 18, 1979, at the age of 77.) He had agreed to help me with this book, he had spoken and written generous things about its predecessors, and he had scorned my disavowal of the proper academic qualifications. As he put it in a letter: "I feel confident that you are far better fitted to undertake the study you propose than any of the current crop of young professional historians, most of whom seem quite incapable of writ-ing a work of analysis and interpretation, or indeed, a major work of any kind." That was my first experience of Creighton's legendary acerbity: there would be many more.

On my first two visits, Creighton met me in the living room, leaning heavily on a cane. (Later he would be confined to a wheel chair.) Always tall and angular, he was now stooped, haggard and very frail. But he was cleanly shaven and impeccably dressed in a blue-grey suit with a shirt and tie in other shades of blue, and his manner was courtly. (I was not just greeted; I was *received*.) For Creighton to sit down was a lengthy exercise, full of pain and labour, but once settled in his chair, he would look up with a beaming, winsome smile, (quite precisely, it lip up his face), and the old, collapsing body became almost invisible, subdued and dominated by the high-domed, oracular head. And then the voice would boom out — deep and orotund, the phrases almost as rich and rhythmical as any in his books — the voice of a Victorian Methodist preacher (such as his father had been) launched on a tumult of castigation and exhortation.

Not that he ignored his illness: apart from the discomfort, his exasperation was palpable. "Old men wear out!" he roared, adding that although his mind was still sharp ("I'm all right up here, thank God!"), he could no longer use his hand to write and had never been comfortable with a dictating machine. ("I need to see the words on the page.") As his final work, he had hoped to write a memoir of his mother, but now he realised this would never happen. There was a long pause. "I think I should die," he finally said. "What's the point in hanging on?" Then he mentioned that he had tried to get pills from one of his doctors, so that he could end himself. (For once this came out quietly, almost under his breath.) Suddenly his eyes sparkled and danced, as he described one of the nurses who had been attending him. After a eulogy of her physical presence, he stopped abruptly, as if recollecting himself, and sadly said: "Oh, my . . ."

Yet these were mere preliminaries. For soon (and this was true of each visit), Creighton would be launched on his big subject — almost his only subject — his beloved Canada. Then it would all come out — his rooted faith in Sir John A. Macdonald's original vision, in British traditions and in strong central government, as well as his total disdain for all Liberals and Americans, collaborators in our downfall, in our loss of independence. "Well, it's still a good place to live, but that's all Canada is now — just a good place to live." This, too, was said quietly, but most of the rest was roared, as if he were addressing not a single guest but an audience of thousands, of many generations, on the subject of our self-betrayal. His vehemence was implacable. My second visit, in the spring of 1979, came just after the Conservatives had won a federal election, but had been denied an over-all majority by the voters of Quebec. "The French Canadians always vote Liberal,"

2

3

4

5

Creighton bellowed. "It's not something they think about. It's a bodily function — like urinating and defecating!" In his books, Creighton castigates Mackenzie King above all other Liberals; now he claimed that Lester Pearson was even worse — "I feel positive hatred toward that man" — and indicated that Pierre Trudeau was almost beneath his contempt. As for Americans — "I have an incredible dislike and hatred of the United States. I've always had it. I never met one I liked." Nor did the emerging nations emerge unscathed: "All those ranks of grinning, idiot black faces at the United Nations . . ." He paused. "I guess I'm what they call a racist." Somehow he sounded both abashed and unrepentant.

6      By now I was feeling distinctly uneasy. These were surely the rantings of a dying man: they could be excused but should never be reported. Yet Creighton was far from senility, and I knew that even in his prime, he had never masked his prejudices. A friend had told me how he once sat behind Creighton at a public lecture given by his fellow historian Arthur Lower. To Creighton, the eminent Lower was anathema, mainly because of his liberal bias against the British tradition as a legitimate part of the Canadian heritage. As my friend recalled: "Donald kept shouting 'Brain damage . . . the man must have brain damage!' He may have thought he was muttering, but his voice carried all around the hall." When I told the anecdote to Creighton, he shook with laughter. Months later, on my final visit, I felt I knew him well enough to broach the subject of his vehemence, and how it should be handled. "Perhaps I've been too outspoken," he conceded, "but you mustn't make me bland. I'm apt to be more vehement verbally than mentally. I love words. I get carried away by them. But I *do* have strong, strong feelings. Everything that hurts the things I love I react against violently — violently!"

7      Much as I admired his passion, this failed to settle my unease. I recalled Leacock's many jibes — much more offensive than amusing — against Germans, Blacks and Orientals — and I wondered whether intolerance, let alone racism, was a distinctive tory trait. It was not a pleasing speculation. But I was only at the start of my journey: there would be time to sort this out.

## VOCABULARY

a. *paragraph 1:* anticipation, yeoman, puritannical, stolid

b. *paragraph 2:* disavowal, acerbity

c. *paragraph 3:* haggard, courtly, winsome, oracular, castigation, exhortation

d. *paragraph 4:* palpable, eulogy

e. *paragraph 5:* vehemence, implacable, defecating, abashed, unrepentant

f. *paragraph 6:* rantings, senility, eminent, anathema, broach

## QUESTIONS

1. In paragraph 1 Taylor develops the second sentence — the main idea of the paragraph — with specific detail about the street. What is the main idea in paragraphs 2 and 4, and how does he use the detail of the paragraphs to develop the main idea in each case?

2. Paragraph 5 moves from specific detail to the main idea. What is that idea, and how does the author give it prominence?

3. Which of the subordinate ideas in paragraph 3 are in turn illustrated or developed?

4. What is Taylor's attitude toward his subject? How does he convey it?

## WRITING ASSIGNMENTS

1. Write several paragraphs describing visits with older people that taught you something about their world and about yourself. Begin with these truths, or build the paragraphs to them.

2. Discuss how contact with a person whose political views were different from yours led you to discoveries about yourself and the world that conflicted with values and ideas held by your parents and teachers. Use this discussion to draw a conclusion about growing up.

## KEN DRYDEN

Ken Dryden *was arguably the best National Hockey League goalie of the 1970s, leading the Montreal Canadiens to a string of Stanley Cups and Team Canada to its dramatic seventh-game win over the Soviet all-stars in the famous "Summit Series" of 1972. He is a graduate of Cornell University, a former "Nader's Raider," and a qualified lawyer. After his retirement from hockey while at the top of his game, Dryden was appointed to a term as Ontario Youth Commissioner in 1984.* The Game *(1983), from which the following reminiscence about backyard hockey is taken, is Dryden's thoughtful and movingly written account of nine typical days in the middle of his last season with the Canadiens.*

## DRYDEN'S BACKYARD

I get out of bed and pull back the curtains. It has snowed overnight and traces are still gently falling. For several minutes I stand there, my forehead pressed to the window, watching the snow, looking out at the backyards of the houses behind, where the Pritchards, the MacLarens, and the Carpenters lived, and down below at the winter's depth of snow, and at the backyard where I spent my childhood. 1

"Dryden's Backyard." That's what it was called in our neighborhood. It was more than 70 feet long, paved curiously in red asphalt, 45 feet wide at "the big end," gradually narrowing to 35 feet at the flower bed, to 25 feet at the porch — our center line — to 15 feet at "the small end." While Steve Shutt and Guy Lafleur were in Willowdale and Thurso on backyard rinks their fathers built, while Larry Robinson was on a frozen stream in Marvelville and Réjean Houle on a road in Rouyn under the only street light that his street had, I was here. 2

It was an extraordinary place, like the first swimming pool on the block, except there were no others like it anywhere. Kids would come from many blocks away to play, mostly "the big guys," friends of my brother, a year or two older than him, seven or eight years 3 older than me. But that was never a problem. It was the first rule of the backyard that they had to let me play. To a friend who complained one day, Dave said simply, "If Ken doesn't play, you don't play."

4    We played "ball hockey" mostly, with a tennis ball, its bounce deadened by the cold. A few times, we got out a garden hose and flooded the backyard to use skates and pucks, but the big end was slightly lower than the small end, and the water pooled and froze unevenly. More important, we found that the more literal we tried to make our games, the less lifelike they became. We could move across the asphalt quickly and with great agility in rubber "billy" boots; we could shoot a tennis ball high and hard. But with skates on, with a puck, we were just kids. So after the first few weeks of the first year, we played only ball hockey.

5    Depending on the day, the time, the weather, there might be any number of kids wanting to play, so we made up games any number could play. With four and less than nine, we played regular games, the first team scoring ten goals the winner. The two best players, who seemed always to know who they were, picked the teams and decided on ends. First choice of players got second choice of ends, and because the size of the big end made it more fun to play in, the small end was the choice to defend. Each team had a goalie — one with goalie pads, a catching glove, and a goalie stick; the other with only a baseball glove and a forward's stick. When we had more than eight players, we divided into three or more teams for a round-robin tournament, each game to five. With fewer than four, it was more difficult. Sometimes we attempted a regular game, often we just played "shots," each player being both shooter and goalie, standing in front of one net, shooting in turn at the other. Most often, however, we played "penalty shots."

6    But the backyard also meant time alone. It was usually after dinner when the "big guys" had homework to do and I would turn on the floodlights at either end of the house and on the porch, and play. It was a private game. I would stand alone in the middle of the yard, a stick in my hands, a tennis ball in front of me, silent, still, then suddenly dash ahead, stickhandling furiously, dodging invisible obstacles for a shot on net. It was Maple Leaf Gardens filled to wildly cheering capacity, a tie game, seconds remaining. I was Frank Mahovlich, or Gordie Howe, I was anyone I wanted to be, and the voice in my head was that of Leafs broadcaster Foster Hewitt: " . . . there's ten seconds left, Mahovlich, winding up at his own line, at center, eight seconds, seven, over the blueline, six — he winds up, he shoots, *he scores!*" The mesh that had been tied to the bottoms of our red metal goalposts until frozen in the ice had been ripped away to hang loose from the crossbars, whipped back like a flag in a stiff breeze. My arms and stick flew into the air, I screamed a scream inside my head, and collected my ball to do it again — many times, for many minutes, the hero of all my own games.

7    It was a glorious fantasy, and I always heard that voice. It was what made my fantasy seem almost real. For to us, who attended hockey games mostly on TV or radio, an NHL game, a Leafs game, was played with a voice. If I wanted to be Mahovlich or Howe, if I moved my body the way I had seen them move theirs and did nothing else, it would never quite work. But if I heard the voice that said their names while I was playing out that fantasy, I could believe it. Foster Hewitt could make me them.

8    My friends and I played every day after school, sometimes during lunch and after dinner, but Saturday was always the big day. I would go to bed Friday night thinking of Saturday, waking up early, with none of the fuzziness I had other days. If it had snowed overnight, Dave and I, with shovels and scrapers, and soon joined by others, would pile the snow into flower beds or high against the back of the garage. Then at 9 a.m. the games would begin.

There was one team in the big end, another in the small; third and fourth teams sat like **9** birds on a telephone wire, waiting their turn on the wall that separated the big end from Carpenter's backyard. Each team wore uniforms identical to the other. It was the Canadian midwinter uniform of the time — long, heavy duffel coats in browns, grays, or blues; tuques in NHL team colors, pulled snug over ears under the watchful eye of mothers, here rolled up in some distinctive personal style; leather gloves, last year's church gloves, now curling at the wrist and separating between fingers; black rubber "billy" boots over layers of heavy woolen socks for fit, the tops rolled down like "low cuts" for speed and style.

Each game would begin with a faceoff, then wouldn't stop again. Action moved quick- **10** ly end to end, the ball bouncing and rolling, chased by a hacking, slashing scrum of sticks. We had sticks without tops on their blades — "toothpicks"; sticks with no blades at all — "stubs." They broke piece by heart-breaking piece, often quickly, but still we used them. Only at the start of a season, at Christmas (Dave and I routinely exchanged sticks until one year he gave me a stick and I gave him a pair of socks) and once or twice more, would we get new ones. All except John Stedelbauer. His father owned a car dealership and during the hockey season gave away hockey sticks to his customers as a promotion. Stedelbauer got all the new sticks he needed, fortunately, as they weren't very good. One year he broke nineteen of them.

A goal would be scored, then another, and slowly the game would leapfrog to five. **11** Bodies grew warm from exertion, fingers and toes went numb; noses ran, wiped by unconscious sleeves; coats loosened, tuques fell off; steam puffed from mouths and streamed from tuqueless heads. Sticks hacked and slashed; tennis balls stung. But in the euphoria of the game, the pain disappeared. Sitting on the wall that overlooked his back- yard, Rick "Foster" Carpenter, younger and not very athletic, gave the play-by-play, but no one listened. Each of us had his own private game playing in his head. A fourth goal, then a fifth, a cheer and the first game was over. Quickly, four duffel coats, four tuques, four pairs of weathered gloves and rubber "billy" boots would jump from the wall to re- place the losers; and the second game would begin. We paused at noon while some went home and others ate the lunch that they had brought with them. At 6 p.m., the two or three who remained would leave. Eighteen hours later, after church, the next game would begin.

When I think of the backyard, I think of my childhood; and when I think of my child- **12** hood, I think of the backyard. It is the central image I have of that time, linking as it does all of its parts: father, mother, sister, friends; hockey, baseball, and Dave — big brother, idol, mentor, defender, and best friend. Yet it lasted only a few years. Dave was already twelve when the backyard was built; I was six. He and his friends played for three or four years, then stopped; I played longer but, without them, less often. Yet until moments ago, I had never remembered that.

The backyard was not a training ground. In all the time I spent there, I don't remember **13** ever thinking I would be an NHL goalie, or even hoping I could be one. In backyard games, I dreamed I *was* Sawchuk or Hall, Mahovlich or Howe; I never dreamed I would be like them. There seemed no connection between the backyard and Maple Leaf Gardens; there seemed no way to get to there from here. If we ever thought about that, it never concerned us; we just played. It was here in the backyard that we *learned* hockey. It was here we got close to it, we got *inside* it, and it got inside us. It was here that our inex- tricable bond with the game was made. Many years have now passed, the game has grown up and been complicated by things outside it, yet still the backyard remains — untouched, unchanged, my unseverable link to that time, and that game.

# VOCABULARY

a. *paragraph   5:* round-robin tournament

b. *paragraph 10:* scrum

c. *paragraph 11:* euphoria

d. *paragraph 12:* mentor

e. *paragraph 13:* inextricable, unseverable


# QUESTIONS

1. Dryden builds to general conclusions through his experiences with backyard hockey. How does he show that these conclusions are the main ideas of his essay?

2. How does Dryden blend fantasy, memory, and reality in his account? Where does the emphasis lie?

3. Why does he spend so much time on details — paragraphs 9, 10, and 11, for example? How do these contribute to the overall effect of the essay?

4. Is this essay primarily about playing hockey as a child, or is it about something else?


# WRITING ASSIGNMENTS

1. Illustrate your reasons for playing a sport or a musical instrument or for performing a similar activity. Let your reader discover your reasons through the details of your essay.

2. Write an essay on one of the following topics or on one of your own choosing.

   a. the art of making friends

   b. on giving advice

   c. a formative event from childhood

   d. living away from home

   e. waiting in line


Give your thesis emphasis by introducing it in a prominent place in the essay — perhaps at the end of the opening paragraph, or in the final paragraph. If you begin the essay with your thesis, you can give it emphasis by repeating or restating it at key points.

# GEORGE GRANT

*George Grant (1918–1988) was born in Toronto and educated at Queen's University (where his grandfather, George Munro Grant, had been principal from 1877 to 1902) and at Oxford. He taught philosophy at Dalhousie University from 1947 to 1960, then became Chairman of the Department of Religion at McMaster University. In 1980 he returned to Dalhousie to become professor of political science and classics. His writings — the best-known of which are* Philosophy in the Mass Age *(1959),* Lament For A Nation *(1965), and* Technology And Empire *(1969) — examine such questions as conservative Canada's survival in the shadow of the U.S.A.'s modern liberalism, and the threat to traditional values embodied in modern technology and Western ideology generally. The following essay discusses the ways in which people represent technology to themselves.*

## THE MORALS OF MODERN TECHNOLOGY

A computer scientist recently made the following statement about the machines he helps to invent: "The computer does not impose on us the ways it should be used." Obviously, that statement is made by someone who is aware that computers can be used for purposes of which he does not approve — for example, the tyrannous control of human beings. This is given in the word should. The scientist makes a statement in terms of his intimate knowledge of computers that transcends that intimacy, in that it is more than a description of any given computer or of what is technically common to all such machines. Because he wishes to state something about the possible good or evil purposes for which computers can be used, he expresses, albeit in negative form, what computers are in a way that is more than technical description. Computers are instruments, made by human skill for the purpose of achieving certain human goals. They are neutral instruments in the sense that the morality of the goals for which they are used is determined outside them. **1**

Many people who have never seen a computer, and only slightly understand its capacity, have the sense from their daily life that they are being managed by computers and have, perhaps, an undifferentiated fear about the potential extent of this management. Our scientist, who knows about the invention and use of these machines, states what they are in order to put our anxiety into perspective; he states what they are to free us from the terrors of such fantasies as the myth of Doctor Frankenstein. His perspective assumes that the machines are instruments because their capacities have been built into them by human beings and because it is human beings who operate those machines for purposes they have determined. All instruments can obviously be used for bad purposes, and the more complex the capacities of the instrument, the more complex its possible bad uses. But if we apprehend computers for what they are, neutral instruments that we in our freedom are called upon to control, we are better able to come to terms rationally with their potential dangers. The first step in coping with these dangers is to see that they are related to human beings' potential decisions about how to use computers, not to the inherent capacities of the machines themselves. Indeed the statement above about the computer is the prevalent "liberal" view of the modern situation, a view so rooted in us that it seems to be common sense, even rationality, itself. We have certain technological capacities; it is up to us to use those capacities for decent purposes. **2**

Yet despite the seeming common sense of the statement "the computer does not impose on us the ways it should be used," when we try to think the sentence, it becomes clear that we are not allowing computers to appear before us for what they are. Indeed the statement **3** (like many similar) obscures what computers are. To begin at the surface: the words "the computer does not impose" are concerned with the capacities of these machines, and these capacities are brought before us as if they existed in abstraction from the events that have made possible their existence. Obviously the machines have been made from a vast variety of materials, consummately fashioned by a vast apparatus of fashioners. The machine's existence has required generations of sustained effort by chemists, metallurgists and workers in mines and factories. Beyond these obvious facts, computers have been made within the new science and its mathematics. That science is a particular paradigm of knowledge and, as any paradigm of knowledge, is to be understood as the relation between an aspiration of human thought and the effective conditions for its realization. It is not my purpose here to describe that paradigm in detail, nor would it be within my ability to show its interrelation with mathematics conceived as algebra. Suffice it to say that what is given in the modern use of the word science is the project of reason to gain "objective" knowledge.

4    Modern "reason" is the summoning of something before a subject and the putting of it to questions, so that something gives us its reasons for being the way it is as an object. A paradigm of knowledge is not something reserved for scientists and scholars. Anybody who is awake in our educational system knows that this paradigm of knowledge stamps the very heart of the institutions and curricula of that system, in what the young are required to know and to be able to do if they are to be called "qualified." That paradigm of knowledge is central to our civilizational destiny and has made possible the existence of computers. I mean by civilizational destiny above all the fundamental presuppositions that the majority of human beings inherit in a civilization and that are so taken for granted as the way things are that they are given an almost absolute status. To describe a destiny is not to judge it. It may indeed be, as many believe, that the development of that paradigm is a great step in the ascent of man, that it is the essence of human liberation, that its development justifies the human experiment itself. Whatever the truth of these beliefs, without this destiny computers would not exist. And like all destinies, it imposes.

5    What has been said about the computer's existence depending upon the paradigm of knowledge is equally true of the earlier machines of industrialism. The western paradigm of knowledge has not been static but has been realized in a dynamic unfolding. One aspect of that realization has been a great extension of what is given in the conception of "machine." We all know that computers are machines for the transmitting of information, not for the transformation of energy. They require software as well as hardware. Computers have required the development of mathematics as algebra and of algebra as almost identical with logic. The existence of computers has required a fuller realization of the western paradigm of knowledge, an extension of the conception of machine. It may well be said that where the steel press may be taken as the image of Newtonian physics and mathematics, the computer can be taken as the image of contemporary physics and mathematics. Yet in making that distinction, it must also be said that contemporary science and Newtonian science are equal moments in the realization of the same paradigm.

6    The phrase "the computer does not impose" misleads because it abstracts the computer from the destiny that was required for its making. Common sense may tell us that the computer is an instrument, but it is an instrument from within the destiny that imposes itself upon us. Therefore the computer does impose.

7    To go further: How are we being asked to take the word ways in the assertion that "the computer does not impose the ways?" Even if the purposes for which the computer's capacities should be used are determined outside itself, do not these capcities limit the kind of ways for which it can be used? To take a simple example from the modern institutions of learning and training: in most institutions there are cards on which children

are assessed as to their "skills" and "behaviour," and this information is retained by computers. It may be granted that such information adds little to the homogenizing vision inculcated throughout society by such means as centrally controlled curricula and teacher training. It may also be granted that as computers and their programming become more sophisticated, the information stored may be able to take more account of differences. Nevertheless, it is clear that the ways computers can be used for storing and transmitting information can only be ways that increase the tempo of the homogenizing processes. Abstracting facts so that they can be stored as information is achieved by classification, and it is the nature of classification to homogenize. Where classification rules, identities and differences can appear only in its terms. Indeed the word information is itself perfectly attuned to the account of knowledge that is homogenizing in its very nature. "Information" is about objects, and comes forth as part of that science that summons objects to give us their reasons.

It is not my purpose to discuss the complex issues of good and evil involved in the **8** modern movement towards homogeneity, nor to discuss the good of heterogeneity, which in its most profound past form was autochthonous. Some modern thinkers state that human beings are beyond the rootlessness characteristic of the present early stages of technological society and are now being called to new ways of being rooted that will be able to accept the benefits of modern homogenization while living out a new form of heterogeneity. These statements are not at issue here. My purpose is to point out that the sentence about computers hides the fact that their ways are always homogenizing. Because this is hidden, the questioning of homogenization is closed down.

To illustrate the matter from another aspect of technological development: the desire of **9** Canadians for the mass-produced car has been a central cause of our political and economic integration and social homogenization with the people of the imperial heartland. This has been not only because of the vast corporate structures necessary for building and keeping in motion such automobiles, and the direct and indirect political power of such corporations, but also because any society with such vehicles tends to become like any other society with the same. Seventy-five years ago somebody might have said "The automobile does not impose on us the ways it should be used," and who would have quarrelled with the statement? Yet it would have been a deluded representation of the automobile.

Human beings may still be able to control the ways that cars are used. Strict administra- **10** tive measures may prevent the pollution of the atmosphere and keep freeways from destroying central city life. It is to be hoped that cities such as Toronto will maintain themselves as communities by winning popular victories over expressways and airports. But whatever efforts may be made, they will not allow us to represent the automobile to ourselves as a neutral instrument.

The ways automobiles and computers can be used hinge on the fact that these machines **11** are investment-heavy and require large institutions for their production. The potential size of such corporations has been imagined by a reliable economist. He says that if the present growth of IBM is extrapolated, that corporation will in the next 30 years be a larger unit than the economy of any presently constituted national state, including that of IBM's homeland. At the simplest factual level, then, computers can be built only in societies in which there are large corporations. This will be the case whatever ways these institutions are related to the states in which they are incorporated, be that relation some form of capitalism or some form of socialism. Computers have been and will continue to be instruments with effect beyond the confines of particular nation states. They are instruments of the imperialism of certain communities towards other communities. They are instruments in the struggle between competing empires, as the present desire of the Soviet Union for

American computers illustrates. It might be that in the long run of progress, humanity will come to the universal and homogeneous state in which individual empires and nations have disappeared. That in itself would be an even larger corporation. But whatever conceivable political and economic alternatives there may be, computers can exist only in societies in which there are large corporate institutions. The ways computers can be used are limited to those situations. In this sense computers are not neutral instruments, but instruments that exclude certain forms of community and permit others.

12    In our era, many believe that the great question about technology is whether the ways it is used will be determined by the standards of justice in one or other of the dominant political philosophies. The rationalism of the west has produced not only modern physical science, but also modern political philosophy. Technology is considered neutral, and its just use will depend upon the victory of true rather than false political philosophy. The appeal of the teachings of political philosophers has been massive in our era, because these teachings have taken the form of ideologies that convince the minds of masses of human beings. The ways that computers should be used can be solved satisfactorily if political regimes are shaped by the true philosophy. The three dominant political alternatives are capitalist liberalism, communist Marxism, and national socialist historicism.

13    The same account of reason that produced the technologies also produced the accounts of justice given in these modern political philosophies. That account of reason led, moreover, to the public manifestation of those political philosophies as ideologies. The statement "the computer does not impose on us the ways it should be used" abstracts from the fact that "the ways" the computer will be used will be determined by politics, in the broadest sense of that term. Politics in our era is dominated by accounts of society that came forth from the same account of reasoning that produced the new co-penetrated arts and sciences.

14    It cannot be my purpose to show the nature of that sameness. Such a demonstration would require a detailed history of the modern West, an explanation of the mutual interdependence of the modern physical and moral sciences as they were defined against the account of science in classical philosophy. Much of the enormous enterprise of modern scholarship has been taken up with the detailed mapping of what was done and thought and made by large numbers of inventors, scientists, artists, philosophers, politicians, religious reformers. Beyond scholarship, the demonstration of this interdependence would require the ability to think what was being thought by the greatest scientists and philosophers. By distinguishing the new science from the account of science in the ancient world, scientists and philosophers laid down the modern affirmations of what science is. Concerning the conception of justice, it would be necessary to follow how great philosophers such as Descartes and Locke, Rousseau and Nietzsche, understood the unity between their accounts of justice and the findings of modern science.

15    Without any of these demonstrations, suffice it to say that the ways computers have been and will be used cannot be detached from modern conceptions of justice, and that these conceptions of justice come forth from the very account of reasoning that led to the building of computers. This is not to say anything about the truth or falsity of modern conceptions of justice, nor is it to prejudge the computer by some reactionary account stemming from a desire to turn our backs on the modern. It is simply to assert that we are not in the position where computers lie before us as neutral instruments, where we use them according to standards of justice reached outside the existence of the computers themselves. The instruments and the standards of justice are bound together; both belong to the same destiny of modern reason. The failure to recognize this hides from us the truth about the "ways" computers can be used.

The force of that destiny is seen in the ambiguity of the word should in the statement **16**
"The computer does not impose on us the ways it should be used." Our novel situation is
presented as if human beings "should" use computers for certain purposes and not for
others. But what has the word should come to mean in advanced technological societies?

"Should" was originally the past tense of "shall." It is still sometimes used in a condi- **17**
tional sense to express greater uncertainty about the future than does the prophetic sense of
"shall." ("I shall get a raise this year" is more certain than "I should get a raise this year."
The colloquialism "I shouldn't wonder" expresses this.) In its origins, "shall" was concerned with "owing," when used as a transitive verb. Chaucer writes: "And by that feyth I
shal to god and yow." But over the centuries "should" took over from "shall" as the word
with the connotation of owing, and could be used for that purpose intransitively.

The sentence "The computer does not impose on us the ways it should be used" is con- **18**
cerned with human actions that are owed. If the statement were in positive form — "The
computer does impose on us the ways it should be used" — the debt would probably be
understood as owed by human beings to machines. We can say of a good car that we owe
it to the car to lubricate it properly. If we want the car to do what it is fitted for — which is,
in traditional usage, its good — then we must look after it. We would mean the same sense
if we were to say we owe it to ourselves to try not to contradict ourselves in trying to think
out some matter clearly. But the "should" in the statement about the computer is clearly
not being used about what is owed by men to machines. The sentence is concerned with
the just use of the machine as instrument. "Should" expresses that we ought to use the
machine justly. But what is the nature of the debt? To what or to whom do we owe it? Is
that debt conditional? For example, if human beings "should" use computers only in ways
that are compatible with constitutional government, and not in ways that promote tyranny,
to what or to whom is this support of constitutional government owed? To ourselves? To
other human beings? To all, or some of them? To nature? To history? To reasonableness?
To God?

Because of the ambiguity that has fallen on all accounts of owing, our era has often **19**
been described as a time of nihilism. Many Europeans came to believe over the last 300
years that their affirmations about goodness could not find foundations in accounts of God
or nature, reason or history. The result for many has been a state of mind well described as
nihilism. This state of mind has had wide public influence because the mass literacy
necessary to technological society made nihilism a situation open not only to the few. In
North America, the organization of training in schools and multiversities has produced
mass "wised-upness," which is the democratic edition of nihilism.

It is necessary to be careful at this point. Characterizing technological society as essen- **20**
tially nihilistic prejudges the question of what that society is. A dismayed reaction is as
likely as any progressivism to close down thought about its nature. If we use the word
good in the simplest way as what we approve, and "bad" as what we deplore, is it not
evident that large majorities now give their shared approval to certain activities and that
from those activities we can apprehend a positive modern conception of goodness? For
example, is it not generally believed that freedom for sexual realization in its varying
particularities should be promoted in societies? If one has any knowledge of the modern
scientific community, is one not aware of the positive expectations about its accomplishments that permeate the community, from which a positive conception of goodness can be
deduced?

A description of the modern era fairer than that of nihilism is that a great change has **21**
taken place in the public conception of goodness. The enucleation of that change is best
made in terms of what is positive in both the past and the prevalent modern accounts. The
original western conception of goodness is that that meets us with the overriding claim of

justice and persuades us that in desiring obedience to that claim we will find what we are fitted for. The modern conception of goodness is of our free creating of richness and greatness of life and all that is advantageous thereto. The presently popular phrase in the modern account of goodness is "quality of life."

22    The modern conception of goodness does not include the assertion of a claim on us that properly orders our desires in terms of owing, and that is itself the route and fulfilment of desire. In the prevalent modern view, owing is always provisional upon what we desire to create. Obviously we live in the presence of others, and our creating may perforce be limited by what we are currently legally permitted to do to others. However, the limitations, whether national or international, put on creating by the claims of others, are understood as contractual; that is, provisional. This exclusion of non-provisory owing from our interpretation of desire means that what is summoned up by the word should is no longer what was summoned up among our ancestors. What moderns hear always includes an "if." The situation is never "beyond all bargains and without an alternative." Moreover, the arrival in the world of this changed interpretation of goodness is related to the arrival of technological civilization. The liberation of human desiring from any supposed excluding claim, so that it is believed we freely create values, is a face of the same liberation in which we overcame chance by technology — gained the liberty to make happen what we want to make happen. We are free, not only in what we want to make happen, but also in choosing the means. Nature becomes more and more at our disposal, as if it were nothing but our raw material.

23    "The computer does not impose on us the ways it should be used" asserts the essence of the modern view, which is that human ability freely determines what happens. The statement then puts that freedom in the service of the very "should" that that same modern novelty has made provisional. The resolute mastery to which we are summoned in "does not impose" is the very source of difficulty in apprehending goodness as "should." Therefore, the "should" in the statement has only a masquerading resonance in the actions we are summoned to concerning computers. Should is a word carried over from the past to be used in a present that is ours only because the assumptions of that past were criticized out of public existence. The statement therefore cushions us from the full impact of the novelties it asks us to consider. It pads us against wondering about the disappearnace of "should" in its ancient resonance and about what this disappearance may portend.

24    I have written at length about this statement to illustrate how difficult it is to apprehend correctly what is novel in our situation. When we represent technology to ourselves as an array of neutral instruments, invented by human beings and under human control, we are expressing a kind of common sense, but it is a common sense from within the very technology we are attempting to represent. The novelness of our novelties is being minimized. We are led to forget that modern destiny permeates our representations of the world and ourselves. The coming to be of technology has required changes in what we think is good, in what we think good is, in how we conceive sanity and madness, justice and injustice, rationality and irrationality, beauty and ugliness.

## VOCABULARY

a. *paragraph  1:* tyrannous

b. *paragraph  3:* consummately, paradigm

c. *paragraph  7:* homogenizing

d. *paragraph 8:* autochthonous

e. *paragraph 9:* deluded

f. *paragraph 11:* extrapolated

g. *paragraph 12:* liberalism, Marxism, historicism

h. *paragraph 15:* reactionary

i. *paragraph 17:* colloquialism

j. *paragraph 19:* affirmation, nihilism

k. *paragraph 22:* provisional, non-provisory

l. *paragraph 23:* masquerading, resonance, portend

## QUESTIONS

1. Grant devotes twenty-four paragraphs to an analysis of the statement quoted at the beginning of his essay. Write a one-sentence outline of each paragraph and trace the development of his argument.

2. As part of his explanation, Grant rejects the view of computers expressed at the outset. How does he show it to be wrong?

3. What is the purpose of the comparison with the view of the automobile (paragraphs 9 and 10)?

4. How does Grant explain the relation between computers and politics (paragraphs 12 and 13)?

5. Why does Grant conclude paragraph 18 with a series of questions? Does he expect the reader to answer them?

6. Why does Grant characterize society as nihilistic (paragraphs 19 through 21)?

## WRITING ASSIGNMENTS

1. Discuss how computers have influenced your own life. Does their influence represent a "tyrannous control of human beings"?

2. Analyse the uses to which other scientific discoveries have been put in our century. How do attitudes toward such discoveries vary?

## NORTHROP FRYE

*One of the century's most influential literary critics,* Northrop Frye *has written seminal books on William Blake (*Fearful Symmetry, *1947), literary theory (*The Anatomy of

Criticism, *1957), and the Bible and literature (*The Great Code, *1982). Born in Sher-
brooke, Quebec, in 1912, and raised in Moncton, New Brunswick, he was educated at
Victoria College, University of Toronto, and has maintained, as Professor of English, a
lifelong association with the university. He has had a lasting influence on such Canadian
writers as Jay Macpherson, James Reaney, and Margaret Atwood. Always interested in
education in the broadest sense, Frye speculates in the following essay on why the conception of literature which is presented to children in school is not what contemporary
scholars regard as being the elementary principles of that subject as now conceived.
Literature for Frye is particularly important because it "gives us not only a means of understanding, but a power to fight. . . . Advertising, propaganda, the speeches of politicians, popular books and magazines, the clichés of rumour, all have their own kind of
pastoral myths, quest myths, hero myths, sacrificial myths, and nothing will drive these
shoddy constructs out of the mind except the genuine forms of the same thing."*

## ELEMENTARY TEACHING

1    The first thing that university teachers want to know is: what is important in the pre-
university study of literature? Most of us, when we complain about our freshmen, base
our complaints on the theme of information or memorized knowledge: our students don't
know enough; they haven't read enough; the chronology of literature is a vague haze in
their minds; some of them could hardly distinguish Chaucer from Tennyson except by the
spelling, and so on. But if students don't have enough information, it is a simple enough
matter to supply it or provide the sources of supply. The trouble is that what they learn
they learn within a mental structure of habits and assumptions, and university comes much
too late in a student's life to alter that structure. For example: many students come to
university assuming that convention is the opposite of originality, and is a sign that a poet
is superficial and insincere. If they are writing poetry themselves, they are apt to get bristly and aggressive about this assumption. They can't be writing in a convention that all
their friends are writing in: they must be conveying unique experiences, because their
poems say that they are. Here is a result of illiterate teaching that makes the most scram-
bled nonsense out of all literary values, yet nothing can really be done about it. We tell
them at university that literary sincerity is quite different from personal sincerity, that it
can only be developed by craftsmanship working within a convention, and that it is the
function of convention to set free the power of expressing emotions, not to provide
formulas for ready-made emotions, though it may do this for dull writers. They listen;
they understand; they may even believe; but the effect on their mental habits is very like
the effect of schoolmarm English on the little boy: "Dar ain't no 'ain't you', is dey? It's
'aren't you', ain't it?"

2    Or, again, I am at an educational conference listening to a speech by a high authority in
the field. I know him to be a good scholar, a dedicated servant of society, and an admirable
person. Yet his speech is a muddy river of clichés, flowing stickily into a delta of banalities at the peroration. The content of the speech does not do justice to his mind: what it
does reflect is the state of his literary education. It is not that he has never read good literature, for he has the literary tastes that one would expect a cultivated man to have. But he
has never been trained to think rhetorically, to visualize his abstractions, to subordinate
logic and sequences to the insights of metaphor and simile, to realize that figures of speech
are not the ornaments of language, but the elements of both language and thought. And
because his main scholarly interests lie outside literature, he has never been compelled to
make up for these deficiencies himself. The result is that he is fluent without being articu-

late, and cannot break out of an armour of ready-made phrases when he tries to express his real convictions. Once again, nothing can now be done for him: there are no courses in remedial metaphor.

The greatest fallacy in the present conception of literary education is the notion that prose is the normal language of ordinary speech, and should form the centre and staple of literary teaching. From prose in this sense we move out to utilitarian English on one side and to the more specialized literary study of poetry on the other. Few subjects can be more futile than a prose-based approach to poetry, an approach which treats poems as documents, to be analysed or summarized or otherwise translated into the language of communication. The root of the fallacy is the assumption that prose represents the only valid form of thought, and that poetry, considered as thought, is essentially decorated or distorted prose. When we suggest that young people try writing poetry, what most of them immediately produce are discontinuous prose statements about their emotions, or what they think their emotions ought to be, when confronted with the outside world. This is not merely because they have been taught to read poetry as a series of statements of this kind — "all that guff about nature," as one freshman expressed it — it is rather that they assume that all verbal expression derives from the attempt to describe something, and that poetry differs from prose, as a mode of thought, in being an attempt to describe subjective emotions. **3**

The main principles of a coherently organized curriculum are simple enough, but very different from the one just mentioned. Poetry should be at the centre of all literary training, and literary prose forms the periphery. In a properly constructed curriculum there would be no place for "effective communication" or for any form of utilitarian English. We still have textbooks on effective writing produced by people who have no notion how to write, mainly because they are trying to be effective about it, but one hopes that the market for them will disappear in our time. The styles employed by journalists and advertisers are highly conventionalized rhetorics, in fact practically trade jargons, and have to be learned as separate skills, without much direct reference to literature at all. A literary training is a considerable handicap in trying to understand, for example, the releases of public relations counsels. I am not saying this just to be ironic: I am stating a fact. I remember a *New Yorker* cartoon of a milkman who found the notice "no milk" on a doorstep, and woke up the household at four in the morning to enquire whether he meant that he had no milk or that he wanted no milk. I suspect that the milkman was a retired teacher of English: certainly he reflects the disadvantages of being sensitive to the nuances of expression. A literary person confronted with most of the verbal technologies of our time is in the position of a genuinely intelligent student confronted with an intelligence test which grossly oversimplifies its categories and calls for an arbitrary choice of half-truths. He is sure to fail the test simply because he is more intelligent than the creature who designed it. The primary function of education is to make one maladjusted to ordinary society; and literary education makes it more difficult to come to terms with the barbarizing of speech, or what *Finnegans Wake* calls the jinglish janglage. **4**

The connections of literature are with the imagination, not with the reason, hence the ideal in literature is one of intensity and power rather than of precision or accuracy, as in science. There can be no intensity without precision, but to aim directly at precision is trying to seize the shadow. Poetry is one of the creative arts, in the context of music and painting, or rhythm and pattern. The rhythmical energy of poetry, its intimate connection with song and dance, is the elementary basis of its appeal, and the primary aspect of it to be presented to children, along with its affinity with the concrete and the sensational, its power of making things vivid by illustration, which has traditionally been expressed in the formula *ut pictura poesis*. **5**

6    I am certainly no expert on the teaching of children, but it seems obvious that all such teaching has to follow the child's own rhythm of thought and development, and not project on him some half-baked adult mystique, whether that mystique claims to derive from the anti-intellectual left or the anti-anti-intellectual right. And it is clear that children recapitulate, as we should expect them to do, the experience of primitive literature, and turn most naturally and easily to the abstract and conventionalized, to riddles, conundrums, and stylized jingles. The authors of *The Lore and Language of Schoolchildren* quote an unremarkable verse:

> Mrs White had a fright
> In the middle of the night,
> She saw a ghost eating toast
> Half-way up the lamp post

and append the comment of a nine-year-old critic: "I think what's so clever about this is the way it all rhymes." Later, in speaking of the child's fondness for tongue twisters and multiple puns, they remark: "It takes children a long time before they cease to be amazed that one word can have more than one meaning." One would hope that this amazement would last the rest of their lives. The speech of a small child is full of chanting and singing, and it is clear that the child understands what many adults do not, that verse is a more direct and primitive way of conventionalizing speech than prose is.

7    This principle, that the physical energy and concrete vividness of verse should normally be presented earlier than the more complex and adulterated rhythm of prose, affects the training in both reading and writing. It is difficult to know how a child thinks, but it is less difficult to know how he talks, once one has gained his confidence, and how he talks might afford an educational clue. Any child who has talked to me has addressed me in an uninhibited stream of burble for which the nearest literary counterpart is the last chapter of *Ulysses*. This chapter has no punctuation, and neither has a child's speech. Surely in teaching writing one should begin by trying to channel this free current of verbal energy and start giving it some precision as it goes along. To teach a child to write as though he were deciphering something from linear B, proceeding from word to phrase, from phrase to sentence, from sentence to paragraph, is to ensure that what he eventually writes will be a dead language. Good writing has to be based on good speech, and good speech is a logical, though complex, development from natural speech. It is a striking feature of our culture that so much creative activity in literature, as in music and painting, should be either explicitly academic or explicitly resistant to education, a culture either of Brahmins or of Dharma bums. In Canada these two aspects of literary culture have reached a curious schizophrenia in which a constant polemic against academic poetry is carried on by poets who are nearly all employed by universities. It seems to me that the source of the feeling that education inhibits spontaneity may be somewhere in the region I have just indicated: in the reversal of the natural rhythms of thought and expression which a prose-based literary education is only too apt to produce.

## VOCABULARY

a. *paragraph 1:* bristly, convention

b. *paragraph 2:* delta, banalities, peroration, rhetorically, metaphor, remedial

c. *paragraph 3:* fallacy, utilitarian

d. *paragraph 4:* periphery, nuances, maladjusted, barbarizing

e. *paragraph 6:* mystique, conundrums, append

f. *paragraph 7:* Brahmins, Dharma bums

## QUESTIONS

1. What points is Frye making about the way in which children are currently taught? How does the way in which Frye presents his main points contribute to his argument?

2. Frye is suggesting what is wrong with the current curriculum and how it might be changed. What are your views on the changes he proposes?

3. Frye ranges widely in his discussion of elementary teaching. Make a list of the subjects he covers and consider how they cohere.

## WRITING ASSIGNMENTS

1. Explain why a literary training can be a handicap in today's society, and show how Frye uses anecdotal humour to illustrate this point. Use your own humorous examples to illustrate an abstract point in a short essay.

2. Compare Frye's argument for education with those of Berry and Huxley. Write a brief account of each writer's beliefs, based on his views of education.

# Beginnings, Middles, and Endings

To make your ideas convincing, you need to capture the attention of your readers and hold it. You will lose their attention if, in beginning the essay, you describe in too much detail how you intend to proceed. Usually you need to indicate a point of view and briefly suggest how you will develop the essay. The following is an ineffective way of doing so:

> I am going to describe how we played bare-handed softball when I was young. I will illustrate with one particular event.

Compare these sentences with the following paragraph from Harry Bruce's essay on playing softball. Bruce states his subject and suggests how he will develop his essay without directly stating his purpose:

> When I tell young softball players I played the game bare-handed, they regard me warily. Am I one of those geezers who's forever jawing about the fact that, in *his* day, you had to walk through six miles of snowdrifts just to get to school? Will I tediously lament the passing of the standing broad jump, and the glorious old days when the only football in the Maritimes was English rugger, when hockey was an outdoor art rather than indoor mayhem and, at decent yacht clubs, men were gentlemen and women were *personae non grata*? No, but I will tell today's softball players that — with their fancy uniforms, batters' helmets, dugouts, manicured diamonds, guys to announce who's at bat over public-address systems and, above all, gloves for every fielder — the game they play is more tarted-up and sissy than the one I knew. — Harry Bruce, "The Softball Was Always Hard"

If you do need to state your purpose and outline the discussion to follow, you can do so with a minimum of personal reference and without sounding stuffy. Here is a paragraph that both states the purpose of the author and outlines the book introduced by the paragraph:

> The aim of this book is to delineate two types of clever schoolboy: the converger and the diverger. The earlier chapters offer a fairly detailed description of the intellectual abilities, attitudes and personalities of a few hundred such boys. In the last chapters, this description is then used as a basis for a more speculative discussion — of the nature of intelligence and originality and of the ways in which intellectual and personal qualities interact. Although the first half of the book rests heavily on the results of psychological tests, and the last two chapters involve psychoanalytic theory, I have done my best to be intelligible, and, wherever possible, interesting to everyone interested in clever schoolboys: parents, school-teachers, dons, psychologists, administrators, clever schoolboys. — Liam Hudson, *Contrary Imaginations*

This author directly challenges the interest of his reader. The bonus, this introductory paragraph promises, will be the wit of the author, evident in the humorous discussion of a seemingly dry subject.

By contrast, the author of the following paragraph eases his readers into the subject without an immediate statement of purpose. But he does make an immediate appeal to an important concern of the reader — the problem of how to deal with their own failures and those of friends and family members:

> The administration of criminal justice and the extent of individual moral responsibility are among the crucial problems of a civilized society. They are indissolubly linked, and together

they involve our deepest emotions. We often find it hard to forgive ourselves for our own moral failures. All of us, at some time or other, have faced the painful dilemma of when to punish and when to forgive those we love — our children, our friends. How much harder it is, then, to deal with the stranger who transgresses. — David L. Bazelon, "The Awesome Decision"

Notice that personal references are not out of place in an opening paragraph — or anywhere else in an essay. The risk of such references is that they can divert the reader from the subject of the essay to the author. For this reason they should be kept to a minimum.

# TRANSITIONS

In the middle, or body, of paragraphs and essays, transitional words and phrases help us to connect ideas and details. We especially need them when we change the subject or course of discussion, as in the following passage by Jacob Bronowski:

> For the main chemical action is to get energy for the muscles by burning sugar there; but three-quarters of that is lost as heat. And there is *another* limit, on the runner and the gazelle equally, which is *more* severe. At this speed, the chemical burn-up in the muscles is too fast to be complete. The waste products of incomplete burning, chiefly lactic acid, now foul up the blood. — Jacob Bronowski, "The Athlete and the Gazelle" [italics added]

The transitional words *another* and *more* show the course of Bronowski's thinking in the sentence: *another* tells us he is adding a detail to intensify his explanation of why muscles tire; *more* shows he is about to compare the effect of lactic acid on the muscles' functioning with the inefficiency of the chemical action in the muscles.

Words like *after* and *since* express relationships of time; words like *above* and *below* express relationships of space. Here are some important transitions that show the relationship of ideas:

- qualification: *however, nevertheless, nonetheless*

- illustration and explanation: *for example, so, thus*

- comparison: *similarly, in the same way, by comparison, likewise*

- contrast: *by contrast, on the one hand, on the other hand*

- consequence: *thus, as a result, consequently, therefore*

- concession: *admittedly, nevertheless, however*

- amplification: *moreover, furthermore, also, in addition, indeed*

- summation: *in conclusion, to sum up, all in all, family*

Punctuation also shows us how ideas are related. A colon tells us that an expansion, explanation, or illustration follows; a semicolon tells us that the ideas joined are closely related or of the same importance.

The opening paragraphs build the expectations of the reader. The body of the essay sustains the reader's interest. An effective ending will not let the discussion drop: the reader should not finish the essay with a sense of loose ends, of lines of thought left uncompleted. In the formal essay, the ending may restate the thesis or perhaps even state it for the first time — if you build to the thesis through explanation and details. One of the most effective conclusions, the reference back to ideas that opened the essay, gives the reader a sense of completion.

> I have my own cabin on that shore now, and though most of those farmyard ballplayers of thirty-seven summers ago have moved away I still see one of them occasionally. He's a mere forty-six, and I like him now as I liked him then. Sometimes I walk along the gravel beach to a patch of grass, from which a footpath once led to a general store. The Ball-maker's shack is gone, but gray planks and ribs and rusty boat nails still endure the lashing of the salt wind that ceaselessly sweeps the bay. They're all that's left of his schooner. Wrecked by time, like bare-handed softball. — Bruce, "The Softball Was Always Hard"

# E.B. WHITE

*E.B. White (1899–1985) was one of America's most distinguished writers — an essayist, poet, a writer of books for children. His life-long association with* The New Yorker *magazine began in 1926. The columns that appeared in* Harper's *magazine under the title "One Man's Meat" were collected in 1942 and published in a book of the same name. Other essays are found in* The Second Tree From the Corner, The Points of My Compass, *and* Essays of E.B. White. *In all of these books there is much about Maine, where White lived for many years, but the city of New York was never far from his thoughts, as you can see in his profile of the city in a later selection in this book.*

## IN AN ELEVATOR

1    In an elevator, ascending with strangers to familiar heights, the breath congeals, the body stiffens, the spirit marks time. These brief vertical journeys that we make in a common lift, from street level to office level, past the missing thirteenth floor — they afford moments of suspended animation, unique and probably beneficial. Passengers in an elevator, whether wedged tight or scattered with room to spare, achieve in their perpendicular passage a trancelike state: each person adhering to the unwritten code, a man descending at five in the afternoon with his nose buried in a strange woman's back hair, reducing his breath to an absolute minimum necessary to sustain life, willing to suffocate rather than allow a suggestion of his physical presence to impinge; a man coming home at one A.M. ascending with only one other occupant of the car, carefully avoiding any slight recognition of joint occupancy. What is there about elevator travel that induces this painstaking catalepsy? A sudden solemnity, perhaps, which seizes people when they feel gravity being tampered with — they hope successfully. Sometimes it seems to us as though everyone in the car were in silent prayer.

## VOCABULARY

a. *paragraph 1*: congeals, animation, perpendicular, adhering, impinge, catalepsy

## QUESTIONS

1. Why does White delay the three main clauses in the first sentence? Why are they short and parallel?

2. What kind of tensions build in elevator rides, according to White?

3. How does White suggest this build-up of tension through the details of various rides?

4. Why do you think he concluded his description of elevator rides with a ride at one A.M.?

5. To what idea or reflection does White build the paragraph? Would the paragraph have the same effect if White had begun with this idea?

## WRITING ASSIGNMENTS

1. White asks the following question:

   What is there about elevator travel that induces this painstaking catalepsy?

   Write your own answer to this question, illustrating through the details of an elevator ride you have taken recently.

2. Describe a similar experience to those described by White, and build the details to a climax as he does. Conclude with your own comment or reflection on the experience as White does.

## WINSTON S. CHURCHILL

*Sir Winston Churchill (1874–1965) had a long and distinguished career in politics before serving Great Britain as prime minister during World War II and later from 1951 to 1955. Churchill was also a historian and one of the most gifted speakers and writers of English. His account of his first day at an English public school (the equivalent of a North American private school) occurs at the beginning of his autobiography* My Early Life, *published in 1930. Churchill tells us that he looked forward to going to school, though "I was perfectly helpless. Irresistible tides drew me swiftly forward. I was no more consulted about leaving home than I had been about coming into the world." Churchill was at this time seven years old. "How I hated this school, and what a life of anxiety I lived there for more than two years," he tells us. Like Lytton Strachey and Alice Munro, Churchill has an eye for detail that give us the sense of place as well as of people.*

## MY FIRST INTRODUCTION TO THE CLASSICS

The school my parents had selected for my education was one of the most fashionable and expensive in the country. It modeled itself upon Eton and aimed at being preparatory for that Public School above all others. It was supposed to be the very last thing in schools. Only ten boys in a class; electric light (then a wonder); a swimming pond; spacious foot-

1

ball and cricket grounds; two or three school treats, or "expeditions" as they were called, every term; the masters all M.A.'s in gowns and mortar-boards; a chapel of its own; no hampers allowed; everything provided by the authorities. It was a dark November afternoon when we arrived at this establishment. We had tea with the Headmaster, with whom my mother conversed in the most easy manner. I was preoccupied with the fear of spilling my cup and so making "a bad start." I was also miserable at the idea of being left alone among all these strangers in this great, fierce, formidable place. After all I was only seven, and I had been so happy in my nursery with all my toys. I had such wonderful toys: a real steam engine, a magic lantern, and a collection of soldiers already nearly a thousand strong. Now it was to be all lessons. Seven or eight hours of lessons every day except half-holidays, and football or cricket in addition.

2    When the last sound of my mother's departing wheels had died away, the Headmaster invited me to hand over any money I had in my possession. I produced my three half-crowns which were duly entered in a book, and I was told that from time to time there would be a "shop" at the school with all sorts of things which one would like to have, and that I could choose what I liked up to the limit of the seven and sixpence. Then we quitted the Headmaster's parlor and the comfortable private side of the house, and entered the more bleak apartments reserved for the instruction and accommodation of the pupils. I was taken into a Form Room and told to sit at a desk. All the other boys were out of doors, and I was alone with the Form Master. He produced a thin greeny-brown, covered book filled with words in different types of print.

3    "You have never done any Latin before, have you?" he said.

4    "No sir."

5    "This is a Latin grammar." He opened it at a well-thumbed page. "You must learn this," he said, pointing to a number of words in a frame of lines. "I will come back in half an hour and see what you know."

6    Behold me then on a gloomy evening, with an aching heart, seated in front of the First Declension.

| Mensa | a table |
|-------|---------|
| Mensa | O table |
| Mensam | a table |
| Mensae | of a table |
| Mensae | to or for a table |
| Mensa | by, with or from a table |

7    What on earth did it mean? Where was the sense of it? It seemed absolute rigmarole to me. However, there was one thing I could always do: I could learn by heart. And I thereupon proceeded, as far as my private sorrows would allow, to memorize the acrostic-looking task which had been set me.

8    In due course the Master returned.

9    "Have you learnt it?" he asked.

10    "I think I can *say* it, sir," I replied; and I gabbled it off.

11    He seemed so satisfied with this that I was emboldened to ask a question.

12    "What does it mean, sir?"

13    "It means what it says. Mensa, a table. Mensa is a noun of the First Declension. There are five declensions. You have learnt the singular of the First Declension."

14    "But," I repeated, "what does it mean?"

"Mensa means a table," he answered. **15**

"Then why does mensa also mean O table," I enquired, "and what does O table mean?" **16**

"Mensa, O table, is the vocative case," he replied. **17**

"But why O table?" I persisted in genuine curiosity. **18**

"O table — you would use that in addressing a table, in invoking a table." And then **19**
seeing he was not carrying me with him, "You would use it in speaking to a table."

"But I never do," I blurted out in honest amazement. **20**

"If you are impertinent you will be punished, and punished, let me tell you, very **21**
severely," was his conclusive rejoinder.

## VOCABULARY

a. *paragraph 1:* preparatory, mortar-boards, formidable

b. *paragraph 6:* declension

c. *paragraph 7:* rigmarole, acrostic

d. *paragraph 11:* emboldened

e. *paragraph 17:* vocative

f. *paragraph 21:* impertinent

## QUESTIONS

1. How important is the opening description of the school to your appreciation of Churchill's feelings about it? How careful is he to specify the physical point of view following his mother's departure?

2. What exactly were his feelings? Does he state them for us or instead imply them in the telling of the episode?

3. What point do you think Churchill is making in the whole account? What in particular does the exchange with the form master contribute?

4. Would you say that Churchill finds humour in the episode? Notice the difference between what Churchill, the man, sees, and what Churchill, the boy, felt. Is the psychological point of view that of the boy or that of the man — or is it possibly both?

5. How does the use of repetition and the use of "conclusive" in the concluding sentence make for an appropriate ending?

## WRITING ASSIGNMENTS

1. Write a characterization of Winston Churchill on the basis of what he reveals about himself in the telling of this episode. Consider what he chooses to emphasize as well as his selection of details.

2. Write a narrative of a similar experience of your own — your first day in a new school, your own first introduction to a forbidding subject, or your discovery that adults could be different from what you had known them to be. Clarify both the physical and psychological point of view for your reader.

## ROBERT FULFORD

Robert Fulford *made his reputation as one of Canada's foremost journalists while a critic for the* Toronto Star, *writing about the arts and a variety of social issues. He was the editor of* Saturday Night *from 1968 to 1987, and made it the most widely read journal of Canadian culture. His books include* Crisis at the Victory Burlesque: Culture, Politics and other Diversions *(1968),* This Was Expo *(1968),* An Introduction to the Arts in Canada *(1977), and* The Journalists *(1981). His program, "Realities," on TVOntario, displays his versatility as an interviewer and the ease with which he can speak about subjects as diverse as day-care for children of single mothers, Churchill's conduct of domestic affairs during World War II, and a moral philosophy of the erotic. In the following essay, he recounts the events of a year that brought great changes to the Canadian West.*

## HOW THE WEST WAS LOST

1   They may never have seen each other's faces, but the two most famous non-whites in late nineteenth-century Canada — Louis Riel and Big Bear — were linked by history and by the events of the crisis year 1885. They were dissimilar in many ways — Riel a Montreal-educated Métis who travelled widely and was three times elected to the Canadian parliament, Big Bear a Plains Cree who knew no world beyond the Prairies. But they were also alike: both were mystics and prophets and both were charismatic leaders of peoples doomed by the westward thrust of the Canadian empire. At the beginning of 1885 Riel was a towering figure in the West, feared as well as respected, and Big Bear was a chief of considerable reputation. By the end of the year Riel was dead, hanged for high treason; and Big Bear was in prison, an object of hatred to the whites and of contempt to the Indians. They were defeated by a process they only dimly understood and could do nothing to resist.

2   This year Canada is marking the hundredth anniversary of the North-West Rebellion with a TV documentary, radio programmes, books, a large exhibition of Métis crafts in Calgary, and half a dozen academic conferences. These events can't be construed as a celebration, because not even the most blissfully unaware Canadian white can regard the destruction of the Métis and Indian societies as an accomplishment. But it isn't exactly an occasion for mourning either; only total hypocrites would pretend to mourn a series of events by which we have all handsomely profited. Perhaps the centenary of the rebellion can serve us best if it broadens our understanding of how we came to be what we are, and of the human price that was paid for modern Canada.

3   Both Louis Riel and Big Bear were products as well as victims of the Europeanization of North America. Descendants of fur traders who married Indian women, the Métis built the brief prosperity of their society (it lasted about seven decades) by feeding the European and white North American markets with buffalo hides and other skins. Big Bear led an Indian community that was heavily influenced by Europe: in the middle of the nineteenth century he and his followers were hunting buffalo on horses brought by the Europeans and shooting them with European guns. In many ways the Europeans were a

curse to the Indians — they brought smallpox (which Big Bear survived in childhood while many of his contemporaries died) — but at times they must also have seemed a blessing. In the short term, Europeans made possible the greatest mobility and freedom the Plains Cree had ever enjoyed.

The events of 1885 brought that period of intense and sometimes happy collaboration **4** to an end. By the beginning of that year, Riel was already a legend. He had behind him the abortive rebellion of 1869–70, which failed to establish a Métis political jurisdiction but nevertheless led to the creation of Manitoba. He had survived his years of exile in Montana and been called back, to the leadership of his people. But what the Métis in general had in mind, and what Riel dreamed, were different. They wanted their land rights: he wanted not only land rights but a new Roman Catholicism in which everyone would be a priest, the pope would be a Canadian, the Métis would be the chosen people, and he himself would be the "Prophet of the New World." Riel's eighteen months in a mental hospital were now years behind him, but his old illness — a kind of megalomania — was upon him again. The man who was about to become one of the central myths of our history was (the evidence seems clear) in the throes of madness.

Riel interpreted the Gospels in a way that made violence acceptable and necessary. **5** "Justice commands us to take up arms," he told his followers. On March 18, at Batoche, in what is now Saskatchewan, he and about sixty supporters ransacked the stores and seized a number of people, including the Indian agent. The next day he formed a provisional government and a few days later took part in a battle in which twelve Mounties and five Métis were killed. It was only a matter of time before the soldiers arrived from the East, defeated the Métis (in early May), and arrested Riel. The war seemed to be over almost before it began. Soon the soldiers were returning to the East, and — as Bob Beal and Rod Macleod write in their absorbing new book, *Prairie Fire: The 1885 North-West Rebellion* (Hurtig) — it was a time of national triumph for the young Dominion of Canada: "Every city and town that had sent a unit greeted their return with ecstatic crowds, and an orgy of banquets, church services, speeches, and plans for memorials followed. By the end of July all the troops were home and the last military operation in which Canadians shot and killed each other was over."

It could be argued that in pursuing their grievances the Métis were blindly impetuous. **6** In 1885 only fools could have imagined that violent action by a tiny, isolated community would win an argument with the government of Canada. And perhaps Riel knew this all along. George Woodcock, in his 1975 book on Riel's general, *Gabriel Dumont*, suggested that Riel was courting martyrdom, consciously or not: "He belonged to a people against whose characteristic culture almost all the forces of the nineteenth century were aligned; even if he had survived, the way of life he defended could hardly have done so, and perhaps that was one of the reasons . . . he decided to die and even made sure of doing so by disputing his defence lawyers' pleas of insanity when he was tried at Regina." But if the Riel rebellion was a kind of madness, the course of patient and peaceful negotiation was no more profitable. The experience of Big Bear was proving that point forcefully.

The year 1885 is mainly remembered for Riel's defeat, but it was also the year the Plains **7** Cree finally collapsed into the arms of white civilization and began their long decades of servitude as wards of the Canadian state. The end of their free civilization on the Prairies was at least as melancholy as the destruction of the Métis.

Big Bear's life — described recently in Hugh A. Dempsey's richly informative *Big* **8** *Bear: The End of Freedom* (Douglas & McIntyre) — encompassed the whole story of nineteenth-century prairie Indians, from triumph on the open plains to humiliation on the reserves. A chief's son, Big Bear won his own reputation in adolescence as a buffalo hunter and a warrior. Like the Métis, the Plains Cree built their lives around the buffalo, which provided most of what they needed — not only food but skins that could be made into clothes and tents, even bones to be made into implements. But the buffalo, while plentiful enough to serve the Indians who hunted them with bow and arrow, didn't last long when attacked by Indians, Métis, and whites with fast horses and repeater rifles. It was said that in the peak years 160,000 buffalo were killed every season, and by the late 1870s they had all but disappeared.

9   The Cree knew no other way to live, and in 1878 Big Bear explained to Lieutenant Governor David Baird: "The Great Spirit has supplied us with plenty of buffalo for food until the white man came. Now as that means of support is about to fail us, the government ought to take the place of the Great Spirit, and provide us with the means of living in some other way." His statement sounded absurd at the time, but it turned out to be a summary of government policies for native peoples for at least the next century.

10   It was commonly said of Big Bear that if he had been white he would have been a great statesman. He approached the whites in a spirit of friendliness and brotherhood, but he was the last major chief in the West to sign a treaty with the government. Other chiefs, promised a few dollars and some provisions, signed away their rights to the land without knowing what their acquiescence meant for the future. Big Bear somehow knew. He never understood the complexities of white power — he seems always to have thought that "government" was the name of a man in Ottawa who controlled everything — but he realized that the whites were taking away all that the Indians had. His dreams often guided the Plains Cree; in his youth, shortly after the smallpox attack, a vision had told him that eventually the whites would come in great number, bearing gifts, and take away the Indian land. That process was set in motion in 1869 when the Hudson's Bay Company sold the West to the new Dominion of Canada for £300,000. The news of this transaction baffled and distressed the Indians, who had believed until then that no-one owned the land.

11   Their reaction illustrated the mutual incomprehension that made a reconciliation between Indians and whites impossible. The whites were bound by their view of the world as something to be owned and conquered. The Indians, as pre-agrarians, knew the world only as something to live with. In the nineteenth century no white man could understand a view so fundamentally alien to his own — or even admit that it existed. Given this profound difference, there was nothing for the whites to do except convert the Indians to Christianity, British justice, and farming.

12   Big Bear never imagined that a war against the whites would be profitable; he counselled peace while he practised the tactics of delay. His followers were not so patient, and in the 1880s his authority began to slip away. Younger men, more attracted to violent action, pushed him aside. In the spring of 1885, when Big Bear and his people were camped near the Frog Lake settlement — north of the North Saskatchewan River, in what is now Alberta — the younger men were in control. When word came that Louis Riel and the Métis had taken control of Batoche, the Plains Cree were ready to join.

13   Mad Louis Riel, the most hated man in the West a century ago, is now a kind of hero: westerners who resent the power of the East join their grievances with his and see him as a pioneer spokesman for western alienation (some even want a posthumous pardon bestowed on him by the government). But there's something perverse in our tendency to idolize him (as we also increasingly idolize Big Bear). It requires us to stand history on its head. Riel and Big Bear remain the natural enemies of those who now populate the West and indeed of all prosperous modern Canadians; it was only after the defeat of the Métis

and the Indians that easterners could move west and begin the settlements that laid the foundation of Saskatchewan and Alberta.

But of course Riel has lived on in another way, his story woven into the larger story of    **14** Canadian politics. Sir John A. Macdonald's decision to let him hang (when there were good grounds to commute his sentence) profoundly alienated Quebec and helped Sir Wilfrid Laurier's Liberals seize that province in a grip so powerful it would not be broken until 1958. Riel had his posthumous revenge, if not on all Canadians then at least on the Conservatives.

## VOCABULARY

a. *paragraph   1:* Métis, mystics, charismatic

b. *paragraph   2:* construed, centenary

c. *paragraph   3:* Europeanization

d. *paragraph   4:* abortive, megalomania, throes

e. *paragraph   5:* provisional

f. *paragraph   6:* impetuous, courting

g. *paragraph   7:* wards

h. *paragraph   8:* implements

i. *paragraph 10:* acquiescence, baffled

j. *paragraph 11:* pre-agrarians

k. *paragraph 13:* alienation, posthumous

## QUESTIONS

1. How does the opening sentence — "They may never . . . 1885" — organize the paragraphs that follow?

2. Many of the transitional words and phrases are chronological, showing how events of the day were connected in time. What examples of such transitions do you find in paragraphs 1, 5, and 13?

3. What transitional ideas do *because, but*, and *either* express in paragraph 2? What about *already, nevertheless*, and *but* in paragraph 4, the semi-colon in 4, the *but* in paragraph 6, and the *when* in 12? Might Fulford have omitted any of these without loss of coherence — that is, without losing the sense of connection between ideas?

4. Does Fulford imply more about Riel and Big Bear than he states? What does he reveal about his own feelings or attitudes?

5. In what way does Fulford's conclusion politicize the North-West Rebellion for Canadians today?

## WRITING ASSIGNMENTS

1. Fulford recounts events of 1885 that were significant to Louis Riel, Big Bear, and Canada. Describe a historical figure or event that has significance for you, and use this description to say something about the effect of the past on the present.

2. Fulford describes the Riel rebellion in paragraph 6 as "a kind of madness." He is thinking of Riel's "megalomania" (see paragraph 4) and the violence of the rebellion. Discuss a conflict in values between the majority and a minority in our society, the origins of this conflict, and the "madness " that has resulted from it.

## MICHAEL IGNATIEFF

*Canadian writer and broadcaster,* Michael Ignatieff *is the author of* A Just Measure of Pain *(1978) and* The Needs of Strangers *(1985). His most recent book,* The Russian Album *(1987), won the Governor General's Award. The following edited excerpt is from this portrait of Russia's* ancien régime *and of the people in his family who belonged to it.*

## PEACE AND WAR

1    In the family album there is a photograph of my grandmother, Natasha Ignatieff, that dates from the period when she and her family came to live in St. Petersburg in the dark and cluttered apartment two blocks from the Neva river. She is dressed for a formal winter evening, a fox fur draped over her shoulders, Brussels lace on the bodice of her velvet gown, her hair swept back in a tight chignon, and a twelve-strand pearl choker around her stiffly upright neck. She is thin and pale, the cheekbones of her long angular face taking the light, the eyes deep-set and dark. Her expression is guarded, and she seems at odds with the occasion. She was a private soul: in the public glare, she shrank back. She hated Petersburg society: paying courtesy calls on the wives of Paul's superiors, making curtsies and small talk and all the while feeling she was up on a high wire one step from a fall.

2    The photograph may be one of those taken by a court photographer during the celebrations at the Winter Palace in honour of the three-hundredth anniversary of the Romanov dynasty in 1913. Perhaps she had just passed through the ritual of presentation to the Empress. Masters of ceremonies in court uniforms, carrying tall gilded sticks, would sort the ladies by rank and form processions to the throne. Natasha went with her sister Sonia and they stood in line, joking like schoolgirls, until they were ushered forward to curtsy quickly. In the blur there was time only for a glance at the glazed frozen face of the Empress.

3    On that evening in 1913 Natasha was in her thirty-sixth year, mistress of a large household, wife of a rising star in the Petersburg bureaucracy, mother of "four little wretches," Nicholas, Vladimir (Dima), Alec, and Lionel. She was also expecting a fifth child — my father George.

4    In that blurred round of middle age, punctuated by the children's whooping coughs and typhoids, their winter colds and summer fevers, she watched, half aware, as the ice

formed at the heart of her marriage. In the bedroom, Count Paul Ignatieff now rose at seven and was assisted in his ablutions and his dressing by his valet. While she remained in bed, Paul would breakfast downstairs with the children and their nannies, then hurry off along the quays of the Neva to the ministry of agriculture. At seven he would return, bolt his dinner, and set to work on the portfolios brought by the office courier. And "so till midnight," she remembered sadly, "every day for years the same routine."

Paul was determined to resist becoming just another bureaucrat. Within months of his    **5** arrival at the ministry he had taken his fight to help the peasantry with loans, education, and technical assistance right to meetings of cabinet, while his minister, Krivoshein, tugged nervously at his coat-tails to make him sit down. When the finance minister muttered that Ignatieff's proposals smacked of socialism, Paul replied that he preferred to experiment rather than wait "until the mob . . . adopts its own simpler solutions and sweeps us away with all our culture."

Natasha tried to interest herself in his work but could not share his worthy fascination    **6** with land banks and credit schemes. When she tried to involve him in her life, a round of children's illnesses and endless petty struggles with the servants, his mind would stray back to his papers. In those moments when they were alone together, she shrank from him, either pregnant or recovering from pregnancy, unable to satisfy him, accumulating a weight of grief and guilt about their relations that burdened her heart until her last night alive.

Paul was a gentle father. He took his breakfast with his sons and read them items from    **7** his morning newspaper. When the *Titanic* went down, in 1912, he read them the whole front page. On most days he let them walk with him to work, before they went back to their lessons with their tutors in the schoolroom of the apartment. He was back again at night for prayers and in the summer he took them sailing on the Baltic. On one of these holidays at a German resort called Misdroy, a picture was taken of the family standing in the sand in front of a cane and canvas beach hut. The boys are in ankle boots and sailor suits. Lionel, still a baby, is making a crazy face in the arms of a stout, brown-faced nurse-maid while Paul has his arm around Dima, who leans against his father. Paul is wearing a cloth cap in honour of the holiday and he is whistling through his moustache, with a vague, happy expression on his face. Natasha is wearing a high blouse fastened at the neck, underneath a full-length travelling coat, and she looks happy and relaxed, her hand resting on Nicholas's shoulder. Near her stands a small round-faced black-haired girl in a white servant's uniform. She was Tonia, the eldest boys' nurserymaid, and next to her stands a new arrival in the family, a firm-jawed Englishwoman of twenty-one, Peggy Meadowcroft.

In 1912, Natasha applied to an agency in London for a governess. The three eldest    **8** boys, by then eight, seven, and six, were getting to be more than either Natasha or a succession of nannies could handle. In due course a stern, fair-skinned girl with golden hair in a broad Edwardian straw hat, lace choker, and white high-waisted dress arrived with her suitcase at the house. Paul took one look at her and announced, "Now hooliganism will be controlled."

Beneath her feminine straw hats Peggy turned out to be a redoubtable Edwardian    **9** adventuress from the lower middle class, armoured with a brisk sense of British superiority. From the beginning, she gave everyone a piece of her mind: the boys for their dirty ears and messy writing, the maids for their slovenly way with a tucked-in corner, the cooks for unpunctuality. The boys, now edging towards adolescence, were dazzled by her good looks, whispered together about what they saw when she was wearing her translucent nightie, and watched open-mouthed as she waded into Russian life. When she took them out on walks and came across a cab driver beating his horse, she did not hesitate. Waving her brolly, she would stride across the street and bring the descending whip to a halt in midair with her high-pitched Putney Russian. The boys would stand on the icy quay, watching the crowd gather, and not know whether to burn with shame or glow with pride.

10    Natasha was guarded with Peggy, irritated with her "bored stiff look" and her humourless bustle. As a wife, she watched the glances that Peggy began casting in her husband's direction and the glances that were returned. Among the photos Peggy took of a family holiday in Switzerland in the hills above Lausanne, during the summer of 1913, there is one, reverently labelled "Count Paul," of him standing in an alpine meadow, leaning jauntily on a walking stick, knapsack over his shoulder, smiling broadly beneath his moustache. His gaze seems to bask in hers. They must have gone walking in the mountains alone together. In the same album, there is one of Natasha back at the hotel, heavily pregnant with my father, sitting in a wicker chair. Peggy has asked her to pose and Natasha's averted gaze flickers with a sense of invaded privacy.

11    My father was born in Petersburg in December, 1913, a child with curly red hair — the only one of her children, Natasha thought, who really looked like his father. He cried solidly for six weeks, and when placed in the baptismal font held onto his blanket with a grip no-one could loosen. At the baptism, the family priest placed around his neck a gold cross given him by his grandmother Ignatieff, which he wears to this day.

12    In January, 1915, Paul was asked to present himself at Tsar Nicholas II's residence at Tsarskoe Selo. The agriculture minister, Krivoshein, in search of liberal allies in the cabinet, had proposed that Paul be chosen to replace a reactionary minister who had just died. Paul presented himself to the sovereign and was surprised and flattered to hear Nicholas recalling the conversation they had had together, nearly twenty years before, over coffee in Paul's tent during regimental manoeuvres of the Preobrajensky Guards. Did Count Ignatieff — the Tsar asked evenly — recall that he had said the people resented the autocracy of the scribe, the clerk, the policeman, the governor, and even the minister? It was a disarming gambit and Paul, who had declined ministerial office before, left the interview as minister of education.

13    The Tsar's eerie feat of memory fostered in Paul the belief that the sovereign would always heed the words of honest men. This illusion drew him into the heart of a regime that both right and left circles in Petrograd regarded as beyond help. In the salons the talk was openly contemptuous of Nicholas II's weakness, and Paul's friends in the Kadet Party believed the only salvation of the country lay in establishing a democratic republic. Yet Paul himself, aware as anyone else of Nicholas's feeble intelligence and puppyish dependence on his wife, retained a mystical reverence for the office of Tsar as father of his people. Here he let himself be betrayed by the Slavophile family traditions and by the belief that, if the bureaucratic wall dividing Tsar from people could be broken down, Russia could chart a middle course between despotism and republicanism. It was on such traditions of service that Paul's very identity was built. Family traditions made him, and family traditions drew him under.

14    He set out to make the Russian school curriculum less remote and scholastic, closer to the needs of agriculture and industry, and instead found himself struggling to maintain teachers' ranks in the face of the steady hemorrhage to the front; he wanted to create a system of popular education open to all with advancement based on merit and instead found himself arguing with cabinet colleagues over whether Jewish children could enrol in Gentile schools. He wanted the school to be the centre of village life; instead, as the ter-

rible retreats of 1915 began, he was organizing the use of schools as dormitories for refugees. He sought to defend the autonomy of the universities from government interference and found instead that the Tsarina insisted on making appointments to the Petrograd University staff.

The cabinet, chaired by I.L. Goremykin, a man Paul regarded as a senile incompetent, **15** was so bitterly divided that some members left the room when others began to speak. It had no jurisdiction over military matters, no collective policy, not even a doctrine-of-cabinet responsibility. Each minister was responsible to the Tsar alone; like the others, Paul put on his court uniform every month or so and journeyed out to Tsarskoe Selo to report to the sovereign; and like the others he was free to criticize — and often did — the decision taken in cabinet. At the same time, cabinet decisions were often reversed by the Tsar. As the months passed, Paul came to understand with increasing despair that the institution of autocracy was incapable of running a modern war. He tried to secure the cooperation of the Russian parliament, the Duma, only to find that other ministers refused to recognize the Duma's authority. Above all, he was aware that power was slipping away from the cabinet — to military headquarters at Mogilev, to the Empress's suite in Tsarskoe Selo, and, worst of all, to the Petrograd salons presided over by the sexually rapacious and mentally disordered holy man, Grigori Rasputin.

In October, 1916, Natasha gave birth prematurely to a boy. They placed him in an incuba- **16** tor and called a priest who christened him Alexander. She lay in bed and heard his weak cries in the next room; halfway between sleep and waking, she recognized Father Nicholas's voice intoning the prayers for the dying. The child died that night. Natasha believed God had taken him to spare him the future that groaned and creaked up ahead like the ice under the Neva bridges.

The bitter Petrograd winter came on: darkness fell in the early afternoon, and the wind **17** howled along the quays at dusk. At dawn the city was enveloped in freezing fog. Now stones were hurled out of the darkness at their car when the Ignatieffs drove into the city.

In November, 1916, Paul attended his last cabinet meeting, convened to consider a **18** response to a motion in the Duma accusing the cabinet of treason. The prime minister lay at the end of a dark and gloomy room, stretched out in an armchair, nursing a gouty foot. All possible stratagems were rejected, one after the other. After a long silence, the prime minister looked at Paul and said in a dismal voice, "Count, you help us." Angrily, Paul answered, "I am kept in this cabinet against my will. It has become clear that this cabinet does not dare, has not the moral standing, to enter into negotiations with the state Duma or the country." He said he would not approach the Duma as a representative of the cabinet, but solely in a personal capacity.

They allowed him one last try. But when he had succeeded in negotiating a softening of **19** the Duma's language, he discovered that the minister of the interior, Protopopoff, had circulated a rumour to the effect that recalcitrant Duma members would be conscripted for service in the trenches if they passed the original motion. The last chance of reconciliation between government and Duma — if it had ever been a real chance at all — had been sabotaged.

Paul journeyed out to headquarters once more. He pointed out to the Tsar that Protopo- **20** poff had made a public statement to the effect that the army had food supplies for four years. "What else can this be described as other than a crime?" he asked. "If it is so, why are the people standing in queues half starved? What else is it than an effort to provoke the people against the army?" Again the Tsar answered, "Thank you. Now my eyes are opened. Stay and work for my sake." Paul was told to report next morning for a further audience. He went the rounds of headquarters pleading with everyone to persuade the Tsar to remove Protopopoff. One of the generals shrugged his shoulders: *"Vous plaidez une cause perdue."*

21    Next morning Paul waited in vain for a summons to the promised audience with the Tsar. At lunch, he watched, with a dawning comprehension, as the Tsar and Tsarina entered, failed to acknowledge his greeting, and turned their backs on the cluster of ministers standing at the end of the room. Other officers and cabinet officials were presented to the Tsarina. He stood apart, aware that she had decided his fate. Two days later he returned for an audience, with a letter of resignation in his hand. He read it to the Tsar in a hoarse and strained voice:

22    "Your Imperial Majesty and Most Gracious Sovereign:

23    "On November 19, at the headquarters of your Majesty, I felt it to be a duty to state that my conscience and my oath of office made it necessary for me to report the apprehensions which cause me concern about the acts of certain persons and the trend of the political life of the country. I implored your Majesty not to force me to be an accomplice of those persons, whose acts my conscience warned me were ruinous to the throne and the fatherland. . . . I esteem it my duty as a loyal subject humbly to beg your Majesty to relieve me from the unbearable burden of serving contrary to the dictates of my conscience. . . .

24    "Even when separated from a direct share in the conduct of affairs in accordance with the principles and examples set by my father, I shall remain the same loyal servant of your Majesty, the throne and the fatherland."

25    The Tsar lifted his eyes and said, "Do not be agitated, go on with your useful work. Your petition will remain with me in my desk." He opened a drawer in the table and put the petition into it.

26    That evening Paul learned from a newspaperman friend that he had been replaced as minister. He made the final round of the ministry. His subordinates assembled in the great hall and they exchanged words of deep feeling. They asked him to speak, but the words would not come and he stood in silence, blinking. He could only recall a line from a poem: "Friends, row hard, row hard." They carried him on their shoulders down the steps of the ministry to his car.

27    He was summoned to Tsarskoe Selo for a farewell audience. Rasputin's body had been found floating in the Neva that morning. The Tsar scarcely seemed to be listening to him when Paul said "it was the mercy of God." Awakened from his reverie, the Tsar looked at him sharply: "You mean, the will of God." "No, your Majesty, I mean the mercy of God. It might have finished worse." Paul said he wished he could have remained to continue the work he had started, to which the Tsar replied, "Do not be afraid. I stay here and guard all that you have done." He then added in a quiet, distant voice: "You told me the truth," and then — after a pause — "as you saw it." With these words, the Tsar clasped him in his arms, and said, "Go to your mother now; take a rest, restore your health, and return to go on with your work." In tears, Paul answered, "Your Majesty, something tells me that I shall never again be in this room. May God protect you."

## VOCABULARY

a. *paragraph   1:* bodice, chignon, choker

b. *paragraph   4:* bureaucrat

c. *paragraph   8:* Edwardian

d. *paragraph 9:* unpunctuality

e. *paragraph 10:* jauntily

f. *paragraph 11:* font

g. *paragraph 12:* autocracy

h. *paragraph 13:* despotism

i. *paragraph 15:* rapacious

j. *paragraph 16:* intoning

k. *paragraph 19:* recalcitrant

## QUESTIONS

1. Ignatieff begins his essay with a description of a photograph. What details in the description prepare us for the world he proceeds to portray? Are the descriptions of other characters also significant?

2. What is the thesis of the essay? Does the essay build to a statement of the thesis, perhaps in the closing paragraph, or instead introduce it early?

3. What impression do you have of the writer, and how is this impression created? Do you notice a special point of view — a way of seeing the people and life in pre-revolutionary Russia? Does the writer seek to be objective in reporting events? In general, what does the point of view contribute to the essay?

4. Why does the writer conclude with a conversation reported in direct speech?

## WRITING ASSIGNMENTS

1. Describe a photograph in your family album. What do the details — clothing, hair-style, pose, background — tell you about the era in which it was taken?

2. Notice how Ignatieff sketches in daily life with a series of typical but specific details — paragraphs 4 and 7, for example. Re-create a period of time from your own past with a similar sampling.

## MARK L. DEMBERT

Mark L. Dembert *is an infectious-disease epidemiologist now serving with the United States Navy in Norfolk, Virginia. Dembert writes about a subject popular with essayists, but he writes with an originality created by his unusual experiences. His economical opening paragraph establishes a point of view and focus for his essay. His concluding paragraph is equally effective.*

## BEING SANTA

1    I look forward to Christmas every year because it enables me to be Santa Claus. Unlike many men who play Santa just for the money or to be the life of the party, I feel as if I actually become Santa Claus in appearance, conversation, mannerisms and in the real sense of enjoyment I derive. Granted, there is a certain amount of ego gratification involved. I look in people's faces and feel really good about their responses to me.

2    My enjoyment of interacting with sick and healthy children during my pediatrics rotations in medical school and internship led me to look for ways to affect children positively. Playing Santa Claus seemed a good challenge. But several years of seagoing medical commitments in the Navy, travel and primary care of adult patients delayed my debut.

3    The idea came back when I went to graduate public health school at Yale in 1981 and became friendly with staff members from a local and innovative teachers' center. They welcomed having a Santa for many of their elementary schools in New Haven. I decided to do it free, so that my creativity would not be limited by numbers of children to see, hours to work, or specific places to visit. I very quickly found that adults appreciated me as much as the children. In the last four years, the role has become a tradition for me.

4    The process begins in the middle of December, when I rerun a videocassette recording of "The Miracle on 34th Street," watching Edmund Gwenn's every nuance. I then reread Raymond Brigg's comic monograph "Father Christmas."

5    I get the suit out of storage in the back of my closet, where it hangs with my tuxedo and other items I rarely use. Before going into storage after Christmas, the suit gets dry-cleaned, and the beard gets a shampoo and a permanent. I have yet to be charged for these services.

6    As my father once told me, "Whatever you do in life, at least dress well for the part." This applies to being Santa. I originally invested $100 in a Santa Claus suit, beard and wig of good quality material, and they have held up well. Christmas is no time for a forlorn Santa Claus. I try to look fat and jolly, a little weatherworn and well-traveled. I use a solid pillow for stuffing, with a belt to keep it up and in place. L.L. Bean suspenders, double-sided Scotch tape for the beard and wig, red and white grease-paint, Sperry sailing boots, and white cotton garden gloves complete the outfit.

7    I choose my transportation around town carefully. I am for high visibility and get a lot of double takes at red traffic lights and at gas-station pumps. I try to be open and spontaneous about where to go. Kindergartens, nursing homes and pediatric wards at hospitals are naturals. Then the originality comes in. It's important to walk the streets a little and get out of buildings. (It is also very cooling; the suit can get quite hot.) I like to stroll down a main business street and look in the windows of restaurants. I wave to passing cars. Almost everyone is happy to see Santa, shake his hand and give a hug or a kiss.

8    There are strict rules about eating and drinking while in the Santa suit. I carry a drinking straw up inside my sleeve, held to my arm with a rubber band. I use it to sip soda and soup at lunch. After much practice, I am adept at quickly slipping in forkfuls of food without dirtying my beard. I avoid biting into pizzas and sipping gravies. Alcoholic drinks are forbidden.

9    It is not in keeping with the spirit of being Santa to prepare lines or answers to questions. Like a good shortstop, I am quick on my feet, and I get a real sense of fun in fielding and parrying such questions and comments as: Where are the reindeer? Where is the snow? Where is Mrs. Santa Claus? I thought you only came out when it snowed. You see every boy and girl in the whole world in one night? Do you have any children? Why did

you come in a car? Where is the Jaguar you promised me last year? What do you do the rest of the year? What are the reindeer's names? Where is the sleigh? And, the toughest was: You're not Santa Claus! To this I shot from the hip and replied, "You're not a kid." Above all, I never deny being Santa Claus, even to the most challenging children. It's important to leave a little bit of uncertainty. If the heat gets bad, I simply go on to the next child. Dissenters, thank goodness, are in a very small minority.

Before the first time I played Santa, I spent several days wondering what I would say **10** and do in this situation or that. However, when I walked into my first classroom, the children were so excited that they made me forget my concerns. Ho-ho-ho-ing came easily; so did winking. I also quickly learned how to handle several children together on my lap.

My beard is taped securely to several places on my face. This prevents slippage during **11** the day or when children pull on it. When I say "Ouch," they love it so much that it makes them try harder. I use my forearms gently but firmly to stop their grabbing. I think it is important for children to see Santa as human, one who can show pain, who can be funny and then serious, who can care and listen and interact with parents and siblings.

My first year, in New Haven, I was the first Santa to be taken to lunch at Mory's. The **12** maître d's upper lip didn't quiver when I signed the guest book as Santa Claus and gave my address as the North Pole. He looked the other way when I sipped my vichyssoise with a straw. But at the end of lunch, he came back to the table and asked me why I hadn't left a blonde under his tree the last three years. Then he grinned. Getting him to smile, according to my professor host, was a first at Mory's.

I now firmly believe that when it comes to instilling in others — and in myself — the **13** virtues of the Christmas spirit, there is no better way than as Santa Claus. How else could I so easily set aside my inhibitions — and my Navy uniform — and become a mirthful, winking, ho-ho-ho-ing, joking, hugging, exuberant man? Being such a person is a wonderful thing to experience.

## VOCABULARY

a. *paragraph  1:* mannerisms, ego gratification

b. *paragraph  2:* pediatrics, rotations, commitments

c. *paragraph  3:* innovative, creativity, tradition

d. *paragraph  6:* forlorn

e. *paragraph  7:* visibility, spontaneous

f. *paragraph  8:* adept

g. *paragraph  9:* dissenters

h. *paragraph 11:* siblings

i. *paragraph 12:* maître d', vichyssoise

j. *paragraph 13:* instilling, inhibitions, exuberant

## QUESTIONS

1. How does Dembert indicate the subject and focus of his essay in the opening paragraph? What is his purpose in writing, and how does it account for his focus?

2. How does Dembert organize the essay? How does his purpose account for this organization?

3. Does Dembert use the concluding paragraph to state or restate his thesis? Or does he use the conclusion for another purpose?

4. What impression do you get of Dembert in reading the essay — specifically, of his interests, sense of humor, general outlook on life? What statements and details convey this impression?

## WRITING ASSIGNMENTS

1. Dembert refers to the "strict rules about eating and drinking while in the Santa suit." Describe your own personal experience involving strict rules of another kind. Explain how these rules affected the experience. In concluding the essay, you might make comment on your attitude toward these rules or on the experience itself.

2. Dembert describes one way to make sick children and other people smile. Discuss your own experiences with sick or unhappy people. You might discuss your own ways of helping people who are sick or in trouble.

## JOAN DIDION

*Joan Didion established her reputation as a magazine columnist and editor and later as a writer of short stories, the screen, and novels. After graduating from the University of California, Berkeley, in 1956, she was an associate editor of* Vogue, *and she was later a columnist for* The Saturday Evening Post *magazine and contributing editor to the* National Review *magazine. In her novels* Play It As It Lays *and* The Book of Common Prayer *and in her many essays, Didion depicts personal and social values often imperceptible to the people who live by them. She explores such values in the following essay on what "home" means to those now approaching middle age.*

## ON GOING HOME

1   I am home for my daughter's first birthday. By "home" I do not mean the house in Los Angeles where my husband and I and the baby live, but the place where my family is, in the Central Valley of California. It is a vital although troublesome distinction. My husband likes my family but is uneasy in their house, because once there I fall into their ways, which are difficult, oblique, deliberately inarticulate, not my husband's ways. We live in dusty houses ("D–U–S–T," he once wrote with his finger on surfaces all over the house, but no one noticed it) filled with mementos quite without value to him (what could the Canton dessert plates mean to him? how could he have known about the assay scales, why

should he care if he did know?), and we appear to talk exclusively about people we know who have been committed to mental hospitals, about people we know who have been booked on drunk-driving charges, and about property, particularly about property, land, price per acre and C-2 zoning and assessments and freeway access. My brother does not understand my husband's inability to perceive the advantage in the rather common real-estate transaction known as "sale-leaseback," and my husband in turn does not understand why so many of the people he hears about in my father's house have recently been committed to mental hospitals or booked on drunk-driving charges. Nor does he understand that when we talk about sale-leasebacks and right-of-way condemnations we are talking in code about the things we like best, the yellow fields and the cottonwoods and the rivers rising and falling and the mountain roads closing when the heavy snow comes in. We miss each other's points, have another drink and regard the fire. My brother refers to my husband, in his presence, as "Joan's husband." Marriage is the classic betrayal.

Or perhaps it is not any more. Sometimes I think that those of us who are now in our     **2**
thirties were born into the last generation to carry the burden of "home," to find in family life the source of all tension and drama. I had by all objective accounts a "normal" and a "happy" family situation, and yet I was almost thirty years old before I could talk to my family on the telephone without crying after I had hung up. We did not fight. Nothing was wrong. And yet some nameless anxiety colored the emotional charges between me and the place that I came from. The question of whether or not you could go home again was a very real part of the sentimental and largely literary baggage with which we left home in the fifties; I suspect that it is irrelevant to the children born of the fragmentation after World War II. A few weeks ago in a San Francisco bar I saw a pretty young girl on crystal take off her clothes and dance for the cash prize in an "amateur-topless" contest. There was no particular sense of moment about this, none of the effect of romantic degradation, of "dark journey," for which my generation strived so assiduously. What sense could that girl possibly make of, say, *Long Day's Journey into Night*? Who is beside the point?

That I am trapped in this particular irrelevancy is never more apparent to me than when     **3**
I am home. Paralyzed by the neurotic lassitude engendered by meeting one's past at every turn, around every corner, inside every cupboard, I go aimlessly from room to room. I decide to meet it head-on and clean out a drawer, and I spread the contents on the bed. A bathing suit I wore the summer I was seventeen. A letter of rejection from *The Nation*, an aerial photograph of the site for a shopping center my father did not build in 1954. Three teacups hand-painted with cabbage roses and signed "E.M.," my grandmother's initials. There is no final solution for letters of rejection from *The Nation* and teacups hand-painted in 1900. Nor is there any answer to snapshots of one's grandfather as a young man on skis, surveying around Donner Pass in the year 1910. I smooth out the snapshot and look into his face, and do and do not see my own. I close the drawer, and have another cup of coffee with my mother. We get along very well, veterans of a guerrilla war we never understood.

Days pass. I see no one. I come to dread my husband's evening call, not only because     **4**
he is full of news of what by now seems to me our remote life in Los Angeles, people he has seen, letters which require attention, but because he asks what I have been doing, suggests uneasily that I get out, drive to San Francisco or Berkeley. Instead I drive across the river to a family graveyard. It has been vandalized since my last visit and the monuments are broken, overturned in the dry grass. Because I once saw a rattlesnake in the grass I stay in the car and listen to a country-and-western station. Later I drive with my father to a ranch he has in the foothills. The man who runs his cattle on it asks us to the roundup, a week from Sunday, and although I know that I will be in Los Angeles I say, in the oblique way my family talks, that I will come. Once home I mention the broken monuments in the graveyard. My mother shrugs.

5    I go to visit my great-aunts. A few of them think now that I am my cousin, or their daughter who died young. We recall an anecdote about a relative last seen in 1948, and they ask if I still like living in New York City. I have lived in Los Angeles for three years, but I say that I do. The baby is offered a horehound drop, and I am slipped a dollar bill "to buy a treat." Questions trail off, answers are abandoned, the baby plays with the dust motes in a shaft of afternoon sun.

6    It is time for the baby's birthday party: a white cake, strawberry-marshmallow ice cream, a bottle of champagne saved from another party. In the evening, after she has gone to sleep, I kneel beside the crib and touch her face, where it is pressed against the slats, with mine. She is an open and trusting child, unprepared for and unaccustomed to the ambushes of family life, and perhaps it is just as well that I can offer her little of that life. I would like to give her more. I would like to promise her that she will grow up with a sense of her cousins and of rivers and of her great-grandmother's teacups, would like to pledge her a picnic on a river with fried chicken and her hair uncombed, would like to give her *home* for her birthday, but we live differently now and I can promise her nothing like that. I give her a xylophone and a sundress from Madeira, and promise to tell her a funny story.

## VOCABULARY

a. *paragraph 1:* oblique, inarticulate, assay scales

b. *paragraph 2:* assiduously

c. *paragraph 3:* lassitude

d. *paragraph 5:* motes

## QUESTIONS

1. Didion begins her essay with a discussion of the significance of "home." Does she view home as an inclusive or exclusive concept? In what ways do the details of the opening paragraph contribute to the meaning of "home"?

2. How do the opening sentences of paragraphs 2 through 5 contribute to the essay's coherence?

3. What details in the body of the essay contribute most to its coherence? Do the sense of coherence and the abundance of details convey a dominant impression? What is it?

4. In the concluding paragraph, Didion returns to her daughter's birthday party. Is this completing of the circuit appropriate or forced?

## WRITING ASSIGNMENT

Return imaginatively to an everyday scene of your childhood, and in a consideration of changes in the landscape, write a meditation on the passage of time and lost youth.

# PART 2

# METHODS OF
# DEVELOPMENT

# INTRODUCTION:
# METHODS OF DEVELOPMENT

Essays traditionally have been classified as *narrative, descriptive, expository*, and *argumentative*. These labels broadly describe essays that narrate events, describe a scene, explain an idea, or argue a point. We customarily refer to novels as narratives, word pictures as descriptions, a set of directions as expositions, and summaries of reasons as arguments. This traditional classification does not, however, tell us everything about narration, description, exposition, and argument. For these also serve other purposes. The novel that depends on narrative seeks to entertain us, or, as with Hugh MacLennan's *Two Solitudes*, to move us or persuade us to take action. Descriptions like William Deverell's picture of a Vancouver slum or Margaret Atwood's of the Canadian North serve these same purposes and others. Argument is an essential means to persuasion, and so is exposition, as in an advertisement that explains what a product does and gives us reasons for buying it.

The paragraphs and essays in this section illustrate narration and description as well as exposition and argument. In particular, they distinguish several methods of development common in exposition — example, comparison and contrast, analogy, classification and division, definition, process, and cause and effect. These methods of analysis occur both in exposition and in argument, as we will see in the next chapter.

As in paragraphs, you can use these methods of analysis singly or in combination in an essay. The more methods your essay requires, the more attention you must give to your organization and transitions. The reader should understand at every point in the essay why you are using a particular method of analysis and how it develops the thesis. Transitions are needed to make these uses clear.

Keep in mind that you know more about the subject than do most of your readers: you are illustrating and analysing ideas for their clarification. Obviously the kind and number of examples you choose depend on how much help you judge that your readers need. How you organize the essay depends, too, on this judgement. Where you place the thesis in an explanatory essay depends on how much information your reader needs to understand it; where you place it in the persuasive essay depends on how disposed they are to accept it.

These essays by no means show all possible ways of organizing and developing ideas. But they do illustrate the choices writers have today in dealing with their experiences and with current ideas and issues. They are models of effective ways to write about experiences and ideas, and can serve as resources to which you can return in planning and revising your own essays.

# DESCRIPTION

Descriptive writing concerns itself with what we see, and is useful in all forms of writing. There are two categories of description: objective and impressionistic. In its choice of words, objective description aims for the value-free and the non-connotative, to approximate scientific writing as far as is possible. Impressionistic description, on the other hand, in its use of language, reveals the writer's reaction to the subject described. In the former, the writer selects details with a view to achieving complete fidelity to the subject; in the latter, with a view to creating a dominant impression. When using this method, it is advisable to order the details spatially, that is, describe the subject as you wish the reader to see it: top to bottom, left to right, etc. The direction of a spatial description can be signalled by the use of such words as *above, on the right, next, adjacent, across, down,* etc.

In a descriptive paragraph or essay you must be careful to specify the place from which the observation is made. Indeed, you may need to specify even the angle of observation. Notice how carefully Annie Dillard controls point of view in describing what lying in bed feels like:

> Later I lay open-mouthed in bed, my arms flung wide at my sides to steady the whirling darkness. At this latitude I'm spinning 836 miles an hour round the earth's axis; I often fancy I feel my sweeping fall as a breakneck arc like the dive of dolphins, and the hollow rushing of wind raises hair on my neck and the side of my face. In orbit around the sun I'm moving 64,800 miles an hour. The solar system as a whole, like a merry-go-round unhinged, spins, bobs, and blinks at the speed of 43,200 miles an hour along a course set east of Hercules. — Annie Dillard, "At Tinker Creek"

Something more than the physical point of view is suggested in these sentences: a dominant mood or attitude. This mood or attitude is often stated directly or conveyed by the details of the description. Alice Munro explains how she and her father differ in their attitudes toward time:

> I try to see that plain before me, dinosaurs walking on it, but I am not able even to imagine the shore of the Lake when the Indians were there, before Tuppertown. The tiny share we have of time appalls me, though my father seems to regard it with tranquillity. — Alice Munro, "Walker Brothers Cowboy"

If you fail to clarify the point of view from which you make the observation, or fail to clarify a change in position, details will seem blurred. Abrupt or unexpected shifts in mood or attitude can also confuse your reader. Using brief transitions that bridge these changes is the remedy. The essays in this book by Cam Stirling and Eric Nicol provide excellent examples.

## GUY VANDERHAEGHE

Guy Vanderhaeghe *was born in 1951 in Esterhazy, Saskatchewan. He studied at the University of Saskatchewan, where he earned a master's degree in history, and at the University of Regina, where he received a Bachelor of Education. He has worked as a teacher, an archivist, and a researcher, but now devotes his time chiefly to writing. He is currently Adjunct Professor in Creative Writing at the University of Ottawa. In the following passage, which is typical of Vanderhaeghe's writing, he combines with ironic subtlety a high rhetorical style and images from everyday life.*

# THE WATCHER

1   It turned out that my grandmother, although she had spent most of her life on that particular piece of ground and eventually died there, didn't care much for the farm and was entirely out of sympathy with most varieties of animal life. She did keep chickens for the eggs, although she admitted that her spirits lifted considerably in the fall when it came time to butcher the hens.

2   Her flock was a garrulous, scraggly crew that spent their days having dust baths in the front yard, hiding their eggs, and, fleet and ferocious as hunting cheetahs, running down scuttling lizards which they trampled and pecked to death while their shiny, expressionless eyes shifted dizzily in their stupid heads. The only one of these birds I felt any compassion for was Stanley the rooster, a bedraggled male who spent his days tethered to a stake by a piece of bailer twine looped around his leg. Poor Stanley crowed heart-rendingly in his captivity; his comb drooped pathetically, and he was utterly crestfallen as he lecherously eyed his bantam beauties daintily scavenging. Grandma kept him in this unnatural bondage to prevent him fertilizing the eggs and producing blood spots in the yolks. Being a finicky eater I approved this policy, but nevertheless felt some guilt over Stanley.

## VOCABULARY

a. *paragraph 2:* garrulous, bedraggled, bailer twine, comb, crestfallen, lecherously, scavenging

## QUESTIONS

1. Descriptions like Vanderhaeghe's work with the meticulous accumulation of details conveyed in precise language. Note some examples of such details and discuss their effectiveness in re-creating the scene.

2. Read aloud the first sentence in paragraph 2, noting the main clauses. In light of the considerable length of the sentence, how are these clauses given emphasis? Read the sentence aloud again, this time breaking it into shorter sentences. What change in effect do you notice? Is there an *equivalence* between the original sentence, particularly in its length, and the experience described?

3. How do the verb forms in paragraph 2 convey movement and confinement? Why does Vanderhaeghe use so many "–ing" forms?

4. Use your dictionary or thesaurus to determine whether there are synonyms for the following words: *butcher, garrulous, scraggly, scuttling, bedraggled, lecherously.* Would any synonyms you found be more suitable than Vanderhaeghe's words?

## WRITING ASSIGNMENT

Write a description of a building, the purpose of which is to convey the viewer's mood of elation. However, nothing in your description should explicitly reveal the viewer's mood.

# LYTTON STRACHEY

*Lytton Strachey (1890–1932), one of England's great biographers, was particularly in-terested in revered figures of the nineteenth century, whose human qualities he wanted to discover. In his biographies Strachey looks at the strengths and failings of his subjects, joining fact with the imagined creation of their inner life. We see this method in his portrait of Queen Victoria. Born in 1819, Victoria became queen in 1837 at the age of eighteen, and in 1840 married a first cousin her own age, the German prince Albert of Saxe–Coburg. When Albert died of a sudden illness in 1861, at the age of 42, she entered a long period of private mourning, for the remainder of her life preserving her physical surroundings as they had existed in his lifetime. Strachey shows how little the author needs to say when the right details are chosen and organized carefully.*

## QUEEN VICTORIA AT THE END OF HER LIFE

[1]She gave orders that nothing should be thrown away — and nothing was. [2]There, in drawer after drawer, in wardrobe after wardrobe, reposed the dresses of seventy years. [3]But not only the dresses — the furs and the mantles and subsidiary frills and the muffs and the parasols and the bonnets — all were ranged in chronological order, dated and com-plete. [4]A great cupboard was devoted to the dolls; in the china room at Windsor a special table held the mugs of her childhood, and her children's mugs as well. [5]Mementoes of the past surrounded her in serried accumulations. [6]In every room the tables were powdered thick with the photographs of relatives; their portraits, revealing them at all ages, covered the walls; their figures, in solid marble, rose up from pedestals, or gleamed from brackets in the form of gold and silver statuettes. [7]The dead, in every shape — in miniatures, in porcelain, in enormous life-size oil-paintings — were perpetually about her. [8]John Brown stood upon her writing-table in solid gold.* [9]Her favorite horses and dogs, endowed with a new durability, crowded round her footsteps. [10]Sharp, in silver gilt, dominated the dinner table; Boy and Boz lay together among unfading flowers, in bronze. [11]And it was not enough that each particle of the past should be given the stability of metal or of marble: the whole collection, in its arrangement, no less than its entity, should be immuta-bly fixed. [12]There might be additions, but there might never be alterations. [13]No chintz might change, no carpet, no curtain, be replaced by another; or, if long use at last made it necessary, the stuffs and the patterns must be so identically reproduced that the keenest eye might not detect the difference. [14]No new picture could be hung upon the walls at Windsor, for those already there had been put in their places by Albert, whose decisions were eternal. [15]So, indeed, were Victoria's. [16]To ensure that they should be the aid of the camera was called in. [17]Every single article in the Queen's possession was photographed from several points of view. [18]These photographs were submitted to Her Majesty, and when, after careful inspection, she had approved of them, they were placed in a series of albums, richly bound. [19]Then, opposite each photograph, an entry was made, indicating the number of the article, the number of the room in which it was kept, its exact position in the room and all its principal characteristics. [20]The fate of every object which had undergone this process was henceforth irrevocably sealed. [21]The whole multitude, once and for all, took up its steadfast station. [22]And Victoria, with a gigantic volume or two of the endless catalogue always beside her, to look through, to ponder upon, to expatiate

1

---

*John Brown (1826–1883) was the Scottish attendant to Victoria's husband, Prince Albert, and after the death of the Prince in 1861, to the Queen herself. — Ed.

over, could feel, with a double contentment, that the transitoriness of this world had been arrested by the amplitude of her might.

## VOCABULARY

a. *paragraph 1:* reposed, mantles, subsidiary, muffs, parasols, mementoes, miniatures, irrevocably, expatiate, amplitude

## QUESTIONS

1. In his description of Victoria in her old age, Strachey develops and illustrates several major ideas that build to his central or topic idea. What are these ideas?

2. Strachey states in sentence 2 that Victoria saved the dresses of seventy years; in sentence 3, that she saved her furs and bonnets, as well as other articles of clothing — and arranged and dated them chronologically. How does the formal transition between these sentences help to show that Strachey is moving from one surprising, even astonishing, fact to an even more surprising one?

3. Compare sentences 11 and 12 with those that follow. How does Strachey indicate that he is building the paragraph to even more suprising details?

4. How do the details of the description build toward the climatic effect of the final sentence of the paragraph?

5. Has Strachey made Queen Victoria human to you? Or is she merely an eccentric?

## WRITING ASSIGNMENTS

1. Write a character sketch of an unusual friend or teacher, centring on a dominant trait and presenting related traits as Strachey does. Present these related traits in the order of rising importance — as illustrations of the dominant trait.

2. Rewrite Strachey's paragraph, beginning with his concluding sentence, and achieving a sense of climax in your reordering of ideas and details.

## DANIELLE CRITTENDEN

Danielle Crittenden *is a writer and journalist whose work has appeared in many Canadian publications, including* Saturday Night, The Idler, *and* The Globe and Mail. *She was born in Toronto, where she still lives, in 1963. The following essay was written as a tribute to a favourite neighbourhood restaurant where she spent many evenings after her shifts as a newspaper reporter. The café, she writes, has since closed.*

## ODE TO A CAFÉ

1    There is a café in Toronto that I do not visit as much as I should since I moved from the neighbourhood. It is in an area known as The Beaches, where it has recently become im-

possible to buy a drink without a parasol in it. This was once a quiet district of clapboard cottages and empty stretches of sand, until the men with the pink neon and the white sportscars moved in. Now it looks something like a seaside village in drag. There are many cafés, and unless you are of a certain romantic temperament, it is unlikely you would wander into this particular one on your own. It is very small, about the size of a dry-cleaning outlet. On some days, depending upon the mood of the proprietress, only a few dishes are available.

Most prefer the café across the street, larger and more fashionable, decorated, like the rest, with black bentwood chairs and marble tables, and modern graphics on the walls. I have watched many people who go there, and it seems to be the choice of the Bohemian set. They sit by the windows wearing their berets and smoking French cigarettes, speaking of whatever is new.    2

Once, when my favourite café was closed, I had no choice but to eat lunch there. I listened to a couple near me discuss a significant development in art: a sculptor who coated small plywood houses with chewed bubblegum. The man was rapturous as he described the metaphysical repercussions this technique could have on the art world. The woman listened intensely, stirring her *espresso* absently many times before she finally sipped it. The waitress appeared to be an unemployed actress, because she put much theatre into taking the orders, rattling off the specials of the day like a succession of memorized lines, sighing dramatically if one took too long to decide, bringing and re-moving plates with great swoops and arabesques. The bill for a stale, paltry amount of food was large (including, I assume, the price of the show), and she was insistent that I pay it immediately and vacate, as she was going "off shift".    3

It made me realize that there are few really good cafés in this city, or any Canadian city. We are not a café society in the tradition of Europe; our eateries are efficient, produc-tive places that use loud music to discourage lingering or prolonged discussion; staff are trained like chained bull terriers. In Paris one can rent a table for several hours for the price of a single cup of coffee, and sit there, watching the other customers in the greasy mirrors along the walls or the passers-by outside as they bustle home in the dying autumn light.    4

There is a photograph that I love, taken in Paris in 1950, of a couple embracing in front of an outdoor café. The two lovers and a nearby table are the only objects in focus — the rest of the world around them is blurred, a mad, monochromatic rush. To me it illustrates what a good café should be, an oasis amidst the swirling, arid winds of society. In North America, we want everything at a fast pace, and our cafés are indicative of this. They are sleek, impressive, and modern, but unwhimsical. The culture they serve is like a bland patty shaped by a production line and fried until flavourless. It sells, people eat it, but ultimately, it is fattening and unhealthy.    5

I had long given up on finding a European-style café in Toronto, until the day I went into the smaller place. It had a large window with "Café Natasha" painted on it in gaudy yellow, next door to a beauty salon and a gourmet candy shop. Inside were eight small tables covered in blue cloths, all taken, except for one seat at a table for four. The woman who appeared to be Natasha looked at me sympathetically, and waved her hand to the empty chair.    6

"Perhaps you would like that one?" she said in a dense accent, and as I opened my mouth to say "No", she was already announcing my arrival to the three diners. They looked up cheerily and waved me over, and I spent the evening with them in a conversa-tion of some sort which was eventually lost in drink, as most good conversations are.    7

It took me many more trips to the café to learn about the woman who ran it. Occasionally,    8
when she was not busy, she would sit with me by the window and smoke one of her skinny

brown cigarettes and muse on the colour of the sky. On evenings when I stopped by for a glass of wine before closing, the lights would be dimmed, and the woman shimmied softly by herself to an old jazz tune.

9    Her age was somewhere between precocious and refined, forty, I think, but it doesn't matter. She belonged in another era: a Berlin coffee house in the 'thirties, perhaps, or a Paris dance hall during the 'twenties. She had deep red hair cut along the line of her chin, and black eyes which reflected the light, or absorbed it, depending on her mood. On a fine day she would be wearing an outrageous, colourful costume with a wide leather belt and lace-up shoes. On bad days she would dress bleakly, her hair would be rumpled, and she would smoke her dreadful cigarettes with particular ferocity. Most of the time I saw her she was between these two extremes, a lyrical creature arranging fresh flowers in a chipped, ceramic jug, or exclaiming about the seasons.

10   It was not her dress or the way she wore her hair that defined Natasha. Something about her reminded me of an exotic, uncatalogued species of bird, next to whom one felt flightless. When she moved, she danced, even to fetch a spoon. The music she played constantly in her café was the kind that evoked memories of other places, and other times. In the spring, it was always Vivaldi; in the hot summer, it would be the sultry pining of Billie Holiday; by autumn, red wine and Piaf; throughout winter, the blues of Bessie Smith.

11   Eventually, I learned that Natasha had left Yugoslavia with her husband many years ago to come to Canada. On the walls she had hung small mirrors and black and white photographs, and a few girlish sketches of people she had drawn at college in Dubrovnik. Natasha worked from eleven in the morning to eleven at night, cooking in the back and serving people out front. She offered simple food which she knew how to cook well: schnitzels and goulash, perogies and chicken soup, with thick, fresh bread. Half of the menu was available at any moment, as long as the dishwasher had not quit earlier that day, or the stove had not broken down, which happened rather frequently. At these times Natasha would be flying around the café like a startled, frantic sparrow, flapping her arms and calling out in her accented English.

12   Yet those who came did not do so for the food but to visit Natasha, and she developed a regular, eclectic clientèle who dropped by to drink and to talk. One pleasant gentleman would take a side table, order a carafe of wine, and sit for hours reading paperback novels. An older woman who lived alone dined every night at the café and often stayed until closing, watching the other customers benignly like an aged cat. One Eastern European fellow was there frequently, a bulky man who wore a dark jacket, steel-toed boots, and had a face like moulded concrete.

13   "Who is that?" I asked Natasha one day.

14   "Shhh," she said furtively. "K.G.B."

15   Sometimes she would stop in the middle of carrying out plates to the kitchen and gaze at her café with fond amusement. There might be an argument going on at one table, drunken outbursts of laughter from another, and two lovers in the corner watching each other as they ate. You could easily spot the new customers. They would sit watching with uncertain grins on their faces. "You know," she would say with great pride, "this has become my private smoking and drinking club."

16   Mostly, though, there were conversations, hundreds of them, now scattered. We would sit with wine, and smoke and speak frivolously, which one does when one is drunk. Sometimes she would shut the café so we could dance late at night, or she would put up the closed sign so we could have privacy to drink in the afternoon. One forgot other things when around her, the world shrank until it could fit in her front window.

17   I left the city for several months, and when I returned, I found a flat in a different neighbourhood. When I saw her again recently, she scolded me for not coming by as often as I did when I lived near the café. I apologized, and we drank quietly, with the resigned

understanding of friends who know that nothing can be done to change the circumstances. She is open less frequently now, and on some days, I have gone by and found the café dark, with a handwritten note taped to the door: "Sorry, dear friends, you are here but I am not."

I noticed that she has been sadder lately, the light catching only the shadows of her eyes. She speaks often about selling the café, opening one in Casablanca, or Havana, or Montparnasse. She knows they are all lost places, but then so are many dreams, and Natasha's café has become more of a state of mind than a place to eat. If she closes, there will be nowhere else. As we talked, I looked out the window at the café across the street. It was full.    **18**

Suddenly Natasha grasped my hand. "But my goodness, look how serious you and I have become!" she exclaimed, standing to fetch more wine. "Come, let's dance . . ."    **19**

## VOCABULARY

a. *paragraph  1:* parasol, in drag

b. *paragraph  2:* Bohemian

c. *paragraph  3:* rapturous, metaphysical, repercussions, arabesques, paltry

d. *paragraph  5:* monochromatic, unwhimsical

e. *paragraph  8:* shimmied

f. *paragraph  9:* precocious

g. *paragraph 10:* exotic

h. *paragraph 11:* schnitzels, goulash, perogies

i. *paragraph 12:* eclectic, benignly

## QUESTIONS

1. Is Crittenden's essay primarily a description of a restaurant, its owner, or about something else that includes both?

2. What does Crittenden say about other restaurants in Toronto and their denizens? Does she establish her own attitude toward modern life?

3. On what aspects of Natasha's behaviour does Crittenden concentrate? Is her opinion of this character implicit or explicit?

4. Analyse the development of the character description in paragraphs 8 through 11. What function do the physical details have? Is the information in this section just a series of random impressions?

5. Why does the essay end with an ellipsis (. . .)? What does Crittenden conclude with this particular convention?

# Writing Assignment

Use Crittenden's description of the restaurant and Natasha as a model for a description of a store that you know well and of its owner. Develop an overall impression or an attitude, and let your selection of details reveal it.

# Annie Dillard

Annie Dillard *lived for several years in the Roanoke Valley of Virginia and wrote about her experiences there in* Pilgrim at Tinker Creek *(1974) — awarded the Pulitzer Prize for Literature. She has also lived in the Pacific Northwest and writes about Puget Sound in another collection of essays,* Teaching a Stone to Talk *(1982). "It's all a matter of keeping my eyes open," Dillard tells us in her essay "Seeing." The mysterious world of nature is the major subject of her writing and the subject of this section of "Seeing."*

# At Tinker Creek

1    ¹Where Tinker Creek flows under the sycamore log bridge to the tear-shaped island, it is slow and shallow, fringed thinly in cattail marsh. ²At this spot an astonishing bloom of life supports vast breeding populations of insects, fish, reptiles, birds, and mammals. ³On windless summer evenings I stalk along the creek bank or straddle the sycamore log in absolute stillness, watching for muskrats. ⁴The night I stayed too late I was hunched on the log staring spellbound at spreading, reflected stains of lilac on the water. ⁵A cloud in the sky suddenly lighted as if turned on by a switch; its reflection just as suddenly materialized on the water upstream, flat and floating, so that I couldn't see the creek bottom, or life in the water under the cloud. ⁶Downstream, away from the cloud on the water, water turtles smooth as beans were gliding down with the current in a series of easy, weightless push-offs, as men bound on the moon. ⁷I didn't know whether to trace the progress of one turtle I was sure of, risking sticking my face in one of the bridge's spider webs made invisible by the gathering dark, or take a chance on seeing the carp, or scan the mudbank in hope of seeing a muskrat, or follow the last of the swallows who caught at my heart and trailed it after them like streamers as they appeared from directly below, under the log, flying upstream with their tails forked, so fast.

2    ⁸But shadows spread, and deepened, and stayed. ⁹After thousands of years we're still strangers to darkness, fearful aliens in an enemy camp with our arms crossed over our chests. ¹⁰I stirred. ¹¹A land turtle on the bank, startled, hissed the air from its lungs and withdrew into its shell. ¹²An uneasy pink here, an unfathomable blue there, gave great suggestion of lurking beings. ¹³Things were going on. ¹⁴I couldn't see whether that sere rustle I heard was a distant rattlesnake, slit-eyed, or a nearby sparrow kicking in the dry flood debris slung at the foot of a willow. ¹⁵Tremendous action roiled the water everywhere I looked, big action, inexplicable. ¹⁶A tremor welled up beside a gaping muskrat burrow in the bank and I caught my breath, but no muskrat appeared. ¹⁷The ripples continued to fan upstream with a steady, powerful thrust. ¹⁸Night was knitting over my face an eyeless mask, and I still sat transfixed. ¹⁹A distant airplane, a delta wing out of nightmare, made a gliding shadow on the creek's bottom that looked like a stingray cruising upstream. ²⁰At once a black fin slit the pink cloud on the water, shearing it in two. ²¹The two halves merged together and seemed to dissolve before my eyes. ²²Darkness pooled in the cleft of the creek and rose, as water collects in a well. ²³Untamed, dreaming lights

flickered over the sky. [24]I saw hints of hulking underwater shadows, two pale splashes out of the water, and round ripples rolling close together from a blackened center.

[25]At last I stared upstream where only the deepest violet remained of the cloud, a cloud so high its underbelly still glowed feeble color reflected from a hidden sky lighted in turn by a sun halfway to China. [26]And out of that violet, a sudden enormous black body arced over the water. [27]I saw only a cylindrical sleekness. [28]Head and tail, if there was a head and tail, were both submerged in cloud. [29]I saw only one ebony fling, a headlong dive to darkness; then the waters closed, and the lights went out. **3**

[30]I walked home in a shivering daze, up hill and down. [31]Later I lay open-mouthed in bed, my arms flung wide at my sides to steady the whirling darkness. [32]At this latitude I'm spinning 836 miles an hour round the earth's axis; I often fancy I feel my sweeping fall as a breakneck arc like the dive of dolphins, and the hollow rushing of wind raises hair on my neck and the side of my face. [33]In orbit around the sun I'm moving 64,800 miles an hour. [34]The solar system as a whole, like a merry-go-round unhinged, spins, bobs, and blinks at the speed of 43,200 miles an hour along a course set east of Hercules. [35]Someone has piped, and we are dancing a tarantella until the sweat pours. [36]I open my eyes and I see dark, muscled forms curl out of water, with flapping gills and flattened eyes. [37]I close my eyes and I see stars, deep stars giving way to deeper stars, deeper stars bowing to deepest stars at the crown of an infinite cone. **4**

## VOCABULARY

a. *paragraph 2:* inexplicable, transfixed, hulking

b. *paragraph 3:* ebony

## QUESTIONS

1. Note all of the first-person references in the passage. Why does Dillard include herself in her essay (unlike Updike, for example)?

2. What implied thesis or idea is Dillard developing in the four paragraphs? What sentence comes closest to stating a thesis?

3. What in the experience at Tinker Creek prompts the feelings Dillard describes in the final paragraph? What is the relationship between water and sky?

4. Break sentence 7 into its component parts and combine them into shorter sentences. Then discuss the differences in effect or meaning from the original sentence.

5. How do the following revisions of sentence 11 change the emphasis and effect:

   a. Startled, a land turtle on the bank hissed the air from its lungs and withdrew into its shell.

   b. Hissing the air from its lungs, a startled land turtle on the bank withdrew into its shell.

# WRITING ASSIGNMENT

Develop an implied thesis of your own through the details of an outdoor experience. You might build your description to the insight you reached into the world of nature as Dillard does.

# JOHN UPDIKE

*Born in Shillington, Pennsylvania in 1932,* John Updike *began his long association with* The New Yorker *magazine early in his career and has published many of his poems, stories, and essays in that magazine. His collection of stories,* The Music School, *won the O. Henry Award in 1966, and he received the National Book Award in 1963 for his novel* The Centaur. *His essay on Central Park in New York shows how details selected from a particular point of view can tell us much about a world without the need of direct commentary. From his casual and humorous description of the park, we get an impression of Updike himself. Notice the sharp contrasts in the details and their arrangement in the essay.*

# CENTRAL PARK

1    On the afternoon of the first day of spring, when the gutters were still heaped high with Monday's snow but the sky itself was swept clean, we put on our galoshes and walked up the sunny side of Fifth Avenue to Central Park. There we saw:

2    Great black rocks emerging from the melting drifts, their craggy skins glistening like the backs of resurrected brontosaurs.

3    A pigeon on the half-frozen pond strutting to the edge of the ice and looking a duck in the face.

4    A policeman getting his shoe wet testing the ice.

5    Three elderly relatives trying to coax a little boy to accompany his father on a sled ride down a short but steep slope. After much balking, the boy did, and, sure enough, the sled tipped over and the father got his collar full of snow. Everybody laughed except the boy, who sniffled.

6    Four boys in black leather jackets throwing snowballs at each other. (The snow was ideally soggy, and packed hard with one squeeze.)

7    Seven men without hats.

8    Twelve snowmen, none of them intact.

9    Two men listening to the radio in a car parked outside the Zoo; Mel Allen was broadcasting the Yanks–Cardinals game from St. Petersburg.

10    A tahr (*Hemitragus jemlaicus*) pleasantly squinting in the sunlight.

11    An aoudad absently pawing the mud and chewing.

12    A yak with its back turned.

13    Empty cages labeled "Coati," "Orang-outang," "Ocelot."

14    A father saying to his little boy, who was annoyed almost to tears by the inactivity of the seals, "Father [Father Seal, we assumed] is very tired; he worked hard all day."

15    Most of the cafeteria's out-of-doors tables occupied.

16    A pretty girl in black pants falling on them at the Wollman Memorial Rink.

17    "BILL & DORIS" carved on a tree. "REX & RITA" written in the snow.

Two old men playing, and six supervising, a checkers game.    **18**

The Michael Friedsam Foundation Merry-Go-Round, nearly empty of children but    **19**
overflowing with calliope music.

A man on a bench near the carrousel reading, through sunglasses, a book on    **20**
economics.

Crews of shinglers repairing the roof of the Tavern-on-the-Green.    **21**

A woman dropping a camera she was trying to load, the film unrolling in the slush and    **22**
exposing itself.

A little colored boy in aviator goggles rubbing his ears and saying, "He really hurt me."    **23**
"No, he didn't," his nursemaid told him.

The green head of Giuseppe Mazzini staring across the white softball field, unblinking,    **24**
though the sun was in its eyes.

Water murmuring down walks and rocks and steps. A grown man tying to block one    **25**
rivulet with snow.

Things like brown sticks nosing through a plot of cleared soil.    **26**

A tire track in a piece of mud far removed from where any automobiles could be.    **27**

Footprints around a KEEP OFF sign.    **28**

Two pigeons feeding each other.    **29**

Two showgirls, whose faces had not yet thawed the frost of their makeup, treading    **30**
indignantly through the slush.

A plump old man saying "Chick, chick" and feeding peanuts to squirrels.    **31**

Many solitary men throwing snowballs at tree trunks.    **32**

Many birds calling to each other about how little the Ramble has changed.    **33**

One red mitten lying lost under a poplar tree.    **34**

An airplane, very bright and distant, slowly moving through the branches of a    **35**
sycamore.

## VOCABULARY

a. *paragraph   2:* brontosaurs

b. *paragraph 10:* tahr

c. *paragraph 11:* aoudad

## QUESTIONS

1. How do Updike's details create a dominant impression, or is he trying to avoid creating
   a dominant impression?

2. What does he gain by presenting these impressions in phrases — actually shortened
   sentences?

3. What impression do you get of Updike from the essay, particularly from what he
   notices and chooses to describe?

# WRITING ASSIGNMENT

Describe an afternoon in a park or athletic field, as Updike does. Make your details as vivid as you can, without developing each impression.

# MORDECAI RICHLER

Mordecai Richler *was born in 1931 in Montreal and attended Sir George Williams University. Since 1959, with the publication of* The Apprenticeship of Duddy Kravitz, *he has earned his living as a writer of screenplays, a journalist, and a novelist. He has written some of the funniest and most important comic novels in recent times, including* St. Urbain's Horseman *(1971), for which he won his second Governor General's Award, and* Joshua Then And Now *(1980). In the following passage Richler displays his talent for detailed description and his skill at capturing a particular time and place, in this instance Montreal in the 1930s.*

# MAIN STREET

1   If the Main was a poor man's street, it was also a dividing line. Below, the French Canadians. Above, some distance above, the dreaded WASPs. On the Main itself there were some Italians, Yugoslavs and Ukrainians, but they did not count as true Gentiles. Even the French Canadians, who were our enemies, were not entirely unloved. Like us, they were poor and coarse with large families and spoke English badly.

2   Looking back, it's easy to see that the real trouble was there was no dialogue between us and the French Canadians, each elbowing the other, striving for WASP acceptance. We fought the French Canadians stereotype for stereotype. If many of them believed that the St. Urbain Street Jews were secretly rich, manipulating the black market, then my typical French Canadian was a moronic gum-chewer. He wore his greasy black hair parted down the middle and also affected an eyebrow moustache. His zoot trousers were belted just under the breastbone and ended in a peg hugging his ankles. He was the dolt who held up your uncle endlessly at the liquor commission while he tried unsuccessfully to add three figures or, if he was employed at the customs office, never knew which form to give you. Furthermore, he only held his liquor commission or customs or any other government job because he was the second cousin of a backwoods notary who had delivered the village vote to the *Union Nationale* for a generation. Other French Canadians were speed cops, and if any of these ever stopped you on the highway you made sure to hand him a folded two dollar bill with your licence.

3   Actually, it was only the WASPs who were truly hated and feared. "Among them," I heard it said, "with those porridge faces, who can tell what they're thinking?" It was, we felt, their country, and given sufficient liquor who knew when they would make trouble?

4   We were a rude, aggressive bunch round the Main. Cocky too. But bring down the most insignificant, pinched WASP fire insurance inspector and even the most arrogant merchant on the street would dip into the drawer for a ten spot or a bottle and bow and say, "Sir."

5   After school we used to race down to the Main to play snooker at the Rachel or the Mount Royal. Other days, when we chose to avoid school altogether, we would take the No. 55 streetcar as far as St. Catherine Street, where there was a variety of amusements

offered. We could play the pinball machines and watch archaic strip-tease movies for a nickel at the Silver Gameland. At the Midway or the Crystal Palace we could see a double feature and a girlie show for as little as thirty-five cents. The Main, at this juncture, was thick with drifters, panhandlers and whores. Available on both sides of the street were "Tourist Rooms by Day and Night", and everywhere there was the smell of french fried potatoes cooking in stale oil. Tough, unshaven men in checked shirts stood in knots outside the taverns and cheap cafés. There was the promise of violence.

As I recall it, we were always being warned about the Main. Our grandparents and   **6** parents had come there by steerage from Rumania or by cattleboat from Poland by way of Liverpool. No sooner had they unpacked their bundles and cardboard suitcases than they were planning a better, brighter life for us, the Canadian-born children. The Main, good enough for them, was not to be for us, and that they told us again and again was what the struggle was for. The Main was for *bummers*, drinkers, and (heaven forbid) failures.

## VOCABULARY

a. *paragraph 1:* WASPs

b. *paragraph 2:* stereotype, zoot, notary

c. *paragraph 5:* archaic, juncture

d. *paragraph 6:* steerage

## QUESTIONS

1. Richler's description of a Montreal neighbourhood depends on an accretion of detail. How would you describe the point of view?

2. How does Richler characterize the typical French-Canadian in paragraph 2? The typical WASP in paragraphs 3 and 4? How does the combination of specific details and general comment contribute to the overall impression?

3. How does the sequence of details in paragraph 5 control the reader's perceptions?

4. How would you characterize the shift in emphasis in the concluding paragraph? Does this shift result from the details, the point of view, the tone?

## WRITING ASSIGNMENT

Create a scene in which you evoke both character and setting without describing the character. Make the concrete details reveal the character and impression you wish to convey.

# NARRATION

Narration is an account of a sequence of events. Narrative writing describes an action; it answers the question, "What happened?" For example, in the following excerpt, Norman Mailer's report of a boxing match captures the intensity of the fight's climactic moment:

> In the twelfth, Griffith caught him. Paret got trapped in a corner. Trying to duck away, his left arm and his head became tangled on the wrong side of the top rope. Griffith was in like a cat ready to rip the life out of a huge boxed rat. He hit him eighteen right hands in a row, an act which took perhaps three or four seconds. — Norman Mailer, "The Death of Benny Paret"

Because narration deals with action in time, the events are usually controlled by verb tenses and the use of such signalling words as *now, when, while, then, before, after, next,* etc. Consider the use of these techniques in E.B. White's account of revisiting a summer camp:

> But when I got back there, with my boy, and we settled into a camp near a farmhouse and into the kind of summertime I had known, I could tell that it was going to be pretty much the same as it had been before — I knew it, lying in bed the first morning, smelling the bedroom, and hearing the boy sneak quietly out and go off along the shore in a boat. I began to sustain the illusion that he was I, and therefore, by simple transposition, that I was my father. — E.B. White, "Once More to the Lake"

Writers often find the flashback technique helpful, either in explaining an action more fully or in providing necessary motivation or context. In White's essay, an event in the present triggers a recollection of his own boyhood:

> My boy loved our rented outboard, and his great desire was to achieve singlehanded mastery over it, and authority, and he soon learned the trick of choking it a little (but not too much), and the adjustment of the needle valve. Watching him I would remember the things you could do with the old one-cylinder engine with the heavy flywheel, how you could have it eating out of your hand if you got really close to it spiritually. Motor boats in those days didn't have clutches, and you would make a landing by shutting off the motor at the proper time and coasting in with a dead rudder. But there was a way of reversing them, if you learned the trick, by cutting the switch and putting it on again exactly on the final dying revolution of the flywheel, so that it would kick back against compression and begin reversing. — White, "Once More to the Lake"

When narrating an action, avoid passive verb forms. Note how Mailer uses active verbs to convey movement succinctly:

> This fight had its turns. Griffith won most of the early rounds, but Paret knocked Griffith down in the sixth. Griffith had trouble getting up, but made it, came alive and was dominating Paret again before the round was over. Then Paret began to wilt. In the middle of the eighth round, after a clubbing punch had turned his back to Griffith, Paret walked three disgusted steps away, showing his hindquarters. — Mailer, "The Death of Benny Paret"

Precise detail is the soul of good narrative. Note the specificity of White's description of handling the motorboat. Writing that lapses into generalities loses its hold not only on the reader but also on the real world.

# Norman Mailer

*Born in New Jersey and raised in Brooklyn,* Norman Mailer *attended Harvard University, where he made the decision to become a writer. After serving in the Pacific in World War II, he wrote* The Naked and the Dead, *the novel that established his reputation as an important American writer. Mailer has maintained that reputation through a series of controversial novels about postwar America, and also through his journalism on a wide range of topics — from boxing to "hip" culture, lunar exploration, and American politics. A remarkable example is his eyewitness account of the knockout of Benny Paret in the twelfth round of a world championship welterweight bout at Madison Square Garden on March 25, 1962. Paret died on April 3, at the age of 24. Later in this book, Norman Cousins discusses the cause of Paret's death.*

# The Death of Benny Paret

[1]Paret was a Cuban, a proud club fighter who had become welterweight champion because of his unusual ability to take a punch. [2]His style of fighting was to take three punches to the head in order to give back two. [3]At the end of ten rounds, he would still be bouncing, his opponent would have a headache. [4]But in the last two years, over the fifteen-round fights, he had started to take some bad maulings.

[5]This fight had its turns. [6]Griffith won most of the early rounds, but Paret knocked Griffith down in the sixth. [7]Griffith had trouble getting up, but made it, came alive and was dominating Paret again before the round was over. [8]Then Paret began to wilt. [9]In the middle of the eighth round, after a clubbing punch had turned his back to Griffith, Paret walked three disgusted steps away, showing his hindquarters. [10]For a champion, he took much too long to turn back around. [11]It was the first hint of weakness Paret had ever shown, and it must have inspired a particular shame, because he fought the rest of the fight as if he were seeking to demonstrate that he could take more punishment than any man alive. [12]In the twelfth, Griffith caught him. [13]Paret got trapped in a corner. [14]Trying to duck away, his left arm and his head became tangled on the wrong side of the top rope. [15]Griffith was in like a cat ready to rip the life out of a huge boxed rat. [16]He hit him eighteen right hands in a row, an act which took perhaps three or four seconds, Griffith making a pent-up whimpering sound all the while he attacked, the right hand whipping like a piston rod which has broken through the crankcase, or like a baseball bat demolishing a pumpkin. [17]I was sitting in the second row of that corner — they were not ten feet away from me, and like everybody else, I was hypnotized. [18]I had never seen one man hit another so hard and so many times. [19]Over the referee's face came a look of woe as if some spasm had passed its way through him, and then he leaped on Griffith to pull him away. [20]It was the act of a brave man. [21]Griffith was uncontrollable. [22]His trainer leaped into the ring, his manager, his cut man, there were four people holding Griffith, but he was off on an orgy, he had left the Garden, he was back on a hoodlum's street. [23]If he had been able to break loose from his handlers and the referee, he would have jumped Paret to the floor and whaled on him there.

[24]And Paret? [25]Paret died on his feet. [26]As he took those eighteen punches something happened to everyone who was in psychic range of the event. [27]Some part of his death reached out to us. [28]One felt it hover in the air. [29]He was still standing in the ropes, trapped as he had been before, he gave some little half-smile of regret, as if he were saying, "I didn't know I was going to die just yet," and then, his head leaning back but still erect, his death came to breathe about him. [30]He began to pass away. [31]As he passed, so his limbs

descended beneath him, and he sank slowly to the floor. [32]He went down more slowly than any fighter had ever gone down, he went down like a large ship which turns on end and slides second by second into its grave. [33]As he went down, the sound of Griffith's punches echoed in the mind like a heavy ax in the distance chopping into a wet log.

## VOCABULARY

a. *paragraph 1:* maulings

b. *paragraph 2:* pent-up, cut man

c. *paragraph 3:* psychic

## QUESTIONS

1. Make a list of the key elements in Mailer's narrative. Why are they ordered in this way? Could you change the sequence of events without sacrificing the story's impact?

2. Locate the climax in the essay. What is gained by delaying it? How does Mailer's commentary make it more effective?

3. How does Mailer's language convey an attitude? Is he scientific and detached or passionate and involved in what he describes? What response does he want to evoke in the reader?

4. Sentence 22 joins a number of actions occurring simultaneously. How does the sentence convey the jarring confusion of the moment?

5. Does sentence 29 describe a continuous action? Would the mood of the paragraph be changed if Mailer broke the sentence into segments or punctuated it differently?

6. How does repetition in sentence 32 reinforce the feeling conveyed in the final paragraph?

## WRITING ASSIGNMENT

Discuss the implications of the passage, including what it tells you about Mailer's attitude toward the death of Paret. Explain how Mailer conveys his attitude about this and about boxing as a sport. (See "Who Killed Benny Paret?" by Norman Cousins for another view of Paret's death.)

## HARRY J. BOYLE

*Journalist and broadcaster* Harry J. Boyle *was born in St. Augustine, Ontario, in 1915, and educated at St. Jerome's College in Kitchener. The author of numerous articles, radio and stage plays, books of essays, novels, and collections of short stories, he has won the Leacock Medal for humour. He has been a program supervisor for* CBC *radio and chair-*

*man of the Canadian Radio-Television Commission. In the following essay, he recounts the type of simple event from childhood that retrospectively acquires an enormous significance.*

## TOBOGGANING

The year I made up my mind Santa Claus was only going to give me useful presents of mittens and scarves and a small treat like a book or a jackknife, he completely surprised me.   **1**

On Christmas morning, in place of the small wooden sleigh I had seen Grandfather working on, there was a toboggan.   **2**

Snow was lean that year and the Big Hill, being sandy and exposed to the sun, had scarcely any sliding surface.   **3**

I went to bed each night after scanning the skies for any sign of snow and praying for a real blizzard. Perversely, the elements would sprinkle a little snow and then blow it into fence drifts or the hollows of the fields.   **4**

It was beginning to look hopeless. I could sit in the kitchen and look out to where the toboggan leaned against the house in the lee of the veranda. It was varnished and new-looking. Pushing it around the yard was frustrating. This long, sleek affair was made for the big slopes and long runs.   **5**

It looked as if I might have to go back to school after the New Year without having had a real outing on the toboggan. Then, on the Saturday before the New Year, the morning was overcast. The world seemed poised and waiting for something. Big snowflakes ruptured from the clouds and floated down to earth. They were melting as fast as they arrived, but the tempo increased and the bare spots soon had a thin coating of white. Mother had a time restraining me from pushing out to the hill.   **6**

The world was a creation of cotton batting by next morning. The teams on the sleigh made a convoy on the way to church. Everyone was sharing in that hearty friendliness that comes when nature has a transformation. Church was secondary in my thoughts to the anticipation of tobogganing, and when we got home I had to be almost forcibly restrained from going to the hill without anything to eat.   **7**

I was swallowing cake as I wallowed through the deep snow to the top of the hill. The toboggan was a delight. On the first run the snow flared out on each side with a great white spume effect. A touch of morning breeze had blown snow off the pond so that when we hit the ice the momentum carried the toboggan part way up the low hill opposite.   **8**

Snap, my old collie, was suspicious of getting on the toboggan at first, but he soon tired of romping through the deep snow and then having to wade back to the top. First time down he jumped halfway and landed head over heels in the snowbank. Next time he crouched and made the journey.   **9**

It had seemed all week that if the snow came my wildest dreams of play and happiness would come true. Yet, somehow I grew tired of being alone.   **10**

Grandfather was the first to wander over to the hill. He stamped around a bit and hedged about going down the hill for a ride. Sensing my mood, he got on, neglecting to take the pipe out of his mouth. He made a wild swipe for it about halfway down and left a foot dragging that sent both of us sprawling into the snow, while the conveyance went wildly to the bottom.   **11**

Father, at the stable door, yelled for us to stay where we were. He retrieved the toboggan and climbed the hill. "Takes some knack to handle one of these things," he suggested to Grandfather.   **12**

13    "You think you're so smart . . . then try it," retorted the older man.

14    "Well, I don't know what you're crowing about.'

15    "Go on . . . just try it."

16    Father got on, adjusted his hands to the ropes, and nodded for a push. He sailed down gracefully, getting an extra boost where the hill bulged a bit, and flashed down to the pond. Lifting both hands in triumph as it came to the ice he flipped off as the toboggan went sideways and hit a clump of grass frozen and protruding above the surface.

17    Grandfather laughed so hard Mother looked out from the kitchen. Soon, in fact before father had trudged up the hill, she came out to investigate, wearing his overcoat and an old stocking cap. "Are you children having a good time?"

18    Father lurched to grab her. "Come on, see for yourself what it's like."

19    Grandfather gave them both a push, and they lost their balance and went sprawling on the toboggan. Down the hill they went but when they reached the bump, both rolled into the snow.

20    By the time Mother and Father came up, our neighbors Ed Higgins and his wife, driving along the concession in a horse and cutter, swung in the laneway.

21    "Do you see what you've done," exclaimed Mother in mock anger. "They thought you were killing me."

22    It developed they were just curious about the toboggan, and it took practically no coaxing to get both of them on the ride. I half expected to go along, but Mother shook her head. Then Father dared Ed to go down the hill standing up, and he did, keeping his balance almost to the pond.

23    After that Father tried it and flipped at the bump. Mother and Mrs. Higgins got on and went down, taking ages to bring the toboggan back.

24    I finally got a chance to go down by myself, but when I looked up they had all gone. I trudged back up the hill, half hoping someone might come back to play with me. No one appeared, and when I went to the house Grandfather was asleep on the sofa in the kitchen, Mother was on the couch in the front room, and Father had gone up to bed for a rest.

25    I kept looking at the models of toboggans in the catalogue until I fell asleep in the old chair. Mother woke me up with the noise as she started to get supper.

26    "Didn't you have a wonderful time with your toboggan?" she said.

27    I didn't answer her, and she was so busy she didn't notice. What was there to say?

## VOCABULARY

a. *paragraph  4:* perversely

b. *paragraph  5:* lee

c. *paragraph  6:* poised

d. *paragraph  8:* spume

e. *paragraph 11:* conveyance

f. *paragraph 12:* knack

g. *paragraph 20:* cutter

# QUESTIONS

1. What is Boyle's purpose in the essay? How does a simple childhood experience acquire depth and resonance as he recounts it?

2. Of what importance are the other characters involved in Boyle's essay? Why does he quote so much actual dialogue?

3. Why are his paragraphs so short? What principle of paragraph development has Boyle used?

4. What sort of emotions does "Tobogganing" convey? What response does it seek to evoke in the reader?

# WRITING ASSIGNMENTS

1. Write an essay that begins in the present, then recounts an episode from the past that illustrates the present mood. Reveal your feelings through the details rather than simply stating them.

2. Compare Boyle's essay with E.B. White's "Once More to the Lake." Think about what makes them so different, despite the similarity of their subject matter.

# JOSEPH CONRAD

*The Polish-born English novelist* Joseph Conrad *(1857–1924) turned to writing as a career after twenty years as a sailor. Conrad served chiefly on English merchant ships, sometimes as first mate, and he commanded his own ship briefly during his years sailing in the East. The section reprinted here from* The Mirror of the Sea, *Conrad's account of his sailing career, shows his extraordinary descriptive power. Conrad uses the episode to say something unusual about the experience of nature.*

# A GALE OF WIND

For after all, a gale of wind, the thing of mighty sound, is inarticulate. It is a man who, in chance phrase, interprets the elemental passion of his enemy. Thus there is another gale in my memory, a thing of endless, deep, humming roar, moonlight, and a spoken sentence.    1

It was off that other cape which is always deprived of its title as the Cape of Good Hope is robbed of its name. It was off the Horn. For a true expression of dishevelled wildness there is nothing like a gale in the bright moonlight of a high latitude.    2

The ship, brought-to and bowing to enormous flashing seas, glistened wet from deck to trucks; her one set sail stood out a coal-black shape upon the gloomy blueness of the air. I was a youngster then, and suffering from weariness, cold, and imperfect oilskins which let water in at every seam. I craved human companionship, and, coming off the poop, took my place by the side of the boatswain (a man whom I did not like) in a comparatively dry spot where at worst we had water only up to our knees. Above our heads the explosive    3 booming gusts of wind passed continuously, justifying the sailor's saying "It blows great guns." And just from that need of human companionship, being very close to the man, I said, or rather shouted:

4   "Blows very hard, boatswain."

5   His answer was:

6   "Ay, and if it blows only a little harder things will begin to go. I don't mind as long as everything holds, but when things begin to go it's bad."

7   The note of dread in the shouting voice, the practical truth of these words, heard years ago from a man I did not like, have stamped its peculiar character on that gale.

8   A look in the eyes of a shipmate, a low murmur in the most sheltered spot where the watch on duty are huddled together, a meaning moan from one to the other with a glance at the windward sky, a sigh of weariness, a gesture of disgust passing into the keeping of the great wind, become part and parcel of the gale. The olive hue of hurricane clouds presents an aspect peculiarly appalling. The inky ragged wrack, flying before a nor'-west wind, makes you dizzy with its headlong speed that depicts the rush of the invisible air. A hard sou'-wester startles you with its close horizon and its low grey sky, as if the world were a dungeon wherein there is no rest for body or soul. And there are black squalls, white squalls, thunder squalls, and unexpected gusts that come without a single sign in the sky; and of each kind no one of them resembles another.

9   There is infinite variety in the gales of wind at sea, and except for the peculiar, terrible, and mysterious moaning that may be heard sometimes passing through the roar of a hurricane — except for that unforgettable sound, as if the soul of the universe had been goaded into a mournful groan — it is, after all, the human voice that stamps the mark of human consciousness upon the character of a gale.

## VOCABULARY

a. *paragraph 1:* inarticulate, elemental

b. *paragraph 2:* deprived, dishevelled

c. *paragraph 8:* appalling, wrack, sou'-wester, squalls

d. *paragraph 9:* goaded

## QUESTIONS

1. Narrative prose can be used simply to recount an incident, as Conrad does here. What else does his account of the storm convey?

2. Conrad builds gradually to his central idea or thesis. What is that idea, and how does the episode with the boatswain illustrate it?

3. Why does the tense shift in the last two paragraphs? How does Conrad move from the particular to the general here?

4. Which part of the passage best re-creates the excitement of the incident?

## WRITING ASSIGNMENTS

1. Describe a suspenseful experience that revealed a truth to you, as the statement of the boatswain revealed a truth to Conrad. Build the details of the experience to this truth. Let your sentences suggest the climactic nature of the experience.

2. Conrad and Dillard reach truths about the world and about themselves through experiences with nature. Compare how they organize their essays to show how they reached these truths.

## ERIC NICOL

Eric Nicol, *one of Canada's best-known humorists and three-time winner of the Leacock Medal for humour, was born in Kingston, Ontario in 1919, but has spent most of his life in Vancouver. He has published many collections of the daily column he writes for* The Vancouver Province, *and also has written many radio plays and television scripts. His subject is often the middle-class anxieties of contemporary urban life. "Parents Night" explores the comic consequences of an adult's revisiting elementary school in a new role.*

## PARENTS NIGHT

It was Parents Night at the school, and since I was a parent I was able to get in.    1

Usually my wife attends these meetings in which the teachers try to communicate with    2 the peer group of Cro-Magnon man. This time I went to spell her off. (I was always a pretty fair speller.)

Entering the school was not all that easy because the main doors were locked. I was    3 delighted to see this tradition being carried on despite the revolution in educative methods and goals. At any school I ever attended as a child (and that was several years ago), the main doors were always locked. Tight.

Schools have a phobia about anybody getting in or out except by the side doors or    4 windows.

They will open the big front doors only in the event of fire, flood or earthquake. A    5 major earthquake. Over the principal's dead body.

Having tried the main doors I entered by the side door and faced another survivor of the    6 old school: the dismembered hand painted on the stairwall, pointing sternly down. The hand never points up. No matter what floor of the school you wish to reach, you follow the unfickle finger downward. Space is curved, in the school as in the universe, and "up" is a concept having reality only in the mind of the janitor.

I followed the finger. It led me through the smells that are peculiar to a school: the basic    7 uric, the occasional whiff of brine from the room where the women teachers dry their tears and blow their noses before going back for another crack at the boy with the pink beard, and the pervasive aroma of something that died in a student's locker.

I passed the inevitable wall covered with framed photos of former principals, each    8 portrait retouched with highlights on the eyes to create the semblance of the will to live.

At the door of the auditorium a teacher placed literature in the hands of the parents    9 filing past. She appeared to be grateful that we were able to grasp the material physically if not mentally.

10      But what grabbed *me*, as proof of the changeless element of education, was the way the parents seated themselves in the auditorium. The first ten rows were empty. Silver-haired couples sat as far to the rear, away from the ominous microphone, as they could without violating the ropes with which the school had denied them the last ten rows.

11      Besides sitting at maximum distance from the source of information, the parents occupied aisle seats, for a faster exit when the buzzer sounded. As I took a seat near the back of the aisle, I realized that this was what we parents had learned best at school: the logistics of laying back and getting the hell out.

12      This was what stuck in our minds. Algebra, history, French — all that stuff had perished in the grey cells, but the defence mechanism against being nailed with a question was as well-oiled as ever.

13      After the principal had, with a blend of resignation and infinite patience, explained the school curriculum to us parents, and we had failed to understand a word, we made for the side doors. There was some good-natured grumbling. Confessions of lack of comprehension. Satisfaction at seeing parents older than oneself.

14      But nobody thought to go up and thank the principal for his gallant effort to instruct us in what was happening in education. We were getting out of school, our ignorance intact. That was enough to make Parents Night a success.

## VOCABULARY

a. *paragraph  2:* peer group

b. *paragraph  4:* phobia

c. *paragraph  6:* dismembered, unfickle

d. *paragraph 10:* ominous

e. *paragraph 11:* logistics

## QUESTIONS

1. How is Nicol's narrative organized? Divide it into its constituent parts.

2. What does Nicol conclude about "parents night"? What do the last two paragraphs show about this conclusion?

3. Nicol's sentence structure reflects the rhythms of ordinary speech. Analyse his story with a view to determining how he achieves this effect. Consider sentence length and structure in your answer.

4. Discuss the blend of colloquial and learned diction in paragraphs 6, 7, and 10. What does Nicol achieve in his narrative with this kind of shift?

5. What is Nicol's tone in the essay? Is he simply pleasantly satiric about his experience, or is the tone more complex?

6. Nicol uses pronouns, conjunctions, and repetition of key words to make transitions between paragraphs. Give some examples of each.

## WRITING ASSIGNMENT

Imagine a reunion of your Grade-eight class and write a short narrative about how this reunion evokes old patterns of behaviour — that is, show your classmates at nineteen still behaving as they did at thirteen.

## E.B. WHITE

*This essay is a poignant evocation of childhood and the passage of time. In his account of a trip to the summer camp of his youth,* E.B. White *meditates on continuity and change.*

## ONCE MORE TO THE LAKE

One summer, along about 1904, my father rented a camp on a lake in Maine and took us all there for the month of August. We all got ringworm from some kittens and had to rub Pond's Extract on our arms and legs night and morning, and my father rolled over in a canoe with all his clothes on; but outside of that the vacation was a success and from then on none of us ever thought there was any place in the world like that lake in Maine. We returned summer after summer — always on August 1st for one month. I have since become a salt-water man, but sometimes in summer there are days when the restlessness of the tides and the fearful cold of the sea water and the incessant wind which blows across the afternoon and into the evening make me wish for the placidity of a lake in the woods. A few weeks ago this feeling got so strong I bought myself a couple of bass hooks and a spinner and returned to the lake where we used to go, for a week's fishing and to revisit old haunts.

    I took along my son, who had never had any fresh water up his nose and who had seen lily pads only from train windows. On the journey over to the lake I began to wonder what it would be like. I wondered how time would have marred this unique, this holy spot — the coves and streams, the hills that the sun set behind, the camps and the paths behind the camps. I was sure that the tarred road would have found it out and I wondered in what other ways it would be desolated. It is strange how much you can remember about places like that once you allow your mind to return into the grooves which lead back. You remember one thing, and that suddenly reminds you of another thing. I guess I remembered clearest of all the early mornings, when the lake was cool and motionless, remembered how the bedroom smelled of the lumber it was made of and of the wet woods whose scent entered through the screen. The partitions in the camp were thin and did not extend clear to the top of the rooms, and as I was always the first up I would dress softly so as not to wake the others, and sneak out into the sweet outdoors and start out in the canoe, keeping close along the shore in the long shadows of the pines. I remembered being very careful never to rub my paddle against the gunwale for fear of disturbing the stillness of the cathedral.

    The lake had never been what you would call a wild lake. There were cottages sprinkled around the shores, and it was in farming country although the shores of the lake were quite heavily wooded. Some of the cottages were owned by nearby farmers, and you

1

2

3

would live at the shore and eat your meals at the farmhouse. That's what our family did. But although it wasn't wild, it was a fairly large and undisturbed lake and there were places in it which, to a child at least, seemed infinitely remote and primeval.

4    I was right about the tar: it led to within half a mile of the shore. But when I got back there, with my boy, and we settled into a camp near a farmhouse and into the kind of summertime I had known, I could tell that it was going to be pretty much the same as it had been before — I knew it, lying in bed the first morning, smelling the bedroom, and hearing the boy sneak quietly out and go off along the shore in a boat. I began to sustain the illusion that he was I, and therefore, by simple transposition, that I was my father. This sensation persisted, kept cropping up all the time we were there. It was not an entirely new feeling, but in this setting it grew much stronger. I seemed to be living a dual existence. I would be in the middle of some simple act, I would be picking up a bait box or laying down a table fork, or I would be saying something, and suddenly it would be not I but my father who was saying the words or making the gesture. It gave me a creepy sensation.

5    We went fishing the first morning. I felt the same damp moss covering the worms in the bait can, and saw the dragonfly alight on the tip of my rod as it hovered a few inches from the surface of the water. It was the arrival of this fly that convinced me beyond any doubt that everything was as it always had been, that the years were a mirage and there had been no years. The small waves were the same, chucking the rowboat under the chin as we fished at anchor, and the boat was the same boat, the same color green and the ribs broken in the same places, and under the floor-boards the same fresh-water leavings and débris — the dead helgramite, the wisps of moss, the rusty discarded fish-hook, the dried blood from yesterday's catch. We stared silently at the tips of our rods, at the dragonflies that came and went. I lowered the tip of mine into the water, tentatively, pensively dislodging the fly, which darted two feet away, poised, darted two feet back, and came to rest again a little farther up the rod. There had been no years between the ducking of this dragonfly and the other one — the one that was part of memory. I looked at the boy, who was silently watching his fly, and it was my hands that held his rod, my eyes watching. I felt dizzy and didn't know which rod I was at the end of.

6    We caught two bass, hauling them in briskly as though they were mackerel, pulling them over the side of the boat in a businesslike manner without any landing net, and stunning them with a blow on the back of the head. When we got back for a swim before lunch, the lake was exactly where we had left it, the same number of inches from the dock, and there was only the merest suggestion of a breeze. This seemed an utterly enchanted sea, this lake you could leave to its own devices for a few hours and come back to, and find that it had not stirred, this constant and trustworthy body of water. In the shallows, the dark, water-soaked sticks and twigs, smooth and old, were undulating in clusters on the bottom against the clean ribbed sand, and the track of the mussel was plain. A school of minnows swam by, each minnow with its small individual shadow, doubling the attendance, so clear and sharp in the sunlight. Some of the other campers were in swimming, along the shore, one of them with a cake of soap, and the water felt thin and clear and unsubstantial. Over the years there had been this person with the cake of soap, this cultist, and here he was. There had been no years.

7    Up to the farmhouse to dinner through the teeming, dusty field, the road under our sneakers was only a two-track road. The middle track was missing, the one with the marks of the hooves and the splotches of dried, flaky manure. There had always been three tracks to choose from in choosing which track to walk in; now the choice was narrowed down to two. For a moment I missed terribly the middle alternative. But the way led past the tennis court, and something about the way it lay there in the sun reassured me; the tape had loosened along the backline, the alleys were green with plantains and other weeds, and the

net (installed in June and removed in September) sagged in the dry noon, and the whole place steamed with midday heat and hunger and emptiness. There was a choice of pie for dessert, and one was blueberry and one was apple, and the waitresses were the same country girls, there having been no passage of time, only the illusion of it as in a dropped curtain — the waitresses were still fifteen; their hair had been washed, that was the only difference — they had been to the movies and seen the pretty girls with the clean hair.

Summertime, oh summertime, pattern of life indelible, the fadeproof lake, the woods **8** unshatterable, the pasture with the sweetfern and the juniper forever and ever, summer without end; this was the background, and the life along the shore was the design, the cottages with their innocent and tranquil design, their tiny docks with the flagpole and the American flag floating against the white clouds in the blue sky, the little paths over the roots of the trees leading from camp to camp and the paths leading back to the outhouses and the can of lime for sprinkling, and at the souvenir counters at the store the miniature birch-bark canoes and the post cards that showed things looking a little better than they looked. This was the American family at play, escaping the city heat, wondering whether the newcomers in the camp at the head of the cove were "common" or "nice," wondering whether it was true that the people who drove up for Sunday dinner at the farmhouse were turned away because there wasn't enough chicken.

It seemed to me, as I kept remembering all this, that those times and those summers **9** had been infinitely precious and worth saving. There had been jollity and peace and goodness. The arriving (at the beginning of August) had been so big a business in itself, at the railway station the farm wagon drawn up, the first smell of the pine-laden air, the first glimpse of the smiling farmer, and the great importance of the trunks and your father's enormous authority in such matters, and the feel of the wagon under you for the long ten-mile haul, and at the top of the last long hill catching the first view of the lake after eleven months of not seeing this cherished body of water. The shouts and cries of the other campers when they saw you, and the trunks to be unpacked, to give up their rich burden. (Arriving was less exciting nowadays, when you sneaked up in your car and parked it under a tree near the camp and took out the bags and in five minutes it was all over, no fuss, no loud wonderful fuss about trunks.)

Peace and goodness and jollity. The only thing that was wrong now, really, was the **10** sound of the place, an unfamiliar nervous sound of the outboard motors. This was the note that jarred, the one thing that would sometimes break the illusion and set the years moving. In those other summertimes all motors were inboard; and when they were at a little distance, the noise they made was a sedative, an ingredient of summer sleep. They were one-cylinder and two-cylinder engines, and some were make-and-break and some were jump-spark, but they all made a sleepy sound across the lake. The one-lungers throbbed and fluttered, and the twin-cylinder ones purred and purred, and that was a quiet sound too. But now the campers all had outboards. In the daytime, in the hot mornings, these motors made a petulant, irritable sound; at night, in the still evening when the afterglow lit the water, they whined about one's ears like mosquitoes. My boy loved our rented outboard, and his great desire was to achieve singlehanded mastery over it, and authority, and he soon learned the trick of choking it a little (but not too much), and the adjustment of the needle valve. Watching him I would remember the things you could do with the old one-cylinder engine with the heavy flywheel, how you could have it eating out of your hand if you got really close to it spiritually. Motor boats in those days didn't have clutches, and you would make a landing by shutting off the motor at the proper time and coasting in with a dead rudder. But there was a way of reversing them, if you learned the trick, by cutting the switch and putting it on again exactly on the final dying revolution of the flywheel, so that it would kick back against compression and begin reversing. Approaching a dock in a strong following breeze, it was difficult to slow up sufficiently by the ordinary coasting method, and if a boy felt he had complete mastery over his motor, he was tempted to keep it running beyond its time and then reverse it a few feet from the dock. It took a cool nerve, because if you threw the switch a twentieth of a second too soon you would catch the flywheel when it still had speed enough to go up past center, and the boat would leap ahead, charging bull-fashion at the dock.

11    We had a good week at the camp. The bass were biting well and the sun shone endlessly, day after day. We would be tired at night and lie down in the accumulated heat of the little bed rooms after the long hot day and the breeze would stir almost imperceptibly outside and the smell of the swamp drift in through the rusty screens. Sleep would come easily and in the morning the red squirrel would be on the roof, tapping out his gay routine. I kept remembering everything, lying in bed in the mornings — the small steamboat that had a long rounded stern like the lip of a Ubangi, and how quietly she ran on the moonlight sails, when the older boys played their mandolins and the girls sang and we ate doughnuts dipped in sugar, and how sweet the music was on the water in the shining night, and what it had felt like to think about girls then. After breakfast we would go up to the store and the things were in the same place — the minnows in a bottle, the plugs and spinners disarranged and pawed over by the youngsters from the boys' camp, the fig newtons and the Beeman's gum. Outside, the road was tarred and cars stood in front of the store. Inside, all was just as it had always been, except there was more Coca Cola and not so much Moxie and root beer and birch beer and sarsaparilla. We would walk out with a bottle of pop apiece and sometimes the pop would backfire up our noses and hurt. We explored the streams, quietly, where the turtles slid off the sunny logs and dug their way into the soft bottom; and we lay on the town wharf and fed worms to the tame bass. Everywhere we went I had trouble making out which was I, the one walking at my side, the one walking in my pants.

12    One afternoon while we were there at the lake a thunderstorm came up. It was like the revival of an old melodrama that I had seen long ago with childish awe. The second-act climax of the drama of the electrical disturbance over a lake in America had not changed in any important respect. This was the big scene, still the big scene. The whole thing was so familiar, the first feeling of oppression and heat and a general air around camp of not wanting to go very far away. In midafternoon (it was all the same) a curious darkening of the sky, and a lull in everything that had made life tick; and then the way the boats suddenly swung the other way at their moorings with the coming of a breeze out of the new quarter, and the premonitory rumble. Then the kettle drum, then the snare, then the bass drum and cymbals, then cracking light against the dark, and the gods grinning and licking their chops in the hills. Afterward the calm, the rain steadily rustling in the calm lake, the return of light and hope and spirits, and the campers running out in joy and relief to go swimming in the rain, their bright cries perpetuating the deathless joke about how they were getting simply drenched, and the children screaming with delight at the new sensation of bathing in the rain, and the joke about getting drenched linking the generations in a strong indestructible chain. And the comedian who waded in carrying an umbrella.

13    When the others went swimming my son said he was going in too. He pulled his dripping trunks from the line where they had hung all through the shower and wrung them out. Languidly, and with no thought of going in, I watched him, his hard little body, skinny and bare, saw him wince slightly as he pulled up around his vitals the small, soggy, icy garment. As he buckled the swollen belt, suddenly my groin felt the chill of death.

# Vocabulary

a. *paragraph  1:* incessant

b. *paragraph  2:* gunwale

c. *paragraph  3:* primeval

d. *paragraph  4:* transposition

e. *paragraph  5:* helgramite

f. *paragraph  6:* undulating

g. *paragraph  7:* teeming, plantains

h. *paragraph  8:* indelible

i. *paragraph 10:* sedative, petulant

j. *paragraph 11:* sarsaparilla

k. *paragraph 12:* melodrama, premonitory

l. *paragraph 13:* languidly, vitals

# Questions

1. How does White at the beginning of his essay set his narrative in a specific time and place?

2. What senses does he appeal to in the essay? Cite specific examples.

3. Why does he use phrases such as "blows across the afternoon" (paragraph 1), "doubling the attendance" (paragraph 6), and "ingredient of summer sleep" (paragraph 10)? How do such details affect the mood of the essay?

4. Discuss the effectiveness of the depiction of the storm in paragraph 12? Why does he use the drama metaphor to describe the incident?

5. Study and comment on the complex stylistic uses of the word "and" in paragraphs 7 and 11.

6. What points does his narrative make about the "indestructible chain" linking the generations?

# Writing Assignment

Using comparison and contrast, tell the story of revisiting a place you knew as a child. Avoid generalizing about impressions by using as many specific details as possible.

# EXAMPLE

The word *example* originally referred to a sample or typical instance. The word still has this meaning, and for many writers it is an outstanding instance — even one essential to the idea under discussion, as in the following explanation of right- and left-handedness in the world:

> The world is full of things whose right-hand version is different from the left-hand version: a right-handed corkscrew as against a left-handed, a right snail as against a left one. Above all, the two hands; they can be mirrored one in the other, but they cannot be turned in such a way that the right hand and the left hand become interchangeable. That was known in Pasteur's time to be true also of some crystals, whose facets are so arranged that there are right-hand versions and left-hand versions. — Jacob Bronowski, *The Ascent of Man*

Examples are essential when we are presenting ideas. Those that seem clear to us might not be clear to our readers. Therefore we must be very careful in selecting the examples we choose to include in an essay. The examples must be typical of the subject, representing the qualities we wish to illustrate. For instance, the crimes Walter Stewart describes in *Good Old Us* were committed by ordinary people, not psychotic criminals.

The examples chosen must be related clearly to the topic. If Walter Stewart had described a riot during the Winnipeg General Strike, it would not illustrate "typical" behaviour but rather the frustration brought on by a particular event. The examples chosen must also be limited in number. Doubtless, Stewart had access to many more examples of crime and corruption in Canada, but chose to use only a select few. We must decide how many examples are needed to illustrate the point and elicit the desired response from the audience.

Examples make ideas concrete and point to the experiences and observations that formed these ideas. Almost all essays depend on examples; some consist entirely of examples. The essays that follow show how indispensable examples are in stating certain ideas.

## E.B. WHITE

*In this excerpt from a profile of New York City, first published in* Holiday Magazine, E.B. White *writes from the point of view of an inhabitant who knows the city well. White conveys through a series of examples a special excitement. Notice how much different the character of New York is from that of John Kenneth Galbraith's Iona Station or Eric Sevareid's Velva, North Dakota.*

## NEW YORK

1  It is a miracle that New York works at all. The whole thing is implausible. Every time the residents brush their teeth, millions of gallons of water must be drawn from the Catskills and the hills of Westchester. When a young man in Manhattan writes a letter to his girl in Brooklyn, the love message gets blown to her through a pneumatic tube — *pfft* — just like that. The subterranean system of telephone cables, power lines, steam pipes, gas mains and sewer pipes is reason enough to abandon the island to the gods and the weevils. Every time an incision is made in the pavement, the noisy surgeons expose ganglia that are tangled beyond belief. By rights New York should have destroyed itself long ago, from panic or fire or rioting or failure of some vital supply line in its circulatory system or from some deep

*Example*   **111**

labyrinthine short circuit. Long ago the city should have experienced an insoluble traffic snarl at some impossible bottleneck. It should have perished of hunger when food lines failed for a few days. It should have been wiped out by a plague starting in its slums or carried in by ships' rats. It should have been overwhelmed by the sea that licks at it on every side. The workers in its myriad cells should have succumbed to nerves, from the fearful pall of smoke-fog that drifts over every few days from Jersey, blotting out all light at noon and leaving the high offices suspended, men groping and depressed, and the sense of world's end. It should have been touched in the head by the August heat and gone off its rocker.

## VOCABULARY

a. *paragraph 1:* implausible, pneumatic, subterranean, weevils, ganglia, labyrinthine, myriad, pall

## QUESTIONS

1. What examples does White give to show that "the whole thing is implausible"?

2. White explicitly compares New York City to a human being. What are the similarities, and how does the comparison help to emphasize the "miracle" he is describing?

3. What is the tone of the paragraph, and how does White achieve it?

## WRITING ASSIGNMENTS

1. In a well-developed paragraph state an idea about your hometown or city and develop it by a series of short examples. Make your examples vivid and lively.

2. Develop one of the following statements by example:

   a. "The insupportable labor of doing nothing." — Sir Richard Steele

   b. "The first blow is half the battle." — Oliver Goldsmith

   c. "Ask yourself whether you are happy, and you cease to be so." — John Stuart Mill

   d. "Parentage is a very important profession; but no test of fitness for it is ever imposed in the interest of the children." — George Bernard Shaw

## WILLIAM DEVERELL

William Deverell *is a Canadian novelist, screenwriter, and criminal lawyer who writes in the impressionistic style popularized by the American "new journalists" Hunter S. Thompson and Tom Wolfe. His latest book is* The Dance of Shiva. *In the following excerpt from an essay published in* Saturday Night Magazine, *Deverell characterizes an aspect of society — the way it treats its welfare cases — by focussing on a typical night in a poor section of Vancouver.*

# WELFARE WEDNESDAY

1  The hundred block East Hastings. Take a walk on the wild side, check out the most manic street in Canada on its most manic night, Welfare Wednesday, a carnival of the desperate and the lonely, wobbling in and out of doorways, hooting at passers-by, seeking salvation from their torment on the one night of the month they have dollars in their pockets.

2  This night the police pound their beat three abreast. An emergency van wails through the lights at Main and Hastings. Cruisers prowl. Forgotten men and women slump in darkened doorways. A man with a black beard matted with blood walks by stroking a small white kitten. Two junkies lean against a pole, nodding, bliss tonight, terror in the morning when they run out of the escape they shoot into pocked veins.

3  A hooker shouts to a man walking by, "Hey, I wanna talk to you! The lawyer says you've got to give him the particulars, it's the only way I'm gonna get off." He refuses to notice her and she follows him. "You heard me, you were there that night, the cops are lying, you have to give the lawyer particulars."

4  Near the doorway of the Smilin' Buddha lounges a short man with a large middle. One of the cops calls to him, "How you doin', Tubs." He joshes with them, but after they've gone he becomes morose. "He called me Tubs," he says. "How do I get that guy's badge?"

5  I ask, "What is your name?"

6  "Call me Levitsky."

7  "What are you selling?"

8  "What are you buying?"

9  "You selling girls or dope?"

10  "Whatever you want," says Levitsky.

11  Gary, a community worker, thin and ragged, fire-eyed, screams at the people slumming, tourists doing the street, daring it. "What are you laughing at? What do you do, just come down to watch the circus on welfare night?"

12  A pervasive smell of piss wafts from the alley as Gary and I talk. He gets frustrated working with the community. "It's a frantic tragedy, it's like Fellini and nothing is being done. It takes two hours to get someone a meal." He tells me his plan is to move all the greenhouses from the Fraser Valley into the inner city so the poor can grow their own food. "We need new paradigms, we've got to get the people working with their own rhythms."

## VOCABULARY

a. *paragraph  2:* pocked

b. *paragraph 12:* paradigms

## QUESTIONS

1. Deverell describes "Welfare Wednesday, a carnival of the desperate and the lonely." What do the details suggest about the Welfare Wednesday mood in this part of Vancouver? Why does he use the word *carnival*?

2. What do the descriptions of the prostitute and Levitsky imply about the world of welfare recipients described by Deverell?

*Example* **113**

3. What effect does the presence of Gary the community worker have on the impression Deverell wishes to convey?

4. Contrast Deverell's view of Vancouver to White's view of New York. What are the advantages and disadvantages of their respective methods?

## WRITING ASSIGNMENTS

1. Every piece of writing suggests something about the personality, interests, and ideas of the author, even when he or she speaks to us through a narrator. Discuss the impression you receive of the author of this selection.

2. Describe one or two people in a situation made pathetic by the setting. Through your choice of examples, allow your reader to visualize the setting as well as the situation.

## JUNE CALLWOOD

June Callwood *was born in 1924 in Chatham, Ontario. She has written many books, including* Love, Hate, Fear & Anger, Canadian Women and the Law, The Law Is Not for Women, Portrait of Canada, Emotions, *and* Twelve Weeks in Spring. *Her interest in the problems of Canadian women is evident in the following article on the availability of abortion.*

## MDs PLAY ROULETTE WITH WOMEN'S LIVES

A few weeks ago, when the Supreme Court of Canada heard the appeal of yet another jury acquittal of Dr. Henry Morgentaler on abortion charges, Mr. Justice Willard Estey appeared to be musing aloud. He observed that a person would have to be affected with "legislative blindness" not to see that there are areas in the country where there is no access to abortion.   **1**

"You've got whole provinces that are carved out of the process," he said. "Is this some kind of local option which has slid into the Criminal Code?"   **2**

The question was, of course, rhetorical. As the judge knows, two provinces, Prince Edward Island and Newfoundland, have slid out of the Criminal Code, as well as regions such as Northern Ontario and virtually all of Alberta.   **3**

Wendy Williams talks about what that means in Newfoundland. She's a nurse who works part-time in the St. John's Family Resources Centre of Planned Parenthood Newfoundland/Labrador. She spends much of her time on the telephone arranging for Newfoundland women to have their abortions in Montreal or Toronto. Newfoundland's only doctor who performs the procedure is recovering from a heart attack, so Wendy Williams and her associates are making off-island arrangements at the rate of 40 a month.   **4**

One-third of the women seeking abortions are teenagers and few of them have flown before or even travelled out of the communities in which they are born. They must learn about youth fares and standby rules. They land in Dorval amid the hustle and confusion of that busy airport and somehow must find their way alone to a hospital located deep within a French-speaking city.   **5**

6    A mother on welfare accompanied her young daughter, despite the hardship of the expense. They brought $100 to cover their living costs but, to their dismay, the doctor wanted that amount up front in cash. Wendy Williams does not know how they survived, penniless in a strange city, for the week they were there.

7    One 14-year-old was 10 weeks pregnant before she summoned the courage to tell her mother. This is not an uncommon situation with teenagers, who keep hoping that what has happened to them is merely an irregularity in their periods. By that time, however, if they wish an abortion, they are likely to qualify only in those rare locations where second-trimester abortions are available. Wendy Williams must call the Toronto General Hospital between the hours of 2 and 3:30 on Friday afternoons and hope that she gets through.

8    Costs, including a $1,000-a-month phone bill, have soared for the volunteer St. John's agency, which receives 300 requests for pregnancy tests every month. Budgeting is now so stringent that the staff has not been able to afford to renew a subscription to a useful journal, *Contraceptive Technology.*

9    In Edmonton, doctors are playing roulette with women's lives. Angered that the provincial Government's fee for abortions is $85 and they no longer are allowed to extra-bill $200 or $250 as they once did, they have chosen to refuse to do the procedure. Heather Halpenny Crocker, co-executive director of the Planned Parents Association in Edmonton, says that well-to-do women manage to negotiate through the boycott, but teenagers, poor women and immigrant women cannot.

10    "It's the same old story," she sighs. "If you have no money and no connections you're out of luck."

11    Edmonton women either try to smuggle themselves into the Calgary Foothills Hospital clinic, pretending to be Calgarians, or else must travel to Seattle, Washington, or Kalispell, Montana, where they will be charged $700 (U.S.). The Montana clinic is doing so much Canadian business this autumn that it is thinking of expanding to another location.

12    "We've been trying to help a 25-year-old with three kids who is pregnant," comments Liz McCord, co-executive director of the Edmonton association. "Her husband tells her that he'll leave her if she has this baby. When she appealed to a doctor for help, his answer was that she should not stay married to such a brute."

13    Glenna Cross, president of the Calgary Birth Control Association, is fuming after a meeting last week of gynecologists and the Alberta Medical Association failed to resolve the deadlock. AMA president Dr. Richard Kennedy commented two weeks ago that a solution to rising health costs in Alberta might be to stop insuring "non-essential" services such as abortion.

14    The number of women seeking abortions has increased 50 per cent at the Calgary centre. Liz McCord says, "I can't see an end in sight. I don't know what we'll do."

15    Statistics Canada recently released figures indicating how many Canadian women have been obliged to go to the United States for abortions, which, theoretically, are medically insured, legal and available in Canada. The numbers certainly do not reflect the reality, because most women in that situation try to avoid crossing the path of a government surveyor, but nonetheless they are dismayingly high. In 1984, for instance, 408 P.E.I. women went to Maine for abortions, 1,200 Ontario women went to New York, 680 Manitoba women went to North Dakota and 700 Alberta women went to Washington state.

16    Only 250 Canadian hospitals (about 30% of public general hospitals) have the Therapeutic Abortion Committees which can authorize abortion, and only 15% of these (39 hospitals) carry the burden of nearly three quarters of the country's legal abortions.

*Example*    **115**

The federal Government is too intimidated by anti-choice forces to contemplate mak-    **17**
ing a law that would provide access to abortion. Quebec has 12 illegal free-standing
clinics that are tolerated by the provincial Government, but the other provinces refuse to
help. Instead, they arrest doctors and close clinics. In this country, access to abortion
requires a travel agent — and money.

## VOCABULARY

a. *paragraph   3:* rhetorical

b. *paragraph   7:* second-trimester

c. *paragraph   8:* stringent

d. *paragraph 16:* therapeutic

## QUESTIONS

1. How general an audience is Callwood addressing, and how do you know?

2. What do the remarks of Mr. Justice Willard Estey show? What purpose is served by the
   specific example in paragraph 12?

3. What other details show that the system of limited access to abortion might be breaking
   down in Canada?

4. How does Callwood convey the dilemma created for Canadian women who cannot
   obtain an abortion? Does Callwood comment on this dilemma or merely illustrate it?

5. How many points is Callwood making about Canada's abortion laws in this essay?
   Does she state a thesis?

6. Do you find that her concluding paragraph is adequately supported by the preceding
   examples and figures?

## WRITING ASSIGNMENT

Narrate an experience that illustrates the injustice or pointlessness of a social code or rule
of etiquette or behaviour in our soceity. Let the details of your narrative make your point.
Do not state it explicitly.

## WALTER STEWART

Walter Stewart *is Professor and Director of the School of Journalism, University of King's
College, Halifax. His essays and journalism have earned him a national reputation as one
of the most clear-sighted and honest observers of Canadian national life. Among his best-
known books are* Shrug: Trudeau In Power *(1971),* But Not In Canada *(1976),* Strike!

*(1977),* Tower of Gold, Feet of Clay: The Canadian Banks *(1982), and* True Blue: The Loyalist Legend *(1985). Stewart argues in the following selection that we as Canadians "are held captive by the myth of the reasonable citizen," despite all the evidence that Canadians can be as violent, racist, and anti-democratic as Americans.*

## GOOD OLD US

1   Williams Lake, British Columbia, 1966. An Indian girl met some youths in a beverage room, and they agreed to give her a lift to her aunt's place. Of course, they didn't take her to her aunt's; they took her to a garbage dump, where the three whites thought they would get a little free loving. Everybody knows about Indian girls.

2   Unfortunately, this girl didn't. She was found dead the next morning, naked and dead by the roadside. The youths, all of good families, admitted that they had wrestled her around some, got fed up with her, and pitched her out of the car into the cold April night. She died of a broken neck, but they said she was alive when they last saw her. What they did wasn't right, maybe, but it wasn't murder, either. A white jury agreed; two of the youths were convicted of assault, and fined $200; the charge against the third was dismissed.

3   The House of Commons, Ottawa, 1938. Premier Maurice Duplessis of Quebec had brought in a law, the Padlock Law, that permitted the seizure and closing of any premises suspected of being used to propagate communism. No proof was required, no defence was permitted, and "communism" was never defined. The law was used against all of Duplessis's political opponents. In Ottawa, J.S. Woodsworth, leader of the CCF, rose in his place in Parliament and, his voice shaking with emotion, declared, "Twice every day for six months the provincial police have carried out execution without judgment, dispossession without due process of law; twenty times a month they have trampled on liberties as old as Magna Carta." Woodsworth was shouted down. Ernest Lapointe, Minister of Justice, told him, "In spite of the fact that the words are so unpleasant to the honourable member for Winnipeg North Centre, I do desire to say that the reign of law must continue in this country, that peace and order must prevail."

4   Outside Vancouver, 1887. A mob of whites, disturbed that indentured Chinese coolie labourers had taken jobs in the mines that God meant white men to have, rushed the Chinese camp and drove the workers out into the January night. There was a twenty-foot cliff behind the camp, and the coolies were driven over it; you could hear them going plump, plump, plump, into the freezing sea.

5   Toronto, 1945. E.B. Jolliffe, provincial leader of the CCF, charged that the Ontario Provincial Police were being used as political spies by the Conservative government, that a special squad was gathering private information for Premier George Drew, and that this information was being used to harass Liberals and CCFers. Jolliffe said the OPP was acting as a private "Gestapo" — an emotive word for that time. He had an impressive amount of evidence, including the testimony of Alvin Rowe, an OPP officer who had worked on the secret squad and who had come to Jolliffe because, he said, he was being used as a political spy, and didn't like it. A royal commission was called to inquire into Jolliffe's charges, but its terms of reference were so narrow that it was barred from conducting a real investigation. Then Alvin Rowe was killed in a plane crash; Jolliffe's party was badly punished at the polls.

6   Sydney, Nova Scotia, 1971. The Sydney police went on strike for higher wages. They had barely left their posts when gangs of toughs took over the town and began drag-racing up and down the main street. Fights, looting, then a general riot broke out; the town was in a state bordering on anarchy until the strike was settled.

*Example*    **117**

Near Seven Oaks, Manitoba, 1816. A disagreement arose between fur traders of the    **7**
North West Company and settlers brought in by Lord Selkirk to found a permanent
community. So the company arranged to have the settlement attacked, and twenty people
were murdered. When Selkirk tried to exact justice, he was blocked by the political
manoeuvrings of his opponents, defeated in court, and eventually driven into near
bankruptcy.

Near Wymark, Saskatchewan, 1967. A man who had complained that the RCMP was    **8**
slow in acting on his earlier charges that he was being harassed by obscene telephone calls
was working in his pasture. An RCMP car pulled up, two constables piled out, and he was
taken away and held for forty days, under the Saskatchewan Mental Health Act, without
ever being charged, or convicted, or even told what he had done wrong.

During the forty days he was subjected to shock treatments and drug therapy and then,    **9**
one day, he was turned loose as suddenly as he had been locked up.

Montreal, 1949. A university professor's house blew up, and his wife and daughter    **10**
were killed, while he was injured. He was clapped into jail and held for three months
under the provincial Coroner's Act. Police had discovered that he had a mistress some
time previously, and they assumed, without a shred of proof, that he had blown up his
own house. He was not charged; he was simply held, while the press seethed with stories
of his infidelity, his callousness, his savagery. Eventually, it turned out that the house had
been destroyed by a natural gas explosion. He was released.

Toronto, 1974. An American sociologist, a controversial figure alleged to hold strong    **11**
and wrong views on the subject of race, had been invited to speak at the University of
Toronto. A group of left-wing students and teachers decreed that he was an inappropriate
speaker; they stormed the lectern, staged a minor riot, and drove the sociologist away. His
speech was never made. Months later, two students were suspended for their part in the
affair; it can be argued that freedom of speech remains suspended at the university.

I am in favour of smugness, to a point; it rounds the figure, deepens the dimples, and aids    **12**
the digestive process. I believe, too, that Canadians have a certain amount to be smug
about; by and large, we have been a reasonable and prosperous people; by and large, we
have avoided mass murder, organized tyranny, and the more public forms of corruption.
However, since 1972, since Watergate, smugness has become a national religion, a national disease. Nothing that has happened on the North American continent since our side
sacked Washington in 1814 has given Canadians such unalloyed pleasure as Watergate.
While the Americans wallow in guilt and self-doubt, we bubble with joy and self-
righteousness. Thank God, we say, for our British traditions and innate Canadian
decency. There may be rot and racism, inequity and injustice, among those fractious,
rebellious Yankees, but not in Canada.

Well, we have never had anything quite like Watergate, but that is a claim we share    **13**
with most nations of the world. We have, however, had major political corruption involving our highest figures — remember Sir John A. and the Pacific Scandal, remember the
McGreevy brothers, remember the Beauharnois Scandal, remember the Ontario High-
ways Scandal? — and we have had extensive cover-ups, political dirty tricks, payoffs, and
— God knows — thousands of examples of the abuse of power.

A major difference between us and the Americans — besides the size, the perva-    **14**
siveness, the sheer bloody-mindedness of Watergate — is our diffidence. Except for the
Pacific Scandal (after all, that was a long time ago), Canadian outbursts of corruption,
venality, brutality, racism, and oppression have gone largely unrecorded. It's not that we
don't want to hear about such subjects — we do — but we don't want to hear them when
they happen in Canada. During the spring of 1975, Canadians flocked to their theatres to
see an American film about authoritarianism in the U.S., called *Hearts and Minds*. At the

same time, they stayed away in droves from a Canadian film about authoritarianism in Canada, called *Les Ordres*. There are some things we would rather not know.

15    We view ourselves as a superior people, a sober, peaceable people, a people of extraordinarily decent instincts and firmly entrenched liberties, and we reject any contrary evidence. Thus, when our federal government comes along, as it did in October 1970, and throws 435 people into jail without charge or trial, when it makes it a crime ever to have belonged to a political organization that was legal five minutes before the law was passed, we are not shocked or upset; we applaud. If the government chooses to establish retroactive crime, our reaction is not to say that our civil liberties are in jeopardy, but that the government must have powerful reasons, secret reasons, reasons that remain secret to this day, to act so arbitrarily. Indeed, some officers of the Canadian Civil Liberties Association give their approval — although the Association itself does not. Because we know we are decent, reasonable people, because our government would never do anything really wrong, really suppressive, whatever is done must, of necessity, be reasonable and right. Indeed, some Canadians are still half-expecting the government to produce secret reasons, one of these days, that will explain the whole thing satisfactorily (just as some of us still wait around on Easter morn for a bunny to drop off a clutch of eggs).

16    One of the problems we face as a nation, perhaps in greater measure than other nations, is that we are held captive by the myth of the reasonable citizen. The Canadian as we see him, the Canadian in the mind of God, is a man who never gives in to extremism; he is a patient man (who shuns violence), a neighbourly man (who spurns racism), a democratic man (who supports free speech, civil liberties, and honesty in politics). He is, in short, all the things your average wild-eyed, gun-toting, bigoted, loud-mouthed, venal, aggressive, tyrannical bastard of an American is not. What is more, his history has made him the gentle citizen he is today. There have been blots on the copybook — things like the Winnipeg General Strike, the Regina Riot, the incarceration of Japanese Canadians during World War II — but these are minor slips, casually recorded or missed entirely in our history of ourselves.

17    Enough. Canadians, as a people, are no better and no worse than anyone else. We were slavers in the eighteenth and early nineteenth centuries, and our treatment of minorities, from Indians to Jehovah's Witnesses, is only marginally different from that of the Americans. We have staged some of the bigger and more bloody-minded riots on the continent, from the Bytown Riots of the 1840s ("Them Bytown days was fightin' days") to the Kenora race riots of 1974. We have not only passed, but applauded, viciously repressive legislation, and our gun laws, to take only one minor example of wrong-headed self-congratulation, are in fact looser and dumber than those in most U.S. states.

## VOCABULARY

a. *paragraph  3:* dispossession, Magna Carta

b. *paragraph  4:* indentured

c. *paragraph  5:* Gestapo, emotive

d. *paragraph  6:* anarchy

e. *paragraph 10:* infidelity, callousness

f. *paragraph 12:* unalloyed, fractious

*Example*  **119**

g. *paragraph 14:* venality

h. *paragraph 16:* tyrannical, incarceration

## QUESTIONS

1. What is Stewart's purpose in beginning with an account of a series of incidents?

2. Consider how Stewart has organized his material. Does it cohere or is it simply a random sample?

3. Why does he include date and place names at the beginning of each example? How does the tone shift in the second part of the essay?

4. What persuasive purposes might Stewart's account serve? How effective do you find his commentary on the examples he cites?

5. Why does he include a comparison with the United States (paragraph 12)? How does this comparison advance his argument?

## WRITING ASSIGNMENT

Stewart lists incidences of Canadian lawlessness, violence, and racism which have not been widely publicized, and uses them to challenge assumptions Canadians have made about themselves and their country. Investigate other aspects of Canadian society that people are reluctant to face up to. Report your findings in a descriptive narrative of your own. Include information on observed or scientifically documented effects and give the sources of your findings.

## BARBARA TUCHMAN

Barbara Tuchman, *born in New York in 1912, is the author of* The Guns of August, *an historical analysis of events preceding, and the early phases of, World War 1. She has dealt with the causes of that war in* The Zimmerman Telegram, *and the pre-war ethos in* The Proud Tower. *In the following essay, she convincingly argues that writers of history have as much claim to the title of artist as do poets and fiction writers.*

## THE HISTORIAN AS ARTIST

I would like to share some good news with you. I recently came back from skiing at Aspen, where on one occasion I shared the double-chair ski-lift with an advertising man from Chicago. He told me he was in charge of all copy for his firm in all media: TV, radio, *and* the printed word. On the strength of this he assured me — and I quote — that "Writing is coming back. *Books* are coming back." I cannot tell you how pleased I was, and I knew you would be too.

Now that we know that the future is safe for writing, I want to talk about a particular kind of writer — the Historian — not just as historian but as artist; that is, as a creative writer on the same level as the poet or novelist. What follows will sound less immodest if you will take the word "artist" in the way I think of it, not as a form of praise but as a category, like clerk or laborer or actor.

3      Why is it generally assumed that in writing, the creative process is the exclusive property of poets and novelists? I would like to suggest that the thought applied by the historian to his subject matter can be no less creative than the imagination applied by the novelist to his. And when it comes to writing as an art, is Gibbon necessarily less of an artist in words than, let us say, Dickens? Or Winston Churchill less so than William Faulkner or Sinclair Lewis?

4      George Macaulay Trevelyan, the late professor of modern history at Cambridge and the great champion of literary as opposed to scientific history, said in a famous essay on his muse that ideally history should be the exposition of facts about the past, "in their full emotional and intellectual value to a wide public by the difficult art of literature." Notice "wide public." Trevelyan always stressed writing for the general reader as opposed to writing just for fellow scholars because he knew that when you write for the public you have to be *clear* and you have to be *interesting* and these are the two criteria which make for good writing. He had no patience with the idea that only imaginative writing is literature. Novels, he pointed out, if they are bad enough, are *not* literature, while even pamphlets, if they are good enough, and he cites those of Milton, Swift, and Burke, are.

5      The "difficult art of literature" is well said. Trevelyan was a dirt farmer in that field and he knew. I may as well admit now that I have always *felt* like an artist when I work on a book but I did not think I ought to say so until someone else said it first (it's like waiting to be proposed to). Now that an occasional reviewer here and there has made the observation, I feel I can talk about it. I see no reason why the word should always be confined to writers of fiction and poetry while the rest of us are lumped together under that despicable term "Nonfiction" — as if we were some sort of remainder. I do not feel like a Non-something; I feel quite specific. I wish I could think of a name in place of "Nonfiction." In the hope of finding an antonym I looked up "Fiction" in Webster and found it defined as opposed to "Fact, Truth and Reality." I thought for a while of adopting FTR, standing for Fact, Truth, and Reality, as my new term, but it is awkward to use. "Writers of Reality" is the nearest I can come to what I want, but I cannot very well call us "Realtors" because that has been pre-empted — although as a matter of fact I would like to. "Real Estate," when you come to think of it, is a very fine phrase and it is exactly the sphere that writers of nonfiction deal in: the real estate of man, of human conduct. I wish we could get it back from the dealers in land. Then the categories could be poets, novelists, and realtors.

6      I should add that I do not entirely go along with Webster's statement that fiction is what is distinct from fact, truth, and reality because good fiction (as opposed to junk), even if it has nothing to do with fact, is usually *founded* on reality and *perceives* truth — often more truly than some historians. It is exactly this quality of perceiving truth, extracting it from irrelevant surroundings and conveying it to the reader or the viewer of a picture, which distinguishes the artist. What the artist has is an *extra* vision and an *inner* vision plus the ability to express it. He supplies a view or an understanding that the viewer or reader would not have gained without the aid of the artist's creative vision. This is what Monet does in one of those shimmering rivers reflecting poplars, or El Greco in the stormy sky over Toledo, or Jane Austen compressing a whole society into Mr. and Mrs. Bennett, Lady Catherine, and Mr. Darcy. We realtors, at least those of us who aspire to write literature, do the same thing. Lytton Strachey perceived a truth about Queen Victoria and the Eminent Victorians, and the style and form which he created to portray what he saw have changed the whole approach to biography since his time. Rachel Carson perceived truth about the seashore or the silent spring, Thoreau about Walden Pond, De Tocqueville and

*Example*    **121**

James Bryce about America, Gibbon about Rome, Karl Marx about Capital, Carlyle about the French Revolution. Their work is based on study, observation, and accumulation of fact, but does anyone suppose that these realtors did not make use of their imagination? Certainly they did; that is what gave them their extra vision.

Trevelyan wrote that the best historian was he who combined knowledge of the evidence with "the largest intellect, the warmest human sympathy and the highest imaginative powers." The last two qualities are no different than those necessary to a great novelist. They are a necessary part of the historian's equipment because they are what enable him to *understand* the evidence he has accumulated. Imagination stretches the available facts — extrapolates from them, so to speak, thus often supplying an otherwise missing answer to the "Why" of what happened. Sympathy is essential to the understanding of motive. Without sympathy and imagination the historian can copy figures from a tax roll forever — or count them by computer as they do nowadays — but he will never know or be able to portray the people who paid the taxes.

When I say that I felt like an artist, I mean that I constantly found myself perceiving a historical truth (at least, what *I* believe to be truth) by seizing upon a suggestion; then, after careful gathering of the evidence, conveying it in turn to the reader, not by piling up a list of all the facts I have collected, which is the way of the Ph.D., but by exercising the artist's privilege of selection.

Actually the idea for *The Proud Tower* evolved in that way from a number of such perceptions. The initial impulse was a line I quoted in *The Guns of August* from Belgian Socialist poet Emile Verhaeren. After a lifetime as a pacifist dedicated to the social and humanitarian ideas which were then believed to erase national lines, he found himself filled with hatred of the German invader and disillusioned in all he had formerly believed in. And yet, as he wrote, "Since it seems to me that in this state of hatred my conscience becomes diminished, I dedicate these pages, with emotion, to the man I used to be."

I was deeply moved by this. His confession seemed to me so poignant, so evocative of a time and mood, that it decided me to try to retrieve that vanished era. It led to the last chapter in *The Proud Tower* on the Socialists, to Jaurès the authentic Socialist, to his prophetic lines. "I summon the living, I mourn the dead," and to his assassination as the perfect and dramatically right ending for the book, both chronologically and symbolically.

Then there was Lord Ribblesdale. I owe this to *American Heritage*, which back in October 1961 published a piece on Sargent and Whistler with a handsome reproduction of the Ribblesdale portrait. In Sargent's painting Ribblesdale stared out upon the world, as I later wrote in *The Proud Tower*, "in an attitude of such natural arrogance, elegance and self-confidence as no man of a later day would ever achieve." Here too was a vanished era which came together in my mind with Verhaeren's line, "the man I used to be" — like two globules of mercury making a single mass. From that came the idea for the book. Ribblesdale, of course, was the suggestion that ultimately became the opening chapter on the Patricians. This is the reward of the artist's eye: It always leads you to the right thing.

As I see it, there are three parts to the creative process: first, the extra vision with which the artist perceives a truth and conveys it by suggestion. Second, medium of expression: language for writers, paint for painters, clay or stone for sculptors, sound expressed in musical notes for composers. Third, design or structure.

When it comes to language, nothing is more satisfying than to write a good sentence. It is no fun to write lumpishly, dully, in prose the reader must plod through like wet sand. But it is a pleasure to achieve, if one can, a clear running prose that is simple yet full of surprises. This does not just happen. It requires skill, hard work, a good ear, and continued practice, as much as it takes Heifetz to play the violin. The goals, as I have said, are clarity, interest, and aesthetic pleasure. On the first of these I would like to quote

Macaulay, a great historian and great writer, who once wrote to a friend, "How little the all important art of making meaning pellucid is studied now! Hardly any popular writer except myself thinks of it."

14    As to structure, my own form is narrative, which is not every historian's, I may say — indeed, it is rather looked down on now by the advanced academics, but I don't mind because no one could possibly persuade me that telling a story is not the most desirable thing a writer can do. Narrative history is neither as simple nor as straightforward as it might seem. It requires arrangement, composition, planning just like a painting — Rembrandt's "Night Watch," for example. He did not fit in all those figures with certain ones in the foreground and others in back and the light falling on them just so, without much trial and error and innumerable preliminary sketches. It is the same with writing history. Although the finished result may look to the reader natural and inevitable, as if the author had only to follow the sequence of events, it is not that easy. Sometimes, to catch attention, the crucial event and the causative circumstance have to be reversed in order — the event first and the cause afterwards, as in *The Zimmermann Telegram*. One must juggle with time.

15    In *The Proud Tower*, for instance, the two English chapters were originally conceived as one. I divided them and placed them well apart in order to give a feeling of progression, of forward chronological movement to the book. The story of the Anarchists with their ideas and deeds set in counterpoint to each other was a problem in arrangement. The middle section of the Hague chapter on the Paris Exposition of 1900 was originally planned as a separate short centerpiece, marking the turn of the century, until I saw it as a bridge linking the two Hague Conferences, where it now seems to belong.

16    Structure is chiefly a problem of selection, an agonizing business because there is always more material than one can use or fit into a story. The problem is how and what to select out of all that happened without, by the very process of selection, giving an over- or under-emphasis which violates truth. One cannot put in everything: The result would be a shapeless mass. The job is to achieve a narrow line without straying from the essential facts or leaving out any essential facts and without twisting the material to suit one's convenience. To do so is a temptation, but if you do it with history you invariably get tripped up by later events. I have been tempted once or twice and I know.

17    The most difficult task of selection I had was in the Dreyfus chapter. To try to skip over the facts about the *bordereau* and the handwriting and the forgeries — all the elements of the Case as distinct from the Affair — in order to focus instead on what happened to France and yet at the same time give the reader enough background information to enable him to understand what was going on, nearly drove me to despair. My writing slowed down to a trickle until one dreadful day when I went to my study at nine and stayed there all day in a blank coma until five, when I emerged without having written a single word. Anyone who is a writer will know how frightening that was. You feel you have come to the end of your powers: you will not finish the book: you may never write again.

18    There are other problems of structure peculiar to writing history: how to explain background and yet keep the story moving: how to create suspense and sustain interest in a narrative of which the outcome (like who won the war) is, to put it mildly, known. If anyone thinks this does not take creative writing, I can only say, try it.

19    Mr. Capote's *In Cold Blood*, for example, which deals with real life as does mine, is notable for conscious design. One can see him planning, arranging, composing his material until he achieves his perfectly balanced structure. That is art, although the hand is too obtrusive and the design too contrived to qualify as history. His method of investigation, moreover, is hardly so new as he thinks. He is merely applying to contemporary material what historians have been doing for years. Herodotus started it more than two

*Example*     **123**

thousand years ago, walking all over Asia Minor asking questions. Francis Parkman went to live among the Indians: hunted, traveled, and ate with them so that his pages would be steeped in understanding; E.A. Freeman, before he wrote *The Norman Conquest*, visited every spot the Conqueror had set foot on. New to these techniques, Mr. Capote is perhaps naïvely impressed by them. He uses them in a deliberate effort to raise what might be called "creative" journalism to the level of literature. A great company from Herodotus to Trevelyan have been doing the same with history for quite some time.

## VOCABULARY

a. *paragraph   5:* antonym

b. *paragraph   7:* extrapolates

c. *paragraph   9:* humanitarian, diminished

d. *paragraph 10:* poignant, evocative

e. *paragraph 11:* globules

f. *paragraph 13:* aesthetic, pellucid

g. *paragraph 15:* Anarchists, counterpoint

h. *paragraph 19:* contrived

## QUESTIONS

1. What does Tuchman gain by turning first to the example of Trevelyan (paragraph 4)?

2. How do the examples in paragraphs 9 through 11 contribute to the argument that the historian is an artist? How do these examples constitute more than a simple recourse to authority?

3. In paragraph 14, Tuchman introduces what appears to be another example, that of Rembrandt, but the example is soon extended to an analogy. Is this analogy convincing? How does it contribute to Tuchman's thesis?

4. How does Tuchman's example from her own work (paragraphs 15 through 17) add to her argument?

5. What purpose, if any, is served by the example of Truman Capote in the concluding paragraph?

## WRITING ASSIGNMENT

Select some other occupation — homemaker, coach, dentist, farmer, etc. — and write an essay like Tuchman's that argues for the view of, for example, "The Coach as Artist."

# CLASSIFICATION AND DIVISION

Classification and divison are essential kinds of analysis in technical writing (for example, in essays and books that describe computers as a class and then subclassify or divide them, distinguishing various kinds of computers and discussing their uses). As with the paragraph, the clarity of the essay depends on a consistent method of analysis — dividing the class of computers, for example, according to a single principle of subclassification or division, and distinguishing the kinds of division if the analysis uses more than one.

There are times when you want to show what various objects have in common. To do so, you engage in the process of *classification* — grouping objects, people, or ideas that share significant qualities. To show the range of cars manufactured in the United States, for example, you might classify Chevrolets, Dodges, and Fords with other American cars. To illustrate the importance of General Motors in the manufacture of cars, you might classify Chevrolets with Buicks, Oldsmobiles, and other General Motors cars. The number of classes into which an object can be fitted is obviously great. Thus Chevrolets, Volkswagens, Toyotas, and Fiats might be classified with other cars manufactured throughout the world.

The process of *division* begins with a class and shows its subclassifications, or divisions. The class may be a broad one, as in the following division of American cars:

**By manufacturer:** GM cars, Chrysler cars, Ford cars, and so on

The same class of American cars may be divided in another way:

**By transmission:** manual, automatic

Any one of the subclasses or divisions can be further divided by some characteristic or principle — for example, General Motors cars can be subdivided according to manufacturing unit:

**By manufacturing units:** Chevrolet, Buick, Oldsmobile, and so on.

Further division might give us Chevrolets divided according to their model, engine size, colour, or place of manufacture, to cite only a few ways. Again the basis or principle of division you choose depends on the purpose of the analysis.

Here is an example of division in a scientific discussion of meteorites:

**purpose of analysis**

**class:** *meteorites*
**division or subclassification**
according to
constituent material
    first type: *stony*
    second type: *iron*
    third type: *stony-iron*

For the investigator of meteorites the basic challenge is deducing the history of the *meteorites* from a bewildering abundance of evidence. The richness of the problem is indicated by the sheer variety of *types* of meteorite. The two main classes are the *stony meteorites* and the *iron meteorites*. The stony meteorites consist mainly of silicates, with an admixture of nickel and iron. The iron meteorites consist mainly of nickel and iron in various proportions. A smaller class is the stony-iron meteorites, which are inter-

**subdivision of
stony meteorites**
according to
presence or absence
of chondrules

**further subdivisions**

mediate in composition between the other two. Stony meteorites are in turn divided into two groups: the chrondites and the achrondites, according to whether or not they contain chondrules, spherical aggregates of magnesium silicate. Within each group there are further subdivisions based on mineralogical and chemical compositions. — I.R. Cameron, "Meteorites and Cosmic Radiation" [italics added]

The essays that follow illustrate the uses of classification and division in both formal and informal essays.

## ROBERTSON DAVIES

Robertson Davies *was born in Thamesville, Ontario, in 1913. He was educated at Upper Canada College, Queen's University, and Balliol College, Oxford. Journalist, editor, dramatist, director, and professor, Davies will undoubtedly be remembered first for his brilliant novels and outstanding essays. He gained his reputation as one of Canada's foremost novelists with* Fifth Business *(1970),* The Manticore *(1972), and* World of Wonders *(1975), the Deptford Trilogy in which he uses the characters from his small-town Ontario world to explore music, Jungian psychology, and the nature of evil, providing along the way his typical wealth of arcana in details about matters as diverse as saints' lives and travelling theatre companies. In essays like this one on superstition, he explores one of his interests by classifying and defining it.*

## A FEW KIND WORDS FOR SUPERSTITION

In grave discussions of "the renaissance of the irrational" in our time, superstition does not figure largely as a serious challenge to reason or science. Parapsychology, UFO's, miracle cures, transcendental meditation and all the paths to instant enlightenment are condemned, but superstition is merely deplored. Is it because it has an unacknowledged hold on so many of us? 1

Few people will admit to being superstitious; it implies naïveté or ignorance. But I live in the middle of a large university, and I see superstition in its four manifestations, alive and flourishing among people who are indisputably rational and learned. 2

You did not know that superstition takes four forms? Theologians assure us that it does. First is what they call Vain Observances, such as not walking under a ladder, and that kind of thing. Yet I saw a deeply learned professor of anthropology, who had spilled some salt, throwing a pinch of it over his left shoulder; when I asked him why, he replied, with a wink, that it was "to hit the Devil in the eye." I did not question him further about his belief in the Devil: but I noticed that he did not smile until I asked him what he was doing. 3

The second form is Divination, or consulting oracles. Another learned professor I know, who would scorn to settle a problem by tossing a coin (which is a humble appeal to Fate to declare itself), told me quite seriously that he had resolved a matter related to university affairs by consulting the *I Ching*. And why not? There are thousands of people on this continent who appeal to the *I Ching*, and their general level of education seems to 4 absolve them of superstition. Almost, but not quite. The *I Ching*, to the embarrassment of rationalists, often gives excellent advice.

5    The third form is Idolatry, and universities can show plenty of that. If you have ever supervised a large examination room, you know how many jujus, lucky coins and other bringers of luck are placed on the desks of the candidates. Modest idolatry, but what else can you call it?

6    The fourth form is Improper Worship of the True God. A while ago, I learned that every day, for several days, a ½ bill (in Canada we have ½ bills, regarded by some people as unlucky) had been tucked under a candlestick on the altar of a college chapel. Investigation revealed that an engineering student, worried about a girl, thought that bribery of the Deity might help. When I talked with him, he did not think he was pricing God cheap, because he could afford no more. A reasonable argument, but perhaps God was proud that week, for the scientific oracle went against him.

7    Superstition seems to run, a submerged river of crude religion, below the surface of human consciousness. It has done so for as long as we have any chronicle of human behavior, and although I cannot prove it, I doubt if it is more prevalent today than it has always been. Superstition, the theologians tell us, comes from the Latin *supersisto*, meaning to stand in terror of the Deity. Most people keep their terror within bounds, but they cannot root it out, nor do they seem to want to do so.

8    The more the teaching of formal religion declines, or takes a sociological form, the less God appears to great numbers of people as a God of Love, resuming his older form of a watchful, minatory power, to be placated and cajoled. Superstition makes its appeareance, apparently unbidden, very early in life, when children fear that stepping on cracks in the sidewalk will bring ill fortune. It may persist even among the greatly learned and devout, as in the case of Dr. Samuel Johnson, who felt it necessary to touch posts that he passed in the street. The psychoanalysts have their explanation, but calling a superstition a compulsion neurosis does not banish it.

9    Many superstitions are so widespread and so old that they must have risen from a depth of the human mind that is indifferent to race or creed. Orthodox Jews place a charm on their doorposts; so do (or did) the Chinese. Some peoples of Middle Europe believe that when a man sneezes, his soul, for that moment, is absent from his body, and they hasten to bless him, lest the soul be seized by the Devil. How did the Melanesians come by the same idea? Superstition seems to have a link with some body of belief that far antedates the religions we know — religions which have no place for such comforting little ceremonies and charities.

10    People who like disagreeable historical comparisons recall that when Rome was in decline, superstition proliferated wildly, and that something of the same sort is happening in our Western world today. They point to the popularity of astrology, and it is true that sober newspapers that would scorn to deal in love philters carry astrology columns and the fashion magazines count them among their most popular features. But when has astrology not been popular? No use saying science discredits it. When has the heart of man given a damn for science?

11    Superstition in general is linked to man's yearning to know his fate, and to have some hand in deciding it. When my mother was a child, she innocently joined her Roman Catholic friends in killing spiders on July 11, until she learned that this was done to ensure heavy rain the day following, the anniversary of the Battle of Boyne, when the Orangemen would hold their parade. I knew an Italian, a good scientist, who watched every morning before leaving his house, so that the first person he met would not be a priest or a nun, as this would certainly bring bad luck.

12    I am not one to stand aloof from the rest of humanity in this matter, for when I was a university student, a gypsy woman with a child in her arms used to appear every year at

examination time, and ask a shilling of anyone who touched the Lucky Baby; that swarthy infant cost me four shillings altogether, and I never failed an examination. Of course, I did it merely for the joke — or so I thought then. Now, I am humbler.

## VOCABULARY

a. *paragraph  1:* renaissance, parapsychology, transcendental

b. *paragraph  2:* naïveté, manifestations

c. *paragraph  3:* theologians

d. *paragraph  4:* oracles, absolve, rationalists

e. *paragraph  5:* jujus

f. *paragraph  8:* minatory, placated, cajoled

g. *paragraph 10:* proliferated, philters

## QUESTIONS

1. On what basis does Davies divide superstitions? What are the four forms he distinguishes?

2. What point is he making through these divisions?

3. In referring to superstitions as a "submerged river of crude religion," what point is Davies making about human nature? What do his examples of the *I Ching*, lucky charms, and bribing the Deity show?

4. What is the order of ideas in the twelve paragraphs? Why does Davies save the example of the gypsy woman and her child for last?

5. Can you think of examples of other kinds of superstitions?

## WRITING ASSIGNMENTS

1. Classify superstitions by another principle and use your classification to make a point, as Davies does.

2. Analyse the significance of a superstiion in your own life. Discuss the ways in which you have attempted to rationalize this superstition.

## LEWIS THOMAS

*The physician and essayist* Lewis Thomas *has served in numerous administrative posts, including chairman of pathology and medicine and dean at New York University and president of The Memorial Sloan-Kettering Cancer Center. His essays in the* New England Journal of Medicine *and other periodicals have been collected in a number of books, including* The Lives of a Cell *and* The Medusa and the Snail. *Though Thomas writes often on medicine, his interests range widely, as this humorous essay on punctuation shows. Like Thurber, Thomas divides a broad class — punctuation marks — in an unusual way.*

## NOTES ON PUNCTUATION

1   There are no precise rules about punctuation (Fowler lays out some general advice (as best he can under the complex circumstances of English prose (he points out, for example, that we possess only four stops (the comma, the semicolon, the colon and the period (the question mark and exclamation point are not, strictly speaking, stops; they are indicators of tone (oddly enough, the Greeks employed the semicolon for their question mark (it produces a strange sensation to read a Greek sentence which is a straightforward question: Why weepest thou; (instead of Why weepest thou? (and, of course, there are parentheses (which are surely a kind of punctuation making this whole matter much more complicated by having to count up the lefthanded parentheses in order to be sure of closing with the right number (but if the parentheses were left out, with nothing to work with but the stops, we would have considerably more flexibility in the deploying of layers of meaning than if we tried to separate all the clauses by physical barriers (and in the latter case, while we might have more precision and exactitude for our meaning, we would lose the essential flavor of language, which is its wonderful ambiguity)))))))))))).

2   The commas are the most useful and usable of all the stops. It is highly important to put them in place as you go along. If you try to come back after doing a paragraph and stick them in the various spots that tempt you you will discover that they tend to swarm like minnows into all sorts of crevices whose existence you hadn't realized and before you know it the whole long sentence becomes immobilized and lashed up squirming in commas. Better to use them sparingly, and with affection, precisely when the need for each one arises, nicely, by itself.

3   I have grown fond of semicolons in recent years. The semicolon tells you that there is still some question about the preceding full sentence; something needs to be added; it reminds you sometimes of the Greek usage. It is almost already a greater pleasure to come across a semicolon than a period. The period tells you that that is that; if you didn't get all the meaning you wanted or expected, anyway you got all the writer intended to parcel out and now you have to move along. But with a semicolon there you get a pleasant little feeling of expectancy; there is more to come; to read on; it will get clearer.

4   Colons are a lot less attractive; for several reasons: firstly, they give you the feeling of being rather ordered around, or at least having your nose pointed in a direction you might not be inclined to take if left to yourself, and, secondly, you suspect you're in for one of those sentences that will be labeling the points to be made: firstly, secondly and so forth, with the implication that you haven't sense enough to keep track of a sequence of notions without having them numbered. Also, many writers use this system loosely and incompletely, starting out with number one and number two as though counting off on their fingers but then going on and on without the succession of labels you've been led to expect, leaving you floundering about searching for the ninethly or seventeenthly that ought to be there but isn't.

5   Exclamation points are the most irritating of all. Look! they say, look at what I just said! How amazing is my thought! It is like being forced to watch someone else's small child jumping up and down crazily in the center of the living room shouting to attract

attention. If a sentence really has something of importance to say, something quite remarkable, it doesn't need a mark to point it out. And if it is really, after all, a banal sentence needing more zing, the exclamation point simply emphasizes its banality!

Quotation marks should be used honestly and sparingly, when there is a genuine quotation at hand, and it is necessary to be very rigorous about the words enclosed by the marks. If something is to be quoted, the *exact* words must be used. If part of it must be left out because of space limitations, it is good manners to insert three dots to indicate the omission, but it is unethical to do this if it means connecting two thoughts which the original author did not intend to have tied together. Above all, quotation marks should not be used for ideas that you'd like to disown, things in the air so to speak. Nor should they be put in place around clichés; if you want to use a cliché, you must take full responsibility for it yourself and not try to fob it off on anon., or on society. The most objectionable misuse of quotation marks, but one which illustrates the dangers of misuse in ordinary prose, is seen in advertising, especially in advertisements for small restaurants, for example "just around the corner," or "a good place to eat." No single, identifiable, citable person ever really said, for the record, "just around the corner," much less "a good place to eat," least likely of all for restaurants of the type that use this type of prose.

6

The dash is a handy device, informal and essentially playful, telling you that you're about to take off on a different tack but still in some way connected with the present course — only you have to remember that the dash is there, and either put a second dash at the end of the notion to let the reader know that he's back on course, or else end the sentence, as here, with a period.

7

The greatest danger in punctuation is for poetry. Here it is necessary to be as economical and parsimonious with commas and periods as with the words themselves, and any marks that seem to carry their own subtle meanings, like dashes and little rows of periods, even semicolons and question marks, should be left out altogether rather than inserted to clog up the thing with ambiguity. A single exclamation point in a poem, no matter what else the poem has to say, is enough to destroy the whole work.

8

The things I like best in T.S. Eliot's poetry, especially in the *Four Quartets*, are the semicolons. You cannot hear them, but they are there, laying out the connections between the images and the ideas. Sometimes you get a glimpse of a semicolon coming, a few lines farther on, and it is like climbing a steep path through woods and seeing a wooden bench just at a bend in the road ahead, a place where you can expect to sit for a moment, catching your breath.

9

Commas can't do this sort of thing; they can only tell you how the different parts of a complicated thought are to be fitted together, but you can't sit, not even take a breath, just because of a comma,

10

# VOCABULARY

a. *paragraph 1:* deploying, exactitude, ambiguity

b. *paragraph 2:* immobilized

c. *paragraph 4:* floundering

d. *paragraph 5:* banality

e. *paragraph 6:* fob off

f. *paragraph 8:* parsimonious

## QUESTIONS

1. By what principle does Thomas divide the class *punctuation marks*? Does he exclude any punctuation marks in his division?

2. How does Thomas illustrate his statement in paragraph 1 that parentheses can complicate the reading of a sentence?

3. What is Thomas showing through the omission of commas in the third sentence of paragraph 2 and the use of commas in the fourth sentence of the same paragraph?

4. In paragraphs 3 and 4, how does Thomas illustrate the uses of the semicolon and the colon?

5. Why does Thomas return to the uses of semicolons and commas?

6. What is the tone of the essay, and what impression do you get of Thomas from the essay?

## WRITING ASSIGNMENTS

1. Write an essay illustrating the uses and misuses of the various punctuation marks that Thomas discusses. Your essay need not be on punctuation, but if you do write on this subject, do so from a different point of view and develop a different thesis.

2. Divide another class — for example, amateurs in sport or amateur cooks — and, like Thomas, discuss the implications of your division.

## JAMES THURBER

James Thurber *(1894–1961) was one of America's great humorists. An artist, playwright, and essayist, he was associated with* The New Yorker *magazine during his entire career. His many books include* My Life and Hard Times, *an account of his youth in Columbus, Ohio;* The Owl in the Attic; *and many collections of essays. Thurber was particularly interested in American popular culture and in the ways we think and write about ourselves. In the essay reprinted here, he gives us an inventory of "a certain kind of Broad Generalization, or Sweeping Statement," abundantly illustrated. Thurber divides this broad class of statements in a humorous way to satirize a common habit of thinking.*

## WHAT A LOVELY GENERALIZATION!

1 I have collected, in my time, derringers, snowstorm paperweights, and china and porcelain dogs, and perhaps I should explain what happened to these old collections before I go on to my newest hobby, which is the true subject of this monograph. My derringer collection may be regarded as having been discontinued, since I collected only two, the second and last item as long ago as 1935. There were originally seventeen snowstorm paperweights, but only four or five are left. This kind of collection is known to the expert as a "diminished collection," and it is not considered cricket to list it in your *Who's Who* bio-

graphy. The snowstorm paperweight suffers from its easy appeal to the eye and the hand. House guests like to play with paperweights and to slip them into their luggage while packing up to leave. As for my china and porcelain dogs, I disposed of that collection some two years ago. I had decided that the collection of actual objects, of any kind, was too much of a strain, and I determined to devote myself, instead, to the impalpable and the intangible.

Nothing in my new collection can be broken or stolen or juggled or thrown at cats. **2** What I collect now is a certain kind of Broad Generalization, or Sweeping Statement. You will see what I mean when I bring out some of my rare and cherished pieces. All you need to start a collection of generalizations like mine is an attentive ear. Listen in particular to women, whose average generalization is from three to five times as broad as a man's. Generalizations, male or female, may be true ("Women don't sleep very well"), untrue ("There are no pianos in Japan"), half true ("People would rather drink than go to the theater"), debatable ("Architects have the wrong idea"), libelous ("Doctors don't know what they're doing"), ridiculous ("You never see foreigners fishing"), fascinating but undemonstrable ("People who break into houses don't drink wine"), or idiosyncratic ("Peach ice cream is never as good as you think it's going to be").

"There are no pianos in Japan" was the first item in my collection. I picked it up at a **3** reception while discussing an old movie called "The Battle," or "Thunder in the East," which starred Charles Boyer, Merle Oberon, and John Loder, some twenty years ago. In one scene, Boyer, as a Japanese naval captain, comes upon Miss Oberon, as his wife, Matsuko, playing an Old Japanese air on the piano for the entertainment of Loder, a British naval officer with a dimple, who has forgotten more about fire control, range finding, marksmanship, and lovemaking than the Japanese commander is ever going to know. "Matsuko," says the latter, "why do you play that silly little song? It may be tedious for our fran." Their fran, John Loder, says, "No, it is, as a matter of —" But I don't know why I have to go into the whole plot. The lady with whom I was discussing the movie, at the reception, said that the detail about Matsuko and the piano was absurd, since "there are no pianos in Japan." It seems that this lady was an authority on the musical setup in Japan because her great-uncle had married a singsong girl in Tokyo in 1912.

Now, I might have accepted the declarations that there are no saxophones in Bessara- **4** bia, no banjo-mandolins in Mozambique, no double basses in Zanzibar, no jew's-harps in Rhodesia, no zithers in Madagascar, and no dulcimers in Milwaukee, but I could not believe that Japan, made out in the movie as a great imitator of Western cuture, would not have any pianos. Some months after the reception, I picked up an old copy of the *Saturday Evening Post* and, in an article on Japan, read that there were, before the war, some fifteen thousand pianos in Japan. It just happened to say that, right there in the article.

You may wonder where I heard some of the other Sweeping Statements I have **5** mentioned above. Well, the one about peach ice cream was contributed to my collection by a fifteen-year-old girl. I am a chocolate man myself, but the few times I have eaten peach ice cream it tasted exactly the way I figured it was going to taste, which is why I classify this statement as idiosyncratic; that is, peculiar to one individual. The item about foreigners never fishing, or, at any rate, never fishing where you can see them, was given to me last summer by a lady who had just returned from a motor trip through New England. The charming generalization about people who break into houses popped out of a conversation I overheard between two women, one of whom said it was not safe to leave rye, Scotch or bourbon in your summer house when you closed it for the winter, but it was perfectly all right to leave your wine, since intruders are notoriously men of insensitive palate, who cannot tell the difference between Nuits-St.-Georges and saddle polish. I would not repose too much confidence in this theory if I were you, however. It is one of those Comfortable Conclusions that can cost you a whole case of Château Lafite.

6    I haven't got space here to go through my entire collection, but there is room to examine a few more items. I'm not sure where I got hold of "Gamblers hate women" — possibly at Bleeck's — but, like "Sopranos drive men crazy," it has an authentic ring. This is not true, I'm afraid, of "You can't trust an electrician" or "Cops off duty always shoot somebody." There may be something in "Dogs know when you're despondent" and "Sick people hear everything," but I sharply question the validity of "Nobody taps his fingers if he's all right" and "People who like birds are queer."

7    Some twenty years ago, a Pittsburgh city editor came out with the generalization that "Rewrite men go crazy when the moon is full," but this is perhaps a little too special for the layman, who probably doesn't know what a rewrite man is. Besides, it is the abusive type of Sweeping Statement and should not be dignified by analysis or classification.

8    In conclusion, let us briefly explore "Generals are afraid of their daughters," vouch-safed by a lady after I had told her my General Wavell anecdote. It happens, for the sake of our present record, that the late General Wavell, of His Britannic Majesty's forces, discussed his three daughters during an interview a few years ago. He said that whereas he had millions of men under his command who leaped at his every order, he couldn't get his daughters down to breakfast on time when he was home on leave, in spite of stern directives issued the night before. As I have imagined it, his ordeal went something like this. It would get to be 7 A.M. and then 7:05, and General Wavell would shout up the stairs demanding to know where everybody was, and why the girls were not at table. Presently, one of them would call back sharply, as a girl has to when her father gets out of hand, "For heaven's sake, Daddy, will you be quiet! Do you want to wake the neighbors?" The General, his flanks rashly exposed, so to speak, would fall back in orderly retreat and eat his kippers by himself. Now, I submit that there is nothing in this to prove that the General was afraid of his daughters. The story merely establishes the fact that his daughters were not afraid of him.

9    If you are going to start collecting Sweeping Statements on your own, I must warn you that certain drawbacks are involved. You will be inclined to miss the meaning of conversations while lying in wait for generalizations. Your mouth will hang open slightly, your posture will grow rigid, and your eyes will take on the rapt expression of a person listening for the faint sound of distant sleigh bells. People will avoid your company and whisper that you are probably an old rewrite man yourself or, at best, a finger tapper who is a long way from being all right. But your collection will be a source of comfort in your declining years, when you can sit in the chimney corner cackling the evening away over some such gems, let us say, as my own two latest acquisitions: "Jewelers never go anywhere" and "Intellectual women dress funny."

10    Good hunting.

## VOCABULARY

a. *paragraph 1:* derringers, monograph, impalpable, intangible

b. *paragraph 2:* libelous, idiosyncratic

c. *paragraph 3:* tedious

d. *paragraph 4:* jew's-harps, zithers, dulcimers

e. *paragraph 8:* flanks, kippers

## QUESTIONS

1. What class does Thurber divide, and by what principle of division or subclassification does he divide?

2. Is Thurber's statement that a woman's "average generalization is from three to five times as broad as a man's" any better founded than other generalizations he cites? How do you think he wants the reader to take this statement?

3. How does each of the examples in paragraph 2 illustrate the labels Thurber gives them? Why is the statement that "People would rather drink than go to the theater" half true?

4. What is the overall tone of the essay, and how is it established? How is this tone related to Thurber's purpose in writing the essay?

## WRITING ASSIGNMENTS

1. Collect examples of generalizations like those in paragraph 2, classify them, and build your examples to a conclusion about the purpose such generalization serve.

2. Write a characterization of Thurber from the way he talks about himself and to the reader of the essay. Consider his qualities as a humorist.

## TERENCE DICKINSON

*Terence Dickinson is Canada's foremost astronomy author. More than 200,000 copies of his seven books are in print and his work has won six national and two international awards. He writes a weekly column on astronomy for the* Toronto Star, *teaches astronomy part-time at St. Lawrence College in Kingston, Ontario, and has been a staff astronomer at several planetariums and science museums in the United States and Canada. This article, from* The Universe and Beyond *(1986), on galaxies is typical of the style he has developed for presenting technical concepts to a lay audience.*

## GALACTIC ENCOUNTERS

By human standards, one cubic light-year is an enormous chunk of space, enough to hold    1
the sun, its orbiting family of planets from Mercury to Pluto, a million roving asteroids and a trillion comets on giant looping paths which carry them so far out that mother sun is reduced to a bright star in the firmament. But on the scale of the universe, it is merely our backyard — just one infinitesimally tiny pocket of the cosmos. The total volume of the known universe is a million trillion trillion cubic light-years.

Suppose one of those million trillion trillion cubic light-years were selected totally at    2
random as a site for exploration and a survey of surrounding space. How would the cosmic landscape vary from one site to another? Ninety-nine times out of a hundred, an intrepid explorer willing to embark on such a blind voyage would emerge in a pristine vacuum embedded in total blackness. Absolutely nothing would be visible to the unaided eye. Resorting to binoculars, the traveller might spy a few smudges of light — some remote galaxies — but statistically, that would be unlikely too.

3    The universe is almost entirely empty space. Planets, stars and galaxies are scattered here and there in an abyss of nothingness (at least as far as human senses are concerned). There is one galaxy for every million trillion cubic light-years of space and one star for every billion cubic light-years. But they are not evenly distributed. Stars are swarmed in galaxies, and galaxies congregate in clusters. On the largest scale, the clusters, which are separated by enormous voids, are themselves arrayed in groups known as superclusters. An observer plunked randomly in the universe would probably land somewhere in one of the voids that occupy most of the cosmos. In regions where galaxies exist, the super-clusters are like island archipelagos scattered across the cosmic ocean.

4    The profusion of stars seen in the dark night skies of Earth is the view from within one of those galaxies. The delicate powdering of the Milky Way is the visible interior of the gigantic pinwheel-shaped galaxy we habit — a system so vast that the unaided eye reveals only a tiny fraction of its bulk. What we see as a sky full of stars is our cosmic neighbour-hood, our corner of the galaxy. The sun resides on the inside edge of one of the curving spiral arms, about two-thirds of the way from the galactic centre, in what astronomer Carl Sagan calls "the galactic boondocks." Stars in our vicinity are, on average, seven light-years apart. The galaxy's total population of stars is at least 200 billion, probably much more.

5    Stars, planets, comets, gas, dust and nebulas are the galactic ingredients. The Milky Way Galaxy is a typical spiral galaxy: an enormous disc about 80,000 light-years from edge to edge, with a bulge at the hub that is 10,000 light-years thick. In our region, 28,000 light-years out from the nucleus, the galaxy is 3,000 light-years thick. If two long-playing records were glued together and a fried egg placed centrally on each, the result would be a correctly proportioned analogy. The glue represents the 200-light-year-thick region where nebulas and newborn stars are concentrated in our galaxy. The sun stays within this zone for most of its nearly circular 200-million-year orbit around the galactic nucleus, regularly oscillating slightly above or below it.

6    There are three basic types of galaxies: spiral galaxies, like the Milky Way; spherical swarms of stars called elliptical galaxies; and loose collections of stars with no distinct structural form, called irregular galaxies. The Large and Small Magellanic Clouds, the Milky Way's satellite galaxies, are irregulars. Two nearby ellipticals are companions of the Andromeda Galaxy and are easily seen in photographs. The smallest eliptical galaxies, called dwarf spheroidal systems, have only a few thousand stars. But giant ellipticals are the titans of the cosmos, with populations of up to 50 trillion stars. Spiral galaxies have a comparatively small size range. The upper limit is marked by NGC 6872 and UGC 2885, both roughly 10 times the size of the Milky Way, while NGC 3928 is only about one-quarter of our galaxy's diameter. Although spiral galaxies are outnumbered by ellipticals, they *appear* to be most common because a typical spiral is larger and brighter than an average elliptical. Irregular galaxies are less numerous than spirals or ellipticals, and most are quite small.

7    Spiral galaxies are undoubtedly among nature's most elegant creations. Their graceful curving arms, traced by millions of giant blue stars and puffs of pink nebulosity, contrast with the bulging nucleus where 100 billion stars are nestled.

8    Compared with spirals, elliptical galaxies are rather dumpy. Ellipticals are star piles, vast spherical or football-shaped blobs of yellow and red stars. Though not ugly, ellipticals certainly lack flair.

9    Why did two main types of galaxies form after the Big Bang? Why are they not all spirals?

10    Until the early 1980s, astronomers assumed that the manner in which the primordial gas clouds collapsed determined the type of galaxy that was born. But that idea is being

seriously questioned. There is growing evidence that the genesis galaxies were of only one type: spiral.

In the new view, ellipticals are the wreckage of spirals that collided within a few billion years of their formation. Because the universe is growing larger, due to continuous expansion since the Big Bang, it must have been much more compact and crowded 14 billion years ago when the galaxies were born — about 1 percent of its present size. But the same amount of matter was in the universe at that time. The newborn galaxies were almost rubbing shoulders, and collisions would have been far more common than they are today.    **11**

A galaxy collision would last for hundreds of millions of years. Once two spirals actually touch, they are likely doomed to loop ever closer to each other before finally merging, although because of the distance between them, individual stars would virtually never collide. Even a gentle merger would create an elliptical galaxy because collisions among the abundant gas clouds in the young galaxies would trigger star formation. Friction from the cloud collisions, plus dynamical friction from the gravitational interaction of the two great star cities, would rip apart the spiral arms and cascade the remains into a chaotic mass of stars — an elliptical galaxy.    **12**

Even a close miss would twist off much of a spiral galaxy's twirling arms, although the nuclear region would remain essentially intact. In such a gravitational tug-of-war between two continents of stars, the outrider stars would receive two sets of signals that would scramble their orbits. As a result, many billions of stars would be flung into intergalactic trajectories and lost from both galaxies forever.    **13**

Further evidence supporting the scenario is that spiral galaxies are almost never located among the denser galaxy clusters. Spirals are usually loners, those that avoided being torn apart when the universe was younger. Galaxy collisions are relatively rare today, although NGC 5128, a nearby galaxy, was recently determined to be the debris from two galaxies that collided two billion years ago. At least one of the originals was a spiral. Elliptical galaxies, it seems, are not born, they are made — heaps of stars from dismembered spirals.    **14**

## VOCABULARY

a. *paragraph 1:* infinitesimally, cosmos

b. *paragraph 2:* pristine

c. *paragraph 3:* archipelagos

d. *paragraph 5:* nebulas, oscillating

## QUESTIONS

1. How does Dickinson divide the class *galaxies*?

2. Why does he begin with a discussion of the universe itself?

3. How does he illustrate his point that "the universe is almost entirely empty space"? Why does he use different kinds of illustrations?

4. What analogies does he use to make comprehensible the vast distances and enormous sizes of the objects in question?

5. What is the tone of the essay? Objective and scientific, or subjective and enthusiastic?

## WRITING ASSIGNMENT

Classify and define the elements of a subject area you know well: stamps, butterflies, vertebrates, mammals, cars, airplanes, etc. Use comparisons that help to bring the subject alive.

## DESMOND MORRIS

Desmond Morris *was born in 1928 in England, and educated at Birmingham and Oxford. He has been curator of mammals at the Zoological Society of London and is now a full-time writer and research fellow at Oxford.* The Naked Ape *(1967) is his most famous book, and he is also the author of* The Human Zoo *(1970),* Intimate Behaviour *(1972), and* Manwatching *(1977), from which the following selection is taken. In it, he classifies kinds of human territory and shows how people, like animals, use signals to prevent confrontation.*

## TERRITORIAL BEHAVIOUR

1    A territory is a defended space. In the broadest sense, there are three kinds of human territory: tribal, family and personal.

2    It is rare for people to be driven to physical fighting in defence of these "owned" spaces, but fight they will, if pushed to the limit. The invading army encroaching on national territory, the gang moving into a rival district, the trespasser climbing into an orchard, the burglar breaking into a house, the bully pushing to the front of a queue, the driver trying to steal a parking space, all of these intruders are liable to be met with resistance varying from the vigorous to the savagely violent. Even if the law is on the side of the intruder, the urge to protect a territory may be so strong that otherwise peaceful citizens abandon all their usual controls and inhibitions. Attempts to evict families from their homes, no matter how socially valid the reasons, can lead to siege conditions reminiscent of the defence of a medieval fortress.

3    The fact that these upheavals are so rare is a measure of the success of Territorial Signals as a system of dispute prevention. It is sometimes cynically stated that "all property is theft," but in reality it is the opposite. Property, as owned space which is *displayed* as owned space, is a special kind of sharing system which reduces fighting much more than it causes it. Man is a co-operative species, but he is also competitive, and his struggle for dominance has to be structured in some way if chaos is to be avoided. The establishment of territorial rights is one such structure. It limits dominance geographically. I am dominant in my territory and you are dominant in yours. In other words, dominance is shared out spatially, and we all have some. Even if I am weak and unintelligent and you can dominate me when we meet on neutral ground, I can still enjoy a thoroughly dominant role as soon as I retreat to my private base. Be it ever so humble, there is no place like a home territory.

Of course, I can still be intimidated by a particularly dominant individual who enters my home base, but his encroachment will be dangerous for him and he will think twice about it, because he will know that here my urge to resist will be dradmatically magnified and my usual subservience banished. Insulted at the heart of my own territory, I may easily explode into battle — either symbolic or real — with a result that may be damaging to both of us.   **4**

In order for this to work, each territory has to be plainly advertised as such. Just as a dog cocks its leg to deposit its personal scent on the trees in its locality, so the human animals cocks its leg symbolically all over his home base. But because we are predominantly visual animals, we employ mostly visual signals, and it is worth asking how we do this at the three levels: tribal, family and personal.   **5**

First: the Tribal Territory. We evolved as tribal animals, living in comparatively small groups, probably of less than a hundred, and we existed like that for millions of years. It is our basic social unit, a group in which everyone knows everyone else. Essentially, the tribal territory consisted of a home base surrounded by extended hunting grounds. Any neighbouring tribe intruding on our social space would be repelled and driven away. As these early tribes swelled into agricultural super-tribes, and eventually into industrial nations, their territorial defence systems became increasingly elaborate. The tiny, ancient home base of the hunting tribe became the great capital city, the primitive war-paint became the flags, emblems, uniforms and regalia of the specialized military, and the war-chants became national anthems, marching songs and bugle calls. Territorial boundary-lines hardened into fixed borders, often conspicuously patrolled and punctuated with defensive structures — forts and look-out posts, checkpoints and great walls, and, today, customs barriers.   **6**

Today each nation flies its own flag, a symbolic embodiment of its territorial status. But patriotism is not enough. The ancient tribal hunter lurking inside each citizen finds himself unsatisfied with membership in such a vast conglomeration of individuals, most of whom are totally unknown to him personally. He does his best to feel that he shares a common territorial defence with them all, but the scale of the operation has become inhuman. It is hard to feel a sense of belonging with a tribe of fifty million or more. His answer is to form sub-groups, nearer to his ancient pattern, smaller and more personally known to him — the local club, the teenage gang, the union, the specialist society, the sports association, the political party, the college fraternity, the social clique, the protest group, and the rest. Rare indeed is the individual who does not belong to at least one of these splinter groups, and take from it a sense of tribal allegiance and brotherhood. Typical of all these groups is the development of Territorial Signals — badges, costumes, headquarters, banners, slogans, and all the other displays of group identity. This is where the action is, in terms of tribal territorialism, and only when a major war breaks out does the emphasis shift upwards to the higher group level of the nation.   **7**

Each of these modern pseudo-tribes sets up its own special kind of home base. In extreme cases non-members are totally excluded, in others they are allowed in as visitors with limited rights and under a control system of special rules. In many ways they are like miniature nations, with their own flags and emblems and their own border guards. The exclusive club has its own "customs barrier": the doorman who checks your "passport" (your membership card) and prevents strangers from passing in unchallenged. There is a government: the club committee; and often special displays of the tribal elders: the photographs or portraits of previous officials on the walls. At the heart of the specialized territories there is a powerful feeling of security and importance, a sense of shared defence against the outside world. Much of the club chatter, both serious and joking, directs itself   **8** against the rottenness of everything outside the club boundaries — in that "other world" beyond the protected portals.

9        In social organizations which embody a strong class system, such as military units and large business concerns, there are many territorial rules, often unspoken, which interfere with the official hierarchy. High-status individuals, such as officers or managers, could in theory enter any of the regions occupied by the lower levels of the pecking order, but they limit this power in a striking way. An officer seldom enters a sergeant's mess or a barrack room unless it is for a formal inspection. He respects those regions as alien territories even though he has the power to go there by virtue of his dominant role. And in businesses, part of the appeal of unions, over and above their obvious functions, is that with their officials, headquarters and meetings they add a sense of territorial power for the staff workers. It is almost as if each military organization and business concern consists of two warring tribes: the officers versus the other ranks, and the management versus the workers. Each has its special home base within the system, and the territorial defence pattern thrusts itself into what, on the surface, is a pure social hierarchy. Negotiations between managements and unions are tribal battles fought out over the neutral ground of a board-room table, and are as much concerned with territorial display as they are with resolving problems of wages and conditions. Indeed, if one side gives in too quickly and accepts the other's demands, the victors feel strangely cheated and deeply suspicious that it may be a trick. What they are missing is the protracted sequence of ritual and counter-ritual that keeps alive their group territorial identity.

10       Likewise, many of the hostile displays of sports fans and teenage gangs are primarily concerned with displaying their group image to rival fan-clubs and gangs. Except in rare cases, they do not attack one another's headquarters, drive out the occupants, and reduce them to a submissive, subordinate condition. It is enough to have scuffles on the border-lands between the two rival territories. This is particularly clear at football matches, where the fan-club headquarters becomes temporarily shifted from the club-house to a section of the stands, and where minor fighting breaks out at the unofficial boundary line between the massed groups of rival supporters. Newspaper reports play up the few accidents and injuries which occur on such occasions, but when they are studied in relation to the total numbers of displaying fans involved, it is clear that the serious incidents represent only a tiny fraction of the overall group behaviour. For every actual punch or kick there are a thousand war-cries, war-dances, chants and gestures.

11       Second: the Family Territory. Essentially, the family is a breeding unit and the family territory is a breeding ground. At the centre of this space, there is the nest — the bedroom — where, tucked up in bed, we feel at our most territorially secure. In a typical house the bedroom is upstairs, where a safe nest should be. This puts it farther away from the entrance hall, the area where contact is made, intermittently, with the outside world. The less private reception rooms, where intruders are allowed access, are the next line of de-fence. Beyond them, outside the walls of the building, there is often a symbolic remnant of the ancient feeding grounds — a garden. Its symbolism often extends to the plants and animals it contains, which cease to be nutritional and become merely decorative — flowers and pets. But like a true territorial space it has a conspicuously displayed boundary line, the garden fence, wall, or railings. Often no more than a token barrier, this is the outer territorial demarcation, separating the private world of the family from the public world beyond. To cross it puts any visitor or intruder at an immediate disadvantage. As he crosses the threshold, his dominance wanes, slightly but unmistakably. He is enter-ing an area where he senses that he must ask permission to do simple things that he would consider a right elsewhere. Without lifting a finger, the territorial owners exert their

dominance. This is done by all the hundreds of small ownership "markers" they have deposited on their family territory: the ornaments, the "possessed" objects positioned in the rooms and on the walls; the furnishings, the furniture, the colours, the patterns, all owner-chosen and all making this particular home base unique to them.

It is one of the tragedies of modern architecture that there has been a standardization of      **12** these vital territorial living units. One of the most important aspects of a home is that it should be similar to other homes only in a general way, and that in detail it should have many differences, making it a *particular* home. Unfortunately, it is cheaper to build a row of houses, or a block of flats, so that all the family living-units are identical, but the territorial urge rebels against this trend and house-owners struggle as best they can to make their mark on their mass-produced properties. They do this with garden-design, with front-door colours, with curtain patterns, with wallpaper and all the other decorative elements that together create a unique and different family environment. Only when they have completed this nest-building do they feel truly "at home" and secure.

When they venture forth as a family unit, they repeat the process in a minor way. On a      **13** day-trip to the seaside, they load the car with personal belongings and it becomes their temporary, portable territory. Arriving at the beach, they stake out a small territorial claim, marking it with rugs, towels, baskets and other belongings to which they can return from their seaboard wanderings. Even if they all leave it at once to bathe, it retains a characteristic territorial quality and other family groups arriving will recognize this by setting up their own "home" bases at a respectful distance. Only when the whole beach has filled up with these marked spaces will newcomers start to position themselves in such a way that the inter-base distance becomes reduced. Forced to pitch between several existing beach territories, they will feel a momentary sensation of intrusion, and the established "owners" will feel a similar sensation of invasion, even though they are not being directly inconvenienced.

The same territorial scene is being played out in parks and fields and on riverbanks,      **14** wherever family groups gather in their clustered units. But if rivalry for spaces creates mild feelings of hostility, it is true to say that without the territorial system of sharing and space-limited dominance, there would be chaotic disorder.

Third: the Personal Space. If a man enters a waiting-room and sits at one end of a long      **15** row of empty chairs, it is possible to predict where the next man to enter will seat himself. He will not sit next to the first man, nor will he sit at the far end, right away from him. He will choose a position about halfway between these two points. The next man to enter will take the largest gap left, and sit roughly in the middle of that, and so on, until eventually the latest newcomer will be forced to select a seat that places him right next to one of the already seated men. Similar patterns can be observed in cinemas, public urinals, airplanes, trains and buses. This is a reflection of the fact that we all carry with us, everywhere we go, a portable territory called a Personal Space. If people move inside this space, we feel threatened. If they keep too far outside it, we feel rejected. The result is a subtle series of spatial adjustments, usually operating quite unconsciously and producing ideal compromises as far as this is possible. If a situation becomes too crowded, then we adjust our reactions accordingly and allow our personal space to shrink. Jammed into an elevator, a rush-hour compartment, or a packed room, we give up altogether and allow body-to-body contact, but when we relinquish our Personal Space in this way, we adopt certain special techniques. In essence, what we do is to convert these other bodies into "nonpersons." We studiously ignore them, and they us. We try not to face them if we can possibly avoid it. We wipe all expressiveness from our faces, letting them go blank. We may look up at the ceiling or down at the floor, and we reduce body movements to a minimum. Packed together like sardines in a tin, we stand dumbly still, sending out as few social signals as possible.

16    Even if the crowding is less severe, we still tend to cut down our social interactions in the presence of large numbers. Careful observations of children in play groups revealed that if they are high-density groupings there is less social interaction between the individual children, even though there is theoretically more opportunity for such contacts. At the same time, the high-density groups show a higher frequency of aggressive and destructive behaviour patterns in their play. Personal Space — "elbow room" — is a vital commodity for the human animal, and one that cannot be ignored without risking serious trouble.

17    Of course, we all enjoy the excitement of being in a crowd, and this reaction cannot be ignored. But there are crowds and crowds. It is pleasant enough to be in a "spectator crowd," but not so appealing to find yourself in the middle of a rush-hour crush. The difference between the two is that the spectator crowd is all facing in the same direction and concentrating on a distant point of interest. Attending a theatre, there are twinges of rising hostility towards the stranger who sits down immediately in front of you or the one who squeezes into the seat next to you. The shared armrest can become a polite, but distinct, territorial boundary-dispute region. However, as soon as the show begins, these invasions of Personal Space are forgotten and the attention is focused beyond the small space where the crowding is taking place. Now, each member of the audience feels himself spatially related, not to his cramped neighbours, but to the actor on the stage, and this distance is, if anything, too great. In the rush-hour crowd, by contrast, each member of the pushing throng is competing with his neighbours all the time. There is no escape to a spatial relation with a distant actor, only the pushing, shoving bodies all around.

18    Those of us who have to spend a great deal of time in crowded conditions become gradually better able to adjust, but no one can ever become completely immune to invasions of Personal Space. This is because they remain forever associated with either powerful hostile or equally powerful loving feelings. All through our childhood we will have been held to be loved and held to be hurt, and anyone who invades our Personal Space when we are adults is, in effect, threatening to extend his behaviour into one of these two highly charged areas of human interaction. Even if his motives are clearly neither hostile nor sexual, we still find it hard to suppress our reactions to his close approach. Unfortunately, different countries have different ideas about exactly how close is close. It is easy enough to test your own "space reaction": when you are talking to someone in the street or in any open space, reach out with your arm and see where the nearest point on his body comes. If you hail from western Europe, you will find that he is at roughly fingertip distance from you. In other words, as you reach out, your fingers will just about make contact with his shoulder. If you come from eastern Europe, you will find you are standing at "wrist distance." If you come from the Mediterranean region, you will find that you are much closer to your companion, a little more than "elbow distance."

19    Trouble begins when a member of one of these cultures meets and talks to one from another. Say a British diplomat meets an Italian or an Arab diplomat at an embassy function. They start talking in a friendly way, but soon the fingertips man begins to feel uneasy. Without knowing quite why, he starts to back away gently from his companion. The companion edges forward again. Each tries in this way to set up a Personal Space relationship that suits his own background. But it is impossible to do. Every time the Mediterranean diplomat advances to a distance that feels comfortable for him, the British diplomat feels threatened. Every time the Briton moves back, the other feels rejected. Attempts to adjust this situation often lead to a talking pair shifting slowly across a room,

and many an embassy reception is dotted with western-European fingertip-distance men pinned against the walls by eager elbow-distance men. Until such differences are fully understood and allowances made, these minor differences in "body territories" will continue to act as an alienation factor which may interfere in a subtle way with diplomatic harmony and other forms of international transaction.

If there are distance problems when engaged in conversation, then there are clearly **20** going to be even bigger difficulties where people must work privately in a shared space. Close proximity of others, pressing against the invisible boundaries of our personal body-territory, makes it difficult to concentrate on non-social matters. Flat-mates, students sharing a study, sailors in the cramped quarters of a ship, and office staff in crowded workplaces, all have to face this problem. They solve it by "cocooning." They use a variety of devices to shut themselves off from the others present. The best possible cocoon, of course, is a small private room — a den, a private office, a study or a studio — which physically obscures the presence of other nearby territory-owners. This is the ideal situation for non-social work, but the space-sharers cannot enjoy this luxury. Their cocooning must be symbolic. They may, in certain cases, be able to erect small physical barriers, such as screens and partitions, which give substance to their invisible Personal Space boundaries, but when this cannot be done, other means must be sought. One of these is the "favoured object." Each space-sharer develops a preference, repeatedly expressed until it becomes a fixed pattern, for a particular chair, or table, or alcove. Others come to respect this, and friction is reduced. This system is often formally arranged (this is my desk, that is yours), but even where it is not, favoured places soon develop. Professor Smith has a favourite chair in the library. It is not formally his, but he always uses it and others avoid it. Seats around a messroom table, or a boardroom table, become almost personal property for specific individuals. Even in the home, father has his favourite chair for reading the newspaper or watching television. Another device is the blinkers-posture. Just as a horse that over-reacts to other horses and the distractions of the noisy race-course is given a pair of blinkers to shield its eyes, so people studying privately in a public place put on pseudo-blinkers in the form of shielding hands. Resting their elbows on the table, they sit with their hands screening their eyes from the scene on either side.

A third method of reinforcing the body-territory is to use personal markers. Books, **21** papers and other personal belongings are scattered around the favoured site to render it more privately owned in the eyes of companions. Spreading out one's belongings is a well-known trick in public-transport situations, where a traveller tries to give the impression that seats next to him are taken. In many contexts carefully arranged personal markers can act as an effective territorial display, even in the absence of the territory owner. Experiments in a library revealed that placing a pile of magazines on the table in one seating position successfully reserved that place for an average of 77 minutes. If a sports-jacket was added, draped over the chair, then the "reservation effect" lasted for over two hours.

In these ways, we strengthen the defences of our Personal Spaces, keeping out in- **22** truders with the minimum of open hostility. As with all territorial behaviour, the object is to defend space with signals rather than with fists and at all three levels — the tribal, the family and the personal — it is a remarkably efficient system of space-sharing. It does not always seem so, because newspapers and newscasts inevitably magnify the exceptions and dwell on those cases where the signals have failed and wars have broken out, gangs have fought, neighbouring families have feuded, or colleagues have clashed, but for every territorial signal that has failed, there are millions of others that have not. They do not rate a mention in the news, but they nevertheless constitute a dominant feature of human society — the society of a remarkably territorial animal.

# VOCABULARY

a. *paragraph 2:* siege

b. *paragraph 4:* intimidated, encroachment, subservience

c. *paragraph 5:* predominantly

d. *paragraph 6:* regalia, conspicuously

e. *paragraph 7:* conglomeration

f. *paragraph 9:* hierarchy, protracted

g. *paragraph 11:* remnant, conspicuously

h. *paragraph 20:* proximity, messroom

# QUESTIONS

1. What is Morris's basic analogy regarding territorial behaviour? What are his broadest categories of territorial behaviour?

2. Morris also uses classification within his three major divisions. How does he classify nationalities in terms of "personal space"? Does he offer any evidence to support his view?

3. What in Morris's opening paragraph suggests that he accepts the view of man as an innately aggressive animal? Does he offer any evidence to support this view?

# WRITING ASSIGNMENT

Consider a number of practices or rituals that people regularly engage in — formal dinners, graduation exercises, moving house, etc. — and classify and divide them according to various criteria. How does your classification help define each item categorized?

# ANALOGY

Illustrative analogy is a special kind of example, a comparison between two quite different things or activities for the purpose of explanation — a child growing like a tender plant and needing sun, water, and a receptive soil as well as proper care from a skilled gardener. The comparison may be point by point. But there are differences also, and if there is danger of the analogy being carried too far (children are not so tender that they need as much protection as plants from the hazards of living), the writer may state these differences to limit the inferences readers may draw. The writer has chosen the analogy for the sake of vivid illustration and nothing more. We will see later that analogy is often used in argument : children *should* be fully protected from various hazards because they are tender plants. The argument will stand or fall depending on how convinced we are of the similarities and of the unimportance of the differences.

Analogy is often used in explanations of scientific ideas. One of the most famous is Fred Hoyle's analogy between the moving apart of the galaxies in the universe and an expanding raisin cake:

> Suppose the cake swells uniformly as it cooks, but the raisins themselves remain of the same size. Let each raisin represent a cluster of galaxies, and imagine yourself inside one of them. As the cake swells, you will observe that all the other raisins move away from you. Moreover, the farther away the raisin, the faster it will seem to move. When the cake has swollen to twice its initial dimensions, the distance between all the raisins will have doubled itself — two raisins that were initially an inch apart will now be two inches apart; two raisins that were a foot apart will have moved two feet apart. Since the entire action takes place within the same time interval, obviously the more distant raisins must move apart faster than those close at hand. So it happens with the clusters of galaxies.

And Hoyle draws a further conclusion from his analogy:

> No matter which raisin you happen to be inside, the others will always move away from you. Hence the fact that we observe all the other galaxies to be moving away from us does not mean that we are situated at the center of the universe. Indeed, it seems certain that the universe has no center. A cake may be said to have a center only because it has a boundary. We must imagine the cake to extend outward without any boundary, an infinite cake, so to speak, which means that however much cake we care to consider there is always more.

Hoyle points out the limits of the analogy in these final sentences. One advantage of the raisin analogy is the disparity of size between a raisin and a galaxy — a system of sometimes billions of stars occupying an enormous amount of space. The disparity in size provides a relative estimate of size in the universe.

Reasoning about everyday decisions and choices also often uses analogy, as in the decision to buy a book similar in subject and setting to an author's earlier book you enjoyed. Since arguments from analogy make predictions only, you cannot be certain that you will in fact enjoy the book. But you can increase the probability that you will enjoy it — by making the comparison with several books of the author and not just one, and by looking for as many similarities as possible.

These are two important characteristics of good arguments from analogy. A candidate for federal office may argue that she has the same record and personal characteristics as a much admired former member of Parliament. This analogical argument will be even stronger if she makes the comparison with several former MPs instead of with one. Thus she points out that, like them, she was mayor of a large city, held office in years of economic hardship, and had a successful career as a provincial legislator.

Dissimilarities between the candidate and the people cited must not be significant enough to weaken the argument. Differences in height or colour of hair are obviously insignificant and not relevant to the conclusion. But the candidate may have to argue that her being a woman is an insignificant difference, too. She may even use other dissimilarities to strengthen her case. If the MPs cited have the same record of service as the candidate yet are different in gender, race, and background — some coming from small towns and some from large cities — the probability increases that qualifications have to do with the similarities she has cited, despite the differences in gender, race, or background.

Finally, the points of similarity must be relevant to the conclusion and give strength to it: the analogy would be weak if the candidate used the similarities cited to claim she had the same kind of education as did previous MPs. But the analogy does support the limited conclusion that she has the experience to deal with unemployment and the federal deficit intelligently. A limited conclusion could be drawn from a limited analogy if the points of similarity are clearly specified or agreed on, if these points are relevant to the conclusions and if inferences are drawn from these points only.

## SIR JAMES JEANS

*Sir James Jeans (1877–1946), British mathematician and physicist, was educated at Cambridge University. He taught at Cambridge, at Princeton in the United States, and worked at the Mount Wilson Observatory in California, where he studied the structure of stars. As well as being an expert in a number of scientific fields, he is a master of the informal essay. In the following essay, he draws on his scientific expertise and his popularizing skill to explain a natural phenomenon.*

## WHY THE SKY LOOKS BLUE

1    Imagine that we stand on an ordinary seaside pier, and watch the waves rolling in and striking against the iron columns of the pier. Large waves pay very little attention to the columns — they divide right and left and reunite after passing each column, much as a regiment of soldiers would if a tree stood in their road; it is almost as though the columns had not been there. But the short waves and ripples find the columns of the pier a much more formidable obstacle. When the short waves impinge on the columns, they are reflected back and spread as new ripples in all directions. To use the technical term, they are "scattered." The obstacle provided by the iron columns hardly affects the long waves at all, but scatters the short ripples.

2    We have been watching a sort of working model of the way in which sunlight struggles through the earth's atmosphere. Between us on earth and outer space the atmosphere interposes innumerable obstacles in the form of molecules of air, tiny droplets of water, and small particles of dust. These are represented by the columns of the pier.

3    The waves of the sea represent the sunlight. We know that sunlight is a blend of many colors — as we can prove for ourselves by passing it through a prism, or even through a jug of water, or as nature demonstrates to us when she passes it through the raindrops of a summer shower and produces a rainbow. We also know that light consists of waves, and that the different colors of light are produced by waves of different lengths, red light by long waves and blue light by short waves. The mixture of waves which constitutes

sunlight has to struggle past the column of the pier. And these obstacles treat the light waves much as the columns of the pier treat the sea-waves. The long waves which constitute red lights are hardly affected but the short waves which constitute blue light are scattered in all directions.

Thus the different constituents of sunlight are treated in different ways as they struggle 4 through the earth's atmosphere. A wave of blue light may be scattered by a dust particle, and turned out of its course. After a time a second dust particle again turns it out of its course, and so on, until finally it enters our eyes by a path as zigzag as that of a flash of lightning. Consequently the blue waves of the sunlight enter our eyes from all directions. And that is why the sky looks blue.

## VOCABULARY

a. *paragraph 1:* impinge

b. *paragraph 2:* interposes

c. *paragraph 4:* constituents

## QUESTIONS

1. Writers use analogies to make something abstract and difficult concrete and simple. How does Jeans succeed in doing this here?

2. Since light waves and ocean waves are different in many respects, what are the limits of Jean's analogy? What would happen if he pushed it too far, if he, for example, considered tidal waves or choppy seas or whitecaps in his account?

3. Contrast the ways in which the analogy illustrates Jean's point here and the way Huxley's chess analogy (in his essay "A Liberal Education") controls his argument.

## WRITING ASSIGNMENT

Consult a science column in *Omni, Scientific American*, or *The Economist* and note how often science writers use analogies to aid in explanation. Develop your own analogy to explain a complex idea from a discipline you know well.

## PAUL DAVIES

Paul Davies *is a professor of theoretical physics at the University of Newcastle upon Tyne in England and the author of* Other Worlds *and other books that explain the new physics to the general reader. Davies uses an analogy to explain how, according to the Big Bang theory of the origin of the universe, matter expanded in all directions from an "initial singularity" or original compact mass of energy. This expansion slowed down after the initial explosion. Davies offers several explanations for this dissipation of energy or, in the analogy, the fatigue of the runners — one explanation being the spontaneous creation of subatomic particles which slow the expansion.*

## THE EXPANDING UNIVERSE

1    There is a helpful analogy to the expanding universe which should clarify the issue. Consider a large group of people in a tight huddle. Each person represents a region of space enclosed within its own horizon — a "bubble" of space — so to represent the fact that there is no communication between bubbles we equip everyone with blindfolds. Thus, each person is ignorant of the behavior of his fellows. The compact group represents the initial singularity, and when a whistle is blown, the people all start to run in straight lines away from the center of the huddle: the universe expands. The group spreads out in a sort of ring. The runners have instructions that they must adjust their stride so that the ring remains as circular as possible as it expands, but none of the runners knows how fast his neighbors are running, so each picks a random speed. The result is, almost certainly, a ragged, distorted line, very far from circular. There is, of course, a small chance that purely by accident all the runners will match their strides, but it is obviously pretty unlikely. What is observed of the universe today corresponds to a ring of runners so nearly circular that there is no detectable distortion in its shape. How can this have happened: is it a miracle? About ten years ago an ingenious suggestion was made to try and explain this curious symmetry. In the language of the runners it amounts to the following. When the group explodes outwards, some runners will inevitably run faster than their neighbors. However, after a while, fatigue will set in and they will slow down. Their colleagues, on the other hand, will not have dissipated their energy so rapidly and will have enough stamina to catch up. The end result will be, after a long enough time, an approximately circular ring of rather exhausted runners, plodding doggedly outwards at a considerably reduced rate.

2    Translated into cosmological language, the idea is this. In the primeval universe, some regions of space expanded rather more energetically (i.e., faster) than others, and some directions were vigorously stretched while others spread out more sluggishly. Dissipative effects began to sap the energy of the more vigorous motions and slow them down, enabling the sluggish motions to catch up. In the end the turbulent and chaotic early state is damped down and reduced to a rather slow and quiescent motion, with a high degree of uniformity, precisely as observed.

## VOCABULARY

a. *paragraph 1:* dissipated, stamina, cosmological

b. *paragraph 2:* primeval, turbulent, quiescent

## QUESTIONS

1. Each runner in the analogy represents a portion of the compact energy that expands in the Big Bang. To explain the Big Bang, why does Davies blindfold each runner?

2. Why was the ring of runners not a perfect circle in earlier stages of the expansion?

3. How does Davies explain the nearly circular ring observable today by astronomers?

4. What questions about the Big Bang does the analogy not explain for you?

# WRITING ASSIGNMENT

Compare the analogy of Davies with Hoyle's raisin-cake analogy, noting both similarities and differences and the advantages of each in explaining the Big Bang. Is one analogy more effective than the other, or are the analogies equally effective?

# T.H. HUXLEY

*Thomas H. Huxley (1825–1895) was one of nineteenth-century England's most brilliant scientists and writers. In the controversy that arose after the publication of Charles Darwin's* Origin of Species *(1859), Huxley was one of Darwin's leading defenders, advocating the value of the scientific method and the need for greater freedom of debate on controversial subjects. An original contributor to educational theory and practice, Huxley was also an early advocate of a woman's right to full education. In the following essay he conveys his ideas on education by discussing life as a game with an elaborate set of rules which people must be taught.*

# A LIBERAL EDUCATION

Suppose it were perfectly certain that the life and fortune of every one of us would, one day or other, depend upon his winning or losing a game of chess. Don't you think that we should all consider it to be a primary duty to learn at least the names and the moves of the pieces; to have a notion of a gambit, and a keen eye for all the means of giving and getting out of check? Do you not think that we should look with a disapprobation amounting to scorn, upon the father who allowed his son, or the state which allowed its members, to grow up without knowing a pawn from a knight? **1**

Yet it is a very plain and elementary truth, that the life, the fortune, and the happiness of every one of us, and, more or less, of those who are connected with us, depend upon our knowing something of the rules of a game infinitely more difficult and complicated than chess. It is a game which has been played for untold ages, every man and woman of us being one of the two players in a game of his or her own. The chessboard is the world, the pieces are the phenomena of the universe, the rules of the game are what we call the laws of Nature. The player on the other side is hidden from us. We know that his play is always fair, just, and patient. But also we know, to our cost, that he never overlooks a mistake, or makes the smallest allowance for ignorance. To the man who plays well, the highest stakes are paid, with that sort of overflowing generosity with which the strong shows delight in strength. And one who plays ill is checkmated — without haste, but without remorse. **2**

My metaphor will remind some of you of the famous picture in which Retzsch has depicted Satan playing at chess with man for his soul. Substitute for the mocking fiend in that picture, a calm, strong angel who is playing for love, as we say, and would rather lose than win — and I should accept it as an image of human life. **3**

Well, what I mean by Education is learning the rules of this mighty game. In other words, education is the instruction of the intellect in the laws of Nature, under which name I include not merely things and their forces, but men and their ways; and the fashioning of the affections and of the will into an earnest and loving desire to move in harmony with those laws. For me education means neither more nor less than this. Anything which professes to call itself education must be tried by this standard, and if it fails to **4** stand the test, I will not call it education, whatever may be the force of authority, or of numbers, upon the other side.

5       It is important to remember that, in strictness, there is no such thing as an uneducated man. Take an extreme case. Suppose that an adult man, in the full vigor of his faculties, could be suddenly placed in the world, as Adam is said to have been, and then left to do as he best might. How long would he be left uneducated? Not five minutes. Nature would begin to teach him, through the eye, the ear, the touch, the properties of objects. Pain and pleasure would be at his elbow telling him to do this and avoid that; and by slow degrees the man would receive an education, which, if narrow, would be thorough, real, and adequate to his circumstances, though there would be no extras and very few accomplishments.

6       And if to this solitary man entered a second Adam, or better still, an Eve, a new and greater world, that of social and moral phenomena, would be revealed. Joys and woes, compared with which all others might seem but faint shadows, would spring from the new relations. Happiness and sorrow would take the place of the coarser monitors, pleasure and pain; but conduct would still be shaped by the observation of the natural consequences of actions; or, in other words, by the laws of the nature of man.

7       To every one of us the world was once as fresh and new as to Adam. And then, long before we were susceptible of any other mode of instruction, Nature took us in hand, and every minute of waking life brought its educational influence, shaping our actions into rough accordance with Nature's laws, so that we might not be ended untimely by too gross disobedience. Nor should I speak of this process of education as past for any one, be he as old as he may. For every man the world is as fresh as it was at the first day, and as full of untold novelties for him who has the eyes to see them. And Nature is still continuing her patient education of us in that great university, the universe, of which we are all members — Nature having no Test Acts.

8       Those who take honors in Nature's university, who learn the laws which govern men and things and obey them, are the really great and successful men in this world. The great mass of mankind are the "Poll," who pick up just enough to get through without much discredit. Those who won't learn at all are plucked; and then you can't come up again. Nature's pluck means extermination.

9       Thus the question of compulsory education is settled so far as Nature is concerned. Her bill on that question was framed and passed long ago. But, like all compulsory legislation, that of Nature is harsh and wasteful in its operation. Ignorance is visited as sharply as willful disobedience — incapacity meets with the same punishment as crime. Nature's discipline is not even a word and a blow, and the blow first; but the blow without the word. It is left to you to find out why your ears are boxed.

10      The object of what we commonly call education — that education in which man intervenes and which I shall distinguish as artificial education — is to make good these defects in Nature's methods; to prepare the child to receive Nature's education, neither incapably nor ignorantly, nor with willful disobedience; and to understand the preliminary symptoms of her displeasure, without waiting for the box on the ear. In short, all artificial education ought to be an anticipation of natural education. And a liberal education is an artificial education, which has not only prepared a man to escape the great evils of disobedience to natural laws, but has trained him to appreciate and to seize upon the rewards, which Nature scatters with as free a hand as her penalties.

11      That man, I think, has had a liberal education, who has been so trained in youth that his body is the ready servant of his will, and does with ease and pleasure all the work that, as a mechanism, it is capable of; whose intellect is a clear, cold, logic engine, with all its parts of equal strength, and in smooth working order; ready, like a steam engine, to be

turned to any kind of work, and spin the gossamers as well as forge the anchors of the mind; whose mind is stored with a knowledge of the great and fundamental truths of Nature and of the laws of her operations; one who, no stunted ascetic, is full of life and fire, but whose passions are trained to come to heel by a vigorous will, the servant of a tender conscience; who has learned to love all beauty, whether of Nature or of art, to hate all vileness, and to respect others as himself.

Such a one and no other, I conceive, has had a liberal education; for he is, as **12** completely as a man can be, in harmony with Nature. He will make the best of her, and she of him. They will get on together rarely; she as his ever beneficent mother; he as her mouthpiece, her conscious self, her minister and interpreter.

## VOCABULARY

a. *paragraph  1:* gambit, disapprobation

b. *paragraph  6:* monitors

c. *paragraph 11:* gossamers, ascetic

d. *paragraph 12:* beneficent

## QUESTIONS

1. Does Huxley offer specific definitions of general terms like "Nature" and "Education"? If so, what are they?

2. Why does he mention a devil and an angel in paragraph 3?

3. In paragraphs 8 and 9, Huxley seems to divide humanity into an educated elite and an uneducated, undifferentiated mass. Why does his essay take this direction at this point?

4. What analogies does he use in paragraph 11? How important are they?

5. Discuss the weaknesses or limitations of Huxley's life/game of chess analogy?

## WRITING ASSIGNMENT

Think of other analogies that would be illuminating for discussing a subject as large and unwieldy as human life. You might want to consider analogies from sports, politics, warfare, drama, business, or computer science.

## NANCY K. HILL

Nancy K. Hill, *a native of Minnesota, has taught at Yale and at the University of Colorado in Boulder. Her essay on teaching, like that of Hugh MacLennan, depends on comparison — but with the difference that Hill explores a number of popular analogies as a way of establishing her idea that teaching is best compared to mountaineering. Hill in this way combines exposition — her explanation of what makes a good teacher — with argumentative analogy, to be considered in a later section of this book.*

## TEACHING AS MOUNTAINEERING

1    Just recently a committee meeting at the University of Colorado was interrupted by the spectacle of a young man scaling the wall of the library just outside the window. Discussion of new interdisciplinary courses halted as we silently hoped he had discipline enough to return safely to the earth. Hope was all we could offer from our vantage point in Ketchum Hall, the impulse to rush out and catch him being checked by the realization of futility.

2    The incident reinforced my sense that mountaineering serves as an apt analogy for the art of teaching. The excitement, the risk, the need for rigorous discipline all correspond, though the image I have in mind is not that of the solitary adventurer rappelling off a wall, but that of a Swiss guide leading an expedition.

3    I remember a mountaineer named Fritz who once led a group up the Jungfrau at the same time a party was climbing the north face of the Eiger. My own mountaineering skill was slender, and my enthusiasm would have faltered had I not felt Fritz was capable of hauling not only me but all the rest of us off that mountain. Strong, self-assured, calm, he radiated that solid authority that encouraged me to tie on to his rope. But I soon realized that my presence on his line constituted a risk for Fritz. Had I been so foolhardy as to try to retrieve my glove which went tumbling off a precipice, or had I slipped into one of those inexplicably opening crevasses, I might well have pulled the noble Fritz down with me. It was a sobering realization. I, the novice, and he, the expert, were connected by the same lifeline in an experience of mutual interdependence. To give me that top of the world exaltation he, too, was taking a risk.

4    The analogy to teaching seems to me apt, and not just for professors who happen to live in Colorado, for the analogy implies an active acceptance of responsibility for one's own fate, whereas most other analogies to teaching suggest passivity. What is needed to restore teachers' confidence that the profession is significant is a new analogy, a new metaphor (I shy away from the PR word, "image") that conveys more of the essence of teaching than the worn-out analogies we have known. Most previous analogies are seriously inadequate, for while they may describe a part of the teaching activity, they also suggest patterns that are not fully applicable to teaching. It is not a simple matter, for those faulty analogies create misunderstandings about the professor's role, not only in the lay public, but in the professoriate itself. These wrong analogies have contributed to growing demoralization within the profession, and have confused the difficult issue of proper evaluation.

5    The most common analogies to the teacher are the preacher, the shepherd, the curator, the actor, the researcher, and, most insidiously, the salesman. None captures the special relationship between teacher and students, a relationship better described by Socrates as a coming together of friends. Rather than emphasizing the mutuality of the endeavor, each of these common analogies turns on a separation between the professional and his clients. Each leads to a certain kind of evaluation.

6    The preacher exhorts, cajoles, pleads with a congregation often so benighted as to exist in a state of somnolence. He measures his success by the number of souls so stirred as either to commit themselves to his cause, or vehemently to reject it. Somewhat like the preacher is the shepherd who gathers and watches over a flock clearly inferior to himself.

The analogy may be apt for the Lord and his subangelic followers, but it will not do for teacher and students, or, especially, for Socrates and his friends. The Shepherd is likely to be evaluated by the gulf separating his wisdom from that of his flock.

If the poor country curate has often furnished an analogy to the bleating professor, so    7
has the curator of a museum. Lips pursed so as to distil a purer essence of hauteur, the curator as connoisseur points out the rarities of classical cultures to the uninitiated who can scarcely be expected to appreciate these finer things. Since they cannot understand him anyway, the curator has no compunction about sprinkling his presentation with Latin and Greek and with English so esoteric as to sound foreign. Chances are high that the professor as connoisseur will succeed in convincing most of the class that the subject is really the province of a secret society with its own arcane practices and language, best left behind its own inaccessible walls. Indeed, colleagues of the connoisseur measure his success by the paucity of devotees allowed in to the society through this winnowing process.

The teacher as actor also plays to a passive audience, but he measures success by larger    8
numbers. A certain aura of the magician clings to him as he lures spectators into witnessing his academic sleight-of-hand without their ever really getting in on the trick. A certain tinge of the stand-up comedian colors the performance as the actor plays to the audience to register laughs big enough to drown out the lecturer droning on next door.

A bastardized version of the actor is that figure now thought so apt an analogy in our    9
consumer-conscious society: the salesman. His predecessors include the snake-oil man and the door-to-door purveyor of anything from brushes to Britannicas. He or she takes the product to the people, wherever they are, and tailors the pitch to their pockets. While all of these analogies create a certain level of despair in the professoriate either struggling to pattern themselves in a particular mode or hopelessly realizing they can never achieve it, the salesman analogy has the most deleterious effects. No longer adhering even to a prepared script, the salesman shamelessly alters his or her presentation so it will draw the largest number of contented consumers.

The researcher as teacher differs from the previous analogies, and that very distinction    10
is often thought to make him or her a good teacher. Taciturn, solitary, he disdains the performing arts and is content merely to mutter out an assortment of scattered facts to the young only dimly perceived beyond his clouded trifocals. His measure of success is his students' capacity to regurgitate factual data.

None of these analogies comes close enough to the essential magic and majesty of a    11
real learning experience. None even dimly anticipates that self-eradicating feature that is built in to the teaching process, for those who have truly mastered what their teacher has presented no longer need him or her. None accepts as a necessary ingredient in the learning process, activity, the sense of an intellectual excitement so compelling that one's whole being is caught up in it. None acknowledges the peril, and the joy, of encountering those mental deeps Hopkins described.

> . . . the mind, mind has mountains; cliffs of fall
> Frightful, sheer, no-man-fathomed. Hold them cheap
> May who ne'er hung there.

Mountaineering furnishes the needed analogy. The Swiss mountain guide, like the true    12
teacher, has a quiet authority about his very person. He or she engenders trust and confidence so that one is willing to join the endeavor. The mountaineer accepts his leadership role, yet recognizes that the success of the journey (measured by the scaling of the

heights) depends upon close co-operation and active participation by each member of the group. He has crossed the terrain before and is familiar with the landmarks, but each trip is new, and generates its own anxiety and excitement. Essential skills must be mastered if the trip is to be successful; lacking them, disaster looms as an ominous possibility. The very precariousness of the situation necessitates keen focus and rapt attention; slackness, misjudgment, or laziness can bring doom.

13    The teacher as mountaineer learns, as E.M. Forster urged, to connect. The guide rope links mountaineers together so that they may assist each other in the ascent. The effective teacher does something similar by using the oral and written contributions of the students as instructional materials. The teacher also makes other connections, locating the text in its historical setting, forging inter- and intradisciplinary links where plausible, joining the material of the course with the lives of the students, where possible, and with the wider national life beyond the classroom where pertinent.

14    Teaching as mountaineering does not encourage the yellowed lecture note syndrome. Indeed, the analogy does not really encourage lecturing at all. If the student as mountaineer is to be challenged, the student must come to each class session ready and prepared to assist in scaling the next peak, ready to test his or her own abilities against those of the master teacher. Only by arduous and sustained effort does the student approach the mastery of the teacher, and only then is the student ready to assume the role of guide — well-trained in the art of mountaineering, able to take controlled risks, ready to lead others to a mountain-top experience. Not a huckster, not a performer, not a pleader, but a confident, exuberant guide on expeditions of shared responsibility.

15    To encourage and further such mountain-top experiences the society must recognize teaching for the sublime art it is — not merely an offshoot of research, not merely a performance before a passive audience, but a guided expedition into the most exciting and least understood terrain on earth — the mind itself.

## VOCABULARY

a. *paragraph  2:* rappelling

b. *paragraph  3:* novice, interdependence

c. *paragraph  4:* demoralization

d. *paragraph  5:* mutuality

e. *paragraph  6:* exhorts, cajoles, benighted, somnolence, vehemently, subangelic

f. *paragraph  7:* curate, hauteur, connoisseur, compunction, esoteric, arcane, paucity, winnowing

g. *paragraph  9:* bastardized, purveyor

h. *paragraph 10:* taciturn, disdains, trifocals

i. *paragraph 11:* self-eradicating

j. *paragraph 12:* terrain, ominous, precariousness, slackness

k. *paragraph 13:* plausible, pertinent

l. *paragraph 14:* syndrome, exuberant

## QUESTIONS

1. What are the similarities between the teacher and the preacher, the shepherd, the curator, the actor, the researcher, and the salesman? And what differences weaken each analogy for Hill?

2. What are the similarities between the teacher and the mountaineer? What is the mind parallel to in the analogy? What are the differences, and why do they not weaken the analogy for Hill?

3. In what way is the teaching process "self-eradicating"? Why is this feature basic to the true teacher?

4. Does Hill begin the essay with a statement of her thesis, or does she build to it? What do you think she has assumed about her audience in organizing the essay?

## WRITING ASSIGNMENTS

1. Discuss the extent to which you hold one or more of the conceptions of the teacher that Hill believes are mistaken, and give your reasons for holding them. Use this discussion to defend your conception of the ideal teacher.

2. Compare your conception of the ideal teacher with that of Hill. Defend your conception through an example, as she does.

3. Compare two effective teachers in your life. Describe their similarities and differences — in attitude toward students and teaching methods, for example. In a concluding paragraph, discuss how closely these teachers meet the definition of teacher as mountaineer.

4. Discuss how close Hill is in her conception of the teacher to that of Northrop Frye in his essay "Elementary Teaching."

## BROOKS ATKINSON

Brooks Atkinson *was associated throughout his career as a journalist with the* New York Times*, as war correspondent, dramatic critic, and essayist. In 1947 he won the Pulitzer Prize for Foreign Correspondence. In later years he became increasingly concerned with the environment. The essay reprinted here, one of his finest on this subject, is particularly effective in its use of analogy.*

# THE WARFARE IN THE FOREST IS NOT WANTON

1    After thirty-five years the forest in Spruce Notch is tall and sturdy. It began during the Depression when work gangs planted thousands of tiny seedlings in abandoned pastures on Richmond Peak in the northern Catskills. Nothing spectacular has happened there since; the forest has been left undisturbed.

2    But now we have a large spread of Norway spruces a foot thick at the butt and 40 or 50 feet high. Their crowns look like thousands of dark crosses reaching into the sky.

3    The forest is a good place in which to prowl in search of wildlife. But also in search of ideas. For the inescapable fact is that the world of civilized America does not have such a clean record. Since the seedlings were planted the nation has fought three castastrophic wars, in one of which the killing of combatants and the innocent continues. During the lifetime of the forest 350,000 Americans have died on foreign battlefields.

4    Inside America civilized life is no finer. A President, a Senator, a man of God have been assassinated. Citizens are murdered in the streets. Riots, armed assaults, looting, burning, outbursts of hatred have increased to the point where they have become commonplace.

5    Life in civilized America is out of control. Nothing is out of control in the forest. Everything complies with the instinct for survival — which is the law and order of the woods.

6    Although the forest looks peaceful it supports incessant warfare, most of which is hidden and silent. For thirty-five years the strong have been subduing the weak. The blueberries that once flourished on the mountains have been destroyed. All the trees are individuals, as all human beings are individuals; and every tree poses a threat to every other tree. The competition is so fierce that you can hardly penetrate some of the thickets where the lower branches of neighboring trees are interlocked in a blind competition for survival.

7    Nor is the wildlife benign. A red-tailed hawk lived there last summer — slowly circling in the sky and occasionally drawing attention to himself by screaming. He survived on mice, squirrels, chipmunks and small birds. A barred owl lives somewhere in the depth of the woods. He hoots in midmorning as well as at sunrise to register his authority. He also is a killer. Killing is a fundamental part of the process. The nuthatches kill insects in the bark. The woodpeckers dig insects out. The thrushes eat beetles and caterpillars.

8    But in the forest, killing is not wanton or malicious. It is for survival. Among birds of equal size most of the warfare consists of sham battles in which they go through the motions of warfare until one withdraws. Usually neither bird gets hurt.

9    Nor is the warfare between trees vindictive. Although the spruces predominate they do not practice segregation. On both sides of Lost Lane, which used to be a dirt road, maples, beeches, ashes, aspens and a few red oaks live, and green curtains of wild grapes cover the wild cherry trees. In the depths of the forest there are a few glades where the spruces stand aside and birches stretch and grow. The forest is a web of intangible tensions. But they are never out of control. Although they are wild they are not savage as they are in civilized life.

10    For the tensions are absorbed in the process of growth, and the clusters of large cones on the Norway spruces are certificates to a good future. The forest gives an external impression of discipline and pleasure. Occasionally the pleasure is rapturously stated. Soon after sunrise one morning last summer when the period of bird song was nearly over, a solitary rose-breasted grosbeak sat on the top of a tall spruce and sang with great resonance and beauty. He flew a few rods to another tree and continued singing: then to another tree where he poured out his matin again, and so on for a half hour. There was no practical motive that I was aware of.

After thirty-five uneventful years the spruces have created an environment in which a    **11**
grosbeak is content, and this one said so gloriously. It was a better sound than the explosion of bombs, the scream of the wounded, the crash of broken glass, the crackle of burning buildings, the shriek of the police siren.

The forest conducts its affairs with less rancor and malevolence than civilized    **12**
America.

## VOCABULARY

a. *paragraph  8:* wanton, malicious

b. *paragraph  9:* segregation, intangible

c. *paragraph 10:* discipline, resonance, matin

d. *paragraph 12:* rancor, malevolence

## QUESTIONS

1. One sometimes hears the argument that violence is natural to human beings, since we
   are a part of a warring natural world. How does Atkinson implicitly reject this analogy?
   More specifically, what are the points of dissimilarity between the world of the forest
   and the world of humans?

2. How might the world of the forest be used to argue that competition in the world of
   humans need not be destructive of some of those competing — as the argument that
   only the "fit" survive in the world of business implies?

3. How does Atkinson increase the probability of his argument through the details he
   marshals in support of it?

## WRITING ASSIGNMENT

Each of the following statements suggests analogy. Write an essay on one of them, discussing points of similarity and dissimilarity and using this discussion to argue a thesis.

a. The family is a small nation.

b. The nation is a large family.

c. University or college examinations are sporting events.

d. Choosing a university or college is like buying a car.

# COMPARISON AND CONTRAST

Comparison shows the similarities between people, things, or ideas; contrast shows the differences. The word *comparison* sometimes refers to both kinds of analysis, as in this block comparison of President Franklin Roosevelt with Great Britain's wartime prime minister, Winston S. Churchill:

> Roosevelt, as a public personality, was a spontaneous, optimistic, pleasure-loving ruler who dismayed his assistants by the gay and apparently needless abandon with which he seemed to delight in pursuing two or more totally incompatible policies, and astonished them even more by the swiftness and ease with which he managed to throw off the cares of office during the darkest and most dangerous moments. Churchill too loves pleasure, and he too lacks neither gaiety nor a capacity for exuberant self-expression, together with the habit of blithely cutting Gordian knots in a manner which often upset his experts, but he is not a frivolous man. His nature possesses a dimension of depth — and a corresponding sense of tragic possibilities — which Roosevelt's light-hearted genius instinctively passed by. — Sir Isaiah Berlin, "Mr. Churchill"

Block comparisons present the details of the first subject as a whole and then the details of the second. But the author may choose to develop the comparison point by point, as in this second paragraph on Roosevelt and Churchill:

> Roosevelt played the game of politics with virtuosity, and both his successes and his failures were carried off in splendid style; his performance seemed to flow with effortless skill. Churchill is acquainted with darkness as well as light. Like all inhabitants and even transient visitors of inner worlds, he gives evidence of seasons of agonized brooding and slow recovery. Roosevelt might have spoken of sweat and blood, but when Churchill offered his people tears, he spoke a word which might have been uttered by Lincoln or Mazzini or Cromwell, but not by Roosevelt, great-hearted, generous and perceptive as he was. — Berlin, "Mr. Churchill"

Both pararaphs build from similarities to differences. Were the similarities more important, the author would probably have built to them instead. Notice also that the purpose of the comparison is to arrive at a relative estimate of the two men as leaders. We discover the qualities of Roosevelt through Churchill, and those of Churchill through Roosevelt.

Relative estimates are useful in explaining abstract concepts such as nationhood, as in the following extended comparison of Canada and the United States:

> The United States was a revolutionary society which had a Declaration of Independence and a belief in self-evident truths about man's inalienable rights to "life, liberty and the pursuit of happiness." Canada was a conservative society with a British North America Act committed to "peace, order, and good government." The United States was a society that had evolved from history, and took its self-image from the past. For Canada borders were important — they defined its separateness from the United States. Greg Curnoe's "Close the 49th Parallel, etc.," could have been painted in the 1850's as easily as in the 1960's, though the style would have been British Imperial rather than American Pop. For Americans not borders but "frontiers" were what was important. Frontiers were not boundaries, but places to go, to expand. — Ramsay Cook, "Canadian and American Culture"

Although the author is concerned with defining the status of Canada as a country, he does so through a relative estimate that illuminates the special situation of each nation. Only through comparison with other countries that have different histories will we understand Canada better.

The whole essay may use comparison and contrast as one of several methods of analysis or as the single method. As with the paragraph, the analysis may consist of a point-by-point comparison or a block comparison — a comparison of wholes. It is best to use one kind of comparison only; mixing the two kinds can produce a disorganized essay. The following essays combine comparison with examples and other methods of analysis.

# JACOB BRONOWSKI

*A distinguished mathematician, scientist, and writer,* Jacob Bronowski *(1908–74) was born in Poland and educated in England. He went to the United States in 1964, where he taught at various universities and did scientific research at the Salk Institute of Biological Studies in San Diego. Bronowski sought in his many books to bridge the sciences and the humanities. "We are a scientific civilization," he states in his book (and television series)* The Ascent of Man; *"that means, a civilization in which knowledge and its integrity are crucial. Science is only a Latin word for knowledge." Bronowski argues that we cannot afford to be ignorant or unconcerned about the values of science. "Knowledge is not a loose-leaf notebook of facts. Above all, it is a responsibility for the integrity of what we are, primarily of what we are as ethical creatures." Bronowski's comparison of the athlete and the gazelle, in* The Ascent of Man, *illustrates how facts of nature can help us understand ourselves as human beings.*

# THE ATHLETE AND THE GAZELLE

Every human action goes back in some part to our animal origins; we should be cold and lonely creatures if we were cut off from that blood-stream of life. Nevertheless, it is right to ask for a distinction: What are the physical gifts that man must share with the animals, and what are the gifts that make him different? Consider any example, the more straightforward the better — say, the simple action of an athlete when running or jumping. When he hears the gun, the starting response of the runner is the same as the flight response of the gazelle. He seems all animal in action. The heartbeat goes up; when he sprints at top speed the heart is pumping five times as much blood as normal, and ninety per cent of it is for the muscles. He needs twenty gallons of air a minute now to aerate his blood with the oxygen that it must carry to the muscles.    1

The violent coursing of the blood and intake of air can be made visible, for they show up as heat on infra-red films which are sensitive to such radiation. (The blue or light zones are hottest; the red or dark zones are cooler.) The flush that we see and that the infra-red camera analyzes is a by-product that signals the limit of muscular action. For the main chemical action is to get energy for the muscles by burning sugar there; but three-quarters of that is lost as heat. And there is another limit, on the runner and the gazelle equally, which is more severe. At this speed, the chemical burn-up in the muscles is too fast to be complete. The waste products of incomplete burning, chiefly lactic acid, now foul up the blood. This is what causes fatigue, and blocks the muscle action until the blood can be cleansed with fresh oxygen.    2

So far, there is nothing to distinguish the athlete from the gazelle — all that, in one way or another, is the normal metabolism of an animal in flight. But there is a cardinal difference: the runner was not in flight. The shot that set him off was the starter's pistol, and what he was experiencing, deliberately, was not fear but exaltation. The runner is like a    3 child at play; his actions are an adventure in freedom, and the only purpose of his breathless chemistry was to explore the limits of his own strength.

4     Naturally there are physical differences between man and the other animals, even between man and the apes. In the act of vaulting, the athlete grasps his pole, for example, with an exact grip that no ape can quite match. Yet such differences are secondary by comparison with the overriding difference, which is that the athlete is an adult whose behavior is not driven by his immediate environment, as animal actions are. In themselves, his actions make no practical sense at all; they are an exercise that is not directed to the present. The athlete's mind is fixed ahead of him, building up his skill; and he vaults in imagination into the future.

5     Poised for that leap, the pole-vaulter is a capsule of human abilities: the grasp of the hand, the arch of the foot, the muscles of the shoulder and pelvis — the pole itself, in which energy is stored and released like a bow firing an arrow. The radical character in that complex is the sense of foresight, that is, the ability to fix an objective ahead and rigorously hold his attention on it. The athlete's performance unfolds a continuous plan; from one extreme to the other, it is the invention of the pole, the concentration of the mind at the moment before leaping, which give it the stamp of humanity.

## VOCABULARY

a. *paragraph 2:* infra-red, lactic acid

b. *paragraph 3:* metabolism, cardinal, exaltation

## QUESTIONS

1. What similarities between humans and animals does Bronowski develop through his example?

2. What are the differences between the pole vaulter and the gazelle and other animals discussed?

3. In general, what are the physical traits that humans share with animals, and what gifts make humans different?

4. What other comparison between humans and animals could Bronowski have used to distinguish human from animal qualities?

## WRITING ASSIGNMENTS

1. Compare and contrast one of the following pairs of activities, or a similar pair, to arrive at a relative estimate of them and to make a point:

   a. softball and hardball

   b. football and touch football

   c. jogging and running

    d. tennis and badminton

    e. checkers and chess

2. Do the same for one of the following pairs, or a similar pair, of activities:

    a. studying for examinations in different subjects

    b. repairing or changing an automobile and a bicycle tire

    c. driving in a small town and in a large city

## HUGH MACLENNAN

Hugh MacLennan *is a novelist whose nationalist concerns have made him a central figure in the debate about Canada's identity. He was educated at Dalhousie University, at Oxford as a Rhodes scholar, and at Princeton University, where he was awarded a* Ph.D. *in Classics in 1935. He taught in McGill's Department of English from 1951 to 1981. His first novel,* Barometer Rising *(1941), and collection of essays,* Cross-Country *(1949), established MacLennan as an interpreter of Canada, a reputation that he strengthened with subsequent books of essays and such novels of national concerns as* Two Solitudes *(1945) and* The Precipice *(1948). Recipient of a Guggenheim Fellowship in 1943, The Lorne Pierce Medal in 1952, and elected F.R.S.C. in 1953, MacLennan has won the Governor General's Award three times for fiction and twice for non-fiction. In the selection below he draws on his knowledge of Scottish history to suggest some important parallels between Scotland's and Canada's political and economic dependence on their great neighbours to the south.*

## SCOTLAND'S FATE, CANADA'S LESSON

Ever since Washington announced its new economic policies two years ago, such parts of Canada as are political have been living in a trance. This is what often happens to people and nations when they are aware of something new they cannot bear to contemplate because, if they do, they will be confronted with unpleasant decisions they don't know how to make.   1

    It happened to millions of individuals immediately after the 1929 stock market crash. Over the centuries is has happened to many a nation — to the United States, for instance, in the decade before the Civil War when the Americans evaded the fact that their country could not endure half-slave and half-free. And to Britain and France in the 1930s, when neither could endure the idea of another war fought to contain the Germans' ambitions. Ultimately, in such situations, the new reality strikes home. But first comes the national trance.   2

    Canada today faces no Fort Sumter or *blitzkrieg*, but unless we soon make up our minds about our future relations with the United States, we will drift or be pushed into such a position that our nation will become a mere territorial expression of American aspirations — as Scotland is a territorial expression of England.   3

    When I was young I often heard people say, "Canada is the Scotland of North America." Only recently did it occur to me that it might be worthwhile considering the extent to which this is true. There are certainly some obvious parallels. As Scotland is the   4 hard northern cap to the British island, with the rich farmlands and cities of England just below her, so is Canada to the United States. Both countries were gouged by the retreating glaciers, which left them on the subsistence level so far as good farmland was concerned. It also gave them a heritage of spectacular beauty uncrowded by cities and towns, and of this they were both inclined to boast. When one of Boswell's friends told Dr. Johnson that Scotland had "many wild, noble prospects," Johnson retorted that Lapland also had wild noble prospects, but that "the noblest prospect which a Scotchman ever sees is the high-road that leads him to England!"

5      A good many high-roads for a good many years led Canadians into the United States, where most of them maintained a pawky pride in the country they had abandoned. So did the Scotch who went to England. A well-known story has it that when an Edinburgh man returned from a week of business in London and was asked how he liked the English, his reply was, "I don't rightly ken; I was only meeting the heads of companies and they were all Scots." (He should have added that these company heads were permanently lost to Scotland, for invariably they sent their sons to English schools and universities.) Still another resemblance is the belief held by Scotsmen and Canadians that they are more moral than their rich southern neighbors. But the most interesting parallels, of course, are political and economic, and here the resemblances are balanced by many important differences.

6      After centures of insane clan warfare and unspeakable treacheries on the part of nearly all her leaders, Scotland finally destroyed her independence for good and all when the chiefs gave the Pretender enough troops to invade England with the purpose of putting him on the throne. After the English had mowed down this feudal army of sword-wielding clansmen at Culloden, they treated the clans with a ruthlessness worthy of Stalin in the Baltic States. Many were hanged, a few were beheaded and thousands were transported to the southern plantations of America.

7      In spite of a half-century of romantic songs about Bonnie Prince Charlie ("Will ye no come back again?") once the reprisals ended, the majority of influential Scots agreed that the total knockout of nationlist hopes was the best thing that had ever happened to them.

8      Having reduced Scottish nationalism to the harmless level of St. Andrew's Day balls, ceremonial bagpipes and clan tartans, England treated Scotland as part of herself, to the almost unanimous applause of the urban Scots in the Lowlands. The order she imposed, together with the investments she made in Scottish industry, made possible Scotland's so-called Golden Age. True, not many Scots participated in it, but the names of some who did are still in the history books of the world: David Hume, James Watt, McAdam and Telford, Adam Smith, Robert Burns, Walter Scott.

9      But Scotland's Golden Age was short-lived. Even during its brief flowering the fate of most poor Scots, above all the Highlanders, was as tragic as it was sordid. Their own chiefs, still trying to live in the style of English lords, decided to copy the methods of English industrial farming. In order to turn the glens into massive sheep runs they evicted nearly all the inhabitants, burned their crofts, killed or transported any who resisted them. Tens of thousands of starving Highlanders emigrated to Canada, my own forebears among them, and now their descendants here number several millions, many of them speaking French.

10      For at least a century these past miseries and betrayals were never spoken of: the pretense was made that the old book was closed and forgotten. But an experience like that can never be forgotten; it lurks underground in the collective unconscious, as Freud proved toward the end of his life. I am convinced that what Freud called "memory traces on the subconscious" have been responsible for Canada's otherwise bewildering diffi-dence and humbleness in most of her dealings with the United States. We hold in our

collective consciousness a memory of Scotland's loss to England. It accounts for our profound distrust of any expression of self-confident, rational nationalism.

## VOCABULARY

a. *paragraph 3: blitzkrieg*

b. *paragraph 4:* subsistence

c. *paragraph 5:* pawky, ken

d. *paragraph 7:* reprisals

e. *paragraph 8:* Golden Age

f. *paragraph 10:* collective unconscious

## QUESTIONS

1. What is MacLennan's thesis, and where does he first state it? Where does he restate it later in the essay?

2. How does he organize the comparison between the Scots and the Canadians? Does he contrast the Scottish and Canadian patterns point by point or instead deal with one set of patterns first and another set afterward? Or does he mix these methods of organization?

3. How does he illustrate these patterns? Does he illustrate all of them?

4. MacLennan traces cause-and-effect relations through historical comparisons and analogies. What are the chief relations he traces? How valid are the analogies he uses?

5. How do the examples explain the phrase *collective unconscious* in the concluding paragraph? What does MacLennan mean by *national trance*?

6. What is the purpose of the short history of Scotland in paragraphs 6 through 9? What conclusion does MacLennan draw from Scottish history?

## WRITING ASSIGNMENT

Using the comparison and contrast technique, write a short essay about comparable people or things: your parents, two close friends, Canada and the Soviet Union, hockey and baseball.

## STEPHEN LEACOCK

Stephen Leacock *(1869–1944) was the English-speaking world's best-known humorist for the period 1910–1925. Born in England, he moved with his family to a bush farm near*

*Ontario's Lake Simcoe when he was five and was educated at Upper Canada College, the University of Toronto, and the University of Chicago (Ph.D. 1903). From 1903 until his retirement in 1936, he was Professor of Political Economy at McGill University. He divided his year between winters in Montreal and summers in Orillia, Ontario, the small town that inspired the creation of Mariposa in* Sunshine Sketches of a Little Town *(1912). Leacock valued traditional institutions over materialistic ideas of progress, the organic over the mechanistic, and the community over the individual — in a word, his values are those usually associated with the term* humanism. *The piece that follows can be seen to display some of Leacock's humanistic and conservative values in the ironic voice that is uniquely his.*

## THE OLD FARM AND THE NEW FRAME

1    When I left the old farm of my childhood which I described in talking about my remarkable uncle, I never saw it again for years and years. I don't think I wanted to. Most people who come off farms never go back. They talk about it, cry about it — but they don't really go. They know better.

2    If they did go back, they would find, as I did, the old place all changed, the old world all gone, in fact no "farms" any more, no cross-road stores, no villages — nothing in the old sense. A new world has replaced it all.

3    I went back the other day in a motor car to have a look round the locality that I hadn't seen since I left it by means of a horse and buggy more than half a century before. I came to do this because I happened to have been looking at one of those typical "motor ads" that you see in the coloured illustrations, motors glistening to an impossible effulgence, a gravelled drive impossibly neat, beside wide lawns of inconceivable grass and unachievable flower beds. In and beside the motor car were super-world beings as impossible as the grass and flowers around them — youths as square in the shoulders as Greek gods, girls as golden as guineas, and even old age, in the persons of the senior generation, smoothed and beautified to a pink and white as immaculate as youth itself. And as I looked at the picture of this transformed world not yet achieved but at least existing, in the creative mind of the artist, I fell to thinking of all the actual transformation that new invention has brought into our lives.

4    I thought particularly of how it has changed the aspect of what we used to call the country — the country of the horse and buggy days that I so easily recall. So I went back.

5    Our farm was up in a lost corner of Ontario, but the locality doesn't particularly matter. They're all the same from Ontario to Ohio.

6    We lived four and a half miles from "the village." To get to it from our farm you went down a lane — heavy going — up to the hubs in bad weather, then on to a road and up a hill, the same hill really you had just come down only on a different angle; then along a splendid "spin" of at least three hundred yards where you "let the mare out," that is, made her go like blazes (eight miles an hour); then, Whoa! steady! another hill, a mighty steep one, to go down. You had to take it pretty easy. In fact, for the hills you had far better get out and walk, as we generally did; it eased the mare to have us walk up the first hill and it eased the buggy to have us walk down the second.

7    After the second hill, a fine spin of about four hundred yards, good road and "room to pass." You couldn't "let the mare out" all along this, as it might "wind" her; but she could keep going at a pretty smart clip just the same. Then came the "big swamp," about three quarters of a mile or more, in fact. I never knew a road from Maine to the Mississippi that

didn't have a swamp in it. A lot of the big swamp was "corduroy" road. The word means *cord du roi*, or king's rope, but the thing meant logs laid side by side with dirt shoveled over them. In the swamp there was no room to pass except by a feat of engineering in chosen spots.

After the swamp you went on over a succession of "spins" and "hills," the mare alternately "eased" and "winded" and "let out" — and at last, there you were, in the village street — yes, sir, right in the village, under an hour, pretty good going, eh? Cover the mare up with a blanket while we go into the tavern or she may get the "heaves" — or the "humps" — or I forget what; anyway it was what a mare got if you stayed too long in the tavern. **8**

And the village street, how well I remember it! Romantic, well, I don't know; I suppose it was. But it was just a street — stores on each side with a square sign over each. Trees here and there. Horses hitched to posts asleep; a grist mill at the end where the river hit the village or the village hit the river, I forget which. There were no fancy signs, no fancy stores. The sole place of entertainment was the tavern — beer 5 cents, whisky 5 cents, mixed drinks (that means beer with whisky or whisky mixed with beer) 5 cents. Food, only at meal times, at a York shilling a meal, later raised to a quarter. **9**

Such was the typical farm road and village of fifty years ago — a "social cell" as I believe the sociologists would call us. **10**

Now look at the change. I visited it, as I say, the other day in a large smooth-running motor car — this "social cell" from which I emerged fifty years ago. Changed? The word isn't adequate. It just wasn't there any more. In the first place some one had changed our old farm-house into a "farmstead". You see, you can't live any longer on a farm if you're going to have people coming to see you in motor cars — golden girls, Apollo boys and Joan and Darby elders. You must turn the place into a "farmstead" — with big shingles all over it in all directions — with a "loggia" in front and a "pergola" at the side. **11**

And the road? All gone, all changed. A great highway swept by in its course and sheared lane and hills into one broad, flat curve; threw aside the second hill into a mere nothing of a "grade," with a row of white posts; and the swamp, it has passed out of existence to become a broad flat with a boulevarded two-way road, set with new shingled bungalows with loggias and pergolas, overgrown with wistaria and perugia, and all trying to live up to the passing motor cars. There's a tea room now where the spring used to be, in the centre of the swamp, the place where we watered the mare to prevent her blowing. **12**

But you hardly see all this — the whole transit from farmstead to village by the sweeping, shortened concrete road is just three minutes. You are in the village before you know it. **13**

And the village itself! Why, it's another place. What charm is this, what magic this transformation? I hardly know the place; in fact, I don't know it. The whole length of it now is neat with clipped grass and the next-to-impossible flowers copied from the motor car advertisements; there are trim little cedars and box hedges, trees clipped to a Versailles perfection and house fronts all aglow with variegated paint and hanging flowers. . . . And the signs, what a multitude of them; it's like a mediaeval fair! "Old English Tea Room"! I didn't know this was England! And no, it isn't; see the next sign, "Old Dutch Tea Room," and "Old Colony Rest House"! and "Normandy Post House"! No, it's not England; I don't know where it is. **14**

But those signs are only a fraction of the total, each one vying with the last in the art of its decoration or the angle of its suspension. "Joe's Garage"! Look at it — built like a little Tudor house, half-timbered in black and white. Joe's grandfather was the village blacksmith, I remember him well, and his "blacksmith shop" was a crazy sort of wooden shed, out of slope, with no front side in particular and a forge in it. If they had it now they would label it "Ye Olde Forge" and make it an out-of-town eating place. **15**

16    But these new signs mean that, for the people who ride from the city, in the motor cars, the village and its little river has become a "fishing resort." You see, it's only fifty-six miles from the city; you run out in an hour or so. You can rent a punt for $1 and a man to go with you and row for another $1 — or he'll fish for you, if you like. Bait only costs about 50 cents and you can get a fine chicken dinner, wine and all, from about $2. In short, you have a wonderful time and only spend $10; yet when I was young if you had $10 in the village no one could change it, and $10 would board you for a month.

17    And the people too! A new kind of people seems to have come into — or, no, grown up in — the village. I find, on examination, that they're really the grandsons and graddaughters of the people who were there. But the new world has taken hold of them and turned them into a new and different sort of people — into super people, as it were.

18    Joe Hayes for example — you remember his grandfather, the blacksmith — has turned into a "garage man," handy, efficient, knowing more than a science college, a friend in distress. What the horse-and-buggy doctor of the countryside was to the sick of fifty years ago, such is now the garage man to the disabled motor car and its occupants towed into his orbit. People talk now of their mimic roadside adventures and tell how there "wasn't a garage man within five miles" as people used to tell of having to fetch the doctor at night over five miles of mud and corduroy.

19    And Joe's brothers and cousins have somehow turned into motor-men of all sorts, taxi-men, and even that higher race, the truckmen. What the "draymen" of Old London were, admired for their bulk and strength even by the fairest of the ladies, so today are the "truckmen" who have stepped into their place in evolution. . . .

20    Nor is it one sex only that the motor has transformed. People who live in a village where motors come and go must needs take thought for their appearance. See that sign BEAUTY PARLOR! You'd hardly think that that means Phoebe Crawford, whose great-aunt was the village seamstress. Or that other sign, GEORGETTE: LINGERIE, that's Mary Ann Crowder. Her grandfather was Old Man Crowder up the river.

21    Changed, isn't it? Wonderfully changed, into a sort of prettier and brighter world. And if a little "social cell" has changed like this, it's only part of the transformation that has redecorated all our world.

22    The only trouble is to live up to it — to be as neat and beautiful as a beauty parlor girl, as friendly as a garage man, as bold and brave as a truck driver and as fit guest to sit down to a frogs' legs dinner in an Old Mill chophouse.

23    Alas! This happy world that might have been, that seemed about to be! The transformation from the grim and sombre country-side to all this light and colour, had it only just begun to be overwhelmed and lost in the shadow of War?

24    Perhaps the old farm had something to it after all.

## VOCABULARY

a. *paragraph   3:* effulgence, guineas

b. *paragraph 11:* loggias, pergolas

c. *paragraph 12:* wistaria, perugia

d. *paragraph 19:* draymen

## QUESTIONS

1. How does Leacock organize his essay? How else could he have compared and contrasted his material?

2. How do the details contrasted in paragraphs 9 and 14 reveal Leacock's attitude toward the village today?

3. What emotions does Leacock convey, and what examples can you cite of details that convey these emotions and create a mood?

4. How well does the essay convey the sense of then and now?

5. Rewrite the last sentence of paragraph 23 as a statement. How does your revision affect the emphasis of ideas in the original sentence?

6. Where does Leacock mix short and long sentences to stress certain perceptions and feelings?

## WRITING ASSIGNMENTS

1. Leacock says in his unfinished autobiography: "I was born in Victorian England, on December thirteenth in 1869, which is exactly the middle of Queen Victoria's reign. . . . I am certain that I have never got over it." Discuss how his comparison of his home town past and present illustrates these statements. Then develop the same idea from your own personal experience and observation.

2. Write a characterization of Stephen Leacock, the man and the humorist, through the details and other revealing features of his essay. Accentuate the qualities that most stand out.

## CASEY MILLER AND KATE SWIFT

Casey Miller *has worked in publishing and as a freelance writer and editor.* Kate Swift *is also a freelance writer and editor and has been a science writer for the American Museum of Natural History, and a news director for the Yale School of Medicine. The discussion reprinted here is taken from* Words and Women *(1976) — a book concerned with the influence of language on the lives of women.*

## "MANLY" AND "WOMANLY"

Webster's Third New International Dictionary (1966) defines *manly* as "having qualities appropriate to a man: not effeminate or timorous; bold, resolute, open in conduct or bearing." The definition goes on to include "belonging or appropriate in character to a man" (illustrated by "manly sports" and "beer is a manly drink"), "of undaunted courage: gallant, brave." The same dictionary's definition of *womanly* is less specific, relying heavily on phrases like "marked by qualities characteristic of a woman"; "possessed of the

1

character or behavior befitting a grown woman"; "characteristic of, belonging to, or suitable to a woman's nature and attitudes rather than to a man's." Two of the examples provided are more informative: "convinced that drawing was a waste of time, if not downright womanly . . . " and "her usual womanly volubility."

2    In its definition of *manly* the Random House Dictionary of the English Language (1967) supplies the words "strong, brave, honorable, resolute, virile" as "qualities usually considered desirable in a man" and cites "feminine; weak, cowardly," as antonyms. Its definitions of *womanly* are "like or befitting a woman; feminine; not masculine or girlish" and "in the manner of, or befitting, a woman." The same dictionary's synonym essays for these words are worth quoting in full because of the contrasts they provide:

> MANLY, MANFUL, MANNISH mean possessing the qualities of a man. MANLY implies possession of the most valuable or desirable qualities a man can have, as dignity, honesty, directness, etc., in opposition to servility, insincerity, underhandedness, etc.: *A manly foe is better than a weak friend.* It also connotes courage, strength, and fortitude: *manly determination to face what comes.* MANFUL stresses the reference to courage, strength, and industry: *manful resistance.* MANNISH applies to that which resembles man: *a boy with a mannish voice.* Applied to a woman the term is derogatory, suggesting the aberrant possession of masculine characteristics: *a mannish girl; a mannish stride.*

> WOMANLY, WOMANLIKE, WOMANISH mean resembling a woman. WOMANLY implies resemblance in appropriate, fitting ways: *womanly decorum, modesty.* WOMANLIKE, a neutral synonym, may suggest mild disapproval or, more rarely, disgust: *Womanlike, she (he) burst into tears.* WOMANISH usually implies an inappropriate resemblance and suggests weakness or effeminacy: *womanish petulance.*

3    What are these parallel essays saying? That we perceive males in terms of human qualities, females in terms of qualities — often negative — assigned to them as females. The qualities males possess may be good or bad, but those that come to mind when we consider what makes "a man" are positive. Women are defined circularly, through characteristics seen to be appropriate or inappropriate to women — not to human beings. In fact, when women exhibit positive attributes considered typical of men — dignity, honesty, courage, strength, or fortitude — they are thought of as aberrant. A person who is "womanlike" may (although the term is said to be "neutral") prompt a feeling of disgust.

4    The broad range of positive characteristics used to define males could be used to define females too, of course, but they are not. The characteristics of women — weakness is among the most frequently cited — are something apart. At its entry for *woman* Webster's Third provides this list of "qualities considered distinctive of womanhood": "Gentleness, affection, and domesticity or on the other hand fickleness, superficiality, and folly." Among the "qualities considered distinctive of manhood" listed in the entry for *man*, no negative attributes detract from the "courage, strength, and vigor" the definers associate with males. According to this dictionary, *womanish* means "unsuitable to a man or to a strong character or either sex."

5    Lexicographers do not make up definitions out of thin air. Their task is to record how words are used, it is not to say how they should be used. The examples they choose to illustrate meanings can therefore be especially revealing of cultural expectations. The American Heritage Dictionary (1969), which provides "manly courage" and "masculine charm," also gives us "Woman is fickle," "brought out the woman in him," "womanly virtue," "feminine allure," "feminine wiles," and "womanish tears." The same dictionary defines *effeminate*, which comes from the Latin *effeminare*, meaning "to make a woman out of," as "having the qualities associated with women; not characteristic of man; unman-

ly" and "characterized by softness, weakness, or lack of force; not dynamic or vigorous." For synonyms one is referred to *feminine*.

*Brother* and *sister* and their derivatives have acquired similar features. A columnist who wrote that "the political operatives known as 'Kennedy men' and 'Nixon men' have been sisters under their skins" could not possibly have called those adversaries "brothers," with all the mutual respect and loyalty that word implies. As the writer explained, "Like the colonel's lady and Judy O'Grady, their styles were different but their unwavering determination to win was strikingly similar." Other kinds of sisters for whom no comparable male siblings exist include the sob sister, the weak sister, and the plain ordinary sissy, whose counterpart in the brotherhood is the buddy, a real pal. Like *effeminate*, these female-related words and phrases are applied to males when a cutting insult is intended. **6**

Masculine, manly, manlike, and other male-associated words used to compliment men are frequently also considered complimentary when applied to women: thus a woman may be said to have manly determination, to have a masculine mind, to take adversity like a man, or to struggle manfully against overwhelming odds. The one male-associated word sometimes used to insult her is *mannish*, which may suggest she is too strong or aggressive to be a true woman, or that she is homosexually oriented, in which case *mannish* can become a code word. **7**

Female-associated words, on the other hand, must be hedged, as in "He has almost feminine intuition," if they are used to describe a man without insulting him. He may be praised for admirable qualities defined as peculiar to women, but he cannot be said to have womanly compassion or womanlike tenderness. In exceptions to this rule — for example, when a medic on the battlefield or a sports figure in some postgame situation of unusual drama is said to be "as gentle as a woman" — the life-and-death quality of the circumstances makes its own ironic and terrible commentary on the standards of "masculinity" ordinarily expected of men. **8**

The role expectations compressed into our male-positive-important and female-negative-trivial words are extremely damaging, as we are beginning to find out. The female stereotypes they convey are obvious, but the harm doesn't stop there. The inflexible demands made on males, which allow neither for variation nor for human frailty, are dehumanizing. They put a premium on a kind of perfection that can be achieved only through strength, courage, industry, and fortitude. These are admirable qualities, but if they are associated only with males, and their opposites are associated only with females, they become sex-related demands that few individuals can fulfill. **9**

## VOCABULARY

a. *paragraph 1:* timorous, undaunted, volubility

b. *paragraph 2:* virile, antonyms, servility, fortitude, derogatory, aberrant, decorum, petulance

c. *paragraph 5:* lexicographers, fickle, allure, wiles

## QUESTIONS

1. The Miller-Swift essay illustrates the use of moderate antithesis in ordinary exposition — antithesis arising naturally from a contrast of ideas. In how many ways do the writers contrast words and attitudes relating to assumed masculine and feminine qualities?

2. What elements in the second sentence of paragraph 3 are antithetical? What elements in later sentences of the same paragraph are also antithetical?

3. Identify antithetical phrases or clauses in the following:

   a. paragraph 5, sentence 2

   b. paragraph 6, sentence 3

   c. paragraph 8, sentence 2

   d. paragraph 9, sentence 1

   How does the antithesis sharpen the contrast of ideas in these sentences?

4. Do you agree that language today makes "sex-related demands that few individuals can fulfill"? Do movies and television make similar demands?

## WRITING ASSIGNMENTS

1. Discuss the extent to which the attitudes toward men and women contained in the dictionary definitions discussed are reflected in prevailing attitudes toward work or recreation. Draw on your own experience for examples. Disagree with Miller and Swift if your experience suggests attitudes different from those they identify.

2. Analyse your own conception of manliness and womanliness, contrasting ideas where possible and using moderate antithesis in some of your sentences.

## GLORIA STEINEM

Gloria Steinem *was co-founder of the pioneering feminist magazine* Ms. *She has written extensively on a wide range of subjects, including her first-hand experience working as a Playboy bunny in one of Hugh Hefner's Playboy Clubs. In the essay that follows she shows how differences between erotica and pornography indicate some of the attitudes that result in sexual violence against women and sexual stereotyping generally.*

## EROTICA VS. PORNOGRAPHY: A CLEAR AND PRESENT DIFFERENCE

1    Human beings are the only animals that experience the same sex drive at times when we can — and cannot — conceive.

2    Just as we developed uniquely human capacities for language, planning, memory, and invention along our evolutionary path, we also developed sexuality as a form of expression; a way of communicating that is separable from our need for sex as a way of perpetuating ourselves. For humans alone, sexuality can be and often is primarily a way of bonding, of giving and receiving pleasure, bridging differentness, discovering sameness, and communicating emotion.

3    We developed this and other human gifts through our ability to change our environment, adapt physically, and in the long run, to affect our own evolution. But as an

emotional result of this spiraling path away from other animals, we seem to alternate between periods of exploring our unique abilities to forge new boundaries, and feelings of loneliness in the unknown that we ourselves have created; a fear that sometimes sends us back to the comfort of the animal world by encouraging us to exaggerate our sameness.

The separation of "play" from "work", for instance, is a problem only in the human world. So is the difference between art and nature, or an intellectual accomplishment and a physical one. As a result, we celebrate play, art, and invention as leaps into the unknown; but any imbalance can send us back to nostalgia for our primate past and the conviction that the basics of work, nature, and physical labor are somehow more worthwhile or even moral.   **4**

In the same way, we have explored our sexuality as separable from conception: a pleasurable, empathetic bridge to strangers of the same species. We have even invented contraception — a skill that has probably existed in some form since our ancestors figured out the process of birth — in order to extend this uniquely human difference. Yet we also have times of atavistic suspicion that sex is not complete — or even legal or intended-by-god — if it cannot end in conception.   **5**

No wonder the concepts of "erotica" and "pornography" can be so crucially different, and yet so confused. Both assume that sexuality can be separated from conception, and therefore can be used to carry a personal message. That's a major reason why, even in our current culture, both may be called equally "shocking" or legally "obscene," a word whose Latin derivative means "dirty, containing filth." This gross condemnation of all sexuality that isn't harnessed to childbirth and marriage has been increased by the current backlash against women's progress. Out of fear that the whole patriarchal structure might be upset if women really had the autonomous power to decide our reproductive futures (that is, if we controlled the most basic means of production), right-wing groups are not only denouncing prochoice abortion literature as "pornographic," but are trying to stop the sending of all contraceptive information through the mails by invoking obscenity laws. In fact, Phyllis Schlafly recently denounced the entire Women's Movement as "obscene."   **6**

Not surprisingly, this religious, visceral backlash has a secular, intellectual counterpart that relies heavily on applying the "natural" behavior of the animal world to humans. That is questionable in itself, but these Lionel Tiger-ish studies make their political purpose even more clear in the particular animals they select and the habits they choose to emphasize. The message is that females should accept their "destiny" of being sexually dependent and devote themselves to bearing and rearing their young.   **7**

Defending against such reaction in turn leads to another temptation: to merely reverse the terms, and declare that *all* nonprocreative sex is good. In fact, however, this human activity can be as constructive or destructive, moral or immoral, as any other. Sex as communication can send messages as different as life and death; even the origins of "erotica" and "pornography" reflect that fact. After all, "erotica" is rooted in *eros* or passionate love, and thus in the idea of positive choice, free will, the yearning for a particular person. (Interestingly, the definition of erotica leaves open the question of gender.) "Pornography" begins with a root meaning "prostitution" or "female captives," thus letting us know that the subject is not mutual love, or love at all, but domination and violence against women. (Though, of course, homosexual pornography may imitate this violence by putting a man in the "feminine" role of victim.) It ends with a root meaning "writing about" or "description of" which puts still more distance between subject and object, and replaces a spontaneous yearning for closeness with objectification and a voyeur.   **8**

The difference is clear in the words. It becomes even more so by example.   **9**

Look at any photo or film of people making love; really making love. The images may be diverse, but there is usually a sensuality and touch and warmth, an acceptance of   **10** bodies and nerve endings. There is always a spontaneous sense of people who are there because they *want* to be, out of shared pleasure.

11    Now look at any depiction of sex in which there is clear force, or an unequal power that spells coercion. It may be very blatant, with weapons of torture or bondage, wounds and bruises, some clear humiliation, or an adult's sexual power being used over a child. It may be much more subtle: a physical attitude of conqueror and victim, the use of race or class difference to imply the same thing, perhaps a very unequal nudity, with one person exposed and vulnerable while the other is clothed. In either case, there is no sense of equal choice or equal power.

12    The first is erotic: a mutually pleasurable, sexual expression between people who have enough power to be there by positive choice. It may or may not strike a sense-memory in the viewer, or be creative enough to make the unknown seem real; but it doesn't require us to identify with a conqueror or a victim. It is truly sensuous, and may give us a contagion of pleasure.

13    The second is pornographic: its message is violence, dominance, and conquest. It is sex being used to reinforce some inequality, or to create one, or to tell us the lie that pain and humiliation (ours or someone else's) are really the same as pleasure. If we are to feel anything, we must identify with conqueror or victim. That means we can only experience pleasure through the adoption of some degree of sadism or masochism. It also means that we may feel diminished by the role of conqueror, or enraged, humiliated, and vengeful by sharing identity with the victim.

14    Perhaps one could simply say that erotica is about sexuality, but pornography is about power and sex-as-weapon — in the same way we have come to understand that rape is about violence, and not really about sexuality at all.

15    Yes, it's true that there are women who have been forced by violent families and dominating men to confuse love with pain, so much so that they have become masochists. (A fact that in no way excuses those who administer such pain.) But the truth is that, for most women — and for men with enough humanity to imagine themselves into the predicament of women — true pornography could serve as aversion therapy for sex.

16    Of course, there will always be personal differences about what is and is not erotic, and there may be cultural differences for a long time to come. Many women feel that sex makes them vulnerable and therefore may continue to need more sense of personal connection and safety before allowing any erotic feelings. We now find competence and expertise erotic in men, but that may pass as we develop those qualities in ourselves. Men, on the other hand, may continue to feel less vulnerable, and therefore more open to such potential danger as sex with strangers. As some men replace the need for submission from childlike women with the pleasure of cooperation from equals, they may find a partner's competence to be erotic, too.

17    Such group changes plus individual differences will continue to be reflected in sexual love between people of the same gender, as well as between women and men. The point is not to dictate sameness, but to discover ourselves and each other through sexuality that is an exploring, pleasurable, empathetic part of our lives; a human sexuality that is unchained both from unwanted pregnancies and from violence.

18    But that is a hope, not a reality. At the moment, fear of change is increasing both the indiscriminate repression of all nonprocreative sex in the religious and "conservative" male world, and the pornographic vengeance against women's sexuality in the secular world of "liberal" or "radical" men. It's almost futuristic to debate what is and is not truly erotic, when many women are again being forced into compulsory motherhood, and the number of pornographic murders, tortures, and woman-hating images are on the increase in both popular culture and real life.

It's a familiar division: wife or whore, "good" woman who is constantly vulnerable to **19** pregnancy or "bad" woman who is unprotected from violence. *Both* roles would be upset if we were to control our own sexuality. And that's exactly what we must do.

In spite of all our atavistic suspicions and training for the "natural" role of motherhood, **20** we took up the complicated battle for reproductive freedom. Our bodies had borne the health burden of endless births and poor abortions, and we had a greater motive for separating sexuality and conception.

Now we have to take up the equally complex burden of explaining that all nonpro- **21** creative sex is *not* alike. We have a motive: our right to a uniquely human sexuality, and sometimes even to survival. As it is, our bodies have too rarely been enough our own to develop erotica in our own lives, much less in art and literature. And our bodies have too often been the objects of pornography and the woman-hating, violent practice that it preaches. Consider also our spirits that break a little each time we see ourselves in chains or full labial display for the conquering male viewer, bruised or on our knees, screaming a real or pretended pain to delight the sadist, pretending to enjoy what we don't enjoy, to be blind to the images of our sisters that really haunt us — humiliated often enough ourselves by the truly obscene idea that sex and the domination of women must be combined.

Sexuality *is* human, free, separate — and so are we. **22**

But until we untangle the lethal confusion of sex with violence, there will be more **23** pornography and less erotica. There will be little murders in our beds — and very little love.

# VOCABULARY

a. *paragraph  2:* perpetuating, bonding

b. *paragraph  4:* primate

c. *paragraph  5:* empathetic, atavistic

d. *paragraph  6:* patriarchal, autonomous

e. *paragraph  7:* visceral, secular

f. *paragraph  8:* nonprocreative, gender, objectification, voyeur

g. *paragraph 10:* diverse, sensuality

h. *paragraph 11:* coercion, blatant, bondage, humiliation

i. *paragraph 12:* contagion

j. *paragraph 13:* sadism, masochism, diminished

k. *paragraph 15:* predicament, aversion

l. *paragraph 18:* indiscriminate, repression, compulsory

m. *paragraph 23:* lethal

## QUESTIONS

1. In what ways does Steinem use comparison and contrast in paragraphs 1 through 5 to establish the basis of her comparison of erotica and pornography?

2. In paragraphs 10 and 11, Steinem establishes an important difference between the messages conveyed by erotica and pornography. How would you describe that difference?

3. Paragraph 14 suggests a similarity between pornography and rape. Does the comparison stand up to analysis?

4. In paragraph 19, Steinem contrasts two extreme views of "woman" and suggests that this radicalization of a woman's role is one of the roots of violent pornography. Does she offer any solution to this "image" problem?

## WRITING ASSIGNMENT

Write a polemical essay that considers the similarities and differences between the male and female attitudes toward sports, children, home, or a subject of your own choosing. Consider the gender stereotyping associated with your chosen subject and whether such sexism is unfair.

# DEFINITION

There are many ways of defining something, and the way we choose depends on our purpose. If we are in a store that advertises "Submarine Sandwiches" and a visitor asks what these are, we can point to one on the counter. But pointing may not be enough: we may have to explain or "denote" what a submarine sandwich is — that is, single the submarine out from all other things like it. In a denotative definition we can start with a classification of things like food and single the submarine out from all other kinds. But since the visitor knows a submarine is something to eat, we can limit our class to sandwiches.

A dictionary definition usually gives us a denotative definition of this sort — identifying first the class or genus of objects to which the word belongs and then distinguishing the word by its specific difference. As we noted, the class or genus may be broad (*food*) or it may be narrow (*sandwich*). The following dictionary definition of a submarine chooses a narrow genus:

> **Sub·ma·rine**[2] a large sandwich consisting of a long roll that is split lengthwise and filled with a variety of cold meats, cheese, tomatoes, onions, coleslaw, etc. — *Gage Canadian Dictionary*

Sometimes we want to do more than merely name or identify an object: we want to present ideas and impressions, the emotional aura we associate with it. The word *rose* has a precise denotation — a particular flower with describable properties. It also has a range of connotations or associations. Thus roses are often associated with success or happiness, and we recognize this association in the popular expression "a rosy future." Connotations may be positive in their implication, or negative. Though the words *inexpensive* and *cheap* both mean low in price, *cheap* usually carries the connotation of poor quality or of something contemptible. *Inexpensive* is an emotionally neutral word; *cheap* is not.

Denotative and connotative definitions tell us how words are used currently. Sometimes we find it helpful to give the original meaning, or etymology, to claify the current meaning — for example, to explain that the word *gravity* comes from the Latin *gravitas* meaning weight or heaviness. But we must be careful not to assume that a current word possesses, or should possess, its original meaning. The word *sinister* originally meant "of or on the left," but this meaning is rare today, and we would certainly be misunderstood if we used *sinister* to refer to a left-handed person. But notice how the etymology of *sinister* helps to explain an expression like a left-handed compliment.

We can use definition to clarify the meanings of words that have become indefinite or confused in popular usage. We sometimes call this kind of definition *precising*. Another use of definition is to stipulate or propose a name or term for a newly discovered phenomenon so that we can refer to it. An example is the term *quasar*, proposed in the 1960s for newly discovered "quasi-stellar" sources of light in the sky that seem not to be stars. Stipulative definitions are proposed with the understanding that the term may change later as more is discovered. By contrast, theoretical definitions propose an explanation or theory of the phenomenon: they do not merely propose a term for discussion and further research. Most textbook definitions of democracy and similar ideas are theoretical. In giving definitions, we should be clear about the use we are making of them. It will matter to the reader whether we are trying to make a commonly used word more exact in its usage or proposing a definition without claiming to know the whole truth about it.

# RICHARD B. WRIGHT

Richard B. Wright *has worked in publishing in Toronto and has taught at Ridley College in St. Catharines, Ontario, though he is now a full-time writer. His works include* In the Middle of a Life *(1973),* Farthing's Fortunes *(1976),* Final Things *(1980), and* Tourists *(1984). His first novel,* The Weekend Man *(1970), from which the following definition of "the weekend man" is taken, is one of the most evocative and compelling novels of the '70s. Its re-creation of a suburban world, as seen through the eyes of a quiet and thoughtful outsider, is an extraordinary blend of vivid detail and extended meditation conveyed by an engagingly original voice.*

## THE WEEKEND MAN

1    What is a weekend man you ask? A weekend man is a person who has abandoned the present in favour of the past or the future. He is really more interested in what happened to him twenty years ago or in what is going to happen to him next week than he is in what is happening to him today. If the truth were known nothing much happens to most of us during the course of our daily passage. It has to be said. Unless we are test pilots or movie stars most of us are likely to wake up tomorrow morning to the same ordinary flatness of our lives. This is not really such a bad thing. It is probably better than fighting off a sabre-tooth tiger at the entrance to the cave. But we weekend men never leave well enough alone. First off we must cast about for a diversion. A diversion is anything that removes us from the ordinary present. Sometimes we divert ourselves into our own pasts. This is more likely to happen as we grow older. I am only thirty, for instance, but in the course of an average day I sometimes shake my head a dozen times to keep from sinking into my own past. Diverting oneself into the past would not be so bad if it didn't bring on the *nostalgies*. But, of course, it does, and a severe case of the *nostalgies* can often as not leave a person worse off than he was before.

2    It is also possible to divert oneself into the future; that is, look forward to something that is going to happen to you on Friday night or next July twenty-third. This is alright except that it never happens the way you imagine it will: in fact it's just as likely to turn into a disappointment. And that can plunge a person into the worst kind of despair. The weekend man simply never learns to live with the thundering ironies. He is forever looking backwards and being afflicted by a painful sense of loss or he is looking forward and being continually disappointed. What to do? Well, you'll have to work it out for yourself. I myself just drift along, hoping that the daily passage will deliver up a few painless diversions. Most of the time, however, I am quietly gritting my teeth and just holding on.

## VOCABULARY

a. *paragraph 2:* ironies, diversions

## QUESTIONS

1. Why is the denotative definition of "weekend" appropriate to Wright's expression "weekend man"?

2. Does the phrase have positive or negative connotations?

3. What part do the expressions "nostalgies" and "thundering ironies" play in the definition of "weekend man"?

4. What is the tone of the paragraph — the voice of the writer that you hear in reading it? Serious, sarcastic, bemused, ironic? What evidence in the passage supports your description of its tone?

## WRITING ASSIGNMENTS

1. Invent an expression that describes a group engaged in what Wright calls a "diversion" from the "ordinary present." Discuss the characteristics of such a group.

2. First give the denotative meaning of the name of a rock group. Then give its connotations and, if you can, explain their origin. Use your definition to make a point.

## TIME

*The following discussion of euphemism is the first of a number of selections in this book concerned with misuses of language. William Zinsser, in the essay on the virtues of simplicity that appears later in this book, discusses the consequences of the "viscous language" of everyday life illustrated here. Notice how* Time *combines etymological with other kinds of definition to explain euphemism.*

## EUPHEMISM

From a Greek word meaning "to use of good omen," euphemism is the substitution of a pleasant term for a blunt one — telling it like it isn't. Euphemism has probably existed since the beginning of language. As long as there have been things of which men thought the less said the better, there have been better ways of saying less. In everyday conversation the euphemism is, at worst, a necessary evil; at its best, it is a handy verbal tool to avoid making enemies needlessly, or shocking friends. Language purists and the bluntspoken may wince when a young woman at a party coyly asks for direction to "the powder room," but to most people this kind of familiar euphemism is probably no more harmful or annoying than, say, a split infinitive. 1

On a larger scale, though, the persistent growth of euphemism in a language represents a danger to thought and action, since its fundamental intent is to deceive. As linguist Benjamin Lee Whorf has pointed out, the structure of a given language determines, in part, how the society that speaks it views reality. If "substandard housing" makes rotting slums appear more livable or inevitable to some people, then their view of American cities has been distorted and their ability to assess the significance of poverty has been reduced. Perhaps the most chilling example of euphemism's destructive power took place in Hitler's Germany. The wholesale corruption of the language under Nazism, notes critic George Steiner, is symbolized by the phrase *endgültige Lösung* (final solution), which "came to signify the death of 6,000,000 human beings in gas ovens." 2

## VOCABULARY

a. *paragraph 1:* wince, coyly

## QUESTIONS

1. The *Time* essay includes the etymology of *euphemism* in the first sentence. What help does the etymology give you in understanding its present meaning? What present meanings are not contained in the etymology?

2. What denotative definition of *euphemism* does *Time* give? How similar is this definition to the one in your dictionary?

3. What examples of negative connotations of the word does *Time* give? Does the word have a positive connotation, and is there an example of it?

4. How do the examples in the second paragraph help you understand Whorf's idea that "the structure of a given language determines, in part, how the society that speaks it views reality"?

## WRITING ASSIGNMENTS

1. Write a paragraph illustrating the positive uses of euphemism. Distinguish these uses carefully through various examples, drawing them from several areas of experience.

2. Write a paragraph illustrating the negative uses of euphemism. Distinguish these uses, and vary your examples.

3. Illustrate Whorf's statement about language and reality through euphemisms relating to death or some other experience. Be careful to state what your examples reveal about the people who use them.

4. Use the *Oxford English Dictionary* and other reference books to investigate the etymology and properties of one of the following, and write an account of the word:

   a. gyroscope   c. cotton gin   e. schooner

   b. alcohol   d. sergeant   f. vaccine

5. Use the *Oxford English Dictionary* and other reference books to show how etymology sheds light on the current meanings of one of the words below. Indicate the extent to which original meanings of the word have been retained in current usage.

   a. silly   c. foolish   e. nice

   b. humorous   d. jargon   f. mediocre

6. Write a definition of one of the following. Relate the details of your definition to the uses of the object:

a. an expressway interchange

b. the playing of a game, such as Monopoly

c. the instrument panel of a video game

d. part of a musical instrument (trumpet valves, violin strings)

e. bicycle chain

f. lawn mower blade

## ALLAN FOTHERINGHAM

*Allan Fotheringham is a political columnist who is well known across Canada for his humourous attacks on public figures. He has published three books in the same style:* Malice in Blunderland, *in which he roasts the Trudeau Liberals;* Look Ma . . . No Hands, *a satiric look at Canada's Conservatives; and* Capitol Offences, *where he examines political life in Washington. His columns appear in* Maclean's *and various newspapers, including the* Vancouver Sun, *in which the following column was published. In it he displays the provocative humour and sophistication that have made him one of Canada's most widely read journalists.*

## WHAT IS A GENTLEMAN?

What, essentially, is a gentleman? We pause to consider the question because I happened to be reading Jilly Cooper's column in the London Sunday Times. "Proverbially," she says, "he prefers blondes and makes love on his elbows." Well, I suppose so, but it strikes me as a rather old-fashioned concept.    1

The English, I know, define a gentleman as one who can conduct a heated argument with both hands in his pockets. True. But, it might be added, one of the things Englishmen do not do — as opposed to North Americans — is put their hands in their pockets. Watch, next time.    2

Nor do they, it has been pointed out to me continually in London, put their feet up — on the table, on the desk, on the nearest available object, a cherished North American habit and very comfortable, too. A gentleman? For one thing, he does not wink. I loathe grown men who wink. Whether girls feel the same, I suppose, is another matter.    3

A gentleman has never heard the story before. A gentleman never corrects someone else's pronunciation. And a gentleman never tells — on you, on his wife, or on himself.    4

The old story used to be that a gentleman never wears brown in town. That's gone by the board, helped by those obviously well-bred English gentlemen who discombobulate their Canadian friends by insisting on wearing brown suede shoes with a blue suit. The essential rule, you must realize, is that the sign of a well-dressed gentleman is that you never notice his attire. Which may be a disappointment to some of those Howe St. flamboyant fops who can be spotted coming a half-block away, rather like a strumpet on the Strand.    5

Miss (presumably) Cooper says gentlemen "don't jump on girls without asking, or off buses without paying." Gentlemen don't ask girls what they would like to do, or what    6 restaurants they would like to go to: they do and they go. Balzac was talking about a gentleman when he said, "A good husband is never the first to go to sleep at night or the last to awake in the morning." A gentleman never takes the garbage out; he convinces his wife early in marriage that it would be beneath him to do so. A gentleman does not zip up his wife; he has, presumably, married a lady and a lady would never ask.

7    A romantic young woman at lunch yesterday insisted his table manners are terribly important. She retains the illusion that this small defect can be quickly corrected once she captures him. It is possible, I suppose, that a chap who eats peas off his knife can be a gentleman, but not plausible. The true grit quickly learn the drill. Shaw felt, "A gentleman is a gentleman the world over. Loafers differ."

8    Gentlemen do not bully at Monopoly. An acquaintance, now an Associate Editor at *Time*, disappointed me terribly in this way. It is almost impossible to think of an Australian as a gentleman. Simma Holt tells me a gentleman is "a tired wolf" — which gives one to think.

9    My secretary, incorrigibly English, says a true gentlemen "knows instinctively when I prefer to light my own cigarette, never serves aces at me on the tennis court, and always removes his wristwatch." Among the few true gentlemen extant, she says, "Captain Horatio Hornblower, Bob Dylan and Pierre Elliott Trudeau come to mind. Richard Burton, Joe Namath and Front Page Tom don't."

10    A gentleman pretends, almost, that he doesn't mind a woman smoking at lunch. It is not a question of whether a gentleman over-drinks: everyone does that once in a while. But it is a mark of a gentleman that he never misbehaves, when he mis-drinks.

11    Miss (we presume) Cooper says, "In other people's houses, gentlemen don't do the cross-word or their hostess without asking." The main concern is not the offence, but the consideration. "The French don't mind what you *do*," went the Alan Jay Lerner lyrics in My Fair Lady, "as long as you pronounce it properly."

12    The myth about is that gentlemen are out of style. In the court house, on the bookshelves outside Supreme Court room 455, is the 1898 version of the B.C. Gazette, detailing the voters list in Revelstoke, professions attached. There is a Railway-wiper, a Tinner, a Car-oiler, a Well-digger, a Servant-man, even a Journalist. Plus "Adelphie Nault of Nakusp, Gentleman." Also David Brown of Trout Lake City — a "Gentleman." Adulteration has set it on the breed, along with everything else: Sheriff Eddy Wells informs us he still occasionally has a "Retired Gentleman" called for jury duty. But true gentlemen — we need more of.

13    The true measure of them is that they are as respected by men as they are by women. Fred Astaire is a gentleman, but you really wouldn't waste the title on Andy Williams. Teddy Kennedy once — no more. Look around you. They are a rare, disappearing breed.

14    A gentleman, said H. L. Mencken, is one who never strikes a woman without provocation. Oscar Wilde had it even more refined: "The gentleman is one who never hurts anyone's feelings unintentionally." All I know is that a gentleman never has more than two ingredients in his drink, never splits the cheque, does not wear a hat in the city, a tie clip or button-down shirts. He does not talk about his money or his wife, or ask about yours.

15    A gentleman always takes the backhand side at tennis, and the seat facing the wall in restaurants. I am partial to the description of the late Stanley Woodward, sports editor of the New York Herald-Tribune, who was, said a colleague, "uncommonly kind to his inferiors, barely tolerant of his equals and openly contemptuous of his superiors." The final test of a gentleman, said some forgotten Englishman, is his respect for those who can be of no possible service to him.

# VOCABULARY

a. *paragraph 1:* proverbially

b. *paragraph 5:* discombobulate, flamboyant, strumpet

c. *paragraph 9:* incorrigibly

d. *paragraph 15:* contemptuous

# QUESTIONS

1. Why does Fotheringham include so many humorous definitions of *gentleman*? Does the subject have a serious side?

2. What are the connotations of *gentleman*? How have they changed in the last hundred years or so?

3. What is the etymology of *gentleman*, and why is it important for a correct understanding of the various connotations?

4. Why do so many of Fotheringham's definitions involve relations between the sexes?

5. The story is told of an American woman who, incensed by the unhelpful remarks of a ticket-taker on a London bus, burst out with: "You're no gentleman!" To which the baffled Cockney replied: "Well, I never said I was!" To what extent are outmoded notions of class bound up with Fotheringham's definitions?

# WRITING ASSIGNMENT

Use the *Gage Canadian Dictionary*, the *Oxford English Dictionary*, or the *Dictionary of American English* and other reference books in the library to trace the history of one of the following terms. In a concluding paragraph, suggest one or more uses to which this history of the term might be put:

| | | |
|---|---|---|
| a.   anarchist | e.   fascist | h.   socialist |
| b.   communist | f.   mugwump | i.   tory |
| c.   Creole | g.   republican | j.   Yankee |
| d.   democrat | | |

# MARGARET ATWOOD

*Novelist, poet, editor, critic, and feminist* Margaret Atwood *is one of Canada's best-known and most respected writers. She was educated at Victoria College, University of Toronto, where she was influenced by the teaching of Northrop Frye. In the following selection she explores the bush country of northern Quebec, which she discovered as a child on field trips with her father, an entomologist.*

## TRUE NORTH

1    Where is the north, exactly? It's not only a place but a direction, and as such its location is relative: to the Mexicans, the United States is the north, to Americans Toronto is, even though it's on roughly the same latitude as Boston.

2    Wherever it is for us, there's a lot of it. You stand in Windsor and imagine a line going north, all the way to the pole. The same line going south would end up in South America. That's the sort of map we grew up with, at the front of the classroom in Mercator projection, which made it look even bigger than it was, all that pink stretching on forever, with a few cities sprinkled along the bottom edge. It's not only geographical space, it's space related to body image. When we face south, as we often do, our conscious mind may be directed down there, towards crowds, bright lights, some Hollywood version of fame and fortune, but the north is at the back of our minds, always. There's something, not someone, looking over our shoulders; there's a chill at the nape of the neck.

3    The north focuses our anxieties. Turning to face north, face the north, we enter our own unconscious. Always, in retrospect, the journey north has the quality of dream.

4    The Acid Rain Dinner, in Toronto's Sheraton Centre, in 1985. The first of these fund-raising events was fairly small. But the movement has grown, and this dinner is huge. The leaders of all three provincial parties are here. So is the minister of the environment from the federal government. So are several labour leaders, and several high-ranking capitalists, and representatives of numerous northerly chambers of commerce, summer residents' associations, tourist-camp runners, outfitters. Wishy-washy urban professionals who say "frankly" a lot bend elbows with huntin', shootin', fishin', and cussin' burnt-necks who wouldn't be caught dead saying "frankly." This is not a good place to be overheard saying that actually acid rain isn't such a bad thing because it gets rid of all that brown scum and leeches in the lake, or who cares because you can water-ski anyway. Teddy Kennedy, looking like a bulky sweater, is the guest speaker. Everyone wears a little gold pin in the shape of a rain drop. It looks like a tear.

5    Why has acid rain become the collective Canadian nightmare? Why is it — as a good cause — bigger than baby-seal bashing? The reasons aren't just economic, although there are lots of those, as the fishing-camp people and foresters will tell you. It's more than that, and cognate with the outrage aroused by the uninvited voyage of the American icebreaker *Polar Sea* through the Northwest Passage, where almost none of us ever goes. It's territorial, partly; partly a felt violation of some area in us that we hardly ever think about unless it's invaded or tampered with. It's the neighbours throwing guck into our yard. It's our childhood dying.

6    In Europe, every scrap of land has been claimed, owned, re-owned, fought over, captured, bled on. The roads are the only no-man's-land. In northern Canada, the roads are civilization, owned by the collective human *we*. Off the road is *other*. Try walking in it, and you'll soon find out why all the early traffic here was by water. "Impenetrable widerness" is not just verbal.

7    And suppose you get off the road. Suppose you get lost. Getting lost, elsewhere and closer to town, is not knowing exactly where you are. You can always ask, even in a foreign country. In the north, getting lost is not knowing how to get out.

8    One way of looking at a landscape is to consider the typical ways of dying in it. Given

the worst, what's the worst it could do? Will it be delirium from drinking salty water on the high seas, shrivelling in the desert, snakebite in the jungle, tidal waves on a Pacific isle, volcanic fumes? In the north, there are several hazards. Although you're probably a lot safer there than you are on the highway at rush hour, given the odds, you still have to be a little wary.

Like most lessons of this sort, those about the north are taught by precept and example, but also, more enjoyably, by cautionary nasty tale. There is death by blackfly, the one about the fellow who didn't have his shirt cuffs tight enough in the spring and undressed at night only to find he was running with blood, the ones about the lost travellers who bloated up from too many bites and who, when found, were twice the size, unrecognizable, and dead. There is death from starvation, death by animal, death by forest fire; there is death from something called "exposure," which used to confuse me when I heard about men who exposed themselves: why would they intentionally do anything that fatal? There's death by thunderstorm, not to be sneered at: on the open lake, in one of the excessive northern midsummer thunderstorms, a canoe or a bush plane is a vulnerable target. The north is full of Struwwelpeter-like stories about people who didn't do as they were told and got struck by lightning. Above all, there are death by freezing and death by drowning. Your body's heat-loss rate in the water is twenty times that in air, and northern lakes are cold. Even in a life jacket, even holding on to the tipped canoe, you're at risk. Every summer the numbers pile up.

Every culture has its exemplary dead people, its hagiography of landscape martyrs, those unfortunates who, by their bad ends, seem to sum up in one grisly episode what may be lurking behind the next rock for all of us, all of us who enter the territory they once claimed as theirs. I'd say that two of the top northern landscape martyrs are Tom Thomson, the painter who was found mysteriously drowned near his overturned canoe with no provable cause in sight, and the Mad Trapper of Rat River, also mysterious, who became so thoroughly bushed that he killed a Mountie and shot two others during an amazing wintertime chase before being finally mowed down. In our retelling of these stories, mystery is a key element. So, strangely enough, is a presumed oneness with the landscape in question. The Mad Trapper knew his landscape so well he survived in it for weeks, living off the land and his own bootlaces, eluding capture. One of the hidden motifs in these stories is a warning: maybe it's not so good to get *too* close to Nature.

I remember a documentary on Tom Thomson that ended, rather ominously, with the statement that the north had taken him to herself. This was, of course, pathetic fallacy gone to seed, but it was also a comment on our distrust of the natural world, a distrust that remains despite our protests, our studies in the ethics of ecology, our elevation of "the environment" to a numinous noun, our save-the-tree campaigns. The question is, would the trees save us, given the chance? Would the water, would the birds, would the rocks? In the north, we have our doubts.

A different part of the north. We're sitting around the table, by lamplight — it is still the old days here, no electricity — talking about bad hunters. Bad hunters, bad fishers, everyone has a story. You come upon a campsite, way in the back of beyond, no roads into the lake, they must have come in by float plane, and there it is, garbage all over the place, beer cans, blobs of human poop flagged by melting toilet paper, and twenty-two fine pickerel left rotting on a rock. Business executives who get themselves flown in during hunting season with their high-powered rifles, shoot a buck, cut off the head, fill their quota, see another one with a bigger spread of antlers, drop the first head, cut off the second. The woods are littered with discarded heads, and who cares about the bodies?

New way to shoot polar bear: you have the natives on the ground finding them for you, then they radio the location in to the base camp, the base camp phones New York, fellow gets on the plane, gets himself flown in, they've got the rifle and the clothing all ready for him, fly him to the bear, he pulls the trigger from the plane, doesn't even get out of the g.d. *plane*, they fly him back, cut off the head, skin it, send the lot down to New York.

14    These are the horror stories of the north, one brand. They've replaced the ones in which you got pounced upon by a wolverine or had your arm chewed off by a she-bear with cubs or got chased into the lake by a moose in rut, or even the ones in which your dog got porcupine quills or rolled in poison ivy and gave it to you. In the new stories, the enemies and the victims of old have done a switch. Nature is no longer implacable, dangerous, ready to jump you; it is on the run, pursued by a number of unfair bullies with the latest technology.

15    One of the key nouns in these stories is "float plane." These outrages, this banditry, would not be possible without them, for the bad hunters are notoriously weak-muscled and are deemed incapable of portaging a canoe, much less paddling one. Among their other badnesses, they are sissies. Another key motif is money. What money buys these days, among other things, is the privilege of no-risk slaughter.

16    As for us, the ones telling the stories, tsk-tsking by lamplight, we are the good hunters, or so we think. We've given up saying we only kill to eat; Kraft dinner and freeze-dried food have put paid to that one. Really there's no excuse for us. However, we do have some virtues left. We can still cast a fly. We don't cut off heads and hang them stuffed on the wall. We would never buy an ocelot coat. We paddle our own canoes.

17    We're sitting on the dock at night, shivering despite our sweaters, in mid-August, watching the sky. There are a few shooting stars, as there always are at this time in August, as the earth passes through the Perseids. We pride ourselves on knowing a few things like that, about the sky; we find the Dipper, the North Star, Cassiopeia's Chair, and talk about consulting a star chart, which we know we won't actually do. But this is the only place you can really *see* the stars, we tell each other. Cities are hopeless.

18    Suddenly, an odd light appears, going very fast. It spirals around like a newly dead firecracker, and then bursts, leaving a cloud of luminous dust, caught perhaps in the light from the sun, still up there somewhere. What could this be? Several days later, we hear that it was part of an extinct Soviet satellite, or that's what they say. That's what they would say, wouldn't they? It strikes us that we don't really know very much about the night sky at all any more. There's all kinds of junk up there: spy planes, old satellites, tin cans, man-made matter gone out of control. It also strikes us that we are totally dependent for knowledge of these things on a few people who don't tell us very much.

19    Once, we thought that if the balloon ever went up we'd head for the bush and hide out up there, living — we naively supposed — off the land. Now we know that if the two superpowers begin hurling things at each other through the sky, they're likely to do it across the Arctic, with big bangs and fallout all over the north. The wind blows everywhere. Survival gear and knowing which moss you can eat is not going to be a large help. The north is no longer a refuge.

20    Driving back towards Toronto from the Near North, a small reprise runs through my head:

> Land of the septic tank,
> Home of the speedboat,
> Where still the four-wheel-drive
> Wanders at will,
> Blue lake and tacky shore,
> I will return once more:

Vroom-diddy-vroom-vroom
Vroom-diddy-vroom-vroom
Vroo-OO-oo-oom.

Somehow, just as the drive north inspires saga and tragedy, the drive south inspires parody. And here it comes: the gift shops shaped like teepees, the maple-syrup emporiums that get themselves up like olde-tyme sugaring-off huts; and, farther south, the restaurants that pretend to offer wholesome farm fare, the stores that pretend to be general stores, selling quilts, soap shaped like hearts, high-priced fancy conserves done up in frilly cloth caps, the way Grandma (whoever she might be) was fondly supposed to have made them.

And then come the housing developments, acres of prime farmland turning overnight into Quality All-Brick Family Homes; and then come the Industrial Parks; and there, in full anti-bloom, is the city itself, looming like a mirage or a chemical warfare zone on the horizon. A browny-grey scuzz hovers above it, and we think, as we always do when facing re-entry, we're going into *that*? We're going to breathe *that*?    21

But we go forward, as we always do, into what is now to us the unknown. And once inside, we breathe the air, not much bad happens to us, we hardly notice. It's as if we've never been anywhere else. But that's what we think, too, when we're in the north.    22

## VOCABULARY

a. *paragraph  2:* Mercator

b. *paragraph  3:* retrospect

c. *paragraph  5:* cognate

d. *paragraph  9:* precept, Struwwelpeter-like

e. *paragraph 10:* hagiography

f. *paragraph 11:* pathetic fallacy, ecology, numinous

g. *paragraph 12:* quota

h. *paragraph 14:* in rut, implacable

i. *paragraph 15:* portaging

j. *paragraph 17:* Perseids, Cassiopeia's Chair

k. *paragraph 18:* luminous

l. *paragraph 20:* reprise, saga, parody, emporiums

m. *paragraph 21:* scuzz

## QUESTIONS

1. Atwood's definition of *north* is a precising definition. How does she try to persuade us of the need for this definition?

2. Atwood begins paragraph 1 with a question. How far does this question take her in the definition of *north*? Why do you think she begins in this way?

3. What are Atwood's various strategies for defining *north*?

4. In paragraphs 13 and 14, Atwood offers two versions of "horror stories of the north." To what purpose?

## WRITING ASSIGNMENT

1. Select some value-laden term or concept, such as "democracy," "obscenity," "freedom," or "work," and write your own definition.

## ASHLEY MONTAGU AND EDWARD DARLING

*In this essay from their book* The Prevalence of Nonsense, *Ashley Montagu and* Edward Darling *give us a special kind of definition — the etymology or history of a phrase — to shed light on its current meaning. Montagu and Darling show one important use of the* Oxford English Dictionary — *the dictionary that records all known meanings of a word from its original appearance to the uses current at the time of the dictionary's publication. Knowing the past meanings of a word often helps us to understand nuances or shades of meaning that a dictionary of contemporary usage fails to illuminate.*

## "THUMBS DOWN" — THE SIGNAL FOR DEATH?

1    In 1873, when the French painter Jean Léon Gérôme exhibited his picture of some of the action at the old Roman Coliseum showing the blood-hungry spectators savagely demanding the death of a gladiator and leaning forward with their thumbes all pointing down, he called it "Pollice Verso." At which point he made more history than he realized, because he clearly gave the meaning of "thumbs down" to "pollice verso," although *verso* really means *turned*, and could mean *extended* or even *rotated*. However, the picture is extremely graphic and is widely known through frequent reproductions — and it is not at all hard to understand why anyone who had seen it would take up the idea: it carries great conviction. We believe that today's meaning of "thumbs down" — which is unquestionably a gesture of rejection — owes its content to Gérôme. For it was not always so. "Latin scholars have advanced almost every other conceivable gesture except that shown by Gérôme. . . . The Latin phrase has been translated 'with thumbs turned inward' and 'with thumbs turned outward,' in either case using the thumb as if it were a dagger pointing at oneself or thrusting into an opponent, much as we 'thumb a ride.'"*

2    The Oxford English Dictionary, however — that vast edifice in thirteen huge volumes, than which there is no thanner — points out that in 1600 Holland translated *Pliny* (XXVIII.ii. 297): "To bend or bow downe the thumbes when wee give assent unto a thing, or doe favour any person." Assuming it's a favor to be allowed to live, "thumbs down" meant "let him live." A 1693 translation of Juvenal's *Satires* (iii. 68) by Dryden renders the Latin "Where . . . with thumbs bent back, they popularly kill." So "thumbs up" was the death gesture. Even after Gérôme there were some stiff-necked scholars who stuck to

*Charles Earl Funk, *A Hog on Ice and Other Curious Expressions* (New York: Harper & Brothers, 1948).

the original meaning; and the OED lists them in due order. But there is nothing that can dam the flow of meaning from a certain direction when enough people begin to use a word for a certain purpose, and it is impossible for scholars to foist neologisms upon the people just because they are "fit." Thus we find even the *Britannica* (11th edition) giving the negative meaning to "thumbs down" first: "If the spectators were in favor of mercy, they waved their handkerchiefs; if they desired the death of the conquered gladiator they turned their thumbs downwards." And then the article adds: "A different account is given by Mayor on *Juvenal* iii. 36, who says: 'Those who wished the death of the conquered gladiator turned their thumbs towards their breasts, as a signal to his opponents to stab him; those who wished him to be spared, turned their thumbs downwards, as a signal for dropping the sword.'"

"Thumbs down" is not the only expression to change or reverse its meaning — the       3
process is going on in every living language all the time. *Undertaker* formerly meant *entrepreneur*, one who undertakes a project, as a manufacturer; now, of course, it means one who undertakes to bury the dead, and the associations are unpleasant so that today's entrepreneurs in the burial business call themselves morticians or funeral directors. A *hussy* was first a simple "housewife," modest and virtuous, just as *wench* was entirely respectable and meant "pupil" or "daughter" or even "orphan" (it derives from Anglo-Saxon *wencel*, "weak" and needing protection). *Catiff* simply meant "captive" from the Old French, and it was applied in pity, since a captive is miserable; but it came to have an indication of odium and took on the meaning of "coward." And so forth.

In connection with the remark a moment ago that the scholars cannot foist a new word       4
upon the language — it won't be used unless the folk pick it up — perhaps some readers will remember that there was a contest during the Prohibition days for some word which would convey scorn, contempt, and general rejection for a person breaking the law; and someone came up with "scofflaw." But you seldom hear it, and scarcely ever see it in print. In short, it carries no emotional weight of any kind. If you call me a scofflaw, I am not insulted, hurt, or even annoyed; instead, I am more likely to laugh.

Once the trend had begun to swing toward "thumbs down" to mean "death to him,"       5
nothing could stop it; and that's what we have today.

## VOCABULARY

a. *paragraph 1:* graphic

b. *paragraph 2:* edifice, foist, neologisms, gladiator

## QUESTIONS

1. What points are Montagu and Darling making about language in their analysis of the phrase *thumbs down*? What lessons might be drawn from their analysis about the language of politics or other uses?

2. Do Montagu and Darling say or imply that the original meaning of a word or phrase is the "correct" meaning even if the word or phrase picks up other meanings in later use?

3. Why do Montagu and Darling cite the 11th edition of the *Britannica* in paragraph 2? If the citation were omitted, would you lose essential information about the change in meaning in the phrase?

4. What value is there in knowing the original meaning of popular phrases like *thumbs down*?

## WRITING ASSIGNMENTS

1. Use reference books (on words and phrases, quotations, popular sayings, historical dictionaries) in the library to discover the origin of one of the following words or phrases. Report your findings in an essay of your own:

   a.   baker's dozen

   b.   fuller's earth

   c.   Hobson's choice

   d.   hoisted with his own petard

   e.   Horatio Alger story

   f.   mess of pottage

   g.   Pyrrhic victory

   h.   survival of the fittest

2. Compare the scientific methods of Montagu and Darling with Desmond Morris's methods in "Territorial Behaviour." Think in terms of evidence, objectivity, and logic.

## JOSEPH WOOD KRUTCH

*A distinguished drama critic and teacher of English,* Joseph Wood Krutch *(1893–1970) taught at Columbia until 1950. He spent the remainder of his life writing about nature, conservation, and American life and values in a series of books, including* The Desert World, If You Don't Mind My Saying So, *and* Human Nature and the Human Condition, *in which his definition of "normal" appears. As his definition suggests, Krutch was opposed to "adjustment" as the measure of good and happiness. "If men are nothing but the product of their society," he writes, "if what is called 'human nature' is actually determined by the existing system of production and distribution, then man will become more and more merely that creature whose desires and convictions and acts are best 'adjusted' to his external condition." Krutch had an unusual gift for writing about complex ideas in plain language — free of clutter and fashionable jargon.*

## THE MEANING OF "NORMAL"

1   The words we choose to define or suggest what we believe to be important facts exert a very powerful influence upon civilization. A mere name can persuade us to approve or disapprove, as it does, for example, when we describe certain attitudes as "cynical" on the one hand or "realistic" on the other. No one wants to be "unrealistic" and no one wants to be "snarling". Therefore his attitude toward the thing described may very well depend upon which designation is current among his contemporaries; and the less critical his mind, the more influential the most commonly used vocabulary will be.

2   It is for this reason that, even as a mere verbal confusion, the use of "normal" to designate what ought to be called "average" is of tremendous importance and serves not only to indicate but actually to reinforce the belief that average ability, refinement, intellectuality, or even virtue is an ideal to be aimed at. Since we cannot do anything to the

purpose until we think straight and since we cannot think straight without properly defined words it may be that the very first step toward an emancipation from the tyranny of "conformity" should be the attempt to substitute for "normal," as commonly used, a genuine synonym for "average."

Fortunately, such a genuine and familiar synonym does exist. That which is "average" is also properly described as "mediocre." And if we were accustomed to call the average man, not "the common man" or still less "the normal man," but "the mediocre man" we should not be so easily hypnotized into believing that mediocrity is an ideal to be aimed at.    **3**

A second step in the same direction would be to return to the word "normal" its original meaning. According to the Shorter Oxford Dictionary it derives from the Latin "norma," which has been Anglicized as "norm" and is, in turn, thus defined: "A rule or authoritative standard." The adjective "normative" is not commonly misused — no doubt because it is not part of that "vocabulary of the average man" by which educators now set so much store. It still generally means "establishing a norm or standard." But "normal" seldom means, as it should, "corresponding to the standard by which a thing is to be judged." If it did, "a normal man" would again mean, not what the average man *is* but what, in its fullest significance, the word "man" should imply, even "what a man *ought* to be." And that is a very different thing from the "average" or "mediocre" man whom we have so perversely accustomed ourselves to regard as most worthy of admiration.    **4**

Only by defining and then attempting to reach up toward the "normal" as properly defined can a democratic society save itself from those defects which the enemies of democracy have always maintained were the necessary consequences of such a society. Until "preparation for life" rather than "familiarity with the best that has been thought and said" became the aim of education every schoolboy knew that Emerson had bid us hitch our wagons to a star. We now hitch them to a mediocrity instead.    **5**

Unless, then, normal is a useless and confusing synonym for average, it should mean what the word *normative* suggests, namely, a *concept of what ought to be* rather than a *description of what is*. It should mean what at times it has meant — the fullest possible realization of what the human being is capable of — the complete, not the aborted human being. It is an *entelechy*, not a mean; something excellent, not something mediocre; something rare, not common; not what the majority are, but what few, if any, actually measure up to.    **6**

Where, it will be asked, do we get this norm, upon what basis does it rest? Upon the answer to that question depends what a civilization will be like and especially in what direction it will move. At various times religion, philosophy, law and custom have contributed to it in varying degrees. When none of these is available poetry and literature may do so. But unless we can say in one way or another, "I have some idea of what men ought to be as well as some knowledge of what they are," then civilization is lost.    **7**

# VOCABULARY

a. *paragraph 1:* designation

b. *paragraph 2:* emancipation, tyranny

c. *paragraph 6:* entelechy

# QUESTIONS

1. Krutch's definition of *normal* is a precising definition: he is seeking to make an uncommon meaning of *normal* its common one. How does Krutch try to persuade us of the need for this definition?

2. How does Krutch account for the present differences in the connotations of *normative* and *normal*, which derive from the same word? Does he state or imply why *normal* came to mean *average?*

3. Can the meaning of *entelechy* be determined from its context? What help does the etymology of the word provide?

4. Use the synonym listings in your dictionary to determine the exact difference in meaning between the following pairs of words. Write sentences using ten of the italicized words to reflect their precise dictionary meanings.

| | | | | |
|---|---|---|---|---|
| a. | *essential*; necessary | g. | element; *factor* |
| b. | *predict*; prophesy | h. | recumbent; *prone* |
| c. | *mimic*; mock | i. | adroit; *deft* |
| d. | sinister; *portentous* | j. | *dextrous*; handy |
| e. | fortitude; *forbearance* | k. | blended; *mingled* |
| f. | phase; *facet* | l. | *perturbed*; agitated |

# WRITING ASSIGNMENTS

1. Define one of the following words by stating what it is *not* as well as what it *is*. Comment on the significance of its etymology.

| | | | | |
|---|---|---|---|---|
| a. | tolerance | c. | barbecue |
| b. | stinginess | d. | soccer |

2. Discuss the different meanings of one of the following words, illustrating these meanings by your use of them.

| | | | | |
|---|---|---|---|---|
| a. | funny | d. | crazy |
| b. | average | e. | tacky |
| c. | cool | f. | weird |

# PROCESS

Like classification and division, process analysis is an essential method in technical writing, as in essays and books that describe how to assemble or repair machinery.

A process is a series of connected actions, each developing from the preceding one, and leading to a result of some kind: a product, an effect, even a decision. Mechanical processes are probably the kind we deal with the most, and three of the examples in this section are of these — the first is the simple process of sharpening a knife; the second and third the complex processes of fly casting and building a rail fence. A mechanical process is one that we create. By contrast, a natural process such as Bronowski describes in his description of the athlete is one we may initiate but do not create:

> He seems all animal in action. The heartbeat goes up; when he sprints at top speed the heart is pumping five times as much blood as normal, and ninety per cent of it is for the muscles.
> — Jacob Bronowski, "The Athlete and the Gazelle"

Both mechanical and natural processes are repeatable. A particular historical process — the events that led to the Riel Rebellion or produce an economic depression — is not, though the general circumstances may repeat themselves at another time.

Although we are committed in describing a process to present the steps chronologically — in the order they occur — we may interrupt the account to discuss the implications or details of a particular stage. In describing a complex process, we need to distinguish the main stages and the steps and procedures each of these contain. Process and causal analysis, discussed in the next section, are closely related and are often combined.

## FLORENCE H. PETTIT

*A designer and professional craftswoman,* Florence Pettit *has written much about the craft arts. Her description of how to sharpen a knife, from her book* How to Make Whirligigs and Whimmy Diddles, *shows how important the consideration of audience is in exposition: Pettit selects her details with beginners in mind, and is careful to define her tools and equipment, focussing on the difficult steps of the process.*

## HOW TO SHARPEN YOUR KNIFE

If you have never done any whittling or wood carving before, the first skill to learn is how     1
to sharpen your knife. You may be surprised to learn that even a brand-new knife needs sharpening. Knives are never sold honed (finely sharpened), although some gouges and chisels are. It is essential to learn the firm stroke on the stone that will keep your blades sharp. The sharpening stone must be fixed in place on the table, so that it will not move around. You can do this by placing a piece of rubber inner tube or a thin piece of foam rubber under it. Or you can tack four strips of wood, if you have a rough worktable, to frame the stone and hold it in place. Put a generous puddle of oil on the stone — this will soon disappear into the surface of a new stone, and you will need to keep adding more oil. Press the knife blade flat against the stone in the puddle of oil, using your index finger. Whichever way the cutting edge of the knife faces is the side of the blade that should get a little more pressure. Move the blade around three or four times in a narrow oval about the size of your fingernail, going *counterclockwise* when the sharp edge is facing right. Now

turn the blade over in the same spot on the stone, press hard, and move it around the small oval *clockwise*, with more pressure on the cutting edge that faces left. Repeat the ovals, flipping the knife blade over six or seven times, and applying lighter pressure to the blade the last two times. Wipe the blade clean with a piece of rag or tissue and rub it flat on the piece of leather strop at least twice on each side. Stroke *away* from the cutting edge to remove the little burr of metal that may be left on the blade.

## QUESTIONS

1. What details help the reader to visualize the mechanical process described in the paragraph?

2. Are the stages of the process presented chronologically? If not, why not?

3. Are any terms defined in context — that is, in the description of how to sharpen a knife?

## WRITING ASSIGNMENTS

1. Describe a mechanical process comparable to sharpening a knife — for example, sharpening the blades of a hand mower or pruning a tree or painting the exterior of a house.

2. Rewrite the paragraph on how to sharpen a knife, explaining the process to a child who is just beginning to learn to carve wood.

## RODERICK HAIG-BROWN

Roderick Haig-Brown *(1908–1976) wrote prolifically about the things he loved: fishing, conservation, the environment. Born in England, he visited the American west coast in 1926 and eventually settled on Vancouver Isaland in 1931. He made his living by logging, trapping, guiding, fishing, and writing. He wrote novels for adults and some excellent children's stories.* Saltwater Summer *won a Governor General's Award, and* A Primer of Fly Fishing, *from which the following excerpt is taken, is considered the standard work on the subject.*

## FLY CASTING

1    The mechanics of fly casting are simply this: the line is thrown back through the air by the impulse of the rod; as it passes the caster's shoulder its weight begins to pull on the rod top; at the moment it straightens out behind the caster the rod is fully flexed, under the maximum desirable tension; at this precise moment the caster exercises the power of this tension by a simple forward movement of hand and wrist and arm; the rod responds, releasing its tension into the forward drive of the line that makes the cast. This is the theory behind the overhead cast that is expressed in the fly-fisherman's axiom: "It must be allowed to straighten out behind if it is to go forward straight."

This theory is not difficult to put into effect; it is simply a matter of timing, and a **2** surprisingly limited amount of practice is enough to develop sufficient accuracy of timing to produce reasonably good and satisfying casts.

The first point to establish is the grip of the hand on the rod. This should be about half- **3** way up the cork handle, absolutely firm and solid, but not tense or rigid. All four fingers are curved round the handle the little finger, third finger and middle finger contributing most of the firmness by pressing the cork solidly into the fleshy part of the palm, near the heel of the hand. The forefinger supports and steadies this grip but supplies its own firm-ness against the thumb, which should be along the upper side of the handle and some-where near the top of the grip. A few casters point the forefinger instead of the thumb along the handle, claiming that greater accuracy and delicacy is obtainable by doing so. But I am satisfied that this is not advisable because it restricts the flexibility of the wrist and materially reduces the firmness and solidity of the grip.

The best place to practice casting and develop timing is on dry land, not out on the **4** water, and a fair-sized lawn is ideal for the purpose. To make a trial cast, put rod and reel down on the grass, draw off about thirty feet of line beyond the rod top and stretch this straight out. Pick up the rod, holding the line against the butt with the forefinger, and throw the line upwards and backwards with a firm, crisp movement that stops the rod in a perpendicular position over the right shoulder. Pause for a moment for the line to straighten out behind, then bring the rod firmly forward to an angle of about twenty degrees from horizontal. The line should come forward and settle out in a straight line along the grass.

It probably will not do so the first time, nor for several times thereafter. The beginning **5** caster almost invariably makes two mistakes: he carries the rod back too far, and he does not wait long enough to let the line straighten out behind him before starting his forward movement. Both of these are crucial because they destroy the timing that develops and uses the tension of the rod. Two other common mistakes are insufficient force in the pickup, or backward movement of the rod, and excessive force in the forward movement. The pickup must be firm and positive, a backward and upward throw of the line that gives it sufficient velocity to straighten out in the air at the level of the rod top. The forward throw calls for slightly less force, since the line is already in the air, but it should still be a firm movement, precisely timed to the full extension of the line behind the caster.

The best and quickest way I know for a beginner to get the feel of these movements and **6** their timing is to allow a skillful caster, standing behind his right shoulder, to make the cast while he himself leaves his hand passively on the rod grip. When this has been done several times the instructor will sense that his pupil is accurately following his movements. A few repetitions, with time in between for trial and error without guidance, should produce a reasonable measure of success.

# VOCABULARY

a. *paragraph 1:* flexed, axiom

b. *paragraph 4:* perpendicular

c. *paragraph 5:* velocity

## QUESTIONS

1. How is Haig-Brown's essay organized? Identify the various parts and explain their purpose.

2. Would you be able to perform the overhead cast on the basis of the details given by Haig-Brown? How does reading this description compare to watching and imitating an expert fisherman?

3. Consider the language of the essay. How does Haig-Brown create a prose that imitates that of an instruction manual? What are the strengths and weaknesses of this kind of writing?

## WRITING ASSIGNMENT

Discuss experiences of your own with a process that you have learned. Make the language as simple and lucid as Haig-Brown's.

## CHARLES LONG

Charles Long *was born in 1943, studied management science at Case Institute of Technology and economics and political science at the University of Queensland in Brisbane, Australia. Since 1975 he has been a full-time writer living in Canada, and has published a variety of "how-to" books, including* The Stonebuilder's Primer *and* How to Survive Without a Salary. *He observes that technical clarity in such writing depends on "explaining the whole before the parts, so the reader has some framework on which to place the details; explaining why, as well as how, a thing is done; ordering the steps in strict sequence; and relating each element to a common reference point." "Getting the Hang of It" admirably illustrates these precepts in action.*

## GETTING THE HANG OF IT

1    Almost as an afterthought, Glen Switzer waves out the truck window at the sturdy rail fence that has tracked us for a mile or more along the narrow Ontario sideroad.

2    "My grandfather built that fence," he says, "more than 60 years ago."

3    It is not a boast, but it should be. This land is not easily reconciled to farms and fences. The rocky, untillable roadside is choked with juniper and grape that grapple with fences until they pull them down. Dying elms drop limbs from above. Wind and snowploughs take their toll. And you don't dig postholes in this inhospitable shield — you prospect for them.

4    Half the secret of the 60-year-fence is arbor vitae, better known as cedar. Eastern white cedar grows from Manitoba to the Maritimes, western red cedar in British Columbia. Both species are light and easily split; both have natural resistance to rot.

5    The important question in terms of function is, what is the fence intended to keep out? Or in? The best fence, in rural tradition, is horse-high, bull-strong and sheep-tight — in imperial measure, that converts to about six feet high for horses, five feet for cattle and at

least four feet for sheep. The size of the rails determines the size of the escape gaps between them, but on average, sheep need a five-rail fence, horses and cattle three or four. A five-foot-high four-rail fence is standard.

Those blessed with an old rail fence that merely needs propping up already have the materials at hand. If it is necessary to cut new rails, peel the poles and look for the smallest taper from butt to top. Substitute for cedar at your peril; birch, for example, will rot after a heavy dew and a fog. Rails should be at least 12 feet long and as straight as possible. They will overlap at the ends, so 12-foot rails make fence sections, or panels, about 10 feet long.    **6**

Stakes (the upright braces, or legs) should be about seven feet long for the usual five-foot-high fence. Lengths vary as the fence goes uphill and down, but the standard practice is to cut them seven feet long and then trim off any excess tops at job's end. Unlike rails, stakes need not be uniform or straight, and taper is not a problem. Use the heavier stakes for main supports and the lighter ones for binders and braces.    **7**

The total quantity of material required depends on the fence style. A patent fence à la Switzer takes three stakes per panel (two supports and a brace). Their "binder" fence uses 3½ stakes per panel. And the "four-stake" fence . . . well, you figure it out. The number of rails per panel depends on the disposition of the livestock and the greenness of the grass on the other side.    **8**

Fencing one side of an acre (approximately 210 feet) requires 21 panels. Thus a four-rail patent-style fence will consume 84 rails (21 times 4) and 63 stakes (21 times 3). Add an extra set of stakes at each end of the fence and two extra sets to incorporate a gate. Fence wire comes by the pound or the roll — the usual type is 12-guage "black" wire. Galvanized wire is also available; it is slower to rust but too brittle to take much twisting and tightening. You will also need a good pair of fencing pliers, a saw for trimming the stake tops and a couple of homemade fence jacks.    **9**

A jack is the fencer's skyhook, the thing that holds the first rails up in the air while the support is built around them. To make one, simply take two sticks about four feet long and cross them near the top. Put a twist of wire around the intersection, then spread the feet outward and connect them at the bottom with a long wire. This should result in a triangle, with a wire for the bottom side and a notch at the top — about hip-high for a five-foot fence.    **10**

Clear the fence line of brush, vines and entanglements. Don't worry about rocks and stumps — the rails can accommodate those. The chief concerns are to make some working room and then to clear away those things that will grow up and strangle the fence the moment your back is turned.    **11**

The first rail laid is the bench rail. Like a keystone, it holds the whole assembly together and so should be the strongest and soundest rail in the panel, although not necessarily the biggest. When the fence is complete, the bench rail will be second from the top. A broken top rail or bottom rail can be replaced easily; if the bench rail breaks, the whole section has to be taken down and rebuilt.    **12**

Set up the first jack about 10 feet down the fencerow, then lay the first bench rail in the notch at the top, and wire the other end to the building or other fence that marks the start of this section. Set the second jack about 10 feet away, and place the next bench rail across both jacks. The first jack is now holding the overlapped ends of both rails. Build the first support at this spot.    **13**

Cross two stout stakes *above* the overlapped rails — the stakes lean against the rails, and the rails rest on the jack. Set the bottoms of the two stakes about five feet apart, and heel them firmly into the ground.    **14**

Now wire the two stakes together *beneath* the two bench rails. Stand on one side of the fence and pass the end of the wire under the bench rails, between the two stakes, around    **15** the far stake, back between the two stakes again — so the wire crosses itself beneath the bench rail — and around the near stake. Cut off the wire, cross the free ends, and twist them tight. The wire forms a figure eight, a sling that holds the bench rails up under the crotch of the crossed stakes. Wriggle the jack out from under the permanent support and leapfrog it 20 feet ahead, 10 feet beyond the second jack.

16    With the first jack out of the way, hang a big loop of wire from the overlapping bench rails to carry the bottom rail. The length of the loop depends on both the girth of the bottom rail and the desired ground clearance. Place the bottom rail high enough to keep it out of the mud and damp weeds yet low enough to block nosy calves or adventurous sheep.

17    Cut the wire to length, and bend each end back on itself, forming two long, flat hooks. Turn one hook to the right and the other to the left, then bend the curve of one hook up and the curve of the other hook down. Pass the wire around the bench rails, slip the two hooks together in reef-knot fashion, and bend the free ends aside. This forms a self-tightening knot that joins the big loop at the top.

18    Rest the bottom rail in the loop. Its weight will tighten the loop and pull down on the bench rails, which will in turn tighten the first key joint at the top, the one that holds the bench rails to the stakes. For this reason, the bottom rail should be the heaviest one in the panel, pulling the whole assembly together. The bench rail, remember, was the strongest — the bottom rail is the heaviest.

19    For a three-rail fence, set the loop so that the bottom rail rests halfway between the bench and the ground. For a four-rail fence, the loop is longer, leaving a wide gap between the bottom rail and the bench. The fourth rail (fourth in terms of design but the third to be put in the fence) goes in this gap.

20    Fix a short length of wire across the loop, just above the overlapping bottom rails, by wrapping each end around the vertical sides of the hanging loop. Lay the fourth rail on the cross wire.

21    Set the top rail in the V of the stakes. Now, all the rails are in place, and the two main supports are up. The only remaining weakness is a tendency toward longitudinal collapse — a slow shift along the length of the fence that lets the whole thing sag to its knees like a centipede lying down in its tracks. The solution is to add a diagonal brace against that longitudinal movement.

22    As with farming and child rearing, fencing with rails is not quite as simple as it appears from the other side of the fence. A fence is an integrated thing that rests on all its parts, and one subtle misstep may lead to grief three panels hence. Gerald Switzer and a partner once fenced a building lot while the owner studied every step. It took them two hours to build 25 panels. Only four panels remained unfinished when the owner sent them home. "Don't worry about the rest," he said. "I've been watching you guys, and I'm sure I can do it myself." He did, but it took him eight hours to finish those last four panels.

23    The Switzers build 600 to 700 feet of fence on an average day. On a really good day, they have done twice that much. They will keep on doing it as long as they can get the rails. And when their grown-up grandchildren drive down the road, chances are those fences will still be there.

## VOCABULARY

a. *paragraph  3:* reconciled, untillable

b. *paragraph  7:* taper, binders

c. *paragraph 8:* disposition

d. *paragraph 9:* incorporate, galvanized

e. *paragraph 11:* accommodate

f. *paragraph 17:* reef-knot fashion

g. *paragraph 21:* longitudinal

h. *paragraph 22:* integrated

## QUESTIONS

1. What in the opening of the essay shows that Long is writing for the general reader and not for specialists?

2. How does Long help the reader visualize the process?

3. What steps in the process require the most explanation, and why?

4. What are some techniques that Long uses to add interest and colour to his account of building a rail fence?

## WRITING ASSIGNMENTS

1. Describe a procedure you know well — for example, doing a lab experiment, preparing a meal. Write for the general reader who knows nothing about the procedure or activity.

2. Each of the following processes contains several main stages; one or more of these stages contain steps or procedures. Give an analysis of one of the processes, or do so for a comparable process you know well. Distinguish the main from the subordinate stages and procedures carefully:

   a.   replacing or repairing a flat tire

   b.   cutting down a dead tree

   c.   painting the outside of a house

   d.   parking on a hill

   e.   refinishing a piece of furniture

## ALEXANDER PETRUNKEVITCH

Alexander Petrunkevitch *was born in Russia and emigrated to America in 1903. He taught at Yale University, where he published two seminal works on spiders. A highly cultured man who works also in history and philosophy, he has translated poetry both from and into Russian. In the following essay he describes in meticulous detail a curious and deadly battle between a spider and a wasp.*

# THE SPIDER AND THE WASP

1   In the feeding and safeguarding of their progeny insects and spiders exhibit some interesting analogies to reasoning and some crass examples of blind instinct. The case I propose to describe here is that of the tarantula spiders and their arch-enemy, the digger wasps of the genus Pepsis. It is a classic example of what looks like intelligence pitted against instinct — a strange situation in which the victim, though fully able to defend itself, submits unwittingly to its destruction.

2   Most tarantulas live in the tropics, but several species occur in the temperate zone and a few are common in the southern U.S. Some varieties are large and have powerful fangs with which they can inflict a deep wound. These formidable looking spiders do not, however, attack man; you can hold one in your hand, if you are gentle, without being bitten. Their bite is dangerous only to insects and small mammals such as mice; for man it is no worse than a hornet's sting.

3   Tarantulas customarily live in deep cylindrical burrows, from which they emerge at dusk and into which they retire at dawn. Mature males wander about after dark in search of females and occasionally stray into houses. After mating, the male dies in a few weeks, but a female lives much longer and can mate several years in succession. In a Paris museum is a tropical specimen which is said to have been living in captivity for 25 years.

4   A fertilized female tarantula lays from 200 to 400 eggs at a time; thus it is possible for a single tarantula to produce several thousand young. She takes no care of them beyond weaving a cocoon of silk to enclose the eggs. After they hatch, the young walk away, find convenient places in which to dig their burrows and spend the rest of their lives in solitude. The eyesight of tarantulas is poor, being limited to a sensing of change in the intensity of light and to the perception of moving objects. They apparently have little or no sense of hearing, for a hungry tarantula will pay no attention to a loudly chirping cricket placed in its cage unless the insect happens to touch one of its legs.

5   But all spiders, and especially hairy ones, have an extremely delicate sense of touch. Laboratory experiments prove that tarantulas can distinguish three types of touch: pressure against the body wall, stroking of the body hair, and riffling of certain very fine hairs on the legs called trichobothria. Pressure against the body, by the finger or the end of a pencil, causes the tarantula to move off slowly for a short distance. The touch excites no defensive response unless the approach is from above where the spider can see the motion, in which case it rises on its hind legs, lifts its front legs, opens its fangs and holds this threatening posture as long as the object continues to move.

6   The entire body of a tarantula, especially its legs, is thickly clothed with hair. Some of it is short and wooly, some long and stiff. Touching this body hair produces one of two distinct reactions. When the spider is hungry, it responds with an immediate and swift attack. At the touch of a cricket's antennae the tarantula seizes the insect so swiftly that a motion picture taken at the rate of 64 frames per second shows only the result and not the process of capture. But when the spider is not hungry, the stimulation of its hairs merely causes it to shake the touched limb. An insect can walk under its hairy belly unharmed.

7   The trichobothria, very fine hairs growing from disclike membranes on the legs, are sensitive only to air movement. A light breeze makes them vibrate slowly, without disturbing the common hair. When one blows gently on the trichobothria, the tarantula reacts with a quick jerk of its four front legs. If the front and hind legs are stimulated at the same time, the spider makes a sudden jump. This reaction is quite independent of the state of its appetite.

8   These three tactile responses — to pressure on the body wall, to moving of the common hair, and to flexing of the trichobothria — are so different from one another that

there is no possibility of confusing them. They serve the tarantula adequately for most of its needs and enable it to avoid most annoyances and dangers. But they fail the spider completely when it meets its deadly enemy, the digger wasp Pepsis.

These solitary wasps are beautiful and formidable creatures. Most species are either a deep shiny blue all over, or deep blue with rusty wings. The largest have a wing span of about four inches. They live on nectar. When excited, they give off a pungent odor — a warning that they are ready to attack. The sting is much worse than that of a bee or common wasp, and the pain and swelling last longer. In the adult stage the wasp lives only a few months. The female produces but a few eggs, one at a time at intervals of two or three days. For each egg the mother must provide one adult tarantula, alive but paralyzed. The mother wasp attaches the egg to the paralyzed spider's abdomen. Upon hatching from the egg, the larva is many hundreds of times smaller than its living but helpless victim. It eats no other food and drinks no water. By the time it has finished its single Gargantuan meal and become ready for wasphood, nothing remains of the tarantula but its indigestible chitinous skeleton. **9**

The mother wasp goes tarantula-hunting when the egg in her ovary is almost ready to be laid. Flying low over the ground late on a sunny afternoon, the wasp looks for its victim or for the mouth of a tarantula burrow, a round hole edged by a bit of silk. The sex of the spider makes no difference, but the mother is highly discriminating as to species. Each species of Pepsis requires a certain species of tarantula, and the wasp will not attack the wrong species. In a cage with a tarantula which is not its normal prey, the wasp avoids the spider and is usually killed by it in the night. **10**

Yet when a wasp finds the correct species, it is the other way about. To identify the species the wasp apparently must explore the spider with her antennae. The tarantula shows an amazing tolerance to this exploration. The wasp crawls under it and walks over it without evoking any hostile response. The molestation is so great and so persistent that the tarantula often rises on all eight legs, as if it were on stilts. It may stand this way for several minutes. Meanwhile the wasp, having satisfied itself that the victim is of the right species, moves off a few inches to dig the spider's grave. Working vigorously with legs and jaws, it excavates a hole 8 to 10 inches deep with a diameter slightly larger than the spider's girth. Now and again the wasp pops out of the hole to make sure that the spider is still there. **11**

When the grave is finished, the wasp returns to the tarantula to complete her ghastly enterprise. First she feels it all over once more with her antennae. Then her behavior becomes more aggressive. She bends her abdomen, protruding her sting, and searches for the soft membrane at the point where the spider's legs join its body — the only spot where she can penetrate the horny skeleton. From time to time, as the exasperated spider slowly shifts ground, the wasp turns on her back and slides along with the aid of her wings, trying to get under the tarantula for a shot at the vital spot. During all this maneuvering, which can last for several minutes, the tarantula makes no move to save itself. Finally the wasp corners it against some obstruction and grasps one of its legs in her powerful jaws. Now at last the harassed spider tries a desperate but vain defense. The two contestants roll over and over on the ground. It is a terrifying sight and the outcome is always the same. The wasp finally manages to thrust her sting into the soft spot and holds it there for a few seconds while she pumps in the poison. Almost immediately the tarantula falls paralyzed on its back. Its legs stop twitching, its heart stops beating. Yet it is not dead, as is shown by the fact that if taken from the wasp it can be restored to some sensitivity by being kept in a moist chamber for several months. **12**

After paralyzing the tarantula, the wasp cleans herself by dragging her body along the ground and rubbing her feet, sucks the drop of blood oozing from the wound in the **13** spider's abdomen, then grabs a leg of the flabby, helpless animal in her jaws and drags it down to the bottom of the grave. She stays there for many minutes, sometimes for several hours, and what she does all that time in the dark we do not know. Eventually she lays her egg and attaches it to the side of the spider's abdomen with a sticky secretion. Then she emerges, fills the grave with soil carried bit by bit in her jaws, and finally tramples the ground all around to hide any trace of the grave from prowlers. Then she flies away, leaving her descendant safely started in life.

14     In all this the behavior of the wasp evidently is qualitatively different from that of the spider. The wasp acts like an intelligent animal. This is not to say that instinct plays no part or that she reasons as man does. But her actions are to the point; they are not automatic and can be modified to fit the situation. We do not know for certain how she identifies the tarantula — probably it is by some olfactory or chemo-tactile sense — but she does it purposefully and does not blindly tackle a wrong species.

15     On the other hand, the tarantula's behavior shows only confusion. Evidently the wasp's pawing gives it no pleasure, for it tries to move away. That the wasp is not simulating sexual stimulation is certain because male and female tarantulas react in the same way to its advances. That the spider is not anesthetized by some odorless secretion is easily shown by blowing lightly at the tarantula and making it jump suddenly. What, then, makes the tarantula behave as stupidly as it does?

16     No clear, simple answer is available. Possibly the stimulation by the wasp's antennae is masked by a heavier pressure on the spider's body, so that it reacts as when prodded by a pencil. But the explanation may be much more complex. Initiative in attack is not in the nature of tarantulas; most species fight only when cornered so that escape is impossible. Their inherited patterns of behavior apparently prompt them to avoid problems rather than attack them. For example, spiders always weave their webs in three dimensions, and when a spider finds that there is insufficient space to attach certain threads in the third dimension, it leaves the place and seeks another, instead of finishing the web in a single plane. This urge to escape seems to arise under all circumstances, in all phases of life, and to take the place of reasoning. For a spider to change the pattern of its web is as impossible as for an inexperienced man to build a bridge across a chasm obstructing his way.

17     In a way the instictive urge to escape is not only easier but often more efficient than reasoning. The tarantula does exactly what is most efficient in all cases except in an encounter with a ruthless and determined attacker dependent for the existence of her own species on killing as many tarantulas as she can lay eggs. Perhaps in this case the spider follows its usual pattern of trying to escape, instead of seizing and killing the wasp, because it is not aware of its danger. In any case, the survival of the tarantula species as a whole is protected by the fact that the spider is much more fertile than the wasp.

## VOCABULARY

a. *paragraph 1:* progeny

b. *paragraph 2:* temperate

c. *paragraph 5:* riffling

d. *paragraph 8:* tactile

e. *paragraph 9:* pungent, chitinous

# QUESTIONS

1. What kind of audience is Petrunkevitch writing for in this essay? What evidence in the essay reveals the audience Petrunkevitch envisions?

2. "The Spider and the Wasp" is primarily a minutely observed factual account, but its power as an essay depends on the author's fascination with his subject. What evidence of this personal involvement can you point to? Are Petrunkevitch's feelings ever explicitly stated? If so, where?

3. Analyse paragraph 12 for ways in which Petrunkevitch links sentences to make time relationships clear and form a coherent sequence. Mark the kinds of transitional devices that you discover in the paragraph.

4. Throughout the essay, identify examples of inductive reasoning.

5. What kinds of transitions does Petrunkevitch use to move from paragraph to paragraph? Explain the transition from paragraph 15 to paragraph 16.

6. What central idea gives unity to the essay? Show how the essay is unified.

# WRITING ASSIGNMENTS

1. Consider the ritual of the spider and the wasp, as Petrunkevitch reports it. Then, as a detached but fascinated observer, write a short process essay (under 1,000 words) describing in detail some human ritual. Here are a few suggestions:

|   |   |   |   |
|---|---|---|---|
| a. | commuting | e. | high-school graduation |
| b. | going to the laundromat | f. | college registration |
| c. | celebrating a birthday | g. | calling for a date |
| d. | eating a lobster or an artichoke | h. | shopping at the supermarket |

2. Closely observe some typical behaviour of your pet or some other animal, such as eating, begging, or stalking, and write a short process essay describing the behaviour in great detail.

# W.S. MERWIN

*W.S. Merwin is a poet, playwright, translator, and essayist whose work appears often in* The New Yorker *magazine. He is a highly gifted writer of the short essay; as his description of unchopping a tree shows, a process analysis can be more than a set of simple instructions. In his essay Merwin talks to the reader in an ironic tone, as if to say, "We share a secret, something that I am hinting at, and I need not say directly." When writer and reader share an understanding of this kind, they share it about a third party — someone who does not know what they do and needs to be enlightened.*

## UNCHOPPING A TREE

1    Start with the leaves, the small twigs, and the nests that have been shaken, ripped, or broken off by the fall; these must be gathered and attached once again to their respective places. It is not arduous work, unless major limbs have been smashed or mutilated. If the fall was carefully and correctly planned, the chances of anything of the kind happening will have been reduced. Again, much depends upon the size, age, shape, and species of the tree. Still, you will be lucky if you can get through this stage without having to use machinery. Even in the best of circumstances it is a labor that will make you wish often that you had won the favor of the universe of ants, the empire of mice, or at least a local tribe of squirrels, and could enlist their labors and their talents. But no, they leave you to it. They have learned, with time. This is men's work. It goes without saying that if the tree was hollow in whole or in part, and contained old nests of bird or mammal or insect, or hoards of nuts or such structures as wasps or bees build for their survival, the contents will have to be repaired where necessary, and reassembled, insofar as possible, in their original order, including the shells of nuts already opened. With spiders' webs you must simply do the best you can. We do not have the spider's weaving equipment, nor any substitute for the leaf's living bond with its point of attachment and nourishment. It is even harder to simulate the latter when the leaves have once become dry — as they are bound to do, for this is not the labor of a moment. Also it hardly needs saying that this is the time for repairing any neighboring trees or bushes or other growth that may have been damaged by the fall. The same rules apply. Where neighboring trees were of the same species it is difficult not to waste time conveying a detached leaf back to the wrong tree. Practice, practice. Put your hope in that.

2    Now the tackle must be put into place or the scaffolding, depending on the surroundings and the dimensions of the tree. It is ticklish work. Almost always it involves, in itself, further damage to the area, which will have to be corrected later. But as you've heard, it can't be helped. And care now is likely to save you considerable trouble later. Be careful to grind nothing into the ground.

3    At last the time comes for the erecting of the trunk. By now it will scarcely be necessary to remind you of the delicacy of this huge skeleton. Every motion of the tackle, every slight upward heave of the trunk, the branches, their elaborately reassembled panoply of leaves (now dead) will draw from you an involuntary gasp. You will watch for a leaf or a twig to be snapped off yet again. You will listen for the nuts to shift in the hollow limb and you will hear whether they are indeed falling into place or are spilling in disorder — in which case, or in the event of anything else of the kind — operations will have to cease, of course, while you correct the matter. The raising itself is no small enterprise, from the moment when the chains tighten around the old bandages until the bole hangs vertical above the stump, splinter above splinter. Now the final straightening of the splinters themselves can take place (the preliminary work is best done while the wood is still green and soft, but at times when the splinters are not badly twisted most of the straightening is left until now, when the torn ends are face to face with each other). When the splinters are perfectly complementary the appropriate fixture is applied. Again we have no duplicate of the original substance. Ours is extremely strong, but it is rigid. It is limited to surfaces, and there is no play in it. However the core is not the part of the trunk that conducted life from the roots up into the branches and back again. It was relatively inert. The fixative for this part is not the same as the one for the outer layers and the bark, and if either of these is involved in the splintered section they must receive applications of the appropriate

adhesives. Apart from being incorrect and probably ineffecive, the core fixative would leave a scar on the bark.

When all is ready the splintered trunk is lowered onto the splinters of the stump. This, **4** one might say, is only the skeleton of the resurrection. Now the chips must be gathered, and the sawdust, and returned to their former positions. The fixative for the wood layers will be applied to chips and sawdust consisting only of wood. Chips and sawdust consisting of several substances will receive applications of the correct adhesives. It is as well, where possible, to shelter the materials from the elements while working. Weathering makes it harder to identify the smaller fragments. Bark sawdust in particular the earth lays claim to very quickly. You must find your own ways of coping with this problem. There is a certain beauty, you will notice at moments, in the pattern of the chips as they are fitted back into place. You will wonder to what extent it should be described as natural, to what extent man-made. It will lead you on to speculations about the parentage of beauty itself, to which you will return.

The adhesive for the chips is translucent, and not so rigid as that for the splinters. That **5** for bark and its subcutaneous layers is transparent and runs into the fibers on either side, partially dissolving them into each other. It does not set the sap flowing again but it does pay a kind of tribute to the preoccupations of the ancient thoroughfares. You could not roll an egg over the joints but some of the mineshafts would still be passable, no doubt. For the first exploring insect who raises its head in the tight echoless passages. The day comes when it is all restored, even to the moss (now dead) over the wound. You will sleep badly, thinking of the removal of the scaffolding that must begin the next morning. How you will hope for sun and a still day!

The removal of the scaffolding or tackle is not so dangerous, perhaps, to the surround- **6** ings, as its installation, but it presents problems. It should be taken from the spot piece by piece as it is detached, and stored at a distance. You have come to accept it there, around the tree. The sky begins to look naked as the chains and struts one by one vacate their positions. Finally the moment arrives when the last sustaining piece is removed and the tree stands again on its own. It is as though its weight for a moment stood on your heart. You listen for a thud of settlement, a warning creak deep in the intricate joinery. You cannot believe it will hold. How like something dreamed it is, standing there all by itself. How long will it stand there now? The first breeze that touches its dead leaves all seems to flow into your mouth. You are afraid the motion of the clouds will be enough to push it over. What more can you do? What more can you do?

But there is nothing more you can do. **7**

Others are waiting. **8**

Everything is going to have to be put back. **9**

## VOCABULARY

a. *paragraph 1:* simulate

b. *paragraph 2:* tackle

c. *paragraph 3:* panoply, bole, complementary, fixative

d. *paragraph 5:* translucent, subcutaneous, thoroughfares

e. *paragraph 6:* struts, joinery

# QUESTIONS

1. What are the chief indications of Merwin's purpose in his essay? Does he state that purpose directly?

2. Examine the following statement from paragraph 4 carefully: "You will wonder to what extent it should be described as natural, to what extent man-made. It will lead you on to speculations about the parentage of beauty itself, to which you will return." What is the tone of the statement — that is, what seems to be the writer's attitude toward his reader as well as toward the act of unchopping a tree? Is an attitude *implied* in the whole essay that no single statement expresses? Could you accept such an implication as embodying the thesis?

3. The writer has chosen a strategy to deal with his idea — that is, he approaches his reader in a particular way to achieve a particular effect. What does he want his reader to think and feel at the end of the essay, and what is his strategy in realizing these aims?

4. The essay ends with three single-sentence paragraphs. To what effect? What is Merwin saying?

5. How well does the writer achieve his purpose?

# WRITING ASSIGNMENT

Write an essay on a similar topic, for example, undoing an insult. Be consistent in conveying a tone and in building to your conclusion. Do not state your thesis directly, let the reader discover it in your tone and details.

# CAUSE AND EFFECT

In many essays and books, causal analysis is the chief method of analysis, as in explanations of the nature and effects of nuclear energy. Causal analysis may take various forms (immediate and mediate or remote causes, formal and material causes, for example). However, writers do not always give the technical names of causes. It is nevertheless important to distinguish several kinds of analysis when the essay uses more than one.

Unlike process analysis, there is not just one kind of causal analysis. The kind of explanation that satisfies the ordinary person — the reason for a cold, for example — will usually not satisfy a scientist. Later in this book we shall consider this more demanding kind of causal explanation as it is used in argument. Usually we look for an event prior to the one we are trying to explain; but often there are many — some close to the event, some remote in time. For example, failure to study for an important exam may lead to a student's eventual failure in a course, and a subsequent drop in grade point average. The course failure — the immediate cause of the drop in the average — will probably be of most concern to college officials considering a scholarship renewal; the remote cause, the failure to study, probably will be of more concern to the student in seeking to improve. In writing about such events, which of them we discuss as the "cause" depends on the purpose of our analysis.

Objects, too, have more than one cause. One useful kind of analysis here distinguishes four related ones. Consider a dictionary. Its material cause is the paper, ink and other materials used in its manufacture. The formal cause is its shape — the alphabetic arrangement of words, and the arrangement of definitions according to a plan. The efficient cause is the dictionary writer, and the final cause, the use intended for the dictionary. The analysis of a chemical compound is more rigorous, demanding an account of substances that form the compound and the process by which the formation occurs. Process analysis ("how") often combines with causal analysis ("why") because we are interested in both the how and why of objects and of events.

## JOHN BROOKS

John Brooks *was a contributing editor of* Time *magazine, and has been on the staff of* The New Yorker *magazine for many years, writing about American business. His books include* The Go-Go Years *(1973) and* The Telephone *(1976), a history of* AT&T, *from which these paragraphs are reprinted. Toward the end of the paragraphs, Brooks refers to the ideas of Marshall McLuhan, summarized earlier in* The Telephone. *He illustrates for us McLuhan's idea that the telephone is a "cool" medium — one requiring full participation since, unlike print, it is empty of content. The user supplies this content, unlike the reader of a book. Brooks says later in his book: "In the uneasy postwar world, people seemed to be coming to associate the telephone with their frustrations, their fears, and their sense of powerlessness against technology."*

## THE TELEPHONE

What has the telephone done to us, or for us, in the hundred years of its existence? A few
effects suggest themselves at once. It has saved lives by getting rapid word of illness, in-

jury, or famine from remote places. By joining with the elevator to make possible the multistory residence or office building, it has made possible — for better or worse — the modern city. By bringing about a quantum leap in the speed and ease with which information moves from place to place, it has greatly accelerated the rate of scientific and technological change and growth in industry. Beyond doubt it has crippled if not killed the ancient art of letter writing. It has made living alone possible for persons with normal social impulses; by so doing, it has played a role in one of the greatest social changes of this century, the breakup of the multigenerational household. It has made the waging of war chillingly more efficient than formerly. Perhaps (though not provably) it has prevented wars that might have arisen out of international misunderstanding caused by written communication. Or perhaps — again not provably — by magnifying and extending irrational personal conflicts based on voice contact, it has caused wars. Certainly it has extended the scope of human conflicts, since it impartially disseminates the useful knowledge of scientists and the babble of bores, the affection of the affectionate and the malice of the malicious.

2    But the question remains unanswered. The obvious effects just cited seem inadequate, mechanistic; they only scratch the surface. Perhaps the crucial effects are evanescent and unmeasurable. Use of the telephone involves personal risk because it involves exposure; for some, to be "hung up on" is among the worst of fears; others dream of a ringing telephone and wake up with a pounding heart. The telephone's actual ring — more, perhaps, than any other sound in our daily lives — evokes hope, relief, fear, anxiety, joy, according to our expectations. The telephone is our nerve-end to society.

3    In some ways it is in itself a thing of paradox. In one sense a metaphor for the times it helped create, in another sense the telephone is their polar opposite. It is small and gentle — relying on low voltages and miniature parts — in times of hugeness and violence. It is basically simple in times of complexity. It is so nearly human, recreating voices so faithfully that friends or lovers need not identify themselves by name even when talking across oceans, that to ask its effects on human life may seem hardly more fruitful than to ask the effect of the hand or the foot. The Canadian philosopher Marshall McLuhan — one of the few who have addressed themselves to these questions — was perhaps not far from the mark when he spoke of the telephone as creating "a kind of extra-sensory perception."

## VOCABULARY

a. *paragraph 1:* famine, quantum, irrational, disseminate

b. *paragraph 2:* mechanistic, evanescent

c. *paragraph 3:* paradox

## QUESTIONS

1. Why does Brooks consider the effects he discusses in paragraph 1 less significant than those in paragraph 2? What does he mean by the statement, "Perhaps the crucial effects are evanescent and unmeasurable"?

2. In what ways is the telephone a paradox? Does the author show it to be a paradox in paragraphs 1 and 2?

3. Has Brooks stated all the effects of the telephone, or has he identified only a few? What central point is he making?

## WRITING ASSIGNMENTS

1. Develop one of the ideas in the essay from your personal experience. You might discuss your own positive and negative attitudes toward the telephone, and the reasons for them, or you might develop the statement, "In some ways it is in itself a thing of paradox."

2. Write an essay describing what it would be like to live without a telephone.

3. Discuss the impact of the telephone on life in your home. Distinguish the various uses and effects of the telephone for various members of your family.

## MARVIN HARRIS

Marvin Harris, *who teaches anthropology at the University of Florida, writes about American life from the point of view of the anthropologist in* Cannibals and Kings *(1977) and* America Now *(1981), from which the selection reprinted below is taken. Harris gives us an interesting illutration of Murphy's Law without trying to explain it. Notice that he combines many of the types of exposition discussed in this section of the book, including definition, process, and example.*

## WHY NOTHING WORKS

According to a law attributed to the savant known only as Murphy, "if anything can go wrong, it will." Corollaries to Murphy's Law suggest themselves as clues to the shoddy goods problem: If anything can break down, it will; if anything can fall apart, it will; if anything can stop running, it will. While Murphy's Law can never be wholly defeated, its effects can usually be postponed. Much of human existence consists of efforts aimed at making sure that things don't go wrong, fall apart, break down, or stop running until a decent interval has elapsed after their manufacture. Forestalling Murphy's Law as applied to products demands intelligence, skill, and commitment. If these human imputs are assisted by special quality-control instruments, machines, and scientific sampling procedures, so much the better. But gadgets and sampling alone will never do the trick since these items are also subject to Murphy's Law. Quality-control instruments need maintenance; gauges go out of order; X rays and laser beams need adjustments. No matter how advanced the technology, quality demands intelligent, motivated human thought and action.

Some reflection about the material culture of prehistoric and preindustrial peoples may help to show what I mean. A single visit to a museum which displays artifacts used by simple preindustrial societies is sufficient to dispel the notion that quality is dependent on technology. Artifacts may be of simple, even primitive design, and yet be built to serve their intended purpose in a reliable manner during a lifetime of use. We acknowledge this when we honor the label "handmade" and pay extra for the jewelry, sweaters, and handbags turned out by the dwindling breeds of modern-day craftspeople.

3    What is the source of quality that one finds, let us say, in a Pomo Indian basket so tightly woven that it was used to hold boiling water and never leaked a drop, or in an Eskimo skin boat with its matchless combination of lightness, strength, and seaworthiness? Was it merely the fact that these items were handmade? I don't think so. In unskilled or uncaring hands a handmade basket or boat can fall apart as quickly as baskets or boats made by machines. I rather think that the reason we honor the label "handmade" is because it evokes not a technological relationship between producer and product but a social relationship between producer and consumer. Throughout prehistory it was the fact that producers and consumers were either one and the same individuals or close kin that guaranteed the highest degree of reliability and durability in manufactured items. Men made their own spears, bows and arrows, and projectile points; women wove their own baskets and carrying nets, fashioned their own clothing from animal skins, bark, or fiber. Later, as technology advanced and material culture grew more complex, different members of the band or village adopted craft specialties such as pottery-making, basket-weaving, or canoe-building. Although many items were obtained through barter and trade, the connection between producer and consumer still remained intimate, permanent, and caring.

4    A man is not likely to fashion a spear for himself whose point will fall off in midflight; nor is a woman who weaves her own basket likely to make it out of rotted straw. Similarly, if one is sewing a parka for a husband who is about to go hunting for the family with the temperature at sixty below, all stitches will be perfect. And when the men who make boats are the uncles and fathers of those who sail them, they will be as seaworthy as the state of the art permits.

5    In contrast, it is very hard for people to care about strangers or about products to be used by strangers. In our era of industrial mass production and mass marketing, quality is a constant problem because the intimate sentimental and personal bonds which once made us responsible to each other and to our products have withered away and been replaced by money relationships. Not only are the producers and consumers strangers but the women and men involved in various stages of production and distribution — management, the worker on the factory floor, the office help, the salespeople — are also strangers to each other. In larger companies there may be hundreds of thousands of people all working on the same product who can never meet face-to-face or learn one another's names. The larger the company and the more complex its division of labor, the greater the sum of uncaring relationships and hence the greater the effect of Murphy's Law. Growth adds layer on layer of executives, foremen, engineers, production workers, and sales specialists to the payroll. Since each new employee contributes a diminished share to the overall production process, alienation from the company and its product are likely to increase along with the neglect or even purposeful sabotage of quality standards.

## VOCABULARY

a. *paragraph 1:* savant, corollaries, forestalling

b. *paragraph 2:* artifacts

c. *paragraph 3:* projectile

d. *paragraph 5:* sentimental, alienation, sabotage

## QUESTIONS

1. What rule does Murphy's Law play in Harris's explanation of why nothing works? Does he say or imply that the law is irreversible and that things inevitably break down?

2. How does Harris prove that quality is not dependent on technology? Has he provided enough evidence to establish this point?

3. Does Harris provide the same kind of evidence for his explanation of the source of quality in the handmade products he discusses in paragraphs 3 through 5? Does he claim that his evidence is certain?

4. We can test the evidence Harris presents in paragraph 2 by examining the museum objects discussed. Can you think of a way to test the explanation in paragraphs 3 through 5 if the evidence cannot be tested directly? How convincing do you find his explanation in these paragraphs?

## WRITING ASSIGNMENTS

1. Write your own explanation of why something you own does not work. In the course of your analysis, discuss the extent to which Harris's ideas offer an explanation.

2. Write an essay on one of the following topics, using causal analysis and examples to develop a thesis. The more limited your focus and discussion, the stronger your thesis will be.

   a. cheating in high school

   b. driving habits of teenagers

   c. family arguments or rivalries

   d. choosing a university or college

## NORMAN COUSINS

Norman Cousins *is inseparably linked with the* Saturday Review, *which he edited from 1940 to 1977. He won numerous awards for his journalism and his work on behalf of world peace, including the Peace Medal of the United Nations in 1971. His columns were collected in a number of books that provide a continuous political commentary on postwar America and the world. His essay on Benny Paret, whose fatal knockout in the ring Norman Mailer describes earlier in this book, raises important questions about boxing and spectator sports generally — and also about the responsibility of the public for the violence encouraged in them.*

## WHO KILLED BENNY PARET?

Sometime about 1935 or 1936 I had an interview with Mike Jacobs, the prize-fight promoter. I was a fledgling newspaper reporter at that time; my beat was education, but dur-

1

ing the vacation season I found myself on varied assignments, all the way from ship news to sports reporting. In this way I found myself sitting opposite the most powerful figure in the boxing world.

2    There was nothing spectacular in Mr. Jacobs's manner or appearance; but when he spoke about prize fights, he was no longer a bland little man but a colossus who sounded the way Napoleon must have sounded when he reviewed a battle. You knew you were listening to Number One. His saying something made it true.

3    We discussed what to him was the only important element in successful promoting — how to please the crowd. So far as he was concerned, there was no mystery to it. You put killers in the ring and the people filled your arena. You hire boxing artists — men who are adroit at feinting, parrying, weaving, jabbing, and dancing, but who don't pack dynamite in their fists — and you wind up counting your empty seats. So you searched for the killers and sluggers and maulers — fellows who could hit with the force of a baseball bat.

4    I asked Mr. Jacobs if he was speaking literally when he said people came out to see the killer.

5    "They don't come out to see a tea party," he said evenly. "They come out to see the knockout. They come out to see a man hurt. If they think anything else, they're kidding themselves."

6    Recently a young man by the name of Benny Paret was killed in the ring. The killing was seen by millions; it was on television. In the twelfth round he was hit hard in the head several times, went down, was counted out, and never came out of the coma.

7    The Paret fight produced a flurry of investigations. Governor Rockefeller was shocked by what happened and appointed a committee to assess the responsibility. The New York State Boxing Commission decided to find out what was wrong. The District Attorney's office expressed its concern. One question that was solemnly studied in all three probes concerned the action of the referee. Did he act in time to stop the fight? Another question had to do with the role of the examining doctors who certified the physical fitness of the fighters before the bout. Still another question involved Mr. Paret's manager; did he rush his boy into the fight without adequate time to recuperate from the previous one?

8    In short, the investigators looked into every possible cause except the real one. Benny Paret was killed because the human fist delivers enough impact, when directed against the head, to produce a massive hemorrhage in the brain. The human brain is the most delicate and complex mechanism in all creation. It has a lacework of millions of highly fragile nerve connections. Nature attempts to protect this exquisitely intricate machinery by encasing it in a hard shell. Fortunately, the shell is thick enough to withstand a great deal of pounding. Nature, however, can protect man against everything except man himself. Not every blow to the head will kill a man — but there is always the risk of concussion and damage to the brain. A prize fighter may be able to survive even repeated brain concussions and go on fighting, but the damage to his brain may be permanent.

9    In any event, it is futile to investigate the referee's role and seek to determine whether he should have intervened to stop the fight earlier. This is not where the primary responsibility lies. The primary responsibility lies with the people who pay to see a man hurt. The referee who stops a fight too soon from the crowd's viewpoint can expect to be booed. The crowd wants the knockout; it wants to see a man stretched out on the canvas. This is the supreme moment in boxing. It is nonsense to talk about prize fighting as a test of boxing skills. No crowd was ever brought to its feet screaming and cheering at the sight of two men beautifully dodging and weaving out of each other's jabs. The time the crowd comes alive is when a man is hit hard over the heart or the head, when his mouthpiece flies out, when blood squirts out of his nose or eyes, when he wobbles under the attack and his pursuer continues to smash at him with poleax impact.

Don't blame it on the referee. Don't even blame it on the fight managers. Put the blame    **10**
where it belongs — on the prevailing mores that regard prize fighting as a perfectly proper
enterprise and vehicle of entertainment. No one doubts that many people enjoy prize fighting and will miss it if it should be thrown out. And that is precisely the point.

## VOCABULARY

a. *paragraph 1:* fledgling

b. *paragraph 2:* colossus

c. *paragraph 3:* adroit, feinting, parrying

d. *paragraph 8:* hemorrhage

e. *paragraph 9:* poleax

## QUESTIONS

1. Cousins distinguishes between the immediate and the remote causes of Paret's death.
   What does he show to be the immediate cause, and why can this cause be stated with
   near certainty?

2. Cousins is concerned chiefly with the remote cause of Paret's death. How is this concern basic to his purpose in writing the essay? What are the chief indications of that
   purpose?

3. How would a different purpose have required Cousins to focus instead on the immediate cause?

4. How does Cousins establish the remote cause? Is his evidence statistical — based on a
   sample of statements of boxing fans? Is it theoretical — based on a discussion of
   "human nature"? Is he concerned with the psychology of the crowd or the sociology of
   boxing? Is his analysis of the event intended to offer a complete explanation?

## WRITING ASSIGNMENTS

1. Analyse a mass sport like pro football or hockey to determine the extent of its appeal to
   violent emotions.

2. Contrast Cousins's view of the causes of Paret's death with Mailer's view in "The
   Death of Benny Paret."

## MICHELE LANDSBERG

Michele Landsberg *is a Canadian author and columnist well known for her work on family and women's issues. Her columns have appeared in the* Toronto Star *and* The Globe and

*Mail. She has also published two books:* Women and Children First, *a collection of her columns dealing with women at home and in the workplace, and* Michele Landsberg's Guide to Children's Literature. *As a wife and mother as well as a professional writer, she has tried to find a middle ground between the ideals of militant feminism and the responsibilities of family life. In this essay she reflects on the way ceremonies mark the passage of time in our lives.*

# CEREMONIES

1   Ceremonies — weddings, christenings, bar mitzvahs, graduations, and even, heaven help me, birthdays and parades — always make me cry.

2   "Now snap out of this sentimental idiocy," I told myself, in what I imagined to be my best Bella Abzug growl, as I sat at the McMaster University convocation last Friday. No use, I felt the old familiar sting under the eyelids as the fanfare rang out, the academics solemnly paraded in their multicoloured gowns, the beaming parents sat tier on tier in the bleachers of what is normally a gym, and the "graduands" began to file endlessly past the chancellor to receive their degrees.

3   Now, in serene ceremony, three or four undignified years (heady new freedom, intellectual passion, beery hangovers, stomach-churning exams) were signed and sealed in dignity. In their hundreds, the young graduands (so much shining hair, so many scrubbed faces) came in an unwinding ribbon of black gowns to kneel before Chancellor Allan Leal. "I admit you Bachelor of Arts," he said to each one, and not even after the 200th did his voice lose its cheery boom of congratulation. Then the academic hood (like a long loop of silk scarf) was slipped over his or her shoulders, and the young graduate turned to march down from the podium and into the world.

4   In the moment of turning, student after student beamed at us a tremendous, exultant, partly-embarrassed smile, lips closed so that they wouldn't burst into an involuntary laugh of delight. And each one, striding down the aisle, sought out his or her family in the crowd to exchange a glance of triumph.

5   Why do moments like that make people cry? The parents of the graduates, of course, have the excitement of pride to justify their moist eyes. But even for bystanders like me, there's an irresistible poignancy about ceremonies. I first started to feel that way in my teens, when it dawned on me that summer did not last forever, and that next year was always turning into this year, and then fading into last year with startling speed.

6   I began to hoard life the way other people hoard elastic bands or vintage wines, latching onto anything which slowed down the quicksilver passage of time. In my mental bank account, I have a peculiar half-conscious ledger system for keeping track of time won and lost. I hate to sleep in, because that steals away part of the day, and I hate to go to sleep at night. I love summer because the days are long and crammed with the sensual treasures which I stockpile in memory against the turn of the year. A day spent picking raspberries in the hot sun is a day wrestled away from the black hole of eternity. But an afternoon spent in a movie is an afternoon lost forever, an afternoon which trickled away while I wasn't there.

7   I gloat over anything ancient — words, or Roman coins, or human rituals — because they have been scooped up and saved from the obliterating flood of time. I once seized on and saved a tattered, yellowing handwritten title deed to a Muskoka log cabin whose ruins I was exploring. And I memorized the flowers still growing in the dooryard; someone had planted them, once. In France, I spent some happy hours exulting over the name of a river,

a name which, according to the books, had come down from pre-history. Imagine: a one-syllable word had survived since before recorded time.

Ceremonies conquer time, too, and I suppose that's why I love them. Participants in **8** ceremony seem to me to step out of time for the moment. Caveboys and cavegirls must have smiled just this way (new dignity struggling with exuberance) when they passed their test of adulthood and went forth from the parental cave.

Weddings, funerals, harvest festivals, and religious rites which have come unchanged **9** through the centuries, all snatch us up from the rush of time and hold us still, linked to those who have felt these feelings before and those who will feel them after we have died.

So I forgave myself for my "sentimental idiocy" at the McMaster convocation. And I **10** only smiled tolerantly when I saw my children rolling their eyes at each other in mock exasperation to tease me for my weakness. Just the way, come to think of it, I used to tease my own mother . . . while wondering a little uneasily what it was that adults knew, what it was that made them blink away tears at ceremonial moments sad and gay.

## VOCABULARY

a. *paragraph 2:* sentimental, fanfare

b. *paragraph 4:* exultant

c. *paragraph 5:* poignancy

d. *paragraph 6:* sensual

e. *paragraph 7:* obliterating

f. *paragraph 8:* exuberance

## QUESTIONS

1. Does Landsberg single out a sufficient cause of emotional reactions to ceremonies, or instead identify a number of related (or unrelated) necessary causes?

2. Does she distinguish psychological from social causes, or does she assume these are one and the same?

3. How do ceremonies foster emotional responses in participants? In observers? How do the memories Landsberg includes in paragraphs 6 and 7 help her make her point?

4. What does Landsberg mean by the statement, "Ceremonies conquer time"?

## WRITING ASSIGNMENT

Describe an encounter with authority (police, customs officials) that you have witnessed or experienced. Analyse the causes of your response on a number of levels: physical, mental, emotional, etc.

# ALAN WERTHEIMER

Alan Wertheimer, *who teaches political science at the University of Vermont, writes often on issues of public policy. His essay, published in the* New York Times *in 1980, explores the dilemma that he believes underlies much discussion today about government spending — the choice between "helping identifiable lives and saving statistical lives." Knowing that a large segment of his audience supports what he refers to as "welfare-state humanitarianism," Wertheimer uses the dilemma to force these people to recognize that the issue is complex, does not present a simple choice between right and wrong, and demands an examination of basic assumptions.*

## STATISTICAL LIVES

**1**     Suppose the following were true:

**2**     At least some money spent on open-heart surgery could be used to prevent heart disease. True, patients in need of such surgery might die, but many more lives would be saved.

**3**     Some money spent treating tooth decay among low-income children might be used on fluoridation and dental hygiene. True, some decay would go untreated, but fewer children would ever need such treatment.

**4**     We could prohibit ransom payments to kidnappers. True, kidnapped children might die, but by lowering the incentive to kidnap, fewer children would be taken.

**5**     We could drastically reduce unemployment compensation. True, the unemployed would suffer, but by converting the money saved to private investment and by lowering the incentive to stay jobless, there would be substantially less unemployment.

**6**     These cases exhibit a similar structure. All involve choosing between a policy designed to help specific persons and one that seeks to prevent the need for such help. These choices are especially difficult because we know who needs help. The patient requiring open-heart surgery, the kidnapped child, the unemployed auto worker — they have names and faces, they are "identifiable" lives. On the other hand, we do not know whose lives will be saved or who will benefit from the prevention of heart disease, tooth decay, kidnappings, or creation of new jobs. Some people will, and we may be able to estimate their numbers with precision. These are real lives, but they are only "statistical" lives.

**7**     We might say we do not have to choose between helping those in need and preventing future needs. After all, we could do both. But resources are scarce, and even when resources are not at issue (as in the kidnapping case), we often must choose between competing persons or goals. We cannot do everything we might like to the extent we might like. We must often choose between helping identifiable lives and saving statistical lives.

**8**     I wish to make three points about these dilemmas. First, we do seem to favor the interests of identifiable lives (saving the kidnapped child) and it may not be irrational to do so. Second, we nevertheless do see the need to attend to the interests of statistical lives, even if this injures identifiable lives. Thus it is now common to hear people advocating directing more medical resources to primary prevention of disease and fewer to treatment. Israel's policy of refusing to negotiate with terrorists may risk the lives of some hostages, but we do see the point. Third, welfare-state policies focus on identifiable lives, whereas conservative economists prefer to focus on statistical lives.

**9**     Monetary theory and other technical issues aside, the new Adam Smiths tell us that however well-intentioned, welfare-state policies have not (always) worked — on the policies' own terms. Minimum-wage laws, unemployment compensation, consumer protection, occupational safety, Medicaid, Social Security — by interfering with market efficiency, by discouraging individual initiative, by impeding private-capital formation, by incurring large-scale expenditures on governmental bureaucracies — all these policies (and others) have been self-defeating. They argue that liberal economics, filled with concern for the genuine needs of identifiable lives, has swelled the future ranks of statistical lives in need. Welfare-state humanitarianism is short-sighted, they say, and is thus less humanitarian than we may believe.

We need not dwell on the accuracy of this account. Conservative economists may be    **10** wrong about the facts. We certainly need not assume that market choices and private-capital formation always serve the interests of all social groups, that regulation always does more harm than good. But suppose conservative economists are (sometimes) right about the facts. Suppose that attempts to serve the needs of identifiable lives do end up harming future statistical lives. Should we turn our back on the needs that we see in order to prevent those that we cannot see? Regrettably, the answer may sometimes be yes.

## VOCABULARY

a. *paragraph 4:* incentive

b. *paragraph 6:* statistical

c. *paragraph 8:* dilemmas

d. *paragraph 9:* impeding, incurring, humanitarianism

## QUESTIONS

1. Wertheimer's argument is in part inductive, that is, he is reasoning from particular instances to a general conclusion (see pages 216–217). He shows that well-established facts and expert testimony make the dilemma real, not fictitious. What are these facts and testimony? What in the wording of paragraphs 9 and 10 shows that Wertheimer considers this evidence highly probable and not certain?

2. If we choose to save specific persons, what would be the consequences? What would they be if we choose to save "statistical" lives?

3. One way of refuting a dilemma is to "grasp the horns" and show that at least one of the alternatives is false or would not lead to the alleged consequences. Another way is to "go between the horns" and show that a third alternative exists — a policy that would save specific persons and "statistical" lives both. In paragraphs 7 and 8 Wertheimer anticipates refutation of the dilemma and answers it. What kind of refutation might be presented, and how does he answer it?

4. Do you agree with Wertheimer's response to the dilemma in paragraph 10? On what evidence do you base your agreement or disagreement — facts, expert testimony, or assumptions that you regard as self-evident?

# WRITING ASSIGNMENTS

1. Present examples of your own of the dilemma Wertheimer presents, and use them to explore their implications of your own beliefs and conclusions.

2. Present a dilemma that you believe should concern North Americans today. Introduce facts or expert testimony to show that the dilemma is a real one, anticipate a refutation of your dilemma and answer it, and state your own views on what can or should be done.

# ARGUMENT

How you choose to build an essay depends on your purpose and audience. The purpose of most of the essays you have read so far in this book has been to illustrate, entertain, or inform, using various techniques of expository writing. Often, however, a writer's purpose is to persuade or convince the audience of the validity of an idea or an action.

The demands of exposition and persuasion are not the same. Your major concern in exposition is to be clear; your major concern in a persuasive argument is not only to be clear, but also to present your ideas in the most convincing way. In describing how to conserve fuel by driving properly, for example, your concern is to make the process clear; if your purpose is also to persuade drivers to change their driving habits, you will have to choose the best means of doing so. These means depend on the nature of your audience. If the audience is hostile to the idea of conservation, you might discuss conservation and make various appeals — for example, to conscience, public spirit, practical concerns — before turning to the matter of driving. If the audience is friendly to your topic, you probably need only remind them of the importance of conservation.

Persuasive arguments present additional challenges. You must construct a sound argument, arouse the interest of the audience through a legitimate appeal to their emotions, and show that you are honest and well-informed on the issue and therefore deserve a hearing. Although some writers seek to avoid all emotional appeals in the belief that the soundness of the argument guarantees its persuasiveness, few arguments are entirely free of emotion. The problem is not how to rid the argument of emotion but how to balance emotion and reason so that the aroused reader considers the argument fully, gives rational assent to it, and can agree with the argument in whole or in part.

Argumentative or persuasive essays have a traditional organization that is easy to learn and put to use. Derived from the oration of the law courts and legislatures of ancient Greece and Rome, this organization shaped the expository essay that we have been considering — in particular the division of the essay into an introduction that states the purpose and gives pertinent background, the main discussion or body, and the conclusion. The argumentative essay today, like the oration of ancient times, contains these divisions but expands them to meet the needs of the argument:

> *introduction*, or what was called the exordium or exhortation to the audience, appealing to the interest and good will of the audience, and stating the subject of the oration or essay;
>
> *division of proofs*, stating the thesis partly or fully and summarizing the evidence and arguments to be presented;
>
> *narration* or background, stating the facts of the case;
>
> *confirmation* or proof, arguing the thesis;
>
> *refutation*, answering opponents;
>
> *conclusion*, reinforcing and summarizing the main argument and reinforcing the original appeal to the audience.

These parts may be combined or arranged in a different order — the narration or background perhaps combined with the confirming arguments, or the refutation coming before the confirmation. Often the division or outline of the argument is omitted, and instead of coming early, the thesis may be delayed until the conclusion.

In explaining your ideas or beliefs, or in debating an issue, you draw on personal experience and observation for illustration and evidence. But often you must turn to other sources of information when you have no experience with the matter under discussion. Opinions need the support of facts.

You may find your evidence in primary sources — first-hand accounts by participants and observers — and in secondary sources — later reports and interpretations by those not present. An eyewitness account is a different kind of evidence from the reconstruction of the event by a historian in later years. Though primary evidence might seem the more reliable, it may be contradictory in itself or be contradicted by other eyewitness evidence. At the time of the Northwest Rebellion of 1885, eyewitnesses disagreed on what they saw and heard. Researchers continue to disagree on what evidence to consider and how to interpret the evidence they do accept.

Establishing the reliability of secondary sources is also difficult. The researcher must discern the reliability of the author by looking for special circumstances or biases that may colour the evidence. Evidence seldom speaks for itself, and no presentation of evidence can be totally neutral or objective, even when the writer seeks to present it fairly; all interpretations are shaped by personal and cultural attitudes. The researcher thus must consider the weight an author gives to various kinds of evidence, as well as its interpretation. Both primary and secondary sources are therefore necessary in the search for facts.

# INDUCTIVE REASONING

After the evidence has been assembled, one process by which we reason from experience and observation is called *induction*. It is a kind of reasoning we engage in daily, for example, in drawing the conclusion that a red and swollen finger is probably infected or that numerous car accidents will follow a heavy snowfall.

Inductive reasoning often makes generalizations or predictions about classes of things or people. An example is the generalization that drivers in a particular age group will probably have a higher number of car accidents, or the broader generalization that as a class another group of people are safe drivers. The prediction may be based on various kinds of evidence — for example, the knowledge of how many of these drivers were in car accidents in a ten-month period, or statistical knowledge of the accident history of this group provincewide or nationwide. No prediction can be made about any single member of the group, however, nor can the prediction be made with absolute certainty.

The problem in inductive reasoning is to choose particular instances that truly represent the group or class about which we are generalizing or making predictions. But, as in the sample precincts that pollsters use to predict the outcome of elections, it is impossible to guarantee that the limited number of people sampled are actually typical or representative. We also may be unaware of special circumstances that, if known, would weaken the generalization. These are important reasons for not claiming certainty for the generalization.

A "hasty generalization" is a judgement made on the basis of insufficient evidence or on the basis of special cases. Thus someone might argue that all people over seventy will have numerous accidents in the future (and therefore should pay higher insurance premiums) because a large number were involved in traffic accidents in a particular three-month period. The argument might be worth considering if the behaviour of these people and driving conditions could be shown to be typical. It would matter, however, if some of the drivers in these accidents proved to have impaired vision (by no means a characteristic only of older people) or if the accidents occurred in a harsh winter months. The generalization in question would then have been based both on special cases and on special circumstances.

Earlier we discussed some ways of analysing cause and effect. These include tracing an effect to its recent or proximate cause (death because of famine) and to its more distant or remote causes (drought, soil erosion, ignorance, indifference, neglect). We also discussed the "four causes" of an object — the materials of its manufacture (material cause), and use (final cause).

Cause may also be analysed through the words *necessary* and *sufficient*, as when we say that getting an "A" on the final exam is necessary but not sufficient for an "A" in the course: an "A" on the final would be sufficient only if the exam solely determined the course grade. Notice what the words *necessary* and *sufficient* imply; they refer to the conditions or circumstances in which this event *might* occur. When scientists say that a necessary condition of getting a cold is exposure to a virus, they mean that a virus of some kind must be present — not that the virus always produces a cold. Other conditions obviously need to be present, but scientists do not now claim to know what these are. If the cold always occurs when a single condition is present, this condition would be sufficient to produce the cold. But scientists still do not claim to know all the causes.

In reasoning about cause in this way, we implicitly recognize that events, like the reasons for our actions, are complex and not simple. Yet this is not what some of our statements show. Statements that generalize about *the* cause of a cold or some other physical or social or political ill, as if a single cause could be identified and dealt with, are hasty generalizations. Another hasty generalization arises from the idea that one event must be the cause of another because it precedes it: I caught the cold "because" I was soaked in a rainstorm. The sequence of events does not necessarily make one event the cause of the next. Clearly we might have caught the cold even if we had not been soaked, and we cannot know whether getting soaked will always give one a cold — even if it always has in the past. This kind of reasoning is given a Latin name — the *post hoc* fallacy, from the expression *post hoc, ergo propter hoc* (after this, therefore because of this).

# DEDUCTIVE REASONING

Induction, then, is reasoning from particular instances to a general conclusion or truth:

> I studied the equations but didn't do the practice problems, and I failed algebra. I studied my French but skipped the language lab and did poorly in French. I studied the formulas and performed the experiments carefully and passed chemistry [*three particular instances*]. Therefore, learning seems to depend on practice as well as study [*probable truth*].

Deduction, by contrast, is the process of inference — of reasoning from a general truth to another general truth or a particular instance:

> Since learning depends on constant study and practice [*general truth*], I passed algebra because I studied the equations and did the practice problems [*particular instance*].

In ordinary conversation we say informally. "I passed algebra because I studied and did the practice problems." This statement is a shortening of the following syllogism or formal argument:

> The act of learning is an act that depends on study and practice.
> The mastery of algebra is an act of learning.
> Therefore, the mastery of algebra is an act that depends on study and practice.

Notice that the first two statements — called the major and minor premises respectively — were left unstated in our shortened statement (called an *enthymeme*). Where the full argument is stated, the premises and conclusion may occur in a different order:

> The child needs to acquire fundamental skills in communication — to learn to read, write, and express himself flexibly and clearly — in order to function as a social creature [*major premise*]. The television experience does not further his verbal development [*conclusion*] because it does not require any verbal participation on his part, merely passive intake [*minor premise*]. — Marie Winn, *The Plug-In Drug*

Where inductive arguments depend on the weight of factual evidence beyond the premises, deductive arguments depend on the premises alone as evidence for the conclusion. No other evidence is required because the premises are regarded to be true — as in Barbara Amiel's argument against unilateral disarmament:

> It is a truism to say that nobody wants nuclear war. Like most truisms, it happens to be true. The Soviet Union would prefer not to cover the Earth in thermonuclear ashes if it could achieve its purposes some other way — and the same goes for the West. — Barbara Amiel, "Of Arms and the Ban I Sing"

From truths such as these, or long-held beliefs, or generalizations well supported by long experience, we make inferences as in our original example. Thus, if it is true that learning depends on study and practice and true also that the mastery of algebra is an act of learning, it must be true that mastering algebra depends on study and practice. Though no other evidence but the premises *need* be provided, I may decide to illustrate or defend one or both. For a true statement is not always obvious to everyone.

Therefore, the argument must satisfy two requirements: the propositions that form the premises must be true, and the process of reasoning must be correct, or to use the technical term, must be valid.

Note that "valid" does not mean "true": an argument may be false in its premises, but still be valid if the process of inference from these premises is correct. Here is a valid argument, both of whose premises are false:

> All Canadians are taxpayers.
> All property owners are Canadians.
> Therefore, all property owners are taxpayers.

We ask of an argument that it be valid in its reasoning and true in its premises. A valid argument whose premises are true is called sound. The argument just cited would be sound if, in fact, all Canadians do pay taxes, and all property owners (everywhere) are Canadians. The argument is, of course, unsound. Logicians have complex techniques for testing the validity of the many kinds of syllogism; we cannot review them here. But we need to keep in mind a few characteristics that invalidate deductive arguments:

Someone says to us: "My neighbours must all be property owners because they all pay taxes." Something strikes us as wrong here, but what is it? We can construct the whole argument as follows:

> All property owners are taxpayers.
> My neighbours are taxpayers.
> Therefore, my neighbours are property owners.

The trouble is with the middle term, "taxpayers." The major term of a syllogism is the predicate term of its conclusion; the subject of the conclusion is the minor term. The term that appears in the premises but not in the conclusion is called the middle term:

| | | | | |
|---|---|---|---|---|
| All | <u>A</u> | is | <u>B</u> | |
| | middle | | MAJOR | |
| All | <u>C</u> | is | <u>A</u> | |
| | MINOR | | middle | |
| All | <u>C</u> | is | <u>B</u> | |
| | MINOR | | MAJOR | |

(The argument may not have more than these three terms.) For the argument to be valid, this middle term must be "distributed" in at least one of the premises; that is, it must refer to — be distributed among — all members of the class named. In the argument above, the middle term, taxpayers, is undistributed in both premises — referring in each to some members of the class taxpayers, but not to all:

> All property owners are taxpayers.
> My neighbours are taxpayers.

Though all property owners are taxpayers, not all taxpayers own property. And though all my neighbours are taxpayers, not all taxpayers are my neighbours. But that is exactly what the conclusion asserts. The argument is thus invalid because the conclusion says more than the premises do.

Other invalid arguments can be analysed more easily. The middle term must not be ambiguous, as in the following argument:

> Whoever helps himself is helped by God.
> A thief helps himself.
> Therefore, a thief is helped by God.

And both premises must be affirmative if the conclusion is so: if one of the premises is negative, so must be the conclusion. And, if both premises are negative, no conclusion follows. The following argument is invalid for this reason:

> No dogs are welcome visitors.
> Children are not dogs.
> Therefore, children are welcome visitors.

In developing arguments of our own, it is important to remember that an argument may seem logical because the process of reasoning is correct, and yet be unsound because the premises are questionable or false. In reading arguments, we need to consider both the premises that form it and the way the writer reasons from them.

# ARTHUR SCHAFER

*Arthur Schafer is a professor at the University of Manitoba. In the following essay from the Toronto* Globe and Mail, *Schafer discusses the widespread belief that "the pursuit of individual self-interest in the marketplace will lead to the general good." Basing his conclusions on his observations of modern society, he warns us about the dangers of using self-interest as the only standard of ethical conduct.*

# MORALS IN THE RAT RACE

1 There are new things under the sun, but political scandal and corruption are not among them. There are dishonest people in every society. No political epoch has been without its share of crooks and charlatans.

2 Canadians have a vague sense, however, that the recent spate of corrupt practices in our society, like those occurring in our neighbor to the south, is a sign of something other than ordinary human fallibility. There seems to be a growing public cynicism, a sense that both personal and public morality have declined drastically. The question irresistibly poses itself: has dishonest behaviour become so widespread that it threatens the very fabric of our society?

3 Is ours a civilization in decline? The evidence is less than conclusive, but it points toward an affirmative answer.

4 The most profoundly important innovation of Western liberal society has been to put the marketplace at the centre of all social transactions. The gospel according to Adam Smith assumes that the pursuit of individual self-interest in the marketplace will lead to the general good. When every citizen rationally pursues his self-interest, all will flourish.

5 Or so the theory would have it. But social reality can be rather disappointing, and the philosophy of liberal individualism is looking distinctly threadbare these days. The very competitive individualism that has produced for us a superabundance of televisions, VCRs, microwave ovens and vacations in Florida now threatens to so undermine civic virtue that our culture crumbles from within. We cannot help but recall that the collapse of earlier civilizations — the Roman Empire comes to mind — was precipitated more powerfully by internal corruption than by external force.

6 Neo-conservatives such as U.S. President Ronald Reagan and British Prime Minister Margaret Thatcher lament the collapse of traditional social values: family, work, patriotism, restraint. They are right, of course. There has been a deep erosion of traditional values, but the process began several hundred years ago. What we are witnessing today is, perhaps, the culmination of a long historical process, a process accelerated by the policies of Mr. Reagan and Mrs. Thatcher.

7 Ironically, it is the very marketplace morality at whose shrine the neo-conservatives worship that produces the social disintegration they lament. The pursuit of individual self-aggrandizement, individual gratification, individual pleasure has led more and more of us into the scramble for wealth and power. Ambition and hedonism prevail. Can any society survive when its citizens are all engaged in a furious competition to carve up the spoils?

8 As long as only a minority is motivated by ruthless self-interest, social bonds can remain largely intact. But when businessmen dishonor their contracts, when ordinary folk cheat on their income tax, when welfare recipients chisel the government, when doctors and nurses and policemen strike for higher pay, when politicians use their power to enrich themselves and their cronies, this should be seen as a dramatic sign that social cohesion is deeply threatened.

9 Business civilization regards work solely as a means to profit, income, consumption. Creative work ceases to be viewed as an end in itself. The cash nexus replaces the spirit of work; the real value of work is lost.

10 A similar process of devaluation occurs within the family. Men have never been slow to abandon their wives and children in the pursuit of self-interest. But the bonds of family solidarity now have become so attenuated that women seek their own freedom as single-mindedly as men. This may be the ultimate "triumph" of individual liberty. "I love your

majesty according to my bond; nor more nor less," Cordelia says to her father. If King Lear had achieved any wisdom along with grey hairs, he would have been thrilled by this testimony. Instead he was outraged. We know better.

Perhaps the most striking paradox of our times is that liberal market society can survive only as long as most people live by the value system that pre-dated the marketplace — the pre-bourgeois values of public-spiritedness, civic virtue, honesty and honor, mutual co-operation, family bonds. Instead, wherever we turn — to government, to business, to work, to the family — we observe a radical loosening of social bonds. It is the rapid spread of marketplace morality throughout society which now threatens the very existence of this society.   **11**

As the political economist Seymour Hirsch has pointed out, the things for which we are now all competing so frantically can, by their very nature, be available only for a small elite. Only a few can be generals. The rest must be privates (except in the Canadian Armed Forces). Only a few can enjoy their vacations on an unspoiled beach. When everyone can afford a car capable of travelling at speeds in excess of 170 kilometres an hour, all are forced by traffic congestion to creep along at 20 kilometres. When everyone achieves a home with a view, the view is likely to be of each other's homes. When everyone gets his PhD, the competitive advantage of this estimable degree tends to diminish, and its holders find themselves driving taxis.   **12**

It is important to realize that the central delusion of the affluent society is not that money does not buy happiness (though it does not). No, the central delusion is the belief that the benefits of affluence can be preserved when nearly everyone becomes "middle class". When everyone has a car, a home in the suburbs and a PhD, none of these things can deliver what they promise.   **13**

We must now face squarely a nightmare vision of our future: endless traffic jams, endless grey, box-like houses in endless, grey Mississauga, unemployed PhDs, businessmen on the make, families split, doctors milking their patients and patients suing their doctors, politicians on the take. And everyone lamenting the decline of morality while heaping praise upon the very institution that has led to this impasse.   **14**

The metaphor of a "rat race," although a cliché, is appropriate because the system ensures that we must run ever faster just to maintain our relative position in the competition. And we must compete as ruthlessly as the most unscrupulous or lose the golden palm.   **15**

A civilization that encourages the motive of self-interested calculation to rule every sphere of social life is on a sure path to moral bankruptcy. The ultimate freedom — from the bonds of community, family, friendship, and neighborliness — becomes the ultimate slavery. This way lies social disintegration.   **16**

Canadians are right to be deeply concerned. We are far richer than our parents and incomparably richer than our great-grandparents. Does anyone believe that we are also happier? Or better people? The challenge that faces us will not be an easy one to meet, for it is nothing less than the creation of a new sense of freedom, a sense of personal liberation that is compatible with the deeper values of community and public-spiritedness.   **17**

# VOCABULARY

a. *paragraph  1:* charlatans

b. *paragraph  2:* spate, fallibility

c. *paragraph  7:* shrine, neo-conservatives

d. *paragraph 8:* chisel

e. *paragraph 9:* nexus

f. *paragraph 15:* unscrupulous

## Questions

1. Schafer argues by means of a series of examples to a generalization supported by them. We call this method of organizing an argument moving from the specific to the general, from particulars of experience to conclusions based on them — inductive. Would the generalization be unclear or difficult to understand if Schafer had begun with it?

2. How various are the examples Schafer presents? How effective are these in helping him make his case?

3. Why does Schafer say that the changes he describes represent a significant decline?

4. What other conclusions about Canadian society do you think are supported by these facts, and how are they supported?

## Writing Assignments

1. In opposition to Schafer, argue that consumerism has had no profound effect on morality. Be careful not to generalize more broadly than your evidence allows.

2. Discuss the extent to which your own experience and observation support the conclusion Schafer reaches. If you believe his conclusion needs qualification, explain why it does.

## H.L. Mencken

*Henry Louis Mencken (1880–1956) wrote for Baltimore newspapers and other periodicals most of his life, and was one of the founders and editors of the* American Mercury *magazine. His satirical essays on American life and politics were collected in six volumes under the title* Prejudices. *His three volumes of autobiography describe his youth in Baltimore and his later career in journalism. Mencken's interests were wide, and he wrote extensively about American democracy and the American language, whose characteristics he describes in a classic book on the subject. His ironic, and often sarcastic, style is well illustrated by these reflections published in* Minority Report *after his death.*

## Reflections on War

1    The thing constantly overlooked by those hopefuls who talk of abolishing war is that it is by no means an evidence of decay but rather a proof of health and vigor. To fight seems to be as natural to man as to eat. Civilization limits and wars upon the impulse but it can never quite eliminate it. Whenever the effort seems to be most successful — that is, whenever man seems to be submitting most willingly to discipline, the spark is nearest to the

powder barrel. Here repression achieves its inevitable work. The most warlike people under civilization are precisely those who submit most docilely to the rigid inhibitions of peace. Once they break through the bounds of their repressed but steadily accumulating pugnacity, their destructiveness runs to great lengths. Throwing off the chains of order, they leap into the air and kick their legs. Of all the nations engaged in the two World Wars the Germans, who were the most rigidly girded by conceptions of renunciation and duty, showed the most gusto for war for its own sake.

The powerful emotional stimulus of war, its evocation of motives and ideals which, **2** whatever their error, are at least more stimulating than those which impel a man to get and keep a safe job — this is too obvious to need laboring. The effect on the individual soldier of its very horror, filling him with a sense of the heroic, increases enormously his self-respect. This increase in self-respect reacts upon the nation, and tends to save it from the deteriorating effects of industrial discipline. In the main, soldiers are men of humble position and talents — laborers, petty mechanics, young fellows without definite occupation. Yet no one can deny that the veteran shows a certain superiority in dignity to the average man of his age and experience. He has played his part in significant events; he has been a citizen in a far more profound sense than any mere workman can ever be. The effects of all this are plainly seen in his bearing and his whole attitude of mind. War may make a fool of man, but it by no means degrades him; on the contrary, it tends to exalt him, and its net effects are much like those of motherhood on women.

That war is a natural revolt against the necessary but extremely irksome discipline of **3** civilization is shown by the difficulty with which men on returning from it re-adapt themselves to a round of petty duties and responsibilities. This was notably apparent after the Civil War. It took three or four years for the young men engaged in that conflict to steel themselves to the depressing routine of everyday endeavor. Many of them, in fact, found it quite impossible. They could not go back to shovelling coal or tending a machine without intolerable pain. Such men flocked to the West, where adventure still awaited them and discipline was still slack. In the same way, after the Franco-Prussian War, thousands of young German veterans came to the United States, which seemed to them one vast Wild West. True enough, they soon found that discipline was necessary here as well as at home, but it was a slacker discipline and they themselves exaggerated its slackness in their imagination. At all events, it had the charm of the unaccustomed.

We commonly look upon the discipline of war as vastly more rigid than any discipline **4** necessary in time of peace, but this is an error. The strictest military discipline imaginable is still looser than that prevailing in the average assembly-line. The soldier, at worst, is still able to exercise the highest conceivable functions of freedom — that is, he is permitted to steal and to kill. No discipline prevailing in peace gives him anything even remotely resembling this. He is, in war, in the position of a free adult; in peace he is almost always in the position of a child. In war all things are excused by success, even violations of discipline. In peace, speaking generally, success is inconceivable except as a function of discipline.

The hope of abolishing war is largely based upon the fact that men have long since aban- **5** doned the appeal to arms in their private disputes and submitted themselves to the jurisdiction of courts. Starting from this fact, it is contended that disputes between nations should be settled in the same manner, and that the adoption of the reform would greatly promote the happiness of the world.

Unluckily, there are three flaws in the argument. The first, which is obvious, lies in the **6** circumstances that a system of legal remedies is of no value if it is not backed by sufficient force to impose its decisions upon even the most powerful litigants — a sheer impossibility in international affairs, for even if one powerful litigant might be coerced, it would be plainly impossible to coerce a combination, and it is precisely a combination of the powerful that is most to be feared. The second lies in the fact that any legal system, to be worthy of credit, must be administered by judges who have no personal interest in the litigation before them — another impossibility, for all the judges in the international court, in the case of disputes between first-class powers, would either be appointees of those powers, or appointees of inferior powers that were under their direct influence, or obliged to consider the effects of their enmity. The third objection lies in the fact, frequently forgotten, that the courts of justice which now exist do not actually dispense justice, but only law, and that this law is frequently in direct conflict, not only with what one litigant honestly believes to be his rights, but also with what he believes to be his honor. Practically every litigation, in truth, ends with either one litigant or the other nursing what appears to him as an outrage upon him. For both litigants to go away satisfied that justice has been done is almost unheard of.

7        In disputes between man and man this dissatisfaction is not of serious consequence. The aggrieved party has no feasible remedy; if he doesn't like it, he must lump it. In particular, he has no feasible remedy against a judge or a juryman who, in his view, has treated him ill; if he essayed vengeance, the whole strength of the unbiased masses of men would be exerted to destroy him, and that strength is so enormous, compared to his own puny might, that it would swiftly and certainly overwhelm him. But in the case of first-class nations there would be no such overwhelming force in restraint. In a few cases the general opinion of the world might be so largely against them that it would force them to acquiesce in the judgment rendered, but in perhaps a majority of important cases there would be sharply divided sympathies, and it would constantly encourage resistance. Against that resistance there would be nothing save the counter-resistance of the opposition — *i.e.*, the judge against the aggrieved litigant, the twelve jurymen against the aggrieved litigant's friends, with no vast and impersonal force of neutral public opinion behind the former.

## VOCABULARY

a. *paragraph 1:* repression, docilely, inhibitions, pugnacity, girded, gusto

b. *paragraph 2:* stimulus, evocation, impel, deteriorating, profound

c. *paragraph 3:* endeavor

d. *paragraph 6:* litigants, coerced

e. *paragraph 7:* aggrieved, feasible, essayed, puny

## QUESTIONS

1. In paragraphs 1 through 4, Mencken argues that war will not be easily abolished, and he states his major premise explicitly: "To fight seems to be as natural to man as to eat." How do the wording of this statement and the wording of others in these paragraphs show that Mencken regards these premises as certain and decisive evidence for his conclusions? What conclusions does he reach based on these premises?

2. Though he regards his premises as certain, Mencken explains and illustrates them. What examples does he present? Does he discuss one civilization or instead generalize about "warlike people" on the basis of observations made over a period of time?

3. Paragraph 1 of Mencken's essay contains the makings of several syllogisms; in the first of these, the major premise may be stated in these words: "The expression of a natural instinct is evidence of health and vigor." What are the minor premise and conclusion?

4. In paragraph 1 Mencken argues that repression of a natural instinct leads to increased destructiveness. What are the minor premise and conclusion?

5. L. A. White, in *Science of Culture*, argues that the need for military conscription refutes the assumption that people are naturally warlike. Given his assumptions and evidence, how might Mencken answer this objection? What do paragraphs 5 through 7 suggest?

6. In paragraphs 5 through 7 Mencken challenges "the hope of abolishing war," a hope based on the assumption that people have long since "submitted themselves to the jurisdiction of courts." What flaws does Mencken find in the argument, and what kind of evidence does he present in refutation? Does he deal with particular instances or instead generalize from observations made over a period of time?

7. Decide whether the following arguments are valid or invalid. It may be necessary to reword the premises:

   a. Since all voters are citizens and I am a voter, I am a citizen.

   b. Since all voters are citizens and I am a citizen, I am a voter.

   c. Since the Irish are vegetarians and Bernard Shaw was Irish, Shaw was a vegetarian.

   d. Those who made 93 or better on the exam will receive an "A" in the course. Seven of us received an "A" in the course and therefore must have made 93 or better on the exam.

   e. Since beneficent acts are virtuous and losing at poker benefits others, losing at poker is virtuous.

8. An *enthymeme* is a condensed syllogism, one of whose premises is implied: Because I did not study the equations, I failed algebra. In the following enthymemes, reconstruct the original syllogism by supplying the missing premise, and evaluate the argument. The premises and conclusion may need rewording:

   a. Pierre Trudeau was a good prime minister because he kept Quebec in Confederation and repatriated the Constitution.

   b. Capital punishment protects society from depraved individuals.

   c. I am a successful businessman because I once had a paper route.

   d. I am an independent voter, just as my father and grandfather were.

# WRITING ASSIGNMENT

Write an argument for or against one of the following. In an additional paragraph identify one or more assumptions that underlie your argument, and explain why you hold these assumptions:

a. building more nuclear power plants

b. a ban on smoking in public transportation

c. periodic examination of licensed drivers

d. required attendance of university and college classes

e. compulsory gun registration

# KENNETH B. CLARK

Kenneth B. Clark *taught psychology at City College of New York from 1942 to 1975, and has taught at other universities including Columbia and Harvard. His writings on black life in America have exerted wide influence on social legislation and judicial thinking on civil rights. Among his influential books are* Dark Ghetto *(1965) and* Pathos of Power *(1974), from which this discussion of the idea of "relevance" in education is taken. Clark raises issues that Frye and Cousins also explore from different points of view and assumptions.*

# THE LIMITS OF RELEVANCE

1    As one who began himself to use the term "relevant" and to insist on its primacy years ago, I feel an obligation to protest the limits of relevance or to propose a redefinition of it to embrace wider terms.

2    Definitions of education that depend on immediate relevance ignore a small but critical percentage of human beings, the individuals who for some perverse reason are in search of an education that is not dominated by the important, socially and economically required pragmatic needs of a capitalist or a communist or a socialist society. Such an individual is not certain what he wants to be; he may not even be sure that he wants to be successful. He may be burdened with that perverse intelligence that finds the excitement of life in a continuous involvement with ideas.

3    For this student, education may be a lonely and tortuous process not definable in terms of the limits of course requirements or of departmental boundaries, or the four- or six-year span of time required for the bachelor's or graduate degree. This student seems unable to seek or to define or to discuss relevance in terms of externals. He seems somehow trapped by the need to seek the dimensions of relevance in relation to an examination and re-examination of his own internal values. He may have no choice but to assume the burden of seeking to define the relevance of the human experience as a reflection of the validity of his own existence as a value-seeking, socially sensitive, and responsive human being. He is required to deny himself the protective, supporting crutch of accepting and clutching uncritically the prevailing dogmatisms, slogans, and intellectual fashions.

If such a human being is to survive the inherent and probably inevitable aloneness of    **4**
intellectual integrity, he must balance it by the courage to face and accept the risks of his
individuality; by compassion and empathetic identification with the frailties of his fellow
human beings as a reflection of his own; by an intellectual and personal discipline which
prevents him from wallowing in introspective amorphousness and childlike self-
indulgence. And, certainly, he must demonstrate the breadth of perspective and human
sensitivity and depth of affirmation inherent in the sense of humor which does not laugh at
others but laughs with man and with the God of Paradox who inflicted upon man the
perpetual practical joke of the human predicament.

American colleges, with few notable exceptions, provide little room for this type of    **5**
student, just as American society provides little room for such citizens. Perhaps it is
enough to see that institutions of higher education do not destroy such potential. One
could hope wistfully that our colleges and even our multi-universities could spare space
and facilities to serve and to protect those students who want to experiment without being
required to be practical, pragmatic, or even relevant.

Is it possible within the complexity and cacophony of our dynamic, power-related, and    **6**
tentatively socially sensitive institutions for some few to have the opportunity to look
within, to read, to think critically, to communicate, to make mistakes, to seek validity,
and to accept and enjoy this process as valid in itself? Is there still some place where relevance can be defined in terms of the quest — where respect for self and others can be
taken for granted as one admits not knowing and is therefore challenged to seek?

May one dare to hope for a definition of education which makes it possible for man to    **7**
accept the totality of his humanity without embarrassment? This would be valuable for its
own sake, but it might also paradoxically be the most pragmatic form of education —
because it is from these perverse, alone-educated persons that a practical society receives
antidotes to a terrifying sense of inner emptiness and despair. They are the font of the continued quest for meaning in the face of the mocking chorus of meaninglessness. They
offer the saving reaffirmation of stabilizing values in place of the acceptance of the disintegration inherent in valuelessness. They provide the basis for faith in humanity and life
rather than surrender to dehumanization and destruction. From these impracticals come
our poets, our artists, our novelists, our satirists, our humorists. They are our models of
the positives, the potentials, the awe and wonder of man. They make the life of the thinking human being more endurable and the thought of a future tolerable.

## VOCABULARY

a. *paragraph 2:* relevance, perverse, pragmatic

b. *paragraph 3:* dimensions, dogmatisms

c. *paragraph 4:* empathetic, introspective, amorphousness, paradox

d. *paragraph 5:* wistfully

e. *paragraph 6:* cacophony, validity

f. *paragraph 7:* antidotes, font, reaffirmation, dehumanization, satirists, humorists

## QUESTIONS

1. How does Clark explain the meanings of the term *relevant*? Why does he briefly review these meanings?

2. What assumptions does Clark make about the educational needs of people?

3. What conclusions does he derive from his assumptions?

4. Do you think that Canadian universities have little room for the kind of student described in paragraph 4? What is your answer to the questions Clark asks in paragraph 6?

5. Does Clark seek to refute those who argue the "pragmatic needs" of education? Or does he present confirming arguments only?

## WRITING ASSIGNMENTS

1. Evaluate the following statement on the basis of your experience and observation:

   " . . . it is from these perverse, alone-educated persons that a practical society receives antidotes to a terrifying sense of inner emptiness and despair."

2. Do you think that most univeristy or college students are guilty of "accepting and clutching uncritically the prevailing dogmatisms, slogans, and intellectual fashions"?

## NORMAN COUSINS

Norman Cousins, *in this column from the* Saturday Review *magazine, turns to the "shucking of responsibility" that he finds pervasive in American life. In arguing that ". . . the school has no right to jettison standards just because of difficulties in enforcing them," he takes a position which challenges those of many educational theorists in the 1960s and early 1970s. Cousins is writing about the world of the late 1970s, but the issues he raises continue to be pertinent today.*

## COP-OUT REALISM

1    On all sides, one sees evidence today of cop-out realism — ostensible efforts to be sensible in dealing with things as they are but that turn out to be a shucking of responsibility.

2    Example: Until fairly recently, off-track betting was illegal in New York State. Gambling on horses was regarded as a disguised form of stealing, run by professional gamblers who preyed upon people who could least afford to lose. Also outlawed was the numbers game, in which people could bet small amounts of money on numbers drawn from the outcome of the day's horse races.

3    Attempts by government to drive out the gambling syndicates had only indifferent results. Finally, state officials decided that, since people were going to throw their money away despite anything the law might do to protect them, the state ought to take over off-track betting and the numbers racket.

It is now possible to assess the effect of that legalization. The first thing that is obvious    **4**
is that New York State itself has become a predator in a way that the Mafia could never
hope to match. What was intended as a plan to control gambling has become a high-
powered device to promote it. The people who can least afford to take chances with their
money are not only not dissuaded from gambling but are actually being cajoled into it by
the state. Millions of dollars are being spent by New York State on lavish advertising on
television, on radio, in buses, and on billboards. At least the Mafia was never able publicly to glorify and extol gambling with taxpayer money. And the number of poor people
who were hurt by gambling under the Mafia is miniscule compared to the number who
now lose money on horses with the urgent blessings of New York State.

A second example of cop-out realism is the way some communities are dealing with    **5**
cigarette-smoking by teenagers and pre-teenagers. Special rooms are now being set aside
for students who want to smoke. No age restrictions are set; freshmen have the same
lighting-up privileges as seniors.

The thinking behind the new school policy is similar to the "realism" behind New    **6**
York's decision to legalize off-track betting and the numbers game. It is felt that since the
youngsters are going to smoke anyway, the school might just as well make it possible for
them to do it in the open rather than feel compelled to do it furtively in back corridors and
washrooms.

Parents and teachers may pride themselves on their "realism" in such approaches. What    **7**
they are actually doing is finding a convenient rationalization for failing to uphold their
responsibility. The effect of their supposedly "realistic" policy is to convert a ban into a
benediction. By sanctioning that which they deplore, they become part of the problem they
had the obligation to meet. What they regard as common sense turns out to be capitulation.

Pursuing the same reasoning, why not set aside a corner for a bar where students can    **8**
buy alcoholic beverages? After all, teenage drinking is a national problem, and it is far
better to have the youngsters drink out in the open than to have them feel guilty about
stealing drinks from the cupboard at home or contriving to snatch their liquor outside the
home. Moreover, surveillance can be exercised. Just as most public bars will not serve
liquor to people who are hopelessly drunk, so the school bartender could withhold alcohol
from students who can hardly stand on their feet.

It is not far-fetched to extend the same "reasoning" to marijuana. If the youngsters are    **9**
going to be able to put their hands on the stuff anyway, why shouldn't they be able to buy
it legally and smoke it openly, perhaps in the same schoolroom that has been converted
into a smoking den?

We are not reducing the argument to an absurdity; we are asking that parents and    **10**
teachers face up to the implications of what they are doing.

The school has no right to jettison standards just because of difficulties in enforcing    **11**
them. The school's proper response is not to abdicate but to extend its efforts in other
directions. It ought to require regular lung examinations for its youngsters. It ought to
schedule regular sessions with parents and youngsters at which reports on these examinations can be considered. It ought to bring in cancer researchers who can run films for
students showing the difference between the brackish, pulpy lungs caused by cigarette
smoking and the smooth pink tissue of healthy lungs. The schools should schedule visits
to hospital wards for lung cancer patients. In short, educators should take the U.S.
Surgeon-General's report on cigarettes seriously.

In all the discussion and debate over cigarette smoking by children, one important fact    **12**
is generally overlooked. That fact is that a great many children *do not* smoke. The school

cannot ignore its obligation to these youngsters just because it cannot persuade the others not to smoke. It must not give the nonsmokers the impression that their needs are secondary or that the school has placed a seal of approval on a practice that is condemning millions of human beings to fatal disease.

13    Still another example of cop-out realism is the policy of many colleges and universities of providing common dormitories and common washrooms for both sexes. The general idea seems to be that it is unrealistic to expect young people not to sleep together. Besides, it is probably reasoned, if people are old enough to vote they are old enough to superintend their own sex habits. So, the thinking goes, the school might just as well allow them to share the same sleeping and toilet facilities.

14    The trouble with such policies is that they put the school in the position of lending itself to the breakdown of that which is most important in healthy relations between the sexes — a respect for privacy and dignity. No one ever need feel ashamed of the human body. But that doesn't mean that the human body is to be displayed or handled like a slab of raw meat. Sex is one of the higher manifestations of human sensitivity and response, not an impersonal sport devoid of genuine feeling. The divorce courts are filled to overflowing with cases in which casual, mechanistic attitudes toward sex have figured in marital collapses. For the school to foster that casualness is for it to become an agent of desensitization in a monstrous default.

15    The function of standards is not to serve as the basis for mindless repressive measures but to give emphasis to the realities of human experience. Such experience helps to identify the causes of unnecessary pain and disintegration. Any society that ignores the lessons of that experience may be in a bad way.

## VOCABULARY

a. *paragraph  1:* ostensible, shucking

b. *paragraph  3:* syndicates

c. *paragraph  4:* assess, predator, dissuaded, cajoled; miniscule

d. *paragraph  7:* rationalization, benediction, sanctioning, deplore, capitulation

e. *paragraph  8:* surveillance

f. *paragraph 11:* jettison, abdicate, brackish

g. *paragraph 14:* manifestations, devoid, mechanistic, desensitization, default

## QUESTIONS

1. Cousins states his major premise in paragraph 1: so-called realism is "a shucking of responsibility." How does he illustrate this premise in paragraphs 2 through 6?

2. In paragraphs 2 through 6 Cousins confirms his premise by showing certain consequences of "cop-out realism." In paragraphs 7 through 10 he shows that if we adopt such a policy, certain consequences follow — consequences that he considers obvious absurdities. What are these absurd consequences?

3. In stating in paragraphs 11 through 14 what the schools should be doing, Cousins draws further conclusions from the policy of "cop-out realism." What are these conclusions? Do you agree with them?

4. In the concluding paragraphs, what basic premises or assumptions concerning human responsibility and dignity emerge? How does Cousins use these premises to summarize his basic argument?

## WRITING ASSIGNMENTS

1. Cousins combines confirmation and refutation in showing that "cop-out realism" entails absurd consequences, and joins narration to these in presenting the background on gambling and schools in New York State. Write an argumentative essay in which you combine narration with confirmation or refutation in the same way. Your refutation need not take the same form as Cousins's. You may prefer to answer objections to your basic premise and proposals directly.

2. Discuss the extent to which, in your view, Cousins would agree with Frye's premise and basic proposals on education. Support your discussion with a comparison of their premises and reasoning.

## SIR JOHN A. MACDONALD

*Canada's first Prime Minister, Sir John A. Macdonald (1815–1891), was born in Glasgow, Scotland and came to Canada in 1820. Even in school he was recognized as a student with rare abilities. A successful lawyer and businessman, he was elected to the Legislative Assembly in 1844 and became a member of the Cabinet in 1847. His political ingenuity, constitutional expertise, and his clear vision of a country united under a strong federal government combined to make him the central player in the deliberations that eventually made Canada a nation. As Prime Minister (1867–73, 1878–91) he built the country, and proceeded to make it secure by imposing high tariffs on imported American goods and by encouraging westward expansion with the building of the transcontinental railway. The following excerpt from a speech in the Legislative Assembly, February 6, 1865, displays Macdonald's political and oratorical skills as he pleads the case for the union of the colonies he had worked so hard to bring about.*

## CONFEDERATION

The whole scheme of Confederation, as propounded by the Conference, as agreed to and sanctioned by the Canadian Government, and as now presented for the consideration of the people, and the Legislature, bears upon its face the marks of compromise. 1

Of necessity there must have been a great deal of mutual concession. When we think of the representatives of five colonies, all supposed to have different interests, meeting together, charged with the duty of protecting those interests and of pressing the views of their own localities and sections, it must be admitted that had we not met in a spirit of conciliation, and with an anxious desire to promote this union; if we had not been im- 2 pressed with the idea contained in the words of the resolution — "That the best interests and present and future prosperity of British North America would be promoted by a Federal Union under the Crown of Great Britain," — all our efforts might have proved to be of no avail. If we had not felt that, after coming to this conclusion, we were bound to set aside our private opinions on matters of detail, if we had not felt ourselves bound to look at what was practicable, not obstinately rejecting the opinions of others nor adhering to our own; if we had not met, I say, in a spirit of conciliation, and with an anxious, over-ruling desire to form one people under one government, we never would have succeeded. With these views, we press the question on this House and the country.

3      I say to this House, if you do not believe that the union of the colonies is for the advantage of the country, that the joining of these five peoples into one nation, under one sovereign, is for the benefit of all, then reject the scheme. Reject it if you do not believe it to be for the present advantage and future prosperity of yourselves and your children. But if, after a calm and full consideration of this scheme, it is believed, as a whole, to be for the advantage of this province — if the House and country believe this union to be one which will ensure for us British laws, British connection, and British freedom — and increase and develop the social, political and material prosperity of the country, then I implore this House and the country to lay aside all prejudices, and accept the scheme which we offer. I ask this House to meet the question in the same spirit in which the delegates met it. I ask each member of this House to lay aside his own opinions as to particular details, and to accept the scheme as a whole if he think it beneficial as a whole.

4      As I stated in the preliminary discussion, we must consider this scheme in the light of a treaty. By a happy coincidence of circumstances, just when an Administration had been formed in Canada for the purpose of attempting a solution of the difficulties under which we laboured, at the same time the Lower Provinces, actuated by a similar feeling, appointed a Conference with a view to a union among themselves, without being cognizant of the position the government was taking in Canada. If it had not been for this fortunate coincidence of events, never, perhaps, for a long series of years would we have been able to bring this scheme to a practical conclusion.

5      But we did succeed. We made the arrangement, agreed upon the scheme, and the deputations from the several governments represented at the Conference went back pledged to lay it before their governments, and to ask the legislatures and people of their respective provinces to assent to it. I trust the scheme will be assented to as a whole. I am sure this House will not seek to alter it in its unimportant details; and, if altered in any important provisions, the result must be that the whole will be set aside, and we must begin *de novo*. If any important changes are made, every one of the colonies will feel itself absolved from the implied obligation to deal with it as a Treaty, each province will feel itself at liberty to amend it *ad libitum* so as to suit its own views and interests; in fact, the whole of our labours will have been for nought, and we will have to renew our negotiations with all the colonies for the purpose of establishing some new scheme.

6      I hope the House will not adopt any such a course as will postpone, perhaps for ever, or at all events for a long period, all chances of union. All the statesmen and the public men who have written or spoken on the subject admit the advantages of a union, if it were practicable: and now when it is proved to be practicable, if we do not embrace this opportunity the present favorable time will pass away, and we may never have it again. Because, just so surely as this scheme is defeated, will be revived the original proposition for a union of the Maritime Provinces, irrespective of Canada; they will not remain as they are now, powerless, scattered, helpless communities; they will form themselves into a power, which, though not so strong as if united with Canada, will, nevertheless, be a powerful and considerable community, and it will be then too late for us to attempt to strengthen

ourselves by this scheme, which, in the words of the resolution, "is for the best interests, and present and future prosperity of British North America."

If we are not blind to our present position, we must see the hazardous situation in    7
which all the great interests of Canada stand in respect to the United States. I am no alarmist. I do not believe in the prospect of immediate war. I believe that the common sense of the two nations will prevent a war; still we cannot trust to probabilities. The Government and Legislature would be wanting in their duty to the people if they ran any risk. We know that the United States at this moment are engaged in a war of enormous dimensions — that the occasion of a war with Great Britain has again and again arisen, and may at any time in the future again arise. We cannot foresee what may be the result; we cannot say but that the two nations may drift into a war as other nations have done before. It would then be too late when war had commenced to think of measures for strengthening ourselves, or to begin negotiations for a union with the sister provinces.

At this moment, in consequence of the ill-feeling which has arisen between England    8
and the United States — a feeling of which Canada was not the cause — in consequence of the irritation which now exists, owing to the unhappy state of affairs on this continent, the Reciprocity Treaty, it seems probable, is about to be brought to an end — our trade is hampered by the passport system, and at any moment we may be deprived of permission to carry our goods through United States channels — the bonded goods system may be done away with, and the winter trade through the United States put an end to. Our merchants may be obliged to return to the old system of bringing in during the summer months the supplies for the whole year. Ourselves already threatened, our trade inter- rupted, our intercourse, political and commercial, destroyed, if we do not take warning now when we have the opportunity, and while one avenue is threatened to be closed, open another by taking advantage of the present arrangement and the desire of the Lower Provinces to draw closer the alliance between us, we may suffer commercial and political disadvantages it may take long for us to overcome.

The Conference having come to the conclusion that a legislative union, pure and    9
simple, was impracticable, our next attempt was to form a government upon federal principles, which would give to the General Government the strength of a legislative and administrative union, while at the same time it preserved that liberty of action for the dif- ferent sections which is allowed by a Federal Union. And I am strong in the belief — that we have hit upon the happy medium in these resolutions, and that we have formed a scheme of government which unites the advantages of both, giving us the strength of a legislative union and the sectional freedom of a federal union, with protection to local interests.

## VOCABULARY

a. *paragraph 1:* propounded, sanctioned

b. *paragraph 2:* obstinately, overruling

c. *paragraph 4:* actuated

d. *paragraph 5:* nought

e. *paragraph 6:* practicable

f. *paragraph 7:* alarmist

g. *paragraph 8:* hampered, intercourse

h. *paragraph 9:* sectional

## QUESTIONS

1. Is Macdonald's appeal primarily to the emotions of his listeners or to their reason? Is it possible to couch an emotional appeal in such formally organized language? How would you describe the tone of this piece?

2. Note the use of negatives ("no", "not") in paragraphs 2, 3, and 6. How do they help Macdonald to organize these paragraphs? Why does he include so many?

3. How does Macdonald use the warnings in paragraphs 5 through 8 to press home his case?

4. Trace Macdonald's argument by writing a one-sentence outline of each paragraph. For example, paragraph 1: "Confederation means compromise"; 2: "Had we been unwilling to compromise, we would not have succeeded." Etc.

## WRITING ASSIGNMENTS

1. Macdonald uses a very formal style to address the Legislative Assembly on matters of great urgency. Rewrite several paragraphs in a conversational style, using shorter, simpler sentences and more colloquial diction.

2. Imitate Macdonald's style in a speech to Parliament on a momentous occasion — the signing of a peace treaty or a threat to national security.

## T.C. (TOMMY) DOUGLAS

*As Premier of Saskatchewan from 1944 to 1961, T.C. (Tommy) Douglas (1904–1986) was the leader of the first socialist government elected in North America. As national leader of the New Democratic Party, he made democratic socialism an important part of Canadian political life, arguing successfully for such programs as Medicare and a comprehensive Canada pension plan. He fervently believed in the power of political action to alleviate suffering, and throughout his political life he made the underprivileged and the exploited his constituency. In the following speech to the House of Commons during a debate on capital punishment, he eloquently makes the case for the abolition of the death penalty.*

## CAPITAL PUNISHMENT

1    There are times, Mr. Speaker, when the House of Commons rises to heights of grandeur and becomes deeply conscious of its great traditions. I think this debate has been one of those rare occasions. There has been a minimum of rancour and there has been no imputation of

motives because I think that the abolitionists and retentionists alike have been sincerely searching their consciences to see if we can honestly resolve a moral problem. This problem is, how can we abolish a brutal punishment without endangering the safety of society?

I am in favour of the motion to abolish capital punishment and I am also supporting the amendment to put it on a five-year trial basis. I doubt that there is much new that can be said in this debate. The entire field has been well covered but I should like to put very briefly four reasons for my opposition to capital punishment. The first is that capital punishment is contrary to the highest concepts of the Judaic-Christian ethic. I do not propose to go into theological arguments, but both in this debate and in the discussions which have taken place outside the House many people have been quoting Scripture in support of retaining the death penalty.

It is always a dangerous practice to quote isolated passages of Scripture. The Bible has been quoted in times past to support slavery, child labour, polygamy, the burning of witches, and subservience to dictators. The Scriptures have to be viewed as a whole. The Bible is not one book; it is many books. It does not have a static concept. It represents man's emerging moral concepts as they have grown through the centuries.

It is true that the Mosaic law provided the death penalty for murder. It is equally true, if one looks particularly at the 20th chapter of the book of Leviticus, that the Mosaic law provided the death penalty for 33 crimes including such things as adultery, bestiality, homosexuality, witchcraft and sacrificing to other gods than Jehovah. It seems to me that those who want to pick out isolated texts from the Bible in support of retaining the death penalty for murder have to be equally consistent and ask that the death penalty be retained for all the other crimes listed in the Mosaic law.

Of course, those who take this position overlook several facts. They overlook, first of all, the fact that the Mosaic law was an advanced law for the primitive times in which it was formulated. It was later succeeded by the Hebrew prophets who introduced the idea of justice superseded by mercy, the possible redemption and reestablishment of the individual. They overlook the fact that if any nation in the world ought to feel itself bound by Mosaic law it should be the state of Israel. The state of Israel abolished the death penalty many years ago except for Nazi war criminals and for treason committed in times of war. The religious hierarchy of the state of Israel enthusiastically supported the Knesset in abolishing the death penalty in that country.

But for those of us who belong to the Christian religion it seems to me we have to remember also that the Christian religion went far beyond the Mosaic law. In the days of the founder of Christianity the Mosaic law still obtained. This law decreed that a woman taken in adultery could be stoned to death. We should remember the statement of Jesus of Nazareth when he came upon a group of people preparing to stone such a woman to death. He said, Let him who is without sin among you cast the first stone.

When the crowd has dwindled away so that only the woman was left he said to the woman, "Go and sin no more." It seems to me that this is the ultimate culmination of the Christian concept of the application of mercy and the possible redemption of the individual.

My second reason for opposing capital punishment is that I believe capital punishment brutalizes the society that uses it without providing any effective deterrent that cannot be provided equally well by life imprisonment. I believe that any society that practises capital punishment brutalizes itself. It has an effect upon that society and I do not believe that society can rid itself of murderers by itself becoming a murderer. Surely if brutality would deter the committing of a crime Great Britain should have been a place of law-abiding citizens because a little over 150 years ago there were over 200 crimes for which an individual could be put to death. Instead of making Britain a nation of law-abiders it was a country where crime abounded, where human sensibilities were dulled by the public execution of criminals. It is rather significant that in that day, as in this, it was often the juries who were more humane than the lawmakers. It was only because juries refused to convict, knowing the terrible punishment which would follow, that the lawmakers were forced 150 years ago to remove the death penalty from a great many of the crimes for which it had been prescribed.

9   All of the evidence which can be gathered seems to indicate that the death penalty is not a unique deterrent and that life imprisonment can be equally effective. . . .

10   I readily agree, Mr. Speaker, that quoting endless statistics is not going to prove either the case for abolition or the case for retention, but there certainly seems to be no convincing volume of evidence which would satisfy any unbiased individual that abolishing the death penalty has resulted in an upsurge of homicide or that those states which have retained the death penalty are any freer of capital crimes than those which have not.

11   After all, Mr. Speaker, who is it that the death penalty deters? It has certainly not deterred the man who commits murder. Will it deter him in the future? Surely he can be deterred in the future by being incarcered for the remainder of his life. Who is deterred if this man is hanged? Is he to be hanged as an example to the rest of the community? I can conceive of nothing more immoral than to break a man's neck as an example to other people, but if that is the argument then surely, as the Leader of the Opposition [Mr. Diefenbaker] said yesterday, we ought to have public executions.

12   The hon. member for Winnipeg South Centre [Mr. Churchill] said that the fear of death will deter men. The fear of death will deter normal men but when a man commits murder, is he normal? Can we understand the motivation that causes a man to take a human life? When a man commits homicide, does he sit down and assess whether he is committing it in a state that has capital punishment or in a state that has abolished capital punishment? I think not. In the main the man who commits homicide is the man who is mentally ill; the man who kills does not make the common, rational judgments that are made by the average individual.

13   An individual who has become so mentally sick that he will take another life or ravage a child is certainly not a mentally healthy or normal individual.

14   The third reason I am opposed to capital punishment, Mr. Speaker, is that I believe there are better ways to ensure the safety of society. I completely disagree with the hon. member for Winnipeg South Centre who argued that we must be concerned about the safety of the public. When he asks which is the more important, the life of an innocent person who may be killed or the life of a murderer, there is no doubt that the life of the innocent person is the more important. But is the fact that we break a man's neck any guarantee that innocent people will not be hurt?

15   We are not suggesting removing the penalty. We are saying that the penalty which ought to be retained is one that will do the two things which are important. First of all, it must be a penalty which will remove the convicted person from human society as long as that person is likely to be a menace to the safety and well-being of his fellow-men. Second, that person should be given an opportunity to receive whatever psychiatric treatment and rehabilitation is possible in the light of his own particular circumstances.

16   What we have to decide is what we are trying to do, Mr. Speaker. Are we thinking purely of punishing somebody because they have done wrong? Are we thinking purely in punitive terms? Are we thinking purely in terms of vengeance or retribution? Or are we thinking of the two things I have mentioned, first, the safety of society by incarcerating the convicted murderer for life and, second, the possible rehabilitation and redemption of that individual? There is additionally the third great advantage that if society has made a mistake it is possible to rectify the mistake because justice is a human institution and like all human institutions it is liable to error.

I maintain that society has no right to take from a man something which it cannot **17**
restore to him. If society makes a mistake and confines a man to prison, depriving him of
his freedom, when that mistake is found out society can at least restore to him his freedom
and provide him with some compensation for the years he has been incarcerated. But if we
hang a man and then find that a mistake has been made there is nothing at all which can be
done to make amends.

My quarrel with the death penalty is that it is purely a negative attempt to promote the **18**
safety of society. We need to adopt positive measures to promote the safety of society. For
instance, we need better law enforcement. In both Canada and the United States every
year a great many unsolved crimes are committed. One of the best deterrents is for the
criminal to know that if he does commit a crime he will be found out, that he will be incarcerated and put in a place where he can no longer be a menace to the community. We need
quicker crime detection methods. For some types of crimes, particularly for those involving psychotics, there ought to be indeterminate sentences.

We all recall a case a few years ago in which a man sexually assaulted a child. He was **19**
sentenced to five years in jail. To my mind this was ridiculous because it was based purely
on the punitive concept and not out of regard for the safety of the community. It was
assumed that at five years less one day, when he was in jail, he was a menace but at five
years plus one day he was no longer a menace. Such an individual ought to be sentenced
to be kept out of circulation until such time as a panel of judges, psychiatrists and social
workers are as certain as a human person can be that the individual is no longer a menace
to the safety of the community. I think that in many cases indeterminate sentences to keep
out of circulation psychotics who are likely to commit crimes would be of great advantage. In the case I referred to the man got out of jail after five years. Within six months he
had not only assaulted another child but had killed the child in the process. Had that individual been sentenced to an indeterminate sentence in the first instance he would not have
committed this second heinous crime.

If we want genuine deterrents in this country we need a program of penal reform for the **20**
segregation of prisoners and for their rehabilitation so that young first offenders do not go
to jail to take what is virtually a postgraduate course in crime.

Let us face the fact that when we talk about retaining capital punishment as a deterrent **21**
we are really trying to take the easy way out from solving our problems. In the long run
society often gets the criminals it deserves.

Why do we have criminals? What is wrong with the society that produces criminals? **22**
Some years ago when I was attending Chicago University I remember that every newspaper in the United States had a heading, "Where Is Crawley?" Crawley was a young gun-
man who was being hunted across the United States for a series of murders.

A very great columnist in the United States wrote a column which he headed, "Why Is **23**
Crawley?" He said that the people of the United States, instead of asking "Where Is
Crawley?", ought to take a little time out to ask "Why Is Crawley?" The columnist went
over his history. He came from a broken home which the father had deserted and where
the mother was out working all day. The boy lived on the streets. He was part of a gang of
hoodlums. He was sent to a reformatory and then was back on the streets. He was without
proper education and without any counseling. He was sent to jail and associated with
hardened criminals. He came out of jail twice as tough as when he went in. By 19 he was a
hardened criminal. By the time he was 21 he was a killer. He was finally shot down by the
police who were trying to capture him.

I suppose one of the most lamentable murders in our time has been the killing of **24**
President John F. Kennedy. Yet, when one reads the story of the man who is believed to
have been responsible for his death, we find that when Lee Oswald was a boy in school he
was recommended to undergo psychiatric treatment because of the dangerous psychotic

tendencies he then displayed. But there were not enough psychiatrists to look after all the children in that particular part of New York city and this boy was not treated. This boy grew up with his psychotic tendencies expanding, and he is believed to have been responsible for extinguishing one of the brightest lights of our generation.

25     If we really want to tackle the problem of eliminating crime, we must tackle the problem of the slums which breed crime and we must tackle the problem of the lack of psychiatric clinics to take care of psychotics and persons who may become criminally dangerous. We need the kind of penal reform that will make possible the rehabilitation of first offenders with proper probation and parole. We need to go to the roots of the cause of crime and to ask ourselves what it is that produces the murderer in society. . . .

26     My final point is that I am opposed to capital punishment because I believe that the measure of a nation is the manner in which it treats its misfits and its offenders. Capital punishment has already been abolished in most of the advanced nations of the Western world. The abolition of capital punishment has come to be taken as the hallmark of a nation's conscience. I want to see Canada take this great forward step, and I want to make a special appeal to the members of the House to consider how important for Canada and for its future will be the vote we shall take tonight.

27     I should not want to be in the shoes of the Prime Minister and the members of his cabinet who have to face up to this very difficult problem. Nobody has been hanged in Canada since 1962. If the motion tonight is defeated the government is going to be in an awkward position. Either it will have to commute those sentenced to death to life imprisonment, knowing that the House of Commons has just rejected a motion suggesting the abolition of the death penalty, or it will have to take the defeat of the motion as an expression of opinion and allow the death sentences to be carried out.

28     I urge the members of the House to consider the predicament which faces the Prime Minister and the cabinet. I want to urge the House to give a five-year trial to the abolition of the death penalty. If the fears that have been expressed prove to be warranted, if there is an upsurge in the rate of homicide, if we are faced with an increase in crime rate, then in five years the members of the House of Commons who are here then can allow the death penalty to become effective again simply by taking no action. But I would urge that we give this a chance, that we step into line with the progressive countries of the world which have already abolished the death penalty.

29     What I plead for is that we pass this resolution tonight, with the amendment, which will declare in principle that the House is in favour of abolishing capital punishment and replacement with life imprisonment. If we do that then I believe the House of Commons will have won a great victory, not a victory that will be accompanied by the blaring of trumpets or the rolling of drums but a victory in that we will have taken a forward, moral step and left behind one of the last relics of barbarianism. We will be moving forward to a more humane approach in dealing with crime.

## VOCABULARY

a. *paragraph 1:* rancour

b. *paragraph 2:* Judaic-Christian, theological

c. *paragraph 3:* polygamy

d. *paragraph 4:* Mosaic law, bestiality, Jehovah

e. *paragraph 5:* superseded

f. *paragraph 7:* culmination

g. *paragraph 16:* punitive, incarcerating

h. *paragraph 19:* indeterminate

i. *paragraph 29:* barbarianism

## QUESTIONS

1. Through what means does Douglas develop his argument — data, historical example, analogy, statistics? Or is his procedure primarily deductive?

2. What do Douglas's ideas about capital punishment, and his style in presenting them, reveal about his general view of human society?

3. Discuss the tone of Douglas's speech. What words does he use to convey it? How does the fact that it is a speech affect us?

4. Are there counter-arguments to each of the points Douglas raises? What are they?

## WRITING ASSIGNMENT

Discuss your own attitude toward capital punishment. Try to re-create Douglas's eloquence by maintaining a clear sense of purpose and by addressing yourself to the plight of mankind itself.

## GEORGE ORWELL

*George Orwell (1903–1950) was the pseudonym of English novelist and essayist Eric Hugh Blair. Orwell was born in India where his father was a customs official for the British colonial government. At the age of 8 he was sent to a school in England, and he later attended Eton on a scholarship. Instead of attending Cambridge University for which he had prepared, Orwell took a job with the Indian Imperial Police and from 1922 to 1927 served in Burma. When he left the service, he returned to Europe where he began his career as journalist and novelist. The rise of totalitarianism in Europe led Orwell to write increasingly about its causes in essays such as the classic study of political language reprinted here and in his most famous novels,* Animal Farm *(1945) and* Nineteen Eighty-Four *(1949).*

## POLITICS AND THE ENGLISH LANGUAGE

Most people who bother with the matter at all would admit that the English language is in a bad way, but it is generally assumed that we cannot by conscious action do anything about it. Our civilization is decadent and our language — so the argument runs — must

**1**

inevitably share in the general collapse. It follows that any struggle against the abuse of language is a sentimental archaism, like preferring candles to electric light or hansom cabs to airplanes. Underneath this lies the half-conscious belief that language is a natural growth and not an instrument which we shape for our own purposes.

2      Now, it is clear that the decline of a language must ultimately have political and economic causes: it is not due simply to the bad influence of this or that individual writer. But an effect can become a cause, reinforcing the original cause and producing the same effect in an intensified form, and so on indefinitely. A man may take to drink because he feels himself to be a failure, and then fail all the more completely because he drinks. It is rather the same thing that is happening to the English language: It becomes ugly and inaccurate because our thoughts are foolish, but the slovenliness of our language makes it easier for us to have foolish thoughts. The point is that the process is reversible. Modern English, especially written English, is full of bad habits which spread by imitation and which can be avoided if one is willing to take the necessary trouble. If one gets rid of these habits one can think more clearly, and to think clearly is a necessary first step toward political regeneration: so that the fight against bad English is not frivolous and is not the exclusive concern of professional writers. I will come back to this presently, and I hope that by that time the meaning of what I have said here will have become clearer. Meanwhile, here are five specimens of the English language as it is now habitually written.

3      These five passages have not been picked out because they are especially bad — I could have quoted far worse if I had chosen — but because they illustrate various of the mental vices from which we now suffer. They are a little below the average, but are fairly representative samples. I number them so that I can refer back to them when necessary:

> (1) I am not, indeed, sure whether it is not true to say that the Milton who once seemed not unlike a seventeenth-century Shelley had not become, out of an experience ever more bitter in each year, more alien [*sic*] to the founder of that Jesuit sect which nothing could induce him to tolerate. — Professor Harold Laski, essay in *Freedom of Expression*

> (2) Above all, we cannot play ducks and drakes with a native battery of idioms which prescribes such egregious collocations of vocables as the Basic *put up with* for *tolerate* or *put at a loss* for *bewilder.* — Professor Lancelot Hogben, *Interglossa*

> (3) On the one side we have the free personality: by definition it is not neurotic, for it has neither conflict nor dream. Its desires, such as they are, are transparent, for they are just what institutional approval keeps in the forefront of consciousness; another institutional pattern would alter their number and intensity; there is little in them that is natural, irreducible, or culturally dangerous. But *on the other side*, the social bond itself is nothing but the mutual reflection of these self-secure integrities. Recall the definition of love. Is not this the very picture of a small academic? Where is there a place in this hall of mirrors for either personality or fraternity? — Essay on psychology in *Politics* (New York)

> (4) All the "best people" from the gentlemen's clubs, and all the frantic fascist captains, united in common hatred of Socialism and bestial horror of the rising tide of the mass revolutionary movement, have turned to acts of provocation, to foul incendiarism, to medieval legends of poisoned wells, to legalize their own destruction of proletarian organizations, and rouse the agitated petty-bourgeoisie to chauvinistic fervor on behalf of the fight against the revolutionary way out of the crisis. — Communist pamphlet

> (5) If the new spirit *is* to be infused into this old country, there is one thorny and contentious reform which must be tackled, and that is the humanization and galvanization of the B.B.C. Timidity here will bespeak canker and atrophy of the soul. The heart of Britain may be sound

and of strong beat, for instance, but the British lion's roar at present is like that of Bottom in Shakespeare's *Midsummer Night's Dream* — as gentle as any sucking dove. A virile new Britain cannot continue indefinitely to be traduced in the eyes or rather ears, of the world by the effete languors of Langham Place, brazenly masquerading as "standard English." When the Voice of Britain is heard at nine o'clock, better far and infinitely less ludicrous to hear aitches honestly dropped than the present priggish, inflated, inhibited, school-ma'amish arch braying of blameless bashful mewing maidens! — Letter in *Tribune*

Each of these passages has faults of its own, but, quite apart from avoidable ugliness, **4** two qualities are common to all of them. The first is staleness in imagery; the other is lack of precision. The writer either has a meaning and cannot express it, or he inadvertently says something else, or he is almost indifferent as to whether his words mean anything or not. This mixture of vagueness and sheer incompetence is the most marked characteristic of modern English prose, and especially of any kind of political writing. As soon as certain topics are raised, the concrete melts into the abstract and no one seems able to think in turns of speech that are not hackneyed: prose consists less and less of *words* chosen for the sake of their meaning, and more and more of *phrases* tacked together like the sections of a prefabricated henhouse. I list below, with notes and examples, various of the tricks by means of which the work of prose-construction is habitually dodged:

*Dying metaphors.* A newly invented metaphor assists thought by evoking a visual **5** image, while on the other hand a metaphor which is technically "dead" (e.g., *iron resolution*) has in effect reverted to being an ordinary word and can generally be used without loss of vividness. But in between these two classes there is a huge dump of worn-out metaphors which have lost all evocative power and are merely used because they save people the trouble of inventing phrases for themselves. Examples are: *Ring the changes on, take up the cudgels for, toe the line, ride rough-shod over, stand shoulder to shoulder with, play into the hands of, no axe to grind, grist to the mill, fishing in troubled waters, rift within the lute, on the order of the day, Achilles' heel, swan song, hotbed.* Many of these are used without knowledge of their meaning (what is a "rift," for instance?), and incompatible metaphors are frequently mixed, a sure sign that the writer is not interested in what he is saying. Some metaphors now current have been twisted out of their original meaning without those who use them even being aware of the fact. For example, *toe the line* is sometimes written *tow the line*. Another example is *the hammer and the anvil*, now always used with the implication that the anvil gets the worst of it. In real life it is always the anvil that breaks the hammer, never the other way about: a writer who stopped to think what he was saying would be aware of this, and would avoid perverting the original phrase.

*Operators* or *verbal false limbs*. These save the trouble of picking out appropriate **6** verbs and nouns, and at the same time pad each sentence with extra syllables which give it an appearance of symmetry. Characteristic phrases are *render inoperative, militate against, make contact with, be subjected to, give rise to, give grounds for, have the effect of, play a leading part (role) in, make itself felt, take effect, exhibit a tendency to, serve the purpose of, etc., etc.* The keynote is the elimination of simple verbs. Instead of being a single word, such as *break, stop, spoil, mend, kill*, a verb becomes a *phrase*, made up of a noun or adjective tacked on to some general-purpose verb such as *prove, serve, form, play, render.* In addition, the passive voice is wherever possible used in preference to the active, and noun constructions are used instead of gerunds (*by examination of* instead of *by examining*). The range of verbs is further cut down by means of the *-ize* and *de-* formations, and the banal statements are given an appearance of profundity by means of the *not* *un-* formation. Simple conjunctions and prepositions are replaced by such phrases as *with respect to, having regard to, the fact that, by dint of, in view of, in the interests of, on the hypothesis that*; and the ends of sentences are saved from anticlimax by such resounding commonplaces as *greatly to be desired, cannot be left out of account, a development to be expected in the near future, deserving of serious consideration, brought to a satisfying conclusion*, and so on and so forth.

7    *Pretentious diction.* Words like *phenomenon, element, individual* (as noun), *objective, categorical, effective, virtual, basic, primary, promote, constitute, exhibit, exploit, utilize, eliminate, liquidate*, are used to dress up simple statements and given an air of scientific impartiality to biased judgments. Adjectives like *epoch-making, epic, historic, unforgettable, triumphant, age-old, inevitable, inexorable, veritable*, are used to dignify the sordid processes of international politics, while writing that aims at glorifying war usually takes on an archaic color, its characteristic words being: *realm, throne, chariot, mailed fist, trident, sword, shield, buckler, banner, jackboot, clarion*. Foreign words and expressions such as *cul de sac, ancien régime, deus ex machina, mutatis mutandis, status quo, gleichschaltung, weltanschauung*, are used to give an air of culture and elegance. Except for the useful abbreviations *i.e., e.g.*, and *etc.*, there is no real need for any of the hundreds of foreign phrases now current in English. Bad writers, and especially scientific, political, and sociological writers, are nearly always haunted by the notion that Latin or Greek words are grander than Saxon ones, and unnecessary words like *expedite, ameliorate, predict, extraneous, deracinated, clandestine, subaqueous*, and hundreds of others constantly gain ground from their Anglo-Saxon opposite numbers.* The jargon peculiar to Marxist writing (*hyena, hangman, cannibal, petty bourgeois, these gentry, lackey, flunkey, mad dog, White Guard*, etc.) consists largely of words and phrases translated from Russian, German, or French; but the normal way of coining a new word is to use a Latin or Greek root with the appropriate affix and, where necessary, the size formation. It is often easier to make up words of this kind (*deregionalize, impermissible, extramarital, nonfragmentary* and so forth) than to think up the English words that will cover one's meaning. The result, in general, is an increase in slovenliness and vagueness.

8    *Meaningless words.* In certain kinds of writing, particularly in art criticism and literary criticism, it is normal to come across long passages which are almost completely lacking in meaning.† Words like *romantic, plastic, values, human, dead, sentimental, natural, vitality*, as used in art criticism, are strictly meaningless, in the sense that they not only do not point to any discoverable object, but are hardly ever expected to do so by the reader. When one critic writes, "The outstanding feature of Mr. X's work is its living quality," while another writes, "The immediately striking thing about Mr. X's work is its peculiar deadness," the reader accepts this as a simple difference of opinion. If words like *black* and *white* were involved, instead of the jargon words *dead* and *living*, he would see at once that language was being used in an improper way. Many political words are similarly abused. The word *Fascism* has now no meaning except in so far as it signifies "something

*An interesting illustration of this is the way in which the English flower names which were in use till very recently are being ousted by Greek ones, *snapdragon* becoming *antirrhinum*, *forget-me-not* becoming *myosotis*, etc. It is hard to see any practical reason for this change of fashion: it is probably due to an instinctive turning away from the more homely word and a vague feeling that the Greek word is scientific.

†Example: "Comfort's catholicity of perception and image, strangely Whitmanesque in range, almost the opposite in aesthetic compulsion, continues to evoke that trembling atmospheric accumulative hinting at a cruel, an inexorably serene timelessness. . . . Wrey Gardiner scores by aiming at simple bull's-eyes with precision. Only they are not so simple, and through this contented sadness runs more than the surface bittersweet of resignation." (*Poetry Quarterly.*)

not desirable." The words *democracy, socialism, freedom, patriotic, realistic, justice*, have each of them several different meanings which cannot be reconciled with one another. In the case of a word like *democracy*, not only is there no agreed definition, but the attempt to make one is resisted from all sides. It is almost universally felt that when we call a country democratic we are praising it: consequently the defenders of every kind of régime claim that is is a democracy, and fear that they might have to stop using the word if it were tied down to any one meaning. Words of this kind are often used in a consciously dishonest way. That is, the person who uses them has his own private definition, but allows his hearer to think he means something quite different. Statements like *Marshal Pétain was a true patriot, The Soviet press is the freest in the world, The Catholic Church is opposed to persecution*, are almost always made with intent to deceive. Other words used in variable meanings, in most cases more or less dishonestly, are: *class, totalitarian, science, progressive, reactionary, bourgeois, equality.*

Now that I have made this catalogue of swindles and perversions, let me give another **9** example of the kind of writing that they lead to. This time it must of its nature be an imaginary one. I am going to translate a passage of good English into modern English of the worst sort. Here is a well-known verse from *Ecclesiastes*:

> I returned and saw under the sun, that the race is not to the swift, nor the battle to the strong, neither yet bread to the wise, nor yet riches to men of understanding, nor yet favour to men of skill; but time and chance happeneth to them all.

Here it is in modern English:

> Objective consideration of contemporary phenomena compels the conclusion that success or failure in competitive activities exhibits no tendency to be commensurate with innate capacity, but that a considerable element of the unpredictable must invariably be taken into account.

This is a parody, but not a very gross one. Exhibit (3), above, for instance, contains **10** several patches of the same kind of English. It will be seen that I have not made a full translation. The beginning and ending of the sentence follow the original meaning fairly closely, but in the middle the concrete illustrations — race, battle, bread — dissolve into the vague phrase "success or failure in competitive activities." This had to be so, because no modern writer of the kind I am discussing — no one capable of using phrases like "objective consideration of contemporary phenomena" — would ever tabulate his thoughts in that precise and detailed way. The whole tendency of modern prose is away from concreteness. Now analyze these two sentences a little more closely. The first contains forty-nine words but only sixty syllables, and all its words are those of everyday life. The second contains thirty-eight words of ninety syllables: eighteen of its words are from Latin roots, and one from Greek. The first sentence contains six vivid images, and only one phrase ("time and chance") that could be called vague. The second contains not a single fresh, arresting phrase, and in spite of its ninety syllables it gives only a shortened version of the meaning contained in the first. Yet without a doubt it is the second kind of sentence that is gaining ground in modern English. I do not want to exaggerate. This kind of writing is not yet universal, and outcrops of simplicity will occur here and there in the worst-written page. Still, if you or I were told to write a few lines on the uncertainty of human fortunes, we should probably come much nearer to my imaginary sentence than to the one from *Ecclesiastes*.

As I have tried to show, modern writing at its worst does not consist of picking out **11** words for the sake of their meaning and inventing images in order to make the meaning clearer. It consists in gumming together long strips of words which have already been set in order by someone else, and making the results presentable by sheer humbug. The attraction of this way of writing is that it is easy. It is easier — even quicker, once you have the habit — to say *In my opinion it is not an unjustifiable assumption that* than to say *I think*. If you use ready-made phrases, you not only don't have to hunt about for words; you also don't have to bother with the rhythms of your sentences, since these phrases are generally so arranged as to be more or less euphonious. When you are composing in a hurry — when you are dictating to a stenographer, for instance, or making a public speech — it is natural to fall into a pretentious, Latinized style. Tags like *a consideration which we should do well to bear in mind* or *a conclusion to which all of us would readily assent* will save many a sentence from coming down with a bump. By using stale metaphors, similes, and idioms, you save much mental effort, at the cost of leaving your meaning vague, not only for your reader but for yourself. This is the signifiance of mixed metaphors. The sole aim of a metaphor is to call up a visual image. When these images clash — as in *The Fascist octopus has sung its swan song, the jackboot is thrown into the melting pot* — it can be taken as certain that the writer is not seeing a mental image of the objects he is naming; in other words he is not really thinking. Look again at the examples I gave at the beginning of this essay. Professor Laski (1) uses five negatives in fifty-three words. One of these is superfluous, making nonsense of the whole passage, and in addition there is the slip — *alien* for akin — making further nonsense, and several avoidable pieces of clumsiness which increase the general vagueness. Professor Hogben (2) plays ducks and drakes with a battery which is able to write prescriptions, and, while disapproving of the everyday phrase *put up with*, is unwilling to look *egregious* up in the dictionary and see what it means; (3), if one takes an uncharitable attitude towards it, is simply meaningless: probably one could work out its intended meaning by reading the whole of the article in which it occurs. In (4), the writer knows more or less what he wants to say, but an accumulation of stale phrases chokes him like tea leaves blocking a sink. In (5), words and meaning have almost parted company. People who write in this manner usually have a general emotional meaning — they dislike one thing and want to express solidarity with another — but they are not interested in the detail of what they are saying. A scrupulous writer, in every sentence that he writes, will ask himself at least four questions, thus: What am I trying to say? What words will express it? What image or idiom will make it clearer? Is this image fresh enough to have an effect? And he will probably ask himself two more: Could I put it more shortly? Have I said anything that is avoidably ugly? But you are not obliged to go to all this trouble. You can shirk it by simply throwing your mind open and letting the ready-made phrases come crowding in. They will construct your sentences for you — even think your thoughts for you, to a certain extent — and at need they will perform the important service of partially concealing your meaning even from yourself. It is at this point that the special connection between politics and the debasement of language becomes clear.

12      In our time it is broadly true that political writing is bad writing. Where it is not true, it will generally be found that the writer is some kind of rebel, expressing his private opinions and not a "party line." Orthodoxy, of whatever color, seems to demand a lifeless, imitative style. The political dialects to be found in pamphlets, leading articles, manifestoes, White Papers and the speeches of undersecretaries do, of course, vary from party to party, but they are all alike in that one almost never finds in them a fresh, vivid, homemade turn of speech. When one watches some tired hack on the platform mechanically repeating the familiar phrases — *bestial atrocities, iron heel, bloodstained tyranny, free peoples of the world, stand shoulder to shoulder* — one often has a curious feeling that one is not watching a live human being but some kind of dummy: a feeling which suddenly becomes

stronger at moments when the light catches the speaker's spectacles and turns them into blank discs which seem to have no eyes behind them. And this is not altogether fanciful. A speaker who uses that kind of phraseology has gone some distance toward turning himself into a machine. The appropriate noises are coming out of his larynx, but his brain is not involved as it would be if he were choosing his words for himself. If the speech he is making is one that he is accustomed to make over and over again, he may be almost unconscious of what he is saying, as one is when one utters the responses in church. And this reduced state of consciousness, if not indispensable, is at any rate favorable to political conformity.

In our time, political speech and writing are largely the defense of the indefensible.     **13**
Things like the continuance of British rule in India, the Russian purges and deportations, the dropping of the atom bombs on Japan, can indeed be defended, but only by arguments which are too brutal for most people to face, and which do not square with the professed aims of political parties. Thus political language has to consist largely of euphemism, question-begging and sheer cloudy vagueness. Defenseless villages are bombarded from the air, the inhabitants driven out into the countryside, the cattle machine-gunned, the huts set on fire with incendiary bullets: this is called *pacification*. Millions of peasants are robbed of their farms and sent trudging along the roads with no more than they can carry: this is called *transfer of population* or *rectification of frontiers*. People are imprisoned for years without trial, or shot in the back of the neck or sent to die of scurvy in Arctic lumber camps: this is called *elimination of unreliable elements*. Such phraseology is needed if one wants to name things without calling up mental pictures of them. Consider for instance some comfortable English professor defending Russian totalitarianism. He cannot say outright, "I believe in killing off your opponents when you can get good results by doing so." Probably, therefore, he will say something like this: "While freely conceding that the Soviet régime exhibits certain features which the humanitarian may be inclined to deplore, we must, I think, agree that a certain curtailment of the right to political opposition is an unavoidable concomitant of transitional periods, and that the rigors which the Russian people have been called upon to undergo have been amply justified in the sphere of concrete achievement."

The inflated style is itself a kind of euphemism. A mass of Latin words fall upon the     **14**
facts like soft snow, blurring the outlines and covering up all the details. The great enemy of clear language is insincerity. When there is a gap between one's real and one's declared aims, one turns as it were instinctively to long words and exhausted idioms, like a cuttlefish squirting out ink. In our age there is no such thing as "keeping out of politics." All issues are political issues, and politics itself is a mass of lies, evasions, folly, hatred, and schizophrenia. When the general atmosphere is bad, language must suffer. I should expect to find — this is a guess which I have not sufficient knowledge to verify — that the German, Russian and Italian languages have all deteriorated in the last ten or fifteen years, as a result of dictatorship.

But if thought corrupts language, language can also corrupt thought. A bad usage can     **15**
spread by tradition and imitation, even among people who should and do know better. The debased language that I have been discussing is in some ways very convenient. Phrases like *a not unjustifiable assumption, leaves much to be desired, would serve no good purpose, a consideration which we should do well to bear in mind*, are a continuous temptation, a packet of aspirins at one's elbow. Look back through this essay, and for certain you will find that I have again and again committed the very faults I am protesting against. By this morning's post I have received a pamphlet dealing with conditions in Germany. The author tells me that he "felt impelled" to write it. I open it at random, and here is almost the first sentence that I see: "[The Allies] have an opportunity not only of

achieving a radical transformation of Germany's social and political structure in such a way as to avoid a nationalistic reaction in Germany itself, but at the same time of laying the foundations of a co-operative and unified Europe." You see, he "feels impelled" to write — feels, presumably, that he has something new to say — and yet his words, like cavalry horses answering the bugle, group themselves automatically into the familiar dreary pattern. This invasion of one's mind by ready-made phrases (*lay the foundations, achieve a radical transformation*) can only be prevented if one is constantly on guard against them, and every such phrase anaesthetizes a portion of one's brain.

16    I said earlier that the decadence of our language is probably curable. Those who deny this would argue, if they produced an argument at all, that language merely reflects existing social conditions, and that we cannot influence its development by any direct tinkering with words and constructions. So far as the general tone or spirit of a language goes, this may be true, but it is not true in detail. Silly words and expressions have often disappeared, not through any evolutionary process but owing to the conscious action of a minority. Two recent examples were *explore every avenue* and *leave no stone unturned*, which were killed by the jeers of a few journalists. There is a long list of flyblown metaphors which could similarly be got rid of if enough people would interest themselves in the job; and it should also be possible to laugh the *not un-* formation out of existence,* to reduce the amount of Latin and Greek in the average sentence, to drive out foreign phrases and strayed scientific words, and, in general, to make pretentiousness unfashionable. But all these are minor points. The defense of the English language implies more than this, and perhaps it is best to start by saying what it does *not* imply.

17    To begin with it has nothing to do with archaism, with the salvaging of obsolete words and turns of speech, or with the setting up of a "standard English" which must never be departed from. On the contrary, it is especially concerned with the scrapping of every word or idiom which has outworn it usefulness. It has nothing to do with correct grammar and syntax, which are of no importance so long as one makes one's meaning clear, or with the avoidance of Americanisms, or with having what is called a "good prose style." On the other hand it is not concerned with fake simplicity and the attempt to make written English colloquial. Nor does it even imply in every case preferring the Saxon word to the Latin one, though it does imply using the fewest and shortest words that will cover one's meaning. What is above all needed is to let the meaning choose the word, and not the other way about. In prose, the worst thing one can do with words is to surrender to them. When you think of a concrete object, you think wordlessly, and then, if you want to describe the thing you have been visualizing you probably hunt about till you find the exact words that seem to fit it. When you think of something abstract you are more inclined to use words from the start, and unless you make a conscious effort to prevent it, the existing dialect will come rushing in and do the job for you, at the expense of blurring or even changing your meaning. Probably it is better to put off using words as long as possible and get one's meaning as clear as one can through pictures or sensations. Afterward one can choose — not simply *accept* — the phrases that will best cover the meaning, and then switch round and decide what impression one's words are likely to make on another person. This last effort of the mind cuts out all stale or mixed images, all prefabricated phrases, needless repetitions, and humbug and vagueness generally. But one can often be in doubt about the effect of a word or a phrase, and one needs rules that one can rely on when instinct fails. I think the following rules will cover most cases:

---

*One can cure oneself of the *not un-* formation by memorizing this sentence: *A not unblack dog was chasing a not unsmall rabbit across a not ungreen field.*

(i)   Never use a metaphor, simile, or other figure of speech which you are used to seeing in print.

(ii)  Never use a long word where a short one will do.

(iii) If it is possible to cut a word out, always cut it out.

(iv)  Never use the passive where you can use the active.

(v)   Never use a foreign phrase, a scientific word, or a jargon word if you can think of an everyday English equivalent.

(vi)  Break any of these rules sooner than say anything outright barbarous.

These rules sound elementary, and so they are, but they demand a deep change of attitude in anyone who has grown used to writing in the style now fashionable. One could keep all of them and still write bad English, but one could not write the kind of stuff that I quoted in those five specimens at the beginning of this article.

I have not here been considering the literary use of language, but merely language as an **18** instrument for expressing and not for concealing or preventing thought. Stuart Chase and others have come near to claiming that all abstract words are meaningless, and have used this as a pretext for advocating a kind of political quietism. Since you don't know what Fascism is, how can you struggle against Fascism? One need not swallow such absurdities as this, but one ought to recognize that the present political chaos is connected with the decay of language, and that one can probably bring about some improvement by starting at the verbal end. If you simplify your English, you are freed from the worst follies of orthodoxy. You cannot speak any of the necessary dialects, and when you make a stupid remark its stupidity will be obvious, even to yourself. Political language — and with variations this is true of all political parties, from Conservatives to Anarchists — is designed to make lies sound truthful and murder respectable, and to give an appearance of solidity to pure wind. One cannot change this all in a moment, but one can at least change one's own habits, and from time to time one can even, if one jeers loudly enough, send some worn-out and useless phrase — some *jackboot, Achilles' heel, hotbed, melting pot, acid test, veritable inferno*, or other lump of verbal refuse — into the dustbin where it belongs.

## VOCABULARY

a. *paragraph   1:* decadent, archaism, hansom cabs

b. *paragraph   3:* ducks and drakes, idioms, egregious, collocations, vocables, integrities, humanization, galvanization, canker, atrophy, virile, effete, languors, brazenly, mewing

c. *paragraph   5:* evocative, perverting

d. *paragraph   6:* symmetry, keynote, banal

e. *paragraph   7:* categorical, virtual, inexorable, expedite, ameliorate, extraneous, deracinated, clandestine, subaqueous, Anglo-Saxon, jargon, slovenliness

f. *paragraph   8:* totalitarian, reactionary, bourgeois

g. *paragraph   9:* commensurate

h. *paragraph 10:* parody

i. *paragraph 11:* humbug, euphonious, superfluous, scrupulous, debasement

j. *paragraph 12:* orthodoxy, phraseology

k. *paragraph 13:* euphemism, pacification, rectification

l. *paragraph 14:* inflated, cuttlefish, schizophrenia

m. *paragraph 15:* anaesthetizes

n. *paragraph 17:* Americanisms, colloquial, dialect

o. *paragraph 18:* quietism

## QUESTIONS

1. Do the examples Orwell cites constitute sufficient evidence to prove his contention of a link between language and politics?

2. Compare the passage from Ecclesiastes quoted in paragraph 9 (King James Version) with modern renderings of it. Do you think these modern renderings are superior to Orwell's parody or to the King James Version? Why?

3. "If you or I were to write a few lines on the uncertainty of human fortunes," why would the writing come nearer to Orwell's parody than to the sentence from Ecclesiastes? (See Harry Bruce's "The Christmas Story Updated" for another parody of obfuscatory language.)

4. Given the assumptions Orwell makes in the whole essay, why are all issues "political issues"?

5. Orwell says in paragraph 17 that his concern has not been to promote a "standard English" or "to make written English colloquial." Explain what he means here. Has he not recommended the use of plain English words? What exceptions would he allow?

6. Is Orwell guilty anywhere of the kind of lazy thinking that makes writers reach for the handy cliché?

## WRITING ASSIGNMENT

Have recent political developments borne out Orwell's argument about the links between tyranny and debased language? Write an essay updating his evidence (some clichés, for instance, date quickly) and draw your own conclusions.

## WENDELL BERRY

Wendell Berry *was born and educated in Kentucky. A full-time farmer and writer, he has also taught at the University of Kentucky. Although a poet and novelist, he is most accomplished in the essay, as is evidenced by such collections as* The Unsettling of America,

Recollected Essays, *and* The Gift of Good Land. *In the following essay, Berry argues that language and literature have an intrinsic value that makes them "not an ornament but a necessity."*

## IN DEFENSE OF LITERACY

In a country in which everybody goes to school, it may seem absurd to offer a defense of literacy, and yet I believe that such a defense is in order, and that the absurdity lies not in the defense, but in the necessity for it. The published illiteracies of the certified educated are on the increase. And the universities seem bent upon ratifying this state of things by declaring the acceptability, in their graduates, of adequate — that is to say, of mediocre — writing skills.   **1**

The schools, then, are following the general subservience to the "practical," as that term has been defined for us according to the benefit of corporations. By "practicality" most users of the term now mean whatever will most predictably and most quickly make a profit. Teachers of English and literature have either submitted, or are expected to submit, along with teachers of the more "practical" disciplines, to the doctrine that the purpose of education is the mass production of producers and consumers. This has forced our profession into a predicament that we will finally have to recognize as a perversion. As if awed by the ascendency of the "practical" in our society, many of us secretly fear, and some of us are apparently ready to say, that if a student is not going to become a teacher of his language, he has no need to master it.   **2**

In other words, to keep pace with the specialization — and the dignity accorded to specialization — in other disciplines, we have begun to look upon and to teach our language and literature as specialties. But whereas specialization is of the nature of the applied sciences, it is a perversion of the disciplines of language and literature. When we understand and teach these as specialties, we submit willy-nilly to the assumption of the "practical men" of business, and also apparently of education, that literacy is no more than an ornament: when one has become an efficient integer of the economy, *then* it is permissible, even desirable, to be able to talk about the latest novels. After all, the disciples of "practicality" may someday find themselves stuck in conversation with an English teacher.   **3**

I may have oversimplified that line of thinking, but not much. There are two flaws in it. One is that, among the self-styled "practical men," the practical is synonymous with the immediate. The long-term effects of their values and their acts lie outside the boundaries of their interest. For such people a strip mine ceases to exist as soon as the coal has been extracted. Short-term practicality is long-term idiocy.   **4**

The other flaw is that language and literature are always *about* something else, and we have no way to predict or control what they may be about. They are about the world. We will understand the world, and preserve ourselves and our values in it, only insofar as we have a language that is alert and responsive to it, and careful of it. I mean that literally. When we give our plows such brand names as "Sod Blaster," we are imposing on their use conceptual limits which raise the likelihood that they will be used destructively. When we speak of man's "war against nature," or of a "peace offensive," we are accepting the limitations of a metaphor that suggests, and even proposes, violent solutions. When students ask for the right of "participatory input" at the meetings of a faculty organization, they are thinking of democratic process, but they are *speaking* of a convocation of robots, and are thus devaluing the very traditions that they invoke.   **5**

Ignorance of books and the lack of a critical consciousness of language were safe enough in primitive societies with coherent oral traditions. In our society, which exists in an atmosphere of prepared, public language — language that is either written or being   **6** read — illiteracy is both a personal and a public danger. Think how constantly "the average American" is surrounded by premeditated language, in newspapers and magazines, on signs and billboards, on TV and radio. He is forever being asked to buy or believe somebody else's line of goods. The line of goods is being sold, moreover, by men who are trained to make him buy it or believe it, whether or not he needs it or understands it or knows its value or wants it. This sort of selling is an honored profession among us. Parents who grow hysterical at the thought that their son might not cut his hair are *glad* to have him taught, and later employed, to lie about the quality of an automobile or the ability of a candidate.

7      What is our defense against this sort of language — this language-as-weapon? There is only one. We must know a better language. We must speak, and teach our children to speak, a language precise and articulate and lively enough to tell the truth about the world as we know it. And to do this we must know something of the roots and resources of our language; we must know its literature. The only defense against the worst is a knowledge of the best. By their ignorance people enfranchise their exploiters.

8      But to appreciate fully the necessity for the best sort of literacy we must consider not just the environment of prepared language in which most of us now pass most of our lives, but also the utter transience of most of this language, which is meant to be merely glanced at, or heard only once, or read once and thrown away. Such language is by definition, and often calculation, not memorable; it is language meant to be replaced by what will immediately follow it, like that of shallow conversation between strangers. It cannot be pondered or effectively criticized. For those reasons an unmixed diet of it is destructive of the informed, resilient, critical intelligence that the best of our traditions have sought to create and to maintain — an intelligence that Jefferson held to be indispensable to the health and longevity of freedom. Such intelligence does not grow by bloating upon the ephemeral information and misinformation of the public media. It grows by returning again and again to the landmarks of its cultural birthright, the works that have proved worthy of devoted attention.

9      "Read not the Times. Read the Eternities," Thoreau said. Ezra Pound wrote that "literature is news that STAYS news." In his lovely poem, "The Island," Edwin Muir spoke of man's inescapable cultural boundaries and of his consequent responsibility for his own sources and renewals:

> Men are made of what is made,
> The meat, the drink, the life, the corn,
> Laid up by them, in them reborn.
> And self-begotten cycles close
> About our way; indigenous art
> And simple spells make unafraid
> The haunted labyrinths of the heart . . .

10     These men spoke of a truth that no society can afford to shirk for long: we are dependent, for understanding, and for consolation and hope, upon what we learn of ourselves from songs and stories. This has always been so, and it will not change.

11     I am saying, then, that literacy — the mastery of language and the knowledge of books — is not an ornament, but a necessity. It is impractical only by the standards of quick profit and easy power. Longer perspective will show that it alone can preserve in us the possibility of an accurate judgment of ourselves, and the possibilities of correction and renewal. Without it, we are adrift in the present, in the wreckage of yesterday, in the nightmare of tomorrow.

# VOCABULARY

a. *paragraph  1:* ratifying

b. *paragraph  2:* subservience, perversion, ascendency

c. *paragraph  3:* willy-nilly

d. *paragraph  6:* premeditated

e. *paragraph  7:* articulate, enfranchise

f. *paragraph  8:* transience, bloating, ephemeral, birthright

g. *paragraph  9:* indigenous, labyrinths

h. *paragraph 10:* consolation

i. *paragraph 11:* perspective

# QUESTIONS

1. To what kind of reader is Berry addressing himself?

2. Does he appeal primarily to reason or to emotion? Cite examples to support your answer.

3. Does he anticipate objections in order to forestall them? How effective are his answers to potential counter-arguments?

4. Compare his argument for education with that of Frye. Do they come to similar conclusions?

# WRITING ASSIGNMENT

Write a persuasive essay arguing that literacy is less essential than Berry contends, that, for example, "computer literacy" is the required skill today.

# CONTROVERSY

Inductive and deductive reasoning often work together, depending on the particular argument and what we consider the point at issue. Proponents of nuclear power plants may, for example, insist that the issue in making the decision to build the plant in a particular region is economic — the increasing power needs of industry. Opponents may argue that the issue is the danger of an accident or the difficulty of disposing of nuclear waste. Much of the debate may be given to establishing the point at issue.

The arguments employed in such a debate can and possibly will be inductive: statistical information on productivity and nuclear fuel, eyewitness accounts of nuclear plant operations, scientific reports on waste disposal, and the like. And the argument will be deductive in the inferences drawn from certain assumptions, perhaps ones on which the participants in the debate agree: that a high standard of living is a desirable goal in the community; that risk must be taken into account in making a decision about nuclear power; that high productivity depends on a dependable source of electrical power.

From such assumptions certain conclusions will be drawn — and used to different advantage. Sometimes both assumptions and conclusions are debated; sometimes the assumptions are accepted as "givens" and not debated. In all debate, fairness and sound argument ideally should prevail. It hardly needs to be said that they often do not. Here are a few important "logical fallacies" a good argument avoids:

*Arguing in a circle* is closely related to begging the question, where we assume as true what we are trying to prove: "No person who cares about jobs would oppose the bill because it is one that those who care about jobs in Cape Breton can support." The speaker has not given a reason to support the bill, but has merely restated the opening assertion.

*Non sequitur* ("it does not follow"): The assertion, "I oppose nuclear power because my father does," contains a hidden assumption — that father knows best. Since this assumption is hidden, the second part of the statement does not follow from the first part clearly. Assumptions of this sort may be hidden because, once stated, the assumption shows the statement to be questionable or absurd.

*Irrelevant conclusion*: If the point at issue is whether nuclear plants present a risk, the argument that they are needed is an irrelevant argument. It may, of course, be relevant to another issue.

*Ad hominem argument* ("to the person"): I may attack my opponents rather than the issue — for example, by arguing that proponents of nuclear power are selfish and greedy. Even if they were people of bad character, their proposals must be judged on their merits. In other circumstances, such as an election campaign, the character of a person may be the issue.

*Ad populum argument* ("to the people"): I may also appeal to popular prejudice to gain support — suggesting that Sir John A. Macdonald or some other revered and usually long-dead person would have favored (or opposed) nuclear power. Such appeals to authority often depend on fear.

*Either/or hypothesis*: I may set up two alternatives — nuclear power or economic depression — without allowing for other solutions.

# MARTIN KITCHEN

Martin Kitchen *is a professor of history at Simon Fraser University. His many books include works on fascism, German military history, and the Cold War. The following essay originated as the opening address to a conference in Vancouver in 1984, and was intended "to give a historical background to disarmament talks and to point out some of the snags they had encountered in the past."*

# PUTTING SWORD TO PAPER

Most agree that war is the greatest man-made disaster and that perhaps, since it is entirely of our own doing, something can be done to limit, civilize and humanize it. The results of such efforts have been woefully meagre but all except the most extreme determinist will agree that, since wars are not natural disasters like volcanic eruptions, their effects can be ameliorated to some extent.

In the inter-war period, the most successful attempt to limit armaments was the Washington Agreement of 1922. The United States, Britain, Japan, France and Italy agreed to scrap more than half their battleships and to freeze the construction of new battleships for 10 years. Limitations were also imposed on the tonnage of other ships, on the calibre of naval guns and on the construction of naval bases in the Pacific. In the years immediately after the First World War, the Americans and Japanese were locked into a dangerous naval rivalry that threatened the traditional naval supremacy of the British empire. Popular protest against this arms race began in the United States and was led by women, particularly the League of Women Voters. The league was soon joined by Church groups, organized labour, the universities and members of congress. Although it was vehemently opposed by the general board of the U.S. navy, President Harding took up the proposal, largely because he was convinced that the British and Japanese would reject the whole idea of arms limitation. The United States would be able to continue their naval-building program while at the same time getting the credit for making a magnanimous gesture. Much to everyone's surprise, the conference was a great success. The United States, Britain, Japan and France signed a four-power treaty pledging to consult one another over any differences arising in the Pacific. All nine nations at the conference pledged to respect the "sovereignty, the independence, and the territorial and administrative integrity of China." Although the treaty was eventually destroyed by the imperialist ambitions of Japan and by the revival of German naval strength after 1933, it did secure a naval holiday for almost 10 years. It was an admirable example of how popular demands for peace and disarmament can result in concrete and practical measures of arms control.

But the agreement did have serious shortcomings. It only limited capital ship-construction and did not halt the building of submarines, a prohibition for which the British were particularly anxious, having suffered serious losses during the war to the German U-boats. Nor did the treaty cover the increasingly destabilizing threat of aircraft construction. Britain's very first Labour government of 1924 agreed to a massive cruiser-building program that had been worked out by the admiralty before they took office even though the Labour party had strongly supported all disarmament initiatives. In spite of the ban on the building of bases in the Pacific, the British government began to modernize the defenses of Singapore, which the Japanese ludicrously claimed presented a major threat to their security. The lesson of the Washington Agreement is that if there are limitations on battle ships, cruisers become more important; if there are limitations on navies, airforces and armies become more important. *Mutatis mutandis*, limitation on nuclear weapons make conventional weapons more important.

4    The history of arms control provides two obvious lessons, the first encouraging, the second somewhat depressing. First, none of the great antagonistic line-ups of the past are fixed and immutable. Alliances change and former enemies become the best of allies. The present division of the world into two hostile power blocs which is the root of all the present problems of disarmament and arms control, will not last forever. However, I am too much of a historian to venture an opinion as to how long we shall have to live in this precarious situation. The second lesson is much less encouraging. It is that disarmament agreements without a fundamental political settlement are useless. The reduction of armaments is a consequence rather than a cause of peace, although the presence of armaments is not in itself a cause of war, as the history of arms races shows. This point was made very trenchantly by the Spanish liberal who was chairman of the League of Nations disarmament commission, Salvador de Madariaga. He wrote: "Nations do not distrust each other because they are armed; they are armed because they distrust each other. Therefore to want disarmament before a minimum of common agreement on fundamentals is as absurd as to want people to go undressed in winter. Let the weather be warm, and people will discard their clothes readily and without committees to tell them how to undress." The historical record suggests that it is not unreasonable to hope for such an improvement in the weather.

5    Disarmament, by which I mean the total renunciation of the use of nuclear weapons, will be every bit as elusive as it has been in the past. But if one believes, as I do, that we are neither heading inexorably towards the final destruction of the human race nor leaving ourselves open to a sudden attack by a ruthless and predatory foe, this should not be a matter for too much wailing and gnashing of teeth. Arms-control discussions are quite another matter, for they do not seek the impossible — the abolition of nuclear weapons. They seek the practical goal of stablizing the international situation and using these frightful weapons as a means towards an understanding. The fear of nuclear war is, after all, paradoxically one of the strongest stabilizing factors in the present-day world. Sheer self-interest and the instinct for self-preservation may force governments to reconsider their positions. Nor should the effect of domestic political considerations, particularly in the United States, be ignored. Popular pressure for arms-control negotiations must be taken into account by democratically elected politians. If it is true that no amount of ingenious formulae for arms control will achieve anything substantial unless the fundamental political questions are addressed fairly and squarely, it is also true that arms-control talks of themselves, if undertaken seriously, can contribute significantly to such a political understanding. As a historian I look at this enterprise with some scepticism, but as a contemporary observer I force myself to be more optimistic. I remember Antonio Gramsci's insistence that "politics demands pessimism of the intelligence and optimism of the will." We may not actually see the lion eat straw like the ox, nor the weaned child put his hand on the cockatrice den. But perhaps we may be able to cast aside some of our winter clothing and rejoice in the pale sun of the thaw.

## VOCABULARY

a. *paragraph 1:* determinist, ameliorated

b. *paragraph 2:* calibre, magnanimous, sovereignty

c. *paragraph 3:* U-boats, initiatives, *Mutatis mutandis*

d. *paragraph 4:* precarious

e. *paragraph 5:* renunciation, inexorably, paradoxically, scepticism

## QUESTIONS

1. Kitchen claims that a case can be made for arms-control discussion, though not for the abolition of nuclear weapons. Is his main purpose to argue for the usefulness of nuclear weapons? If not, what is his main purpose?

2. What audience is Kitchen addressing — the arms negotiators of the super powers, the military establishment, the Canadian public? How do you know?

3. If the difficulties that Kitchen discusses in paragraphs 3 and 4 could be overcome, do you think he would then support total nuclear disarmament?

## WRITING ASSIGNMENTS

1. Kitchen uses an analogy in comparing disarmament and political understanding between the super powers to dressing appropriately for the prevalent weather conditions. Discuss how the dissimilarities weaken the analogy and therefore the argument.

2. Kitchen states that arms-control discussions "do not seek the impossible — the abolition of nuclear weapons. They seek the practical goal of stabilizing the international situation and using these frightful weapons as a means towards an understanding." Agree or disagree with this statement, and give your reasons.

## DAVID SUZUKI

*A geneticist and broadcaster on radio (*Quirks and Quarks) *and television (*The Nature of Things), *David Suzuki was educated at Amherst and the University of Chicago (Ph.D. 1961). He is an international speaker and lecturer, and the recipient of numerous awards and honorary degrees. What distinguishes David Suzuki from the majority of his colleagues is his social conscience and his skills as a media personality: his willingness to "go public" with — and to make the public care about — his concerns about various kinds of scientific research. As the following essay shows, Suzuki's social conscience often prompts him to bring to bear upon matters not strictly scientific his keen scientific training and concerns for mankind's future.*

## NUCLEAR WEAPONS . . . CULPABILITY, SUBJECTIVITY, AND LOSS OF CONTROL

Like everyone else, I've been thinking a lot about nuclear weapons lately and I'd like to    **1** make three points that I think have yet to be considered.

2    (1) *Many prominent scientists are at the forefront of the movement to halt the arms race, but I have yet to hear one of them acknowledge that scientists may be especially culpable for the insane spiral of armaments.* Philip Morrison, who actually armed the first American atomic bomb, who was one of the first Americans to see Hiroshima after the A-bomb blast, who is a passionate opponent of nuclear armaments, nevertheless bristled in disagreement when I suggested that scientists had a special responsibility. But I stick by that claim. I don't believe that military strategists come up with the ideas for neutron bombs, binary nerve gases, new biological weapons, particle beam space platforms, and laser devices. They come out of the imaginative minds of scientists and are created by engineers and technologists, people who are often our colleagues and our students. There is intense pressure on science students in university to focus only on science, and this precludes any time for other courses like philosophy, literature, religion, or history. The result is that few scientists and engineers today are aware of the history of their professions, a history that might put their current activity into a different social perspective. The morality and ethics of science and technology and the social responsibilities that accompany professional careers are not matters of discussion during our training. The implications of the tight linkage between research and applications for military and industrial use are simply not considered by ambitious graduate students. I think that scientists have a lot of thinking to do about their own peers when it comes to the nuclear issue and perhaps such thinking could eventually evolve a code of ethics for scientists.

3    (2) *My second point concerns the nature of the nuclear weapons debate and the part that personal and emotional considerations play in it.* If you've ever talked to someone whose position is different from your own on abortion, religion, or politics, you know that the factors influencing such positions are seldom based on reason. This is evident when two great scientists, Linus Pauling and Edward Teller, use the *same data* to reach opposite conclusions on the nuclear arms issue. In arguments, one person is often heard to exclaim, "You're being too emotional," or "You're taking this far too personally," as if emotions or personal involvement are irrelevant to the debate. If issues were simply problems like a mathematical puzzle, they would be readily solved with an unequivocal single answer. But human problems are incredibly more complicated by the emotional, nonrational, culturally shaped reactions that tend to overwhelm the analytical functions of the brain.

4    I don't think we pay enough attention to this reality. In all of the talk about arms limitation and defence strategies, people are depicted as rational creatures. But the current climate of mistrust between the two superpowers must be seen in the historical and personal backgrounds of the leaders involved. In the end, the biases, the limitations in experience and knowledge of individual human beings, will be the overwhelming factors determing how nuclear weapons are used.

5    (3) *And finally, the technology to deliver nuclear weapons is now so accurate and quick, that it is literally out of human control.* All military strategy with respect to nuclear weapons is based on the assumption that both offensive and defensive strategies are rationally thought out and acted upon. I submit that it is impossible for people to respond as planned. Consider this:

6    The deployment of the Pershing II and SS-20 missiles in central Europe now bring targets within a 10-minute range. To cope with that stark reality, about three-quarters of the 4000-odd satellites are there to spy for the military. In principle, they can detect a missile launch seconds after it leaves its silo and can relay the information to military headquarters at the speed of light. Both the Soviet Union and the United States have invested billions of dollars to build "supercomputers" for the military. Yet over the past decade, NATO's computers have mistakenly identified flying objects as missiles over 150 times! Of course, it can be argued that the system must work because there hasn't been a nuclear

launch but that is hardly reassuring in the knowledge that we can only have one mistake. The supercomputers are supposed to determine the nature of the attack instantly — the payloads, trajectories, targets, and probable damage. Yet we have to assume that several minutes of the 10-minute window will be used by human brains attempting to verify the computer's analysis, to assimilate the implications, and to take action. If it is indeed a deliberate attack, I would expect it to be started at an "inconvenient" time for the enemy, say at 3:00 a.m. Christmas night. When the commander-in-chief is finally roused with the news, can we assume that he or she will be (1) instantly awake, (2) able to ignore concerns for personal safety, family, possessions, and the world, (3) able to comprehend the information, the options, and the consequences, and (4) make the most reasonable decision? This simple scenario shows the absurdity of all the military planning. The technology of nuclear weapons is out of control because human beings simply cannot function quickly enough under the incredible pressures and time constraints. If the military thinkers realize this, then I assume that the supercomputer is programmed to analyze the incoming data and to determine the options and their consequences from moment to moment. Very quickly, in the 10-minute interval, the machine will indicate that there is only one option left and that it must be taken immediately or it's too late. Since, I believe, no human being can act on it, then the programmers must put the final decision in control of the computer. The technology, then, is literally out of control.

## VOCABULARY

a. *paragraph 2:* culpable, bristled

b. *paragraph 3:* unequivocal

c. *paragraph 6:* trajectories, scenario

## QUESTIONS

1. Through what means does Suzuki develop his argument — personal experience, eyewitness accounts, statistics, analogy, causal analysis, or a statement of beliefs or truths and deduction from them?

2. What is Suzuki's main argument and what are his subordinate arguments? How does he distinguish his main argument from these others?

3. What false images of human beings is he attacking in the essay and how does he identify these images?

4. How convincing is Suzuki's claim that technology is out of human control?

## WRITING ASSIGNMENT

Discuss the extent to which you agree with the views attributed to scientists today, including the attitude toward culpability and toward scientific research in theory and in application. How responsible are scientists for what has happened?

# BARBARA AMIEL

*Barbara Amiel was born in England and educated at the University of Toronto. She has written (with George Jonas)* By Persons Unknown *(1977), an account of Peter Demeter's murder of his wife and the sensational trial that followed. She is also the author of* Confessions *(1980). The essay that follows is taken from* Maclean's *magazine, the national weekly magazine for which Amiel has written an acerbic, right-wing column since 1976.*

## OF ARMS AND THE BAN I SING

1    In recent months U.S. Secretary of State Alexander Haig has made the reasonable statement that the defence of Europe could best be achieved by the deployment of a new generation of nuclear weapons. This seemed reasonable to everyone but the people who would be most helped — the Europeans on whose terra firma the weapons would have to be placed. In London, 100,000 marchers dusted off their 1960s' Campaign For Nuclear Disarmament signs and took to the streets with hand-crayoned placards announcing, WE WANT TO LIVE. In Bonn, a quarter of a million ban-the-bomb demonstrators followed suit.

2    All the predictable elements can be found in this latest manifestation of the peace movement. Soviet involvement — no surprise to anyone — was confirmed by the recent arrest in the Netherlands of an intelligence agent, under orders to use his cover as a TASS correspondent to infiltrate and direct the peace movement. The pacifism of many of Europe's youthful protestors appears to reduce itself to a fear of defeat in war rather than of war itself. This attitude seems to be the inevitable product of a new generation of Europeans who have thrived under the seeming security of detente, menaced only by a distant war in Vietnam — the signal message of which seemed to be that the United States could not win.

3    All the same, youthful pacifism and Soviet influence notwithstanding, a quarter of a million marchers in West Germany cannot be dismissed as a fringe movement. What must be tackled by Western policymakers if they wish to defuse the anti-bomb movement and give the Western alliance a chance of survival, is the irrational fear that animates the movement. The irrational, however, by its very nature is often impervious to reason. Still, it is worthwhile to go through the exercise — even if it is only to document the obvious once again.

4    It is a truism to say that nobody wants nuclear war. Like most truisms, it happens to be true. The Soviet Union would prefer not to cover the Earth in thermonuclear ashes if it could achieve its purposes some other way — and the same goes for the West. The question is, what are the purposes of the Soviet Union as opposed to those of the Western alliance? By now, it is clear that the West merely wishes to retain its independence, institutions and as much of its prosperity as it can. The Soviet Union — to use the most charitable word — has a more *dynamic* purpose. It wishes to spread its values, institutions and influence and acquire the prosperity it cannot produce by its own efforts through political, economic and, if need be, military conquest.

5    Curiously enough, this has not been denied even by those who advocate unilateral disarmament in the West. The old slogan "Better Dead Than Red" was an intriguing subconscious acknowledgment of the fact that if the balance of power tilted significantly in favor of the Soviet Union, it would be followed — even in the view of Bertrand Russell's Committee of 100 — by the spread of communism. Otherwise their slogan would have been "Why Blow Up the World for Nothing?" or maybe, "Why Go Up in Smoke For a

Joke?" But, with a few fringe exceptions, even devoted ban-the-bombers recognize that Soviet imperialism is no joking matter. They merely prefer it to nuclear death.

It is puzzling to rational thought why other forms of death — a hail of bullets, slow **6** starvation in a labor camp or being garroted with both arms fractured — seem preferable to so many to the swift obliteration of a nuclear explosion. These forms of death, of course, have been the consequences for literally millions in every country that has come under communist influence. Nor are the sufferings caused by conventional warfare, as in Vietnam, less horrible to their victims than atomic horrors. Napalm burns are no more of a picnic than radiation sickness. As to the scale of destruction — the total number of victims — there is every reason to believe that in an all-out Third World War of a nonnuclear kind, the havoc would merely be spread over a longer period of time. Nuclear war, alas, would claim the same number of victims — although in a shorter period of time.

Banning the bomb, of course, is strictly a Western affair. The Soviet Union supports it **7** only in Stockholm, Amsterdam and Toronto — not Moscow. For Europe, where conventional forces are no match for Soviet might, rejection of the latest nuclear devices leaves it with few alternatives. The most obvious would be immediate surrender. Such a surrender could range from the actual acceptance of Soviet military presence on Western soil to, at best, an undertaking to alter national policy, institutions and ideals to models acceptable to the Kremlin. This may be the wisest choice under such circumstances. The alternative of resisting with conventional forces a nuclear Soviet Union would simply be to invite all the horrors of the bomb without even the most forlorn hopes of successful resistance. A third option is to pin one's hopes on Brezhnev's assurances that he will not go to war against nonnuclear countries, and assume that a power that marched into Afghanistan at the risk of nuclear war will refrain from similar actions when it can do so with utter impunity.

The real alternative, of course, is to accept the truism we started with, namely that no- **8** body wants nuclear war, including the Soviet Union. Since nuclear *war*, as opposed to one-sided nuclear slaughter, could come about only if the West continues to maintain and update its own nuclear defences, the only way to avoid nuclear war is by doing precisely that.

## VOCABULARY

a. *paragraph 1:* terra firma

b. *paragraph 2:* detente

c. *paragraph 3:* animates, impervious

d. *paragraph 4:* dynamic

e. *paragraph 5:* unilateral

f. *paragraph 6:* garroted

## QUESTIONS

1. What values and arguments relating to nuclear disarmament does Amiel assume are evident to the readers of *Maclean's* and need not be stated or argued? What is gained by not doing so?

2. What issues related to nuclear disarmament does Amiel refer to in the essay? Which one does she make the point at issue in the debate about nuclear disarmament — the specific issue argued in the essay?

3. Why does she reject unilateral disarmament as an alternative to the maintenance of nuclear arsenals by both super powers?

4. What appeals to the reader does Amiel make? Does she appeal to emotion — to a sense of outrage at the madness of nuclear weaponry? Does she appeal to conscience?

## WRITING ASSIGNMENTS

1. Amiel and Suzuki deal with the issues they discuss in different ways. Discuss these differences and also similarities, if you see any. Use your comparison to draw a conclusion about effective or ineffective persuasive arguments.

2. Amiel writes that "the irrational . . . by its very nature is often impervious to reason." Against whom is she directing this ad hominem argument? What is its effect?

## MARGARET LAURENCE

*Margaret Laurence (1926–1986) was born in Neepawa, Manitoba, the small town that inspired the creation of the fictional Manawaka of such well-known novels as* The Stone Angel *(1964),* A Jest of God *(1966), and* The Diviners *(1974). She travelled widely, living in Africa and England, and much of her writing is set in Africa (Somaliland and Ghana). Generally her fiction set in Canada portrays female characters in search of freedom and selfhood, winning battles against patriarchal forces that constrict them. Near the end of her life, Margaret Laurence became an energetic campaigner for disarmament, a commitment which is displayed with characteristic humour and passion in the following essay.*

## MY FINAL HOUR

1 My generation was the first in human history to come into young adulthood knowing that the human race now had the dreadful ability to destroy all life on earth and possibly the earth itself. Only later did we realize the full extent of the destruction of life, a continuing destruction passed on to the then-unborn children of survivors, but we *did* know that after Hiroshima, August 6, 1945, the world would never be the same again. The annihilation caused by the first atomic bombs was unthinkable, but it had happened. Also, we had taken it for granted that through wars, through disasters, yet would the earth endure forever. It was clear to many of us in 1945 that this was no longer to be taken for granted. We have lived with that thought ever since, and have yet borne our children, lived our lives, done our work. The will to survive and to pass on important caring to future generations is very strong. But today we have to realize that the bombs used at Hiroshima and Nagasaki were *small* bombs, compared to today's nuclear weapons.

2 I ask you to think of the Holocaust in Europe, when the Nazis murdered a very great part of all the Jewish communities. That horror, surely, must *never* be forgotten. No amount of mourning will *ever* be enough for those millions of children, women, and men

whose lives were torn from them by the group of de-humanized humans who had taken power in Hitler's Germany. Are we to remember the Holocaust and the horrors of Hiroshima and Nagasaki and yet remain silent when we hear today about a "winnable" nuclear war or a "limited" nuclear war? I think not.

Our lives and the lives of all generations as yet unborn are being threatened, as never before, by the increasing possibility of a nuclear war. I believe that the question of disarmament is the most pressing practical, moral, and spiritual issue of our times. I'm not talking about abstractions. I'm talking about my life and your life and my kids' lives and the lives of people everywhere. If we value our own lives, and the lives of our children and all children everywhere, if we honour both the past and the future, then we must do everything in our power to work non-violently for peace. These beliefs are not only an integral part of my social and moral stance but of my religious faith as well. Human society now possesses the terrible ability to destroy all life on earth, and our planet itself. Can anyone who has ever marvelled at the miracle of creation — who has ever borne or fathered a beloved child, who has ever looked closely at a tree or a plant or a river — fail to feel concerned and indeed anguished, every single day, at this thought?

A central disagreement, of course, exists between those who think that more and yet more nuclear arms will ensure that nuclear arms will never be used, and those of us who believe that the proliferation of nuclear weapons brings us closer all the time to the actuality of nuclear war — a war that no side could possibly win; a war that would be so devastating that we cannot begin to imagine that horror. Whatever we are being told about a "limited" or a "winnable" nuclear war, the fact remains that such a war could destroy all that we, as humankind, have aspired to, have achieved. It could destroy the future, not only of the world's peoples but of all creatures that share our planet with us.

As America and Russia develop more and more nuclear arms, so the other will inevitably respond in kind. Nuclear arms have long since ceased to be a "deterrent," if indeed they were ever so, and have become by their very existence a monstrous threat. Daily, the chances are increasing for a nuclear war to break out by accident, by a failure of the intricate and not totally reliable control and warning systems on either side, or simply by human panic and a mutual mistrust between the superpowers.

It is precisely this failure of the imagination on the part of militarists and leaders that is so dangerous today, the failure to visualize what a nuclear holocaust would mean, the apparent inability to imagine the scorched and charred bodies of children . . . our children or children of Russian parents or parents anywhere, and to know, by an extension of imagination that *all* children are our children. The jargon of the militarists is a distortion and a twisting of language, of our human ability to communicate. Language itself becomes the vehicle of concealment and deception. Such words as "overkill" and "megadeath" do not convey in any sense at all what would really happen — the dead, mutilated, and dying people clogging the ruined cities and towns like so much unvalued discarded rubbish, the suffering humans screaming for help with no medical help available, no water, no relief at all for the unbearable pain of millions of humans except finally the dark relief of death for all. Any shelters that the few might reach would in time turn into tombs. Civil defence plans are a sham. In a nuclear war there would be nowhere to hide, and nowhere except a dead and contaminated world to emerge back into.

I profoundly believe that we must proclaim that *this must not happen.*

Yes, but what about the Russians? If we try to persuade our government to refuse Cruise missile testing, aren't we playing into the hands of the bad guys? Won't the Soviet Union, as soon as they have clear superiority in nuclear arms, blow us all to hell without a second's thought? I do not think so. Isn't it necessary to have more and ever more nuclear weapons in the hands of the Americans so that we can feel *safe*? I do not think so. Let me make it clear that I hold no brief for the present Russian system of government. I hold no brief for *any* system of government that is repressive and cruel, and this includes those far-right regimes in countries such as El Salvador, to whom the U.S.A. is determinedly giving so much military aid. The U.S.A. and Russia, the two superpowers, must, I believe, co-exist in this world, even if there are some terrible things wrong in *both* systems, and *there are*. Russia suffered horribly in World War II, whereas war has not been fought on American soil since the Civil War. I cannot believe that the Russian leaders are all that anxious to begin nuclear war in which the Soviet Union would be, if not totally annihilated, then certainly decimated beyond any hope of recovery.

9    Quite frankly, I can't believe that Russia any longer has hopes of a world revolution. I can believe, though, that the Russian people, the ordinary people who love their children just as much as I love mine, are frightened, just as I am frightened, just as a very large proportion of the American people are frightened and are expressing that fear and outrage. The American people are indeed our cousins, and a very great many of them, young and old, are saying virtually the same things as I am saying here.

10    Do we care so little about our children? Do we honour life so little that we will not speak out? I believe we do care, passionately and profoundly. Indeed, one thing that gives me hope is that so many of our churches and synagogues, so many people of all faiths, of all professions and trades, of all ages, are speaking out against the arms race and the descent into total madness. *Physicians For Social Responsibility*, active in this country as well as in America and elsewhere, are telling us what human damage would be done, and how impossible any thought of medical aid would be in a nuclear war. Inter-church groups such as *Project Ploughshares* are making strong representations to our government, as are labour unions, academics, and indeed and perhaps most importantly, women and men everywhere, in every walk of life. This is true in so very many places in the world today.

11    The money spent on arms, including nuclear arms, continues to mount. Recently I read that $550 billion dollars are being spent, world-wide, yearly, on arms. An even more recent estimate puts it at $600 billion dollars. That sum is so great we cannot really comprehend it. But we *can* comprehend that for the cost of *one* Trident nuclear submarine, malaria could be wiped out from the world. Think of that for one minute. I think of the people in the world who are suffering from thirst, from starvation, from preventable diseases, from ceaseless fighting, and the brutality of oppressive regimes. I think, too, of the growing number of unemployed people in our own land. I think of the Reagan program in America — more and yet more money spent on nuclear arms; less and less spent on social programs and help to the poor and the disabled.

12    I have to speak about how I feel as a writer. I don't like calling myself "an artist," but I guess I am, and would join with my tribal sisters and brothers in many ways. I believe that as a writer . . . an artist, if you will . . . I have a responsibility, a moral responsibility, to work against the nuclear arms race, to work for a recognition on the part of governments and military leaders that nuclear weapons must never be used and must systematically be reduced. Throughout human history, artists have affirmed and celebrated life. Whether we work in words, in music, in painting, in film, in bronze or stone or whatever our medium may be, the artist affirms the value of life itself and of our only home, the planet Earth. Art mirrors and ponders the pain and joy of our experience as human beings. In many parts of the world, and over many centuries, artists have risked and even given their own lives to portray the society around them as they perceived it, and to speak out against injustices. Since the most ancient times, artists have passed on to succeeding generations the tales, the histories, the songs, the sagas, the skills of their trade. Can we conceive of a

world in which there would be no succeeding generations? A world in which all the powerful works of the human imagination would be destroyed, would never again be seen or listened to or experienced? We must conceive that this is now a possibility, and one not too far in our uncertain future, either. We must not, as artists, or so I feel, stand by and passively allow this to happen. The death of the individual is the end which we will all one day meet, but in the knowledge that our children and their children will live, that *someone's* children will go on, that the great works of humankind will endure in art, in recorded history, in medicine, in the sciences and philosophies and technologies that our species has developed with devotion and a sense of vocation throughout the ages. The individual is the leaf on the tree. The leaves fall but the tree endures. New leaves are born. This concept has been the mainstay of our species from time immemorial. Now the tree itself is threatened. All art is a product of the human imagination. It is, deeply, an honouring of the past, a perception of the present in one way or another, and a looking towards the future. Whatever the medium of any particular artist, art is reaching out, an attempt to communicate those things which most concern us seriously in our sojourn here on earth. Artists, the real ones, the committed ones, have always sought, sometimes in ways prophetic and beyond their own times, to clarify and proclaim and enhance life, not to obscure and demean and destroy it. Even the so-called literature of despair is not really that at all. Despair is total silence, total withdrawal. Art, by its very nature of necessary expression, is an act of faith, an acknowledgement of the profound mystery at the core of life.

As a writer, therefore, I feel I have a responsibility. Not to write pamphlets, not to write **13** didactic fiction. That would be, in many ways, a betrayal of how I feel about my work. But my responsibility seems to me to be to write as truthfully as I can, about human individuals and their dilemmas, to honour them as living, suffering, and sometimes joyful people. My responsibility also must extend into my life as a citizen of my own land and ultimately of the world.

I do not claim to have done this well. There are no personal victories in those areas. **14** The individual, here, becomes part of a community and only as a part of that community can one person ever be effective and true to herself or himself. There has to be the resolve not to give up, and to join with all others who believe that life itself is more important than our own individual lives, important though these certainly are.

So, if this were indeed my Final Hour, these would be my words to you. I would not **15** claim to pass on any secret of life, for there is none, or any wisdom except the passionate plea of caring. In your dedication to your own life's work, whatever it may be, live as though you had forever, for no amount of careful and devoted doing is too great in carrying out that work to which you have set your hands. Cultivate in your work and your life the art of patience, and come to terms with your inevitable human limitations, while striving also to extend the boundaries of your understanding, your knowledge, and your compassion. These words are easily said; they are not easily lived. Learn from those who are older than you are; learn from your contemporaries; and never cease to learn from children. Try to feel, in your heart's core, the reality of others. This is the most painful thing in the world, probably, and the most necessary. In times of personal adversity, know that you are not alone. Know that although in the eternal scheme of things you are small, you are also unique and irreplaceable, as are all your fellow humans everywhere in the world. Know that your commitment is above all to life itself. Your own life and work and friendships and loves will come to an end, because one day you will die, and whatever happens after that, or if anything happens at all, it will not be on this earth. But life and work and friendship and love will go on, in others, your inheritors. The struggle for peace and for social justice will go on — provided that our earth survives and that caring humans still live. It is up to you, now, to do all that you can, and that means a commitment, at this perilous moment in our human history, to ensure that life itself *will* go on.

16    In closing, I want to quote one verse from that mighty book . . . more like a vast library . . . that Dr. Northrop Frye calls "The Great Code," and which has so shaped, sometimes so ambiguously, the imagination, the art, and the many facets of faith in our world. This verse is from Deuteronomy, Chapter 30:

17    "I have set before you life and death, blessing and cursing; therefore choose life, that both thou and thy seed may live."

## VOCABULARY

a. *paragraph  1:* annihilation

b. *paragraph  4:* proliferation

c. *paragraph 13:* didactic

d. *paragraph 16:* ambiguously

## QUESTIONS

1. Laurence makes emotional appeals to her readers in presenting her thoughts on the threat of nuclear war. How does she do this?

2. Emotional appeals combine with reason in good persuasive arguments, but such arguments also can sway readers without the author's making an appeal to reason. Does Laurence appeal to both your reason and emotion? If you find her essay persuasive, why do you?

3. Paragraph 4 presents the chief argument against nuclear disarmament. What is that argument? Does Laurence answer it convincingly?

4. In paragraphs 12 through 14, Laurence argues from personal authority. Do you find this to be an effective strategy?

## WRITING ASSIGNMENTS

1. Write your own argumentative essay in favour of or opposing the presence of nuclear arsenals. Trace your reasoning on the issue, and distinguish main from subordinate issues.

2. Write an argumentative essay on a current issue with which you have had personal experience. In the course of your argument, state what that experience is and how much authority it grants you in analysing the issue and stating what should be done.

# PART 3

# MATTERS OF
# STYLE

# INTRODUCTION:
# MATTERS OF STYLE

None of us speaks or writes in the same way on all occasions: the differences depend on how formal the occasion is. A letter of application for a job will be more formal than a letter to a friend; a graduation speech will sound different from a locker-room conversation.

Each of us has a formal and informal language and, whether we know it or not, standards for judging their effectiveness. These standards come from the different groups we belong to — each group with its special idioms and vocabulary. Teenagers share a common language, which sometimes they have to translate for their parents; teenagers of a particular racial or ethnic background share a special dialect or language. So do teenagers of a particular city or region of the country. Though teenagers in Vancouver share expressions and idioms with all other teenagers in the city, they may share a special dialect with their families and with their friends. At school they may share a language with their teachers different from the dialect they speak at home. Even a family may have its own private language — special words and expressions to describe acts and feelings.

Cutting across these differences is a standardized English we hear on television and read in newspapers — a language sometimes less colourful and personal than these other languages, but serving as a medium for communication among diverse groups of people, not only in Canada but in other English-speaking countries. This standard is of long growth, and it changes less than the informal language and slang of particular groups. This standard, represented in the readings in this book, falls between two extremes — one formal and abstract in its content and sentences, the other informal and concrete:

> [*Formal*] Of the influences that shape men's actions, none is more powerful than the images we carry in our heads. Every subject is apt to invoke in our minds a specific image, made up of concrete information, misinformation, folklore, desire and prejudice. Thus, how people see themselves as a nation determines to a large extent how they will respond to any new challenge. The roles we play in our family life, particularly with respect to our children, depend greatly on what roles we assign ourselves in the society around us. — Gerald Holton, "The False Images of Science"

> [*Informal*] As I stopped for a moment outside a love shop, where the red satin lips dangling in the window had a "Going Out of Business" sign pinned to them, the full horror of the situation dawned on me. The sensual thrill of erotica had been all but eclipsed by the new mangiamania.
>
> Well, damn it all, I thought. The old libidinous order can't be allowed to just pass away. Not while there's breath in this oh-so-willing body. I squared my shoulders and, turning my back forever on lettuce driers, marched bravely into the love shop.
>
> *L'Amour français* was the promising title of the video cassette I selected and carried home with me in the deepening dusk.
>
> Ah, what a treat. Curled up in bed with a lushly smutty movie, devouring lustful images more eagerly than champagne truffles from Fauchon . . . — Erika Ritter, "Mangiamania"

The abstract ideas of Holton could be stated less formally. But usage is a matter of convention and occasion as well as personal choice, and if we would not be surprised to find his ideas stated informally, we probably would be surprised to find the rental of a pornographic movie described in formal language.

As a rule, informal writing is closer to the patterns of everyday speech; formal writing seems impersonal if it departs widely from these patterns. Much standard writing today has both formal and informal features: we find colloquialisms (*grabs a half-pound of beef, slaps it onto*) in company with abstract or less familiar words (*envision*). We also find striking balance and antithesis — a feature of formal sentences — in company with looser, more familiar phrasing and expressions:

> What I would like to know is: how should I feel about the earth, these days? Where has all the old nature gone? What became of the wild, writhing, unapproachable mass of the life of the world, and what happened to our old, panicky excitement about it? Just in fifty years, since I was a small boy in a suburban town, the world has become a structure of steel and plastic intelligible and diminished. — Lewis Thomas, "A Trip Abroad"

# TONE

By the tone of a piece of writing, we mean the reflection of the writer's attitude toward the subject or reader. The possibilities are many: a piece of writing may be sarcastic, bitter, angry, mocking, whimsical, facetious, joyful, admiring, or indifferent. And we can reveal this attitude in numerous ways — most commonly by stating it directly:

> There should be more sympathy for school children. The idea that they are happy is of a piece with the idea that the lobster in the pot is happy. — H.L. Mencken, "Travail"

Or we can express our attitude indirectly — perhaps by exaggerating, sometimes to the point of absurdity, for a humorous or satirical effect, as in this parody of a soul-searching journal:

> I am plagued by doubts. What if everything is an illusion and nothing exists? In that case, I definitely overpaid for my carpet. If only God would give me some clear sign! Like making a large deposit in my name at a Swiss bank. — Woody Allen, *The Allen Notebooks*

Or we can write sarcastically with a militant irony that tells the reader more directly what we mean:

> Exam from 8 a.m. to 10:30. About 150 students — unwashed, unshaven young males and reasonably well-groomed young females. A general sense of tedium and disaster. Half-past eight. Little coughs, the clearing of nervous throats, coming in clusters of sound, rustling of pages. Some of the martyrs plunged in meditation, their arms locked behind their heads. I meet a dull gaze directed at me, seeing in me with hope and hate the source of forbidden knowledge. . . . The great fraternity of C-minus, backbone of the nation, steadily scribbling on. — Vladimir Nabokov, *Strong Opinions*

Irony arises from an obvious discrepancy between what we show and what we say. A common form of irony is understatement:

> I was born at Swanmoor, Hants, England, on December 30, 1869. I am not aware that there was any particular conjunction of the planets at the time, but should think it extremely likely. My parents migrated to Canada in 1876, and I decided to go with them. — Stephen Leacock, *Sunshine Sketches of a Little Town*

Paradoxical statements also can be ironic:

> The only way to get rid of temptation is to yield to it. — Oscar Wilde, *The Picture of Dorian Gray*

And so can statements that prepare us for one ending and then turn around and surprise us with another:

> A little sincerity is a dangerous thing, and a greal deal of it is absolutely fatal. — Oscar Wilde, *The Critic as Artist*

As these examples suggest, the tone of a sentence, a paragraph, or an essay is conveyed by the *voice* we try to express in writing. Voice depends on the rhythms and nuances of speech, carried into the modulations and rhythms of the sentences and paragraphs. False starts in writing are often failures to discover the right voice or tone. Too formal a sentence or choice of words may create the impressions of distance or unconcern; a highly informal style may suggest lack of seriousness or flippancy. Not surprisingly, we often find as we write that we need to adjust the tone. An essay need not express a single dominant tone, however: the expression of our attitude often changes as we turn to new ideas and details.

## HARRY BRUCE

Harry Bruce *was born in Toronto in 1934 and educated at Mount Allison University and the London School of Economics. He began his career as a reporter for the* Ottawa Journal *in 1955. Since then he has worked as an editor, author and freelance journalist, and has contributed to the major Canadian magazines and newspapers. His books and articles have won a number of awards, including the Brascan Award for Culture. The section that follows is from the title piece of his book* Each Moment As It Flies *(1984).*

## THE SOFTBALL WAS ALWAYS HARD

When I tell young softball players I played the game bare-handed, they regard me warily. Am I one of those geezers who's forever jawing about the fact that, in *his* day, you had to walk through six miles of snowdrifts just to get to school? Will I tediously lament the passing of the standing broad jump, and the glorious old days when the only football in the Maritimes was English rugger, when hockey was an outdoor art rather than indoor mayhem and, at decent yacht clubs, men were gentlemen and women were *personae non grata*? No, but I will tell today's softball players that — with their fancy uniforms, batters' helmets, dugouts, manicured diamonds, guys to announce who's at bat over public-address systems and, above all, gloves for every fielder — the game they play is more tarted-up and sissy than the one I knew.

Softball bloomed in the Dirty Thirties because it was a game the most impoverished deadbeat could afford to play. For schools, it had the edge that soccer still has over North American football: it required no expensive equipment. It was the people's game in the worst of times. Unlike baseball, which calls for a field the size of a town, softball could flourish in one corner of a city park, on a vacant lot, in any schoolyard. The only gear you needed was a ball, a bat, a catcher's glove and mask, and a first baseman's glove, a floppy affair which I knew as a "trapper." Two amiable teams might even use the same gloves — two gloves for eighteen players.

In the Toronto gradeschool league of the Forties, gloves for all other players were outlawed. This meant that early in the season the hands of a boy shortstop felt as though a 300-lb. vice-principal had given him the strap. Any team that lasted long enough to reach the city finals, however, boasted little infielders with palms like saddle-leather. They learned to catch a line drive with both hands, not by snaring it with a glove big enough to hold a medicine ball. They cushioned the ball by drawing back their cupped hands at the split-second of impact. They fielded sizzling grounders by turning sideways, dropping one knee to the ground, getting their whole bodies in front of the ball, then scooping it up, again with both small, bare hands.

A word about balls. The *New Columbia Encyclopedia* says, "Despite the name, the ball used is not soft," which may be the understatement of the tome's 3,052 pages. There were three kinds of softballs, and each was about as soft as anthracite. The best was simply a big baseball, with seams that were pretty well flush with the horsehide cover. Then there was a solid rubber ball with fake seams. After a while, this ball did soften up, but on grounds it no longer hurt enough for competition, it was then retired for use only in practice. Then there was the "outseam" ball. Perhaps it was not a sadist who invented it. Perhaps it was merely someone who sought durability in lean times. But the outseam was a quarter-inch ridge of leather so hard that, when you fielded a rifling, spinning grounder, the ball felt as though its real function was to rip the skin off your palms. The outseam ball was a character-builder.

5    We had no uniforms, but if you reached the city finals team sweaters might magically emerge from some secret cache in the school basement. Certain coaches had the stern theory that even these were bad news, that boys would be so captivated by their own spiffy appearance they'd lose that vital concentration on the game itself, and commit errors. Some boys played in the only shoes they owned, scampers or black oxfords. Others had beaten-up sneakers and, on most teams, some wore short pants and some long. But these youngsters, gangs of ragamuffins by today's standards of sartorial elegance in softball, played furiously competitive, heads-up ball.

6    If you played outside the school system, for a team sponsored by a camera shop, dairy, hardware store or greasy spoon, then you did get a sweater. You swaggered in it. You'd earned it. Not every kid was good enough to make a team with sweaters. They were advertisements of ability. Nowadays, of course, any kid with the money can buy an Expos' jacket or a Pirates' cap. They're merely advertisements of disposable income, much like the $25 million worth of gear that the chains of athletic-shoe stores expected to sell in Canada during recession-ridden 1982.

7    But as a celebrator of softball austerity, I am a pipsqueak beside an eighty-year-old tycoon I know. As a boy in a Nova Scotia coal-mining town, he played cricket and street baseball with home-made bats and balls. To make a ball, boys hoarded string and wrapped it around a rock, or if they were lucky a small rubber ball. "We made very good balls," he said, "and we had just as much fun as kids have today with all their expensive stuff." In line with Canada's hoariest hockey tradition, he added, "We used a piece of frozen manure for a puck. It worked just about as good." It wasn't as durable as rubber, but in those days there was no shortage of horse poop.

8    I once played with a home-made baseball myself. Indeed, I placed the order for its construction. In the summer of '46, when I turned twelve, my father exiled me from Toronto to spend two months at the Bruce homestead on a Nova Scotian shore. That shore, even now, is as sleepy a spot as you're ever likely to find. Not even most Nova Scotians know where it is. But in 1946, the community was not merely remote, it was an anachronism. It hadn't changed much since Victoria had been queen, and to a kid from what he fancied as a bustling, modern metropolis, its empty beauty was at first desolating. This was the ultimate sticks, the boondocks with a vengeance, and I worked off my loneliness by playing catch with myself. Hour after hour, I hurled a Toronto tennis ball against a bluenose barn, catching it on the rebound.

9    Then I discovered potential ballplayers.

10   They lived on the farm next door. They were a big, cheerful family, and my knowing them then started my life-long love affair with the neighborhood. As things are unfolding now, I'll end up there for good. Anyway, several of these farm kids — the oldest was a gentle man of fifteen who, with one paralysing hand, pinned me to a hayfield while I endured the sweet, excruciating humiliation of having his giggling, thirteen-year-old sister plant saliva on my face — were old enough to play a form of softball. Amazingly, however, they'd never played it, nor seen it. They'd never even heard the word.

11   I told the fifteen-year-old a softball bat was *this* long, and *this* thick at one end, and *this* thin at the other. He made one in half an hour. It wasn't exactly a Louisville Slugger but it had heft to it, and at the same time it was light enough to enable the smaller kids to take a good cut at the ball. What ball? My tennis ball had split. When I knowledgeably declared that the heart of a real baseball was cork, the fifteen-year-old took me down to the stony

shore to negotiate with a character I've preserved in memory as "the Ball-maker." He was a hermit who had just given up commercial fishing on his own. He would never again sail the small schooner he'd built, and she'd begun to rot where she lay, a few feet closer to Chedabucto Bay than the ramshackle hut where he somehow survived the seasons.

He was a "beach person," as surely as the salt-stunted spruce were beach trees, and therefore disreputable. If he had known women they had not been church-going women. He was thin, stooped, gnarled, and smelled as though he'd been embalmed in brine, rum, tar, tobacco juice, his own sweat and sinister doings. There was something wrong with one of his eyes and some of his fingers, and though he may only have been as old as I am now (forty-eight), I thought he was ancient enough, and certainly evil enough, to have slit throats for Blackbeard.    **12**

The Ball-maker conversed with grunts, snarls, illogical silences, and an accent so thick that, to me, it was a foreign language. But we struck a deal. He gave me a dime. If I would walk inland, following a brookside path through a forest of spruce and fir, and on past a sawmill to a general store, and if I would use the dime to buy him a plug of chewing tobacco and, further, if I would then take the tobacco to him . . . well, he would meanwhile sculpt a baseball-sized sphere of cork. And he did. He fashioned it from three pieces: a thick, round disc and two polar caps, all jammed together with a single spike. That ball was so flawless it was spooky. I can still see it and feel it in my hand, a brown globe so perfect I wondered if the Ball-maker was a warlock.    **13**

Back at my friend's farm, we encased the cork in scratchy manila twine till we had something bigger than a hardball but smaller than a softball. For bases, we dropped sweaters among the cowflaps in a pasture, and the lesson began. We would play the kind of teamless ball that's been known in a million schoolyards: as each batter went out, the fielders would all change positions to guarantee that every player got a crack at batting. As the ace from Toronto, I naturally led off. Trouble was, I adored the afternoon's first pitcher. It was she who'd kissed me in the hayfield.    **14**

She had hair like a blonde waterfall, eyes like dark chocolate, and skin I ached to touch and smell. Whenever we wrestled, she won. I still dislike that adult sneer, "puppy love." A boy of twelve can love a girl of thirteen with agonizing power. To make matters worse, he hasn't a hope in hell of even understanding the emotion that's racking his skinny being, much less satisfying it. All he knows is that she obsesses him, he yearns for her, he must always appear fine in her eyes.    **15**

She had never pitched in her life so it surprised me when she tossed her waterfall in the sunlight and floated the ball gently into the strike zone. Her first pitch. It crept towards me, letter-high. It could have been hanging there in front of me on a string from the sky, and I stepped into it with all the style I'd learned from a hundred Toronto afternoons. Thwack! A line drive so fast no one saw it, and down she went. She crumpled in a heap of blouse, skirt, hair and bare, beloved arms and legs. I had smacked her with the cursed, hairy ball square on her right eye. Her big brother got her sitting up, and we all huddled round her, with me bleating horrified apologies. She never cried. She managed a smile, got to her feet, and shakily went home.    **16**

When she turned up for our second game, she had the ugliest black eye I have ever seen on a child. To me, it was a beauty mark. She never blamed me for it. It became a bond, proof of a famous incident we'd shared. She was a tough, forgiving farm girl, and she and her brothers and sisters taught me something I'd not forget about the rough grace of the country folk down home. We played ball for weeks. We played till we pounded the ball to bits, till her eye was once more perfect, and summer was gone.    **17**

The car that drove me to the train station passed their farm. Sheets on the clothesline billowed in the usual south-westerly. With her brothers and sister, she was horsing around with their wolfish mutt. They stopped to watch the car moving along the dirt road, and    **18** then they all waved goodbye. I was glad they were too far away to see my face. I still lacked her control.

19     I have my own cabin on that shore now, and though most of those farmyard ballplayers of thirty-seven summers ago have moved away I still see one of them occasionally. He's a mere forty-six, and I like him now as I liked him then. Sometimes I walk along the gravel beach to a patch of grass, from which a footpath once led to a general store. The Ball-maker's shack is gone, but gray planks and ribs and rusty boat nails still endure the lashing of the salt wind that ceaselessly sweeps the bay. They're all that's left of his schooner. Wrecked by time, like bare-handed softball.

## VOCABULARY

a. *paragraph  1:* geezers, rugger, mayhem

b. *paragraph  4:* anthracite, sadist

c. *paragraph  5:* spiffy, scampers, oxfords

d. *paragraph  8:* boondocks, bluenose

e. *paragraph 11:* ramshackle

f. *paragraph 12:* embalmed

g. *paragraph 13:* warlock

h. *paragraph 14:* cowflaps

## QUESTIONS

1. To what extent does Bruce depend on colloquial or everyday spoken expressions in writing about softball?

2. How does he vary sentence length for effect? Is his writing loose in sentence construction, or is he writing at a general or formal level?

3. Is Bruce merely describing a pastime from his youth, or is he making a judgement about this world and developing a thesis?

4. Why does Bruce begin with a short history of softball? How does he signal the shift to a different aspect of his subject?

5. What technique does Bruce use in his conclusion? Does he effectively summarize the essay's central concerns? Does he avoid sentimentality?

## WRITING ASSIGNMENT

Describe a restaurant through its appearance, the food it serves, and the speech of its employees and possibly its owner. Let your details express a judgement or make a point about the restaurant.

# CAM STIRLING

Cam Stirling *is a chemical engineer in Toronto who works as a consultant to the nuclear industry. Using his technical expertise, he has worked as a technical writer in Britain and as an editor for the United Nations at the Atomic Energy Agency in Vienna. He is currently the technology correspondent for* The Idler. *The following essay, which was published in* The Idler, *is a light-hearted reflection of the author's long-standing interest in technology, how it is (mis)understood (both by those who develop it and by those who use it), and how it affects people's outlook and judgement.*

## THE FALL, RISE, AND FALL OF ELEVATORS

On Fridays, I muse. Last Friday, while musing on aeroplanes, and railway carriages, among other things, a man interrupted my thoughts. **1**

"Excuse me," he began nervously. "I think there's something wrong with this elevator." **2**

He was short, fiftyish, and gave rapid sideways glances at whatever drew his attention. I had seen him before in the building but knew nothing about him. He was eminently forgettable, and right now he was badly frightened. Sweat glistened on his brow and upper lip; in one hand he had twisted a glove into a grotesque half-Nelson; his other hand clutched the small rail on the elevator wall with a white-knuckled death grip. **3**

"Oh? In what way?" I asked. **4**

This was, to be honest, a naïve question, because the lights on the indicator panel above the doors *had* gone out. We didn't know what floor we were passing, and the elevator *was* moving slowly with sudden downward jerks. **5**

After flicking several more nervous glances at me, he cleared a dry throat, and said, a bit too loudly, "Do you think we should call for help?" **6**

I pondered this briefly. My first thought was that he could easily reach for the telephone in its little brass box next to the emergency button, and call for help himself. Then I realized that he didn't dare let go of the railing. His type was familiar to me. One finds people like him in aeroplanes, but not in railway carriages. What I mean is that they are quite evident in aeroplanes. Their fear pervades the cabin for several seats in each direction. Sweat stands out in beads on their faces at take-off and landing, during periods of turbulence, at the sight of thunder cells (no matter how distant), and even on overhearing frivolous remarks, for instance, "Why do you suppose there's a hole out there in the wing?" In railway carriages, persons of this type blend with the upholstery, say nothing, and become invisible for all social purposes. **7**

They are to be pitied, because railway carriages are perhaps the best places to meet people. This is particularly so in the European carriages, which are divided into compartments. There isn't the problem of crowds, one can exchange sections of newspaper, and there is usually relaxing and interesting scenery to remark upon: hares starting from the trackside, cattle watching uncertainly as the train passes, donkeys munching thistle in bliss and ignorance. **8**

My companion cleared his throat again, bringing me back to a late Friday afternoon in an elevator. But I had found a point worth pursuing. Ignoring his outstanding query, I countered with a question of my own. "Why do you think that elevators are unlikely places to meet people?" I began. "Of course, one doesn't expect to spend hours in them, but even so, nobody says a thing when they enter an elevator. Don't you find that odd?" **9**

He took my conversational gambit in the wrong sense altogether, casting me a glance such as a beleaguered brigadier might, on being told that the enemy has opened a second front. He did not reply, because at that moment the elevator began to pick up speed, and **10** soon we were descending normally. My companion's Moray-like grip on the railing relaxed, and he smiled wanly, at the same time rolling his eyes indulgently at the imperfections of our technological society and the dullard engineers who fashion it.

11   This was a mistake. The kindly spirit which guided Thomas Telford and I.K. Brunel may well have taken umbrage. The elevator decelerated suddenly and stopped. The light on the indicator panel came on briefly, showing that we were still at the thirty-sixth floor. A buzzer sounded somewhere distantly in the building. The elevator began to rise, slowly.

12   At this, my companion was transformed into a virtual factory of adrenaline. He clutched the railing ferociously, raising the stress in it almost to the plastic flow region.

13   "Oh, bother," I sighed.

14   He responded immediately this time, with alarm and outrage. "Bother? We might be killed!"

15   "Surely that's a bit melodramatic," I observed sceptically. "You realize, don't you, that elevators are perfectly safe. Nothing can happen to us besides some slight inconvenience." He did not look convinced.

16   His glove was dead. A seam had opened on the index finger. It was time to do the humane thing. Although not a Marxist, I reasoned that the truth might help to free him from the thrall of his anxieties.

17   "The trouble today," I began, "is that people take things too much for granted. They never stop to think about things, like elevators. And I would wager that if asked what made the greatest impression on their lives, most people would list entirely trivial items: cake mixes, fibre-reinforced golf clubs, early ripening tomatoes. What about elevators? Without elevators there would be no tall buildings. Our cities would be transformed; buildings would only be tall enough to allow the average worker to carry a photocopy machine to the top floor. Traffic patterns would be radically different; our lives would be utterly changed. Without tall buildings there would be no midtown canyons, no gale force winds, no huddle of banks, with their executive eyries. The pressure on land values would be much reduced. Elevators are one of the main reasons for the high price of houses today."

18   He was transfixed, but I couldn't tell whether he was genuinely interested in the subject, or immobilized by fear. May as well take the hopeful view, I told myself.

19   "There's another side to them though, enrapturing for the mechanically minded. They are exceptionally interesting machines, with long pedigrees. Vitruvius wrote about elevating devices. Did you know that at one time, elevators were driven by steam? Dates back to the late eighteen century, that one, but it is true that the first steam passenger elevator didn't appear until 1857. Haughwout Department Store, New York City. There were a couple here in Toronto, as well. One in a building up near Yorkville Avenue, I think. Hardly Flash Gordon stuff, though. Four or five storeys a minute, and a lot of hissing and clanking. And you probably didn't know that the early elevator cages were suspended on hempen ropes? Not very reliable."

20   True, I was being a shade unreasonable. My companion had probably had a hard week, I could scarcely ask him to take in so much information at once. Little wonder that his expression was blank. Regardless, I decided to continue.

21   "It's just because they are so ordinary, so uninspiring, that people don't think twice about elevators. If they did, if they took the time to inform themselves, they would be amazed how far we have come. Take the cables that are holding us up right now: high quality steel, regularly maintained and inspected, a healthy safety factor."

22   I paused here to consider where my thoughts were leading: the impromptu philosopher adjusting his loin cloth.

23   To this moment the elevator had been rising slowly; but now it stopped and waited, almost as if listening to my address, waiting for the next gyration in logic.

I came, at last, to the most comforting part of my topic. "Elevators also have fail-safe **24** systems, powerful jaws that are held open by the weight of the elevator itself. If anything should happen, like a broken cable, those jaws would snap shut on the guide rails, and hold the elevator where it was. In fact, it was just this kind of demonstrated safety that made elevators thinkable on the large scale. Without mechanisms of that sort, people would be plunging to their deaths every day."

Silence fell between us as I watched his hand knead the limp glove. It was be- **25** ing eviscerated through the index finger. I was forced to conclude, in the sight of this gruesome necropsy, that there was no point in speaking further. He was oblivious to me, to the glove, to the world. His own private Hell was upon him: eternal free fall in an elevator.

I had failed. Failed to convey to him the image of those almost unbreakable, gleaming **26** steel cables; failed to inspire in him an appreciation of that harmony of motor and sheaves, of cable and weights; failed to convince him that mankind's wealth of experience with elevators could be his, allowing him to face his present situation and, through the use of fact and logic, sweep aside his demon fears. Most upsetting, I had failed to open his heart to the innate attractions, the delights, the exhilaration of elevators. "Oh, I have slipped the surly bonds of earth." Elevators summon to my mind's eye visions of twelve-foot silk scarves, castor oil, thick woollen socks, and biplanes. Even now, out of respect for my sweat-sodden companion, I had to suppress a smile of elation as passages from the *Bandy Journals* tumbled joyously into memory. Elevators do that to me. Controlled flight; Leonardo, Bleriot, McCurdy . . .

I became aware of a straining and groaning; we were decelerating strongly. The cabin **27** began to creak. The sound of my companion's stertorous breathing filled the small space, and now the sweat poured into his open mouth.

Then suddenly we were there. A bell sounded, and the doors tripped open. My passen- **28** ger sprang out of the elevator with the speed of a famished mongoose. He stood panting, resting his head against the cool marble of the lobby wall. I had to try one last time.

"I can help you to overcome your fear. I can show you that riding elevators can be **29** exciting."

His breathing stopped. At first he looked distant and uncomprehending, but then he **30** giggled. The giggle rose to a laugh, then to a piercing *falsetto* peal. He began to dance about the lobby, skipping and cackling. His gloves and hat he threw into the fountain, and they were followed by a handful of change and some keys. As the security guard became suspicious and approached us, my erstwhile companion did a little jump, clicked his heels in mid-air, and then, still shrieking wildly, whooshed through the revolving doors.

## VOCABULARY

a. *paragraph 3:* half-Nelson

b. *paragraph 7:* pervades

c. *paragraph 10:* gambit, beleaguered, Moray-like

d. *paragraph 16:* thrall

e. *paragraph 17:* eyries

f. *paragraph 18:* transfixed

g. *paragraph 19:* hempen

h. *paragraph 22:* impromptu

i. *paragraph 23:* gyration

j. *paragraph 25:* knead, eviscerated, necropsy

k. *paragraph 26:* exhilaration

l. *paragraph 27:* stertorous

m.*paragraph 28:* mongoose

n. *paragraph 30: falsetto*, erstwhile

## QUESTIONS

1. Why does Stirling's essay begin with musings on musing? Why do we learn that he is stuck in an elevator only in paragraph 5?

2. How does the language of paragraph 3 contrast with the spoken words in 2 and 4?

3. Why does Stirling contrast passengers in airplanes with those in railway carriages?

4. Why does Stirling digress so casually in paragraph 8?

5. How would you characterize the exchange in paragraphs 13 through 15?

6. How does Stirling change the tone again in paragraph 17? Why is the language here so formal? How does it compare with that of paragraph 19?

7. How does paragraph 26 prepare us for the conclusion? When the last attempt to assuage fear fails, why does Stirling's passenger react in such a hysterical way?

8. Trace the shifts in tone in the essay. Is Stirling interested in anything besides entertaining us?

## WRITING ASSIGNMENT

Imagine you are in a predicament that requires you to comfort those trapped with you. Create a dialogue that characterizes the speakers by conveying their respective reactions.

## ERIKA RITTER

Erika Ritter *has earned an international reputation as a comic playwright since the production of her first play,* Automatic Pilot. *She has also displayed her ready wit as hostess for two years of the* CBC *radio program* Dayshift, *and as a radio, television, and magazine writer. Her most recent book is* Ritter in Residence *(1987).* Urban Scrawl, *from which the following piece is taken, comprises a selection of her essays on the foibles of contemporary urban society.*

## MANGIAMANIA

It happened when I called up a friend to find out about her first date with a new man the night before.    1

"So how was it?"    2

"Terrific. We went to that new restaurant, the Italian place."    3

"Sounds romantic."    4

"No, Northern Italian, actually. The cuisine of Rome is spicier. This place has white sauces to die for and — "    5

"Wait a sec. What about your date?"    6

"Oh, he started with the *zuppa del giorno*, then moved on to — "    7

"No, what I'm asking is: How did the evening go?"    8

"Not bad. Sixty bucks for two, including wine and tip."    9

Click.    10

As I hung up the receiver, I suddenly recalled how my friend had met this new man. Over a tray of green peppercorns in a gourmet food shop. Somehow, it seemed significant.    11

And what also seemed significant, now that I thought about it, was the means by which three of my other friends had recently met *their* new guys. One in a cooking course titled "French Without Fear". Another while browsing through a copy of *Gourmet* magazine in a bookstore. And the third, reaching for the same package of *linguine verde* on the grocery shelf.    12

Click. Click. Click.    13

Yes, something was definitely happening here. I decided that a walk downtown would help me sort it all out.    14

Food, I realized, as I passed the fourth store window in a row proclaiming a sale on wine thermometers and lettuce driers, had completely taken over. The kind of enthusiasm people used to pour into collecting stamps and breeding chinchillas was now being squandered on *crème anglaise* and red lettuce.    15

And that wasn't all. As I stopped for a moment outside a love shop, where the red satin lips dangling in the window had a "Going Out of Business" sign pinned to them, the full horror of the situation dawned on me. The sensual thrill of erotica had been all but eclipsed by the new mangiamania.    16

Well, damn it all, I thought. The old libidinous order can't be allowed to just pass away. Not while there's breath in this oh-so-willing body. I squared my shoulders and, turning my back forever on lettuce driers, marched bravely into the love shop.    17

*L'Amour français* was the promising title of the video cassette I selected and carried home with me in the deepening dusk.    18

Ah, what a treat. Curled up in bed with a lushly smutty movie, devouring lustful images more eagerly than champagne truffles from Fauchon . . .    19

The film opened with a pouty young French man picking up a pouty young French girl on a wharf in Marseilles. Exactly *how* he picked her up, however, I failed to notice, because for some reason my interest was caught by all the fish strewn on the pier. I could just imagine them pan-fried with a soupçon of butter, and some freshly crushed garlic.    20

By the time I pulled myself back to the story line, the pouty French couple (I didn't catch their names, I was too busy watching them nibble flaky croissants from a *patisserie*) were back at his place, feverishly removing their clothes.    21

22    At that point, things got pretty hot and heavy — at least, I imagine they did. Unfortunately, my attention had been totally captivated by a still-life painting over their bed, featuring a neatly peeled Seville orange, some Anjou pears, a pomegranate (out of season), and a loaf of crusty bread, sprinkled with —

23    Click.

24    Trembling and furious with myself, I snapped off the set. What on earth was happening to me?

25    Frantic now, I rummaged in my dresser drawer for a novel I'd picked up in the drugstore a day or two before. Ah, here it was. *First Blissful Encounter.* Now, surely a chapter or two of that was all I needed to reaffirm that what I was looking for was the food of love, not vice versa.

26    Trying to feel confident, I opened the book on the first page. "It all began," I read, "with a kiss from my companion." Now that, I thought, was a very routine way for an evening to begin. And did they *both* have to start with the kiss? Couldn't her companion have ordered something different?

27    "At first," the book went on, "his caresses seemed bland." Yes, I could imagine the kind of bland caresses her companion would serve up, seasoned without inspiration. Fondly I cast my mind back to some truly outstanding kisses I had read about, kisses of the delectable sort available in the great European capitals, where the men not only make them spicy, but also totally fresh.

28    "At last, he took me in his arms, tenderly, delicately." Good grief, I scoffed, you call *that* a hug? A hug should always be robust and full-bodied, and heated to such a temperature that it can completely melt any resistance that —

29    On my God. I slammed shut the covers of the book, the cold sweat pouring down my neck. Could it be that mangiamania had claimed another victim?

30    Striving to be calm, I padded out to the kitchen to see what I could find in the fridge. I don't know why, but I always think better with something to eat. A wedge of perfectly aged Gorgonzola, accompanied by fragrant muscat grapes, and perhaps a chilled glass of that incomparable Bordeaux that everyone is . . .

## VOCABULARY

a. *paragraph 17:* libidinous

b. *paragraph 20:* soupçon

c. *paragraph 27:* delectable

## QUESTIONS

1. What is the tone of the essay? How seriously are we to take the propositions it advances?

2. Ritter states her thesis in paragraph 16. What is it, and why does she delay stating it until then? Would such an organization be appropriate to a more formal essay?

3. How does the second half of the essay differ from the first? How does it provide support for the thesis?

4. Why does Ritter choose a movie on video cassette and a book to test her idea? Why not, for example, a romantic night out?

5. How detailed are the various descriptions of food in the essay? What is the effect of this kind of description?

## WRITING ASSIGNMENTS

1. Ritter humorously suggests that she and her friends are not in complete control of their behaviour. In a deliberately colloquial tone, discuss the ways in which your tastes may have been fashioned by various fads or trends.

2. Listen to your friends talk over lunch, reproduce their conversation, and draw some conclusions about their tastes and preoccupations.

## JONATHAN SWIFT

*Jonathan Swift (1667–1745), the son of English Protestant parents, was born and educated in Ireland. In 1688 he went to England to seek a career in literature. Swift wrote satirical poems, essays, pamphlets, and tracts on the major issues of the day and became involved in many of its political and religious controversies. In 1713 he became Dean of St. Patrick's Cathedral in Dublin and in the succeeding years wrote widely on various questions bearing on Ireland and England. His most famous satirical work,* Gulliver's Travels, *was published in 1726. Swift was deeply concerned about the sufferings that he had observed in his country from boyhood. Ireland, under the control of the British government, was an impoverished country — restricted in selling its goods and incapable of producing enough food to feed the population. Most of the poor were Catholic, a point that Swift emphasizes in his "modest proposal" — written in 1729 to suggest a remedy for the widespread starvation and misery of the country. Swift writes as a distinguished observer, anxious to perform a service to both the English and the Irish with his proposal. The persuasive means that Swift uses deserves the closest study.*

## A MODEST PROPOSAL

### FOR PREVENTING THE CHILDREN OF POOR PEOPLE IN IRELAND FROM BEING A BURDEN TO THEIR PARENTS OR COUNTRY, AND FOR MAKING THEM BENEFICIAL TO THE PUBLIC

It is a melancholy object to those who walk through this great town, or travel in the country, when they see the streets, the roads, and cabin-doors crowded with beggars of the female sex, followed by three, four, or six children, all in rags, and importuning every passenger for an alms. These mothers, instead of being able to work for their honest livelihood, are forced to employ all their time in strolling to beg sustenance for their helpless infants: who, as they grow up, either turn thieves for want of work, or leave their dear native country to fight for the Pretender in Spain, or sell themselves to the Barbadoes.     1

I think it is agreed by all parties, that this prodigious number of children in the arms, or on the backs, or at the heels of their mothers, and frequently of their fathers, is in the     2 present deplorable state of the kingdom, a very great additional grievance; and, therefore, whoever could find out a fair, cheap, and easy method of making these children sound and useful members of the commonwealth, would deserve so well of the public, as to have his statue set up for a preserver of the nation.

3    But my intention is very far from being confined to provide only for the children of professed beggars; it is of a much greater extent, and shall take in the whole number of infants at a certain age, who are born of parents in effect as little able to support them as those who demand our charity in the streets.

4    As to my own part, having turned my thoughts for many years upon this important subject, and maturely weighed the several schemes of other projectors, I have always found them grossly mistaken in their computation. It is true, a child, just dropped from its dam, may be supported by her milk for a solar year with little other nourishment; at most, not above the value of two shillings, which the mother may certainly get, or the value in scraps, by her lawful occupation of begging; and it is exactly at one year old that I propose to provide for them in such a manner, as, instead of being a charge upon their parents or the parish, or wanting food and raiment for the rest of their lives, they shall, on the contrary, contribute to the feeding, and partly to the clothing, of many thousands.

5    There is likewise another great advantage in my scheme, that it will prevent those voluntary abortions, and that horrid practice of women murdering their bastard children, alas, too frequent among us, sacrificing the poor innocent babes, I doubt more to avoid the expense than the shame, which would move tears and pity in the most savage and inhuman breast.

6    The number of souls in this kingdom being usually reckoned one million and a half, of these I calculate there may be about two hundred thousand couple whose wives are breeders; from which number I subtract thirty thousand couple, who are able to maintain their own children (although I apprehend there cannot be so many, under the present distresses of the kingdom); but this being granted, there will remain an hundred and seventy thousand breeders. I again subtract fifty thousand for those women who miscarry, or whose children die by accident or disease within the year. There only remain a hundred and twenty thousand children of poor parents annually born. The question therefore is how this number shall be reared and provided for? which, as I have already said, under the present situation of affairs, is utterly impossible by all the methods hitherto proposed. For we can neither employ them in handicraft or agriculture; we neither build houses (I mean in the country) nor cultivate land: they can very seldom pick up a livelihood by stealing until they arrive at six years old, except where they are of towardly parts; although I confess they learn the rudiments much earlier; during which time they can, however, be properly looked upon only as probationers; as I have been informed by a principal gentleman in the county of Cavan, who protested to me, that he never knew above one or two instances under the age of six, even in a part of the kingdom so renowned for the quickest proficiency in that art.

7    I am assured by our merchants that a boy or a girl before twelve years old is no salable commodity; and even when they come to this age they will not yield above three pounds or three pounds and half-a-crown at most, on the exchange; which cannot turn to account either to the parents or kingdom, the charge of nutriment and rags having been at least four times that value.

8    I shall now, therefore, humbly propose my own thoughts, which I hope will not be liable to the least objection.

9    I have been assured by a very knowing American of my acquaintance in London, that a young healthy child, well nursed, is, at a year old, a most delicious, nourishing, and

wholesome food, whether stewed, roasted, baked, or boiled; and I make no doubt that it will equally serve in a fricassee or a ragout.

I do therefore humbly offer it to public consideration, that of the hundred and twenty    **10** thousand children already computed, twenty thousand may be reserved for breed, whereof only one-fourth part to be males; which is more than we allow to sheep, black cattle, or swine; and my reason is, that these children are seldom the fruits of marriage, a circumstance not much regarded by our savages, therefore one male will be sufficient to serve four females. That the remaining hundred thousand may, at a year old, be offered in sale to the persons of quality and fortune through the kingdom; always advising the mother to let them suck plentifully in the last month, so as to render them plump and fat for a good table. A child will make two dishes at an entertainment for friends; and when the family dines alone, the fore or hind quarter will make a reasonable dish, and, seasoned with a little pepper or salt, will be very good boiled on the fourth day, especially in winter.

I have reckoned, upon a medium, that a child just born will weigh twelve pounds, and    **11** in a solar year, if tolerably nursed, increaseth to twenty-eight pounds.

I grant this food will be somewhat dear, and therefore very proper for landlords, who,    **12** as they have already devoured most of the parents, seem to have the best title to the children.

Infants' flesh will be in season throughout the year, but more plentifully in March, and    **13** a little before and after: for we are told by a grave author, an eminent French physician, that fish being a prolific diet, there are more children born in Roman Catholic countries about nine months after Lent that at any other season; therefore, reckoning a year after Lent, the markets will be more glutted than usual, because the number of popish infants is at least three to one in this kingdom; and therefore, it will have one other collateral advantage, by lessening the number of papists among us.

I have already computed the charge of nursing a beggar's child (in which list I reckon    **14** all cottagers, labourers, and four-fifths of the farmers) to be about two shillings per annum, rags included; and I believe no gentleman would repine to give ten shillings for the carcass of a good fat child, which, as I have said, will make four dishes of excellent nutritive meat, when he has only some particular friend, or his own family, to dine with him. Thus, the squire will learn to be a good landlord, and grow popular among his tenants; the mother will have eight shillings net profit, and be fit for work till she produces another child.

Those who are more thrifty (as I must confess the times require) may flay the carcass;    **15** the skin of which artificially dressed, will make admirable gloves for ladies, and summerboots for fine gentlemen.

As to our city of Dublin, shambles* may be appointed for this purpose in the most con-    **16** venient parts of it, and butchers we may be assured will not be wanting; although I rather recommend buying the children alive, and dressing them hot from the knife, as we do roasting pigs.

A very worthy person, a true lover of his country, and whose virtues I highly esteem,    **17** was lately pleased, in discoursing on this matter, to offer a refinement upon my scheme. He said, that many gentlemen of this kingdom, having of late destroyed their deer, he conceived that the want of venison might be well supplied by the bodies of young lads and maidens, not exceeding fourteen years of age, nor under twelve; so great a number of both sexes in every country now being ready to starve for want of work and service; and these to be disposed of by their parents, if alive, or otherwise by their nearest relations. But, with due deference to so excellent a friend, and so deserving a patriot, I cannot be

*Butcher shops. (All notes in this section are the editors'.)

altogether in his sentiments; for as to the males, my American acquaintance assured me from frequent experience, that their flesh was generally tough and lean, like that of our schoolboys, by continual exercise, and their taste disagreeable; and to flatten them would not answer the charge. Then as to the females, it would, I think, with humble submission, be a loss to the public, because they soon would become breeders themselves: and besides, it is not improbable that some scrupulous people might be apt to censure such a practice (although indeed very unjustly) as a little bordering upon cruelty; which, I confess hath always been with me the strongest objection against any project, how well soever intended.

18    But in order to justify my friend, he confessed that this expedient was put into his head by the famous Psalmanazar,* a native of the island Formosa, who came from thence to London above twenty years ago; and in conversation told my friend, that in his country, when any young person happened to be put to death, the executioner sold the carcass to persons of quality as a prime dainty; and that in his time the body of a plump girl of fifteen, who was crucified for an attempt to poison the emperor, was sold to his Imperial Majesty's prime minister of state, and other great mandarins of the court, in joints from the gibbet, at four hundred crowns. Neither indeed can I deny, that if the same use were made of several plump young girls in this town, who, without one single groat to their fortunes, cannot stir abroad without a chair, and appear at playhouse and assemblies in foreign fineries which they never will pay for, the kingdom would not be the worse.

19    Some persons of a desponding spirit are in great concern about the vast number of poor people who are aged, diseased, or maimed; and I have been desired to employ my thoughts what course may be taken to ease the nation of so grievous an encumbrance. But I am not in the least pain upon that matter, because it is very well known, that they are every day dying, and rotting, by cold and famine, and filth and vermin, as fast as can be reasonably expected. And so to the younger labourers, they are now in almost as hopeful a condition: they cannot get work, and consequently pine away for want of nourishment, to a degree, that if at any time they are accidentally hired to common labour, they have not strength to perform it; and thus the country and themselves are happily delivered from the evils to come.

20    I have too long digressed, and therefore shall return to my subject. I think the advantages by the proposal which I have made are obvious and many, as well as of the highest importance.

21    For first, as I have already observed, it would greatly lessen the number of papists, with whom we are yearly overrun, being the principal breeders of the nation as well as our most dangerous enemies; and who stay at home on purpose with a design to deliver the kingdom to the Pretender, hoping to take their advantage by the absence of so many good Protestants, who have chosen rather to leave their country than stay at home and pay tithes against their conscience to an idolatrous Episcopal curate.†

22    Secondly, the poorer tenants will have something valuable of their own, which by law may be made liable to distress, and help to pay their landlord's rent; their corn and cattle being already seized, and money a thing unknown.

23    Thirdly, whereas the maintenance of a hundred thousand children, from two years old and upwards, cannot be computed at less than ten shillings a piece per annum, the nation's

---

*Psalmanazar (1679?–1763), literary imposter born in southern France, who posed as a Formosan and wrote a description of the island.

†Swift is attacking the prejudice against Irish Catholics in his time, and also the motives of a number of Protestant dissenters from the Church of England.

stock will be thereby increased fifty thousand pounds per annum; besides the profit of a new dish introduced to the tables of all gentlemen of fortune in the kingdom who have any refinement in taste. And the money will circulate among ourselves, the goods being entirely of our own growth and manufacture.

Fourthly, the constant breeders, besides the gain of eight shillings sterling per annum by the sale of their children, will be rid of the charge of maintaining them after the first year. **24**

Fifthly, this food would otherwise bring great custom to taverns; where the vintners will certainly be so prudent as to procure the best receipts for dressing it to perfection, and, consequently, have their houses frequented by all the fine gentlemen, who justly value themselves upon their knowledge in good eating: and a skillful cook, who understands how to oblige his guests, will contrive to make it as expensive as they please. **25**

Sixthly, this would be a great inducement to marriage, which all wise nations have either encouraged by rewards, or enforced by laws and penalties. It would increase the care and tenderness of mothers towards their children, when they were sure of a settlement for life to the poor babes, provided in some sort by the public, to their annual profit instead of expense. We should soon see an honest emulation among the married women, which of them could bring the fattest child to the market. Men would become as fond of their wives during the time of their pregnancy, as they are now of their mares in foal, their cows in calf, or sows when they are ready to farrow; nor offer to beat or kick them (as is too frequent a practice) for fear of a miscarriage. **26**

Many other advantages might be enumerated. For instance, the addition of some thousand carcasses in our exportation of barrelled beef; the propagation of swine's flesh, and improvement in the art of making good bacon, so much wanted among us by the great destruction of pigs, too frequent at our tables, which are no way comparable in taste or magnificence to a well-grown, fat yearling child, which, roasted whole, will make a considerable figure at a Lord Mayor's feast, or any other public entertainment. But this, and many others, I omit, being studious of brevity. **27**

Supposing that one thousand families in this city would be constant customers for infants' flesh, besides others who might have it at merry meetings, particularly weddings and christenings, I compute that Dublin would take off annually about twenty thousand carcasses; and the rest of the kingdom (where probably they will be sold somewhat cheaper) the remaining eighty thousand. **28**

I can think of no one objection that will possibly be raised against this proposal, unless it should be urged, that the number of people will be thereby much lessened in the kingdom. This I freely own, and it was indeed one principal design in offering it to the world. I desire the reader will observe that I calculate my remedy for this one individual kingdom of Ireland, and for no other that ever was, is, or I think ever can be, upon earth. Therefore let no man talk to me of other expedients: of taxing our absentees at five shillings a pound: of using neither clothes nor household furniture except what is of our own growth and manufacture: of utterly rejecting the materials and instruments that promote foreign luxury: of curing the expensiveness of pride, vanity, idleness, and gaming in our women; of introducing a vein of parsimony, prudence, and temperance: of learning to love our country, wherein we differ even from Laplanders, and the inhabitants of Topinamboo:* of quitting our animosities and factions, nor act any longer like the Jews, who were murdering one another at the very moment their city was taken:† of being a little cautious not to **29**

*A district of Brazil notorious for its barbarism and ignorance.

†Swift is referring to the fall of Jerusalem to the Babylonians.

sell our country and consciences for nothing: of teaching landlords to have at least one degree of mercy towards their tenants: lastly, of putting a spirit of honesty, industry, and skill into our shopkeepers; who, if a resolution could now be taken to buy only our native goods, would immediately unite to cheat and exact upon us in the price, the measure, and the goodness, nor could ever yet be brought to make one fair proposal of just dealing, though often and earnestly invited to it.

30      Therefore I repeat, let no man talk to me of these and the like expedients, till he hath at least some glimpse of hope that there will ever be some hearty and sincere attempt to put them in practice.

31      But, as to myself, having been wearied out for many years with offering vain, idle, visionary thoughts, and at length utterly despairing of success, I fortunately fell upon this proposal; which, as it is wholly new, so it hath something solid and real, of no expense and little trouble, full in our own power, and whereby we can incur no danger in disobliging England. For this kind of commodity will not bear exportation, the flesh being of too tender a consistence to admit a long continuance in salt, although perhaps I could name a country which would be glad to eat up our whole nation without it.

32      After all, I am not so violently bent upon my own opinion as to reject any offer proposed by wise men which shall be found equally innocent, cheap, easy, and effectual. But before something of that kind shall be advanced in contradiction to my scheme, and offering a better, I desire the author, or authors, will be pleased maturely to consider two points. First, as things now stand, how they will be able to find food and raiment for a hundred thousand useless mouths and backs? And, secondly, there being a round million of creatures in human figure throughout this kingdom, whose whole subsistence put into a common stock would leave them in debt two millions of pounds sterling, adding those who are beggars by profession, to the bulk of farmers, cottagers, and labourers, with the wives and children who are beggars in effect; I desire those politicians who dislike my overture, and may perhaps be so bold as to attempt an answer, that they will first ask the parents of these mortals, whether they would not at this day think it a great happiness to have been sold for food at a year old, in the manner I prescribe, and thereby have avoided such a perpetual scene of misfortunes as they have since gone through, by the oppression of landlords, the impossibility of paying rent without money or trade, the want of common sustenance, with neither house nor clothes to cover them from the inclemencies of weather, and the most inevitable prospect of entailing the like, or greater miseries, upon their breed for ever.

33      I profess, in the sincerity of my heart, that I have not the least personal interest in endeavouring to promote this necessary work, having no other motive than the public good of my country, by advancing our trade, providing for infants, relieving the poor, and giving some pleasure to the rich. I have no children by which I can propose to get a single penny; the youngest being nine years old, and my wife past child-bearing.

## VOCABULARY

a. *paragraph  1:* importuning

b. *paragraph  2:* prodigious

c. *paragraph  4:* schemes, projectors, raiment

d. *paragraph  5:* bastard

e. *paragraph   6:* apprehend, rudiments, probationers, renowned

f. *paragraph   9:* fricassee, ragout

g. *paragraph 13:* prolific, papists

h. *paragraph 14:* squire

i. *paragraph 15:* flay

j. *paragraph 17:* venison

k. *paragraph 18:* mandarins, gibbet

l. *paragraph 19:* encumbrance

m. *paragraph 20:* digressed

n. *paragraph 21:* tithes, idolatrous, Episcopal curate

o. *paragraph 25:* vintners

p. *paragraph 26:* emulation, foal, farrow

q. *paragraph 27:* yearling

r. *paragraph 29:* expedients, parsimony, animosities

s. *paragraph 31:* consistence

t. *paragraph 32:* effectual, entailing

# QUESTIONS

1. How would you describe the tone of "A Modest Proposal"? Cite examples to account for your description.

2. How does Swift use tone to establish the basic character and motives of his proposer in the opening paragraphs?

3. How does Swift reveal his attitude toward the proposer? Is Swift in accord with the proposer's general views of English motives? Are those motives stated directly or instead implied?

4. How persuasive do you find the essay? Is it an essay of historical interest or literary interest only, or does it have something to say to people today?

# WRITING ASSIGNMENTS

1. Write your own "modest proposal" for dealing with a current social or political evil. You may wish to write as yourself or, like Swift, impersonate someone who wishes to

make a modest proposal. Maintain a consistent tone throughout your essay, or at least make any shifts in tone consistent with the character of your speaker and his or her motives in writing.

2. Contrast the tone of Swift's attack on the English with Orwell's discussion of political language. Distinguish the various rhetorical devices that they employ.

# Figurative Language

Figurative language can increase the vividness of expository and persuasive writing. In the following section, some common figures of speech are defined and illustrated.

A simile is an explicit comparison (using *like* or *as*) that usually develops or implies one or more simple points of resemblance:

> I felt like a *flower*: a little parched, of course, a little gone in the neck, and with no real life to come, perhaps, only sham life, bowl life, easing its petals and lifting its head to start feeding on the day. — Martin Amis, *Money*

A metaphor is an implicit comparison in which an object is presented as if it were something else:

> Each life is a game of chess that went to hell on the seventh move, and now the flukey play is cramped and slow, a dream of constraint and cross-purpose, with each move forced, all pieces pinned and skewered and zugzwanged . . . But here and there we see these figures who appear to run on the true lines, and they are terrible examples. They're rich, usually. — Amis, *Money*

Personification is the attribution of human qualities to abstract ideas or objects. Simile, metaphor, and personification unite in the following passage:

> Then Sunday light raced over the farm as fast as the chickens were flying. Immediately the first straight shaft of heat, solid as a hickory stick, was laid on the ridge. — Eudora Welty

One purpose of figures of speech is to evoke the quality of experience and give shape or substance to an emotion or awareness that up to the moment of its expression may be indefinite. In exposition a writer will depend on metaphor because of its property of expressing an attitude as well as representing an idea:

> England is not the jewelled isle of Shakespeare's much-quoted passage, nor is it the inferno depicted by Dr. Goebbels. More than either it resembles a family, a rather stuffy Victorian family, with not many black sheep in it but with all its cupboards bursting with skeletons. It has rich relations who have to be kowtowed to and poor relations who are horribly sat upon, and there is a deep conspiracy of silence about the source of the family income. It is a family in which the young are generally thwarted and most of the power is in the hands of irresponsible uncles and bedridden aunts. — George Orwell, "England, Your England"

# Imagery

A writer uses imagery to make an observation or impression perceptible to the senses. Eric Sevareid makes concrete the changes that occurred in his hometown in North Dakota:

> Sounds have changed; I heard not once the clopping of a horse's hoof, nor the mourn of a coyote. I heard instead the shriek of brakes, the heavy throbbing of the once-a-day Braniff airliner into Minot, the shattering sirens born of war, the honk of a diesel locomotive which surely cannot call to faraway places the heart of a wakeful boy like the old steam whistle in the night. — Eric Sevareid, "Velva, North Dakota"

Images convey impressions of sight, hearing, smell, taste, or touch. The following passages from an essay by Harry Bruce and from a novel by Alice Munro illustrate some of these:

> Back at my friend's farm, we encased the cork in scratchy manila twine till we had something bigger than a hardball but smaller than a softball. For bases, we dropped sweaters among the cowflaps in a pasture, and the lesson began. — Harry Bruce, "The Softball Was Always Hard"

> He turned and swore at us to get off, but we hung on, bloated with cheerful defiance like criminals born with cauls; we hung on with the rim of the sleigh cutting into our stomachs and our feet spraying snow, until we reached the corner of Mason Street, and there we flung off into a snowbank. — Alice Munro, *Lives of Girls and Women*

We think in images constantly. Neither Bruce nor Munro could have expressed a sense of these particular experiences in abstract language. The more evocative our imagery when the situation calls for vivid impressions, the more directly will our words express experience. A passage will seem overwritten if a vivid representation of experience is not needed; so-called fine writing tries to be too evocative of sense experience. In the passages quoted above, the authors select primarily those details that will give the reader an impression of the physical sensations experienced.

Figurative language is particularly important in descriptive writing such as the following, which conveys an unusual experience and sensation:

> There is something quite deceptive in the sense of acceleration that comes just before a rapid. The word "rapid" itself is, in a way, a misnomer. It refers only to the speed of the white river relative to the speed of the smooth water that leads into and away from the rapid. The white water is faster, but it is hardly "rapid". The Colorado, smooth, flows about seven miles per hour, and, white, it goes perhaps fifteen or, at its whitest and wildest, twenty miles per hour — not very rapid by the standards of the twentieth century. Force of suggestion creates a false expectation. The mere appearance of the river going over those boulders — the smoky spray, the scissoring waves — is enough to imply a rush to fatality, and this endorses the word used to describe it. You feel as if you were about to be sucked into some sort of invisible pneumatic tube and shot like a bullet into the dim beyond. But the white water, though faster than the rest of the river, is categorically slow. Running the rapids in the Colorado is a series of brief experiences, because the rapid themselves are short. In them, with the raft folding and bending — sudden hills of water filling the immediate skyline — things happen in slow motion. The projector of your own existence slows way down, and you dive as in a dream, and gradually rise, and fall again. The raft shudders across the ridgeline of water cordilleras to crash softly into the valleys beyond. Space and time in there are something other than they are out here. Tents of water form overhead, to break apart in rags. Elapsed stopwatch time has no meaning at all. — John McPhee, "Running the Rapids"

# LARRY WOIWODE

Larry Woiwode, *born and raised in North Dakota, has written much about the Middle West in his fiction and essays. His writing about outdoor life is particularly impressive, as his description of the killing of a deer, from an essay on guns in America published in* Esquire *magazine, shows.*

# KILLING A DEER

Once in the middle of a Wisconsin winter I shot a deer, my only one, while my wife and    1
daughter watched. It had been hit by a delivery truck along a country road a few miles
from where we lived and one of its rear legs was torn off at the hock; a shattered shin and
hoof lay steaming in the redbeaded snow. The driver of the truck and I stood and watched
as it tried to leap a fence, kicked a while at the top wire it was entangled in, flailing the
area with fresh ropes of blood, and then went hobbling across a pasture toward a wooded
hill. Placid cows followed it with a curious awe. "Do you have a rifle with you?" the
driver asked. "No, not with me. At home." He looked once more at the deer, then got in
his truck and drove off.

I went back to our Jeep where my wife and daughter were waiting, pale and with-    2
drawn, and told them what I was about to do, and suggested that they'd better stay at
home. No, they wanted to be with me, they said; they wanted to watch. My daughter was
three and a half at the time. I got my rifle, a .22, a foolishly puny weapon to use on a deer
but the only one I had, and we came back and saw that the deer was lying in some low
brush near the base of the hill; no need to trail its blatant spoor. When I got about a hundred yards off, marveling at how it could have made it so far in its condition through snow
that came over my boot tops, the deer tried to push itself up with its front legs, then
collapsed. I aimed at the center of its skull, thinking, *This will be the quickest*, and heard
the bullet ricochet off and go singing through the woods.

The deer was on its feet, shaking its head as though stung, and I fired again at the same    3
spot, quickly, and apparently missed. It was now moving at its fastest hobble up the hill,
broadside to me, and I took my time to sight a heart shot. Before the report even registered
in my mind, the deer went down in an explosion of snow and lay struggling there, spout-
ing blood from its stump and a chest wound. I was shaking by now. Deer are color-blind
as far as science can say, and as I went toward its quieting body to deliver the coup de
grace, I realized I was being seen in black and white, and then the deer's eye seemed to
home in on me, and I was struck with the understanding that I was its vision of approaching death. And then I seemed to enter its realm through its eye and saw the countryside
and myself in shades of white and grey. *But I see the deer in color*, I thought.

A few yards away, I aimed at its head once more, and there was the crack of a shot, the    4
next-to-last round left in the magazine. The deer's head came up, and I could see its eye
clearly now, dark, placid, filled with an appeal, it seemed, and then felt the surge of black
and white surround and subsume me again. The second shot, or one of them, had pierced
its neck; a grey-blue tongue hung out over its jaw; urine was trickling from below its tail; a
doe. I held the rifle barrel inches from its forehead, conscious of my wife's and daughter's
eyes on me from behind, and as I fired off the final and fatal shot, felt myself drawn by
them back into my multicolored, many-faceted world again.

# VOCABULARY

a. *paragraph 1:* flailing, placid

b. *paragraph 2:* blatant, spoor, ricochet

c. *paragraph 3:* coup de grace

d. *paragraph 4:* subsume, many-faceted

## QUESTIONS

1. How does Woiwode use colour and its absence to convey his sense of the difference between the human and the animal worlds?

2. To what senses does Woiwode appeal in describing the killing of the doe?

3. The killing of the doe is a necessary one, a fact Woiwode emphasizes through details of the suffering of the wounded animal. What are his other details meant to show?

4. Why does he stress the difference between his view of the doe and what he imagines is the doe's view of him?

## WRITING ASSIGNMENTS

1. Rewrite the description from the viewpoint of the wounded doe — beginning with the circumstances of the wounding, and ending with her death. Let your details make the point of the essay.

2. Narrate an experience in which you learned something unexpected about the world of nature. Let your reader see that world and undergo the experience as you did. Choose images that appeal to several of the senses, not just to one.

## JOHN FERGUSON

John Ferguson *is an architect in Toronto who has published essays on a variety of subjects. His belief that "a point can be made by a more or less entertaining voyage around the serious concern at the heart of a matter" is nicely illustrated by the subterranean exploration he embarks on here.*

## THE IVORY CELLAR

1    In the year 1909, one million, two hundred and fifty-eight thousand, six hundred and twenty-six people used the underground conveniences of Toronto. It has often been said, in the intervening years, that at least one of them is still down there.

2    This statement is problematic, not because it strains belief, but because it is not amenable to disproof — all of these conveniences have been sodded or paved or otherwise roofed over. Although they have not been destroyed, they are not inaccessible.

3    A subterranean lavatory is not, in itself, a mysterious place. If cleanliness is next to godliness, it may seem perverse to go underground in search of it; but that is a minor paradox. Busy streets simply demand a small collection of toilets and handbasins at this corner or that — so it was in Toronto in the early years of this century, and so it remains in such cities as London and Paris, which continue to acknowledge the merits of a gentle, periodic descent. It is not a mystery that they appeared. It is rather a mystery that they disappeared.

4    Toronto's first one seems to have been built just as Queen Victoria was exhaling for the last time. No one is quite sure — records were not kept until five years later. Like many more or less obscure painters from the hazier centuries, the birth of the downstairs lav in

Toronto must be noted as "*circa* 1901". But while the demise of such painters was quite often recorded, that of the underground lavatory remains troublesome.

The first was certainly at Adelaide and Toronto Streets, which was then the heart of the     5
financial district (and remains approximately so — like a magnetic pole, the centre of a city may shift and waver). In this neighbourhood, flush with new wealth and etched with lines of influence along which errand boys skipped, some retreat was needed. Cities draw people together with ease, and make it difficult to draw apart. It was time to start building lavatories.

By 1906, Yonge-at-Cottingham had opened for business. Soon after, a grand con-     6
venience was opened at Queen, whose entrance was embedded in the richly forested island that ran plumb up the middle of Spadina. Two years later, Cottingham had added a women's room, either as a novelty, or as a concession to the emancipators, who swept a plume of hygienic equality through the smoke and dust of the city.

In the following year, Queen-at-Broadview appeared on the east side of the Don River,     7
itself a moist and infernal presence. This one was fashioned for both men and women, from the beginning; it was an age of sophistication and convenience. The City Engineer's report to City Council requested more conveniences, using the argument of necessity. We see a vision of Toronto, dotted with underground redoubts like the vast and permeable home of the prairie dog. And, for some years afterwards, business appears to have been brisk. Yet the trail grows cold.

Rumours of other lavatories have, of course, made the rounds. College-at-St. George,     8
tiled and spotless, was glimpsed some years ago during a sewer excavation when the overburden was for a moment stripped away, then quickly replaced, as if in embarrassment. Subway riders on the Bloor line report the ghostly appearance of a few shining cubicles midway between stations; they cannot agree which two. (Perhaps they see mere reflections in the windows. Our experience of the city is more and more like this.) I have even heard sudden scaldings in the shower explained by some nearby sepulchral flushing. It is possible that the dog who barks across the street when one is sleeping, awaits no squirrel, but rather a long-dead dandy, who will climb up softly from his midnight ablutions.

What actually happened to the underground lavatory? I asked the oldest member of the     9
Public Works Department (the robust organization that once controlled the lavatory layer of the city). He cast his mind back forty years, but was unable to pull up anything more than a memory of vague recesses growing shabby at street corners. At some point, they disappeared entirely. There may have been problems with drainage; with dirt; with danger and neglect. The lavatories may have filled with the umbrellas and hats that were so often left behind, until the stairs became impassable.

In their day, they were minor palaces, partitioned with marble, heated generously in     10
winter, and attended by paid sprites, with a clean towel and a jaunty word — every man's servant, for a moment. They are no more. In common with other disappearances, as of money or friends, we must look for ramifications and lessons.

An iron gate surfaced recently in an antique store north of Toronto. Like most antiques, it     11
was of uncertain beauty, dubious history, and intolerable price, but it seemed to be a "convenience gate", nicely worked and solid. In all respects, it was like the low gates that once separated the sidewalk from the top of the stair. On a small plate beside the handle, a verse survived faintly:

> If at your backside
> You can hear
> Time's chariot
> Then enter here.

12     This is a fair example of the Victorian propensity to disguise a lively ribaldry with delicate allusiveness. Our modern habit is to replace allusion with a somewhat forced, obligatory ribaldry; we are no nearer than the Victorians to the happy state that might be compared with both aiming, and actually loosing, at the mark. As a palpable artifact, the gate at least proves that public lavatories once existed. It is less certain, however, that gate and verse are native to Toronto. An inscription of similar metre —

> For all men's comfort
> No man's sin —
> Upon these terms
> You may come in

— is still to be found in mosaic over the vomitory of a large convenience set into the cliff that overlooks the Hudson River near Grant's Tomb in New York; it survived as a lavatory until the sixties, when it fell to the inner decay, both of its structure and its customers. The gate may have come from there. To trace the lavatorial relic is to chance a view of a whole world, knottily intertwined.

13     There is much evidence of the public lavatory, through many centuries and countless cities. Toronto came late to this gathering, stayed only briefly, and told few stories that had not already made the rounds. It is a long history, that is reputed to begin with the emperor Vespasian in the first century. He had large clay vessels set out at street corners, later constructing (I quote a contemporary account) "diverse places of fair polished marble" with which to divert the flow of rich Roman waste away from otherwise impressive gutters. French *pissoirs* are still formally known as *vespasiennes* — an indication that service to humanity, though seldom recognized at the time, is almost never entirely forgotten.

14     Development thereafter was swift. Overseen by the benevolent Sterculius and Crepitus — the gods of ordure and convenience, respectively — the Romans soon supplemented the grandeur of their public baths with refined latrines that seated up to twenty. There are hints of communal pursuits such as choral singing; Petronius notes in a military chronicle that —

> None but Orpheus sang as sweet
> As our lads sing on each hard seat.

With the descent of the Dark Ages, however, there was a lengthy retrogression in the march of convenience.

15     The mediaeval period may be considered an age of ferocity, pageantry, and inadequate plumbing. Europe was, at best, spotted with civic cesspits that required periodic cleaning by "rakers" or "gongfermors", who put the mincing heroism of a Galahad in the shade. At worst, it was believed that digestion, like fate, must take its course, indifferent to time and place.

16     This unhappy condition afflicted all of the Western world. The more controlled civilizations of the Orient could resort to such wonderful contrivances as the small public room, suspended on stilts, several storeys above the street, and reached by attenuated ladder or by rope. From these, ordure, falling free, is said to have disappeared before it struck the ground, whether through dissipation or air friction or from some other cause. Change came slowly to the West. Into the eighteenth century, to be caught short in a public place presented problems that were often best confronted by facing it out. Bashfulness seems to have made a later appearance (and remains with us — the blush has not wholly lost its power to recommend).

When privacy was wanted, however, men could be found, wandering the streets, who  **17**
would offer a bucket, and a cloak to conceal the machinations thereon, for a very reasonable sum. In some cities, carts circulated with portable privies on the back; their approach was often announced by a crier (like the ice cream trucks of Toronto that bedevil quiet neighbourhoods with annunciatory tunes); all of this in an attempt to beat back the advance of civic filth, which continued to be deposited, flung, disgorged, evacuated, heaved, catapulted, emptied, and generally placed in the public way.

A hope of victory can be detected in the first patent for a water closet, taken out in 1596  **18**
by a retainer of Queen Elizabeth (who herself wore several strata of skirtings and a heady perfume, in preference to regular attendance at the still-primitive "with-drawing cupboard"), but it was not much used. By the end of the eighteenth century, a series of similar inventions had appeared — like hands thrown in at the end of a game that has gone too long without result. The trajectory of the public convenience accelerated and steadied its course towards London's Great Exhibition of 1851, where the commodious public toilet, and indeed the pay toilet, was at last to be found.

A long journey, and perhaps less fabled than the development of the flying field, or of  **19**
the symphony, though even Shakespeare has honoured it with his attention, as in the scurrilous prologue of *Henry VII* —

> There men have come, and stood or sat within
> Th'impartial vault where echoes chase the wind
> Unleash'd by surfeit — capon, butt of sack,
> Comestibles that fury raise or bate;

The public convenience had at least been given amicable shape. From there, it is a  **20**
short leap into the underground lavatories of Toronto.

The surface of a city is a skin of sorts — creased and furrowed, dotted with protuberant  **21**
features by which it is known and sometimes loved, often defaced with motes and scars, a surface upon which the wrecker's ball can be seen as a brutal depilatory. One must go under the skin, to the *viscera*, to find the underlying character of a place. The underground convenience is close to this fundament. It wasn't long before the public lavatory, once steady on its feet, felt the inward pull of what might be called the "intestinal city", and began to sink below the streets.

At the same time, there was a hum of curiosity about the world below. There were  **22**
public tours of the sewers of Paris — ladies of society slid through huge, damp tunnels, seated in barges while rows of silent men held gas lamps aloft along the littoral. (It should be remarked that these sewers conducted rain water only, while horse-drawn carts carried off the more noisome effluvia along the road above. Such a practice was not unknown, even in a city like Tokyo, and as late as 1950.) At the end of the Second World War, the sewers of Vienna were still accessible by stair from the street, although the entrances were disguised as news kiosks, liberally faced with posters. Through these subterranean passages, fugitives were conducted from the Russian occupation to the West.

The downward imperative was first documented by the photographer Eadweard  **23**
Muybridge, in such sequences as his "Athlete descending a staircase" of 1880. The descent expressed the human quest for deeper knowledge, or for the satisfaction of dire human necessity or, perhaps, for both. By the time Marcel Duchamp painted "Nude Descending the Staircase" in 1912 (coincidentally assisting the emergence of Dada, Cubism, and Reticulism, with a single canvas), there was public recognition of the burrowing tendency.

24    In this febrile, and perhaps dangerous, atmosphere, Toronto entered both the twentieth century and the subterranean lavatory. When, in 1901, a declivity appeared in the pavement at Adelaide and Toronto Streets, it was the civic equivalent of a Freudian slip. It revealed more than it knew, offered not only commodity and relief but also a first gesture towards the acknowledgement of the modern city as a compound of essential urges and unsightly operations — a spade was called a spade, for all its decorative handle.

25    Our underground lavatories disappeared when discretion became the enemy of public convenience. By mid-century, the innocent cry of the lavatory attendant at closing — "Button up!" — had been distorted into the belligerent equivalent to "Be quiet!". Many of the euphemisms associated with the public lavatory had soured into dysphemy.

26    In the half-century or so since, the inwards of the city have been withheld from public view. The subway might offer an opportunity to peek at the sinew and gristle beneath us, but its chambers are sealed. The subway is meant to transport us horizontally; it parallels and mimics motion on the roads above, and is rarely entered and left by the same stairway. Even when a repairman lifts a manhole, the view below is coyly concealed from us, by a canvas or plastic veil.

27    I have heard accounts of a giant alligator who lives in the sewers, surfacing rarely. This has been said in many places, and for all I know, the same alligator may travel from one city to another, like a circuit judge in a dark and aqueous world.

28    I have read, moreover, accounts of sea-snakes, piranha fish, and other dangerous pets, flushed down the toilet but surviving in the subterranean jungle. Many things disappear under the streets, and perhaps much of what has been lost may be attributed to the appetite of these creatures. Of course, this is mere hearsay; but it is nonetheless true that a peculiar psychological alligator has descended, and has consumed Toronto's underground lavatories whole.

## VOCABULARY

a. *paragraph  2:* problematic, amenable

b. *paragraph  4:* demise

c. *paragraph  6:* emancipators

d. *paragraph  7:* redoubts, permeable

e. *paragraph  8:* sepulchral, ablutions

f. *paragraph 10:* sprites, ramifications

g. *paragraph 12:* allusiveness, ribaldry, palpable, artifact, vomitory

h. *paragraph 14:* retrogression

i. *paragraph 17:* annunciatory

j. *paragraph 18:* retainer, trajectory

k. *paragraph 19:* surfeit, capon, butt, sack, comestibles, bate

l. *paragraph 21:* protuberant, *viscera*

m. *paragraph 22:* littoral, effluvia

o. *paragraph 25:* euphemisms, dysphemy

## QUESTIONS

1. What images does Ferguson use in paragraphs 6 through 8? What effects is he trying to create with this kind of language?

2. Consider the last two sentences of paragraph 9. How do the images function here? Are they realistic, surrealistic, or both?

3. Why does Ferguson quote actual inscriptions in paragraphs 11 and 12? What do they tell us about the lavatories?

4. Why does he include a historical account of his subject in paragraphs 13 through 20? What image does he use to enliven this history?

5. What does he mean by "psychological alligator" (paragraph 28)? What significance does the image of a "subterranean jungle" have for Ferguson's thesis?

6. Ferguson says that "to trace the lavatorial relic is to chance a view of a whole world knottily intertwined." Does the essay bear out his claim?

7. What is the tone of the essay? What words or phrases give us a clue to Ferguson's attitude toward his subject?

## WRITING ASSIGNMENTS

1. Describe some aspect of your own neighbourhood or environment that has disappeared over time. Use images that re-create a physical scene and that convey your attitudes to what has happened.

2. The newspaper of a town or city often publishes letters from local readers responding to a column or editorial or commenting on a recent local event. Use several of these letters to comment on the concerns and attitudes of the writers, and to single out a similarity or difference that would give people living in another community or country a sense of your town or city and its concerns.

## K.C. COLE

*A former editor of* Saturday Review *and* Newsday, *K.C. Cole has written articles for numerous periodicals including the* New York Times *and* Psychology Today. *Her book* Between the Lines *(1982) discusses the contemporary issues of feminism, and Cole has also written much about physics as a profession. She draws on her knowledge of physics in this unusual essay on the literal and metaphorical meanings of resonance.*

# RESONANCE

1   Metaphor is a truly marvelous thing. We speak of being in tune with the times or out of tune with each other. We speak of sympathetic vibrations and being on the same wavelength. We speak of going through phases, of ideas that resonate and descriptions that ring true. I wonder how many of us know that all the time we are talking physics?

2   Resonance is the physics lesson all children learn the first time they try to pump themselves on a swing. Pushing forward or leaning backward at the wrong place or time in the swing gets them nowhere. But pushing and pulling precisely in tune with the natural period of swing will get them as high as they want to go. Being in tune means pushing in the same direction that the swing naturally wants to go. It means going with the flow. Pushing at any other time goes against the swing and bucks the current. It saps energy instead of adding it. Eventually, it will bring the highest swinger to a halt.

3   Resonance is music to our ears. A violin bow slips along the string, imperceptibly catching it at precise intervals that push it at the proper time to keep vibrating. The air in a flute resonates at many different frequencies, depending on how far the vibration can travel between lips and mouthpiece. But the stops in a flute are not spaced just anywhere. Beware the flute player who sets the air vibrating at a frequency not natural to the flute; the sound is not a note at all, only an amorphous, irritating hiss.

4   Being out of tune is always irritating because the energy we put into our efforts doesn't seem to get us anywhere. It goes against our grain instead of with it. It steals our harmony and leaves us noise. We can be in or out of tune with ourselves — like the flute and the violin — or in or out of tune with others. Two flutes played beautifully but slightly out of tune with each other can be just as unpleasant as one played badly. Partners in a marriage who are perfectly in tune with their professional or personal lives can be badly out of tune with each other too.

5   To resonate means to sound again, to echo. The trick is to have something that re-sounds again and again. Two can play this game much better than one because one can feed energy to the other. That's what sympathetic vibrations are all about.

6   Though almost everything — and everyone — can resonate to many different frequencies, it is rare to find ourselves exactly in resonance with something or someone else. When we do, it is the click of recognition that comes with finding a friend who laughs at your jokes and whose understanding goes without saying, who reads correctly the exact meaning of the tilt of your slightly raised eyebrow and who provides the ingredients that make the occasion.

7   It's like the car with the unbalanced wheel that starts to shimmy at exactly 62 miles per hour. At other speeds the wheel still wobbles but the springs of the car can't respond; only at 62 miles an hour do the two frequencies coincide and the two vibrations become completely sympathetic. Then the car shakes like mad. It's all a matter of timing.

8   With resonance, a small unnoticed vibration can add up to large, often lovely effects. Lasers are the result of sympathetic vibrations of light. The opera singer's aria is an ode to resonance. Each pure tone that fills the opera house is the tiny vibration of a vocal cord amplified by the shape of chest and throat. The same pure tone can shatter a crystal glass. Resonance can be dangerous. Soldiers marching in step across a bridge can cause it to start swinging at its natural frequency, straining its supports and making it collapse. A lot of little pushes in an angry crowd can add up to a full-scale riot. A lot of little digs over the dinner table can lead to a divorce.

9   Resonance can also be deceiving: a politician who senses dissatisfaction over inflation and taxes can get a large resonant response with a very small input of energy or new ideas

— and winds up playing in a vacuum, with no result. A woman who comes into a man's life at the moment he happens to be looking for a wife (or vice versa) may find herself quickly, but in the long run unhappily, married. Being in tune can easily be a matter of superficial coincidence, not lasting harmony.

It is not easy, that is, to stay in tune even when we start out that way. I am always **10** unprepared for the precipitate ups and downs in my marriage and my relations with friends. One week we seem never to be together enough, seem never to have enough time to say what we want to say, seem so closely attuned to each other's needs and fancies that we are irrevocably inseparable. A week or month later the feelings of being in tune evaporate as invisibly — but surely — as water from a dry stream. Suddenly we seem to have nothing to say to each other and everything we do say is misunderstood. Arguments and hurt feelings lie beneath the surface like spikes, waiting to trip us up.

Anything that resonates necessarily oscillates; it swings or vibrates back and forth. Just **11** because you start out swinging in the same direction doesn't mean you will reverse direction at the same time. Each part of the swing has its phases: ups and downs, stops and starts. If your timing is not right you will soon find yourself up when your partner is down, just starting when your partner has already stopped. Even flutes get out of tune as they warm up. People or things that make beautiful music together must continually be adjusted, fine-tuned. Resonance is a delicate thing.

Still, it is amazing how much of the world around us is colored by resonance. Each **12** atom resonates with one or, often, several natural frequencies. Sodium light is yellow because the sodium atom resonates with the frequency of radiation we see as the color yellow. Grass is green because all the colors of sunlight except green resonate within the grass and become stuck; green is the only color left to reflect to our eyes. Ultraviolet wavelengths of light become stuck within the molecules of a windowpane and prevent us from getting a suntan indoors. The ozone layer of the atmosphere, like suntan lotion, also absorbs resonant ultraviolet rays and protects us from potentially damaging light.

Resonance determines what is transparent, what is invisible, what we see and hear. **13** Tuning into a radio or television station merely means putting your receiver on the same wavelength as the station's transmitter. In the process of tuning into one channel, of course, we ignore all the others. We do the same thing when we tune in to certain people or ideas. When a woman becomes pregnant she focuses on her condition and sometimes ceases to pay attention to anything else. Teen-agers tune into teen-agers; kids into other kids.

It's important to have something around that responds when you push against it, of **14** course; a resounding board, so to speak. I never felt so lonely as when I was bringing up my son and all my friends, childless, were bringing up their careers. I'd throw out experiences and insights only to have them land with a thud. My friends had nothing to give back, nothing to reinforce my joys or help to lessen the sting of my sorrows. On the other hand, I felt just as isolated when I was surrounded by women whose lives were exclusively submerged in homes and children. They could not have commiserated with my conflicts even if they had wanted to.

My friend Alice, who is 73, joked that I would never find a compatible neighborhood **15** because I would never find neighbors who shared my eclectic collection of experiences. It reminded me of a middle-aged woman who was visiting a museum I work in and complained that people like herself probably couldn't relate to our teen-age guides. She had a good point. And yet I wonder how many teen-agers have been permanently put off museums by middle-aged guides like myself. And how much easier it would be if we could vibrate to a large collection of resonances. How sad it would be if we could relate only to people exactly like ourselves.

16    Resonance determines what goes right through and what sinks in. It even determines what we are. Particles of matter, it turns out, are really just resonances of energy. A certain frequency of vibration and presto! a proton. Change the frequency and presto! you have something else.

17    Fortunately, in addition to the sharp focus of single resonance, we can have a rich spectrum of resonances called harmonics. Harmonics sounds the difference between a twanging string and a violin. Changing our tunes every now and then may not be such a bad idea.

## VOCABULARY

a. *paragraph 3:* amorphous

b. *paragraph 8:* lasers

c. *paragraph 10:* precipitate

d. *paragraph 14:* commiserated

e. *paragraph 15:* eclectic

## QUESTIONS

1. What is *resonance*, and where does Cole first define it? How does she develop this definition in the course of the essay?

2. Cole concludes with the statement that "changing our tunes every now and then may not be such a bad idea." How does she develop this metaphorical statement through the physical resonance of music?

3. What other metaphorical meanings of resonance does Cole discuss? How does she illustrate them?

4. Is the essay an account of the many uses of a single metaphor, or is Cole making a point about people or life through the metaphor of resonance?

## WRITING ASSIGNMENTS

1. Illustrate one of the points Cole makes about resonance through experiences and observations of your own. You might begin your essay by restating her definition of resonance and commenting on it.

2. Give the dictionary meaning of one of the following words, then discuss the various metaphorical meanings of the word in your own experience:

   a. resilience          c. toughness

   b. flexibility         d. tenacity

# RICHARD SELZER

*A surgeon and member of the faculty of the Yale School of Medicine,* Richard Selzer *has written on medicine and the art of surgery in* Confessions of a Knife, Letters to a Young Doctor, *and* Mortal Lessons, *in which these final sections of the essay "Lessons from the Art" appear. Selzer writes about medicine and physiology with unusual exuberance and feeling. His metaphorical style is used to powerful effect in these pages on what it means to be a surgeon.*

## LESSONS FROM THE ART

A man of letters lies in the intensive care unit. A professor, used to words and students. He has corrected the sentences of many. He understands punctuation. One day in his classroom he was speaking of Emily Dickinson when suddenly he grew pale, and a wonder sprang upon his face, as though he had just, for the first time, *seen* something, understood something that had eluded him all his life. It was the look of the Wound, the struck blow that makes no noise, but happens in the depths somewhere, unseen. His students could not have known that at that moment his stomach had perforated, that even as he spoke, its contents were issuing forth into his peritoneal cavity like a horde of marauding goblins. From the blackboard to the desk he reeled, fell across the top of it, and turning his face to one side, he vomited up his blood, great gouts and gobbets of it, as though having given his class the last of his spirit, he now offered them his fluid and cells.    1

In time, he was carried to the operating room, this man whom I had known, who had taught me poetry. I took him up, in my hands, and laid him open, and found from where he bled. I stitched it up, and bandaged him, and said later, "Now you are whole."    2

But it was not so, for he had begun to die. And I could not keep him from it, not with all my earnestness, so sure was his course. From surgery he was taken to the intensive care unit. His family, his students were stopped at the electronic door. They could not pass, for he had entered a new state of being, a strange antechamber where they may not go.    3

For three weeks he has dwelt in that House of Intensive Care, punctured by needles, wearing tubes of many calibers in all of his orifices, irrigated, dialyzed, insufflated, pumped, and drained . . . and feeling every prick and pressure the way a lover feels desire spring acutely to his skin.    4

In the room a woman moves. She is dressed in white. Lovingly she measures his hourly flow of urine. With hands familiar, she delivers oxygen to his nostrils and counts his pulse as though she were tellings beads. Each bit of his decline she records with her heart full of grief, shaking her head. At last, she turns from her machinery to the simple touch of the flesh. Sighing, she strips back the sheet, and bathes his limbs.    5

The man of letters did not know this woman before. Preoccupied with dying, he is scarcely aware of her presence now. But this nurse is his wife in his new life of dying. They are close, these two, intimate, depending one upon the other, loving. It is a marriage, for although they own no shared past, they possess this awful, intense present, this matrimonial now, that binds them as strongly as any promise.    6

A man does not know whose hands will stroke from him the last bubbles of his life. That alone should make him kinder to strangers.    7

I stand by the bed where a young woman lies, her face post-operative, her mouth twisted in palsy, clownish. A tiny twig of the facial nerve, the one to the muscles of her mouth,    8 has been severed. She will be thus from now on. The surgeon had followed with religious fervor the curve of her flesh; I promise you that. Nevertheless, to remove the tumor in her cheek, I had cut the little nerve.

9     Her young husband is in the room. He stands on the opposite side of the bed, and together they seem to dwell in the evening lamplight, isolated from me, private. Who are they, I ask myself, he and this wry-mouth I have made, who gaze at and touch each other so generously, greedily? The young woman speaks.

10     "Will my mouth always be like this?" she asks.

11     "Yes," I say, "it will. It is because the nerve was cut."

12     She nods, and is silent. But the young man smiles.

13     "I like it," he says. "It is kind of cute."

14     All at once I *know* who he is. I understand, and I lower my gaze. One is not bold in an encounter with a god. Unmindful, he bends to kiss her crooked mouth, and I so close I can see how he twists his own lips to accommodate to hers, to show her that their kiss still works. I remember that the gods appeared in ancient Greece as mortals, and I hold my breath and let the wonder in.

15     Far away from the operating room, the surgeon is taught that some deaths are undeniable, that this does not deny their meaning. To *perceive* tragedy is to wring from it beauty and truth. It is a thing beyond mere competence and technique, or the handsomeness to precisely cut and stitch. Further, he learns that love can bloom in the stoniest desert, an intensive care unit, perhaps.

16     These are things of longest memory, and like memory, they cut. When the patient becomes the surgeon, he goes straight for the soul.

17     I do not know when it was that I understood that it is precisely this hell in which we wage our lives that offers us the energy, the possibility to care for each other. A surgeon does not slip from his mother's womb with compassion smeared upon him like the drippings of his birth. It is much later that it comes. No easy shaft of grace this, but the cumulative murmuring of the numberless wounds he has dressed, the incisions he has made, all the sores and ulcers and cavities he has touched in order to heal. In the beginning it is barely audible, a whisper, as from many mouths. Slowly it gathers, rises from the streaming flesh until, at last, it is a pure *calling* — an exclusive sound, like the cry of certain solitary birds — telling that out of the resonance between the sick man and the one who tends him there may spring that profound courtesy that the religious call Love.

## VOCABULARY

a. *paragraph 1:* perforated, peritoneal cavity, marauding, gouts, gobbets

b. *paragraph 4:* orifices, dialyzed, insufflated

c. *paragraph 8:* palsy

d. *paragraph 9:* wry-mouth

e. *paragraph 17:* cumulative, resonance

# QUESTIONS

1. How does Selzer personify the wound in paragraph 1, and to what purpose?

2. What is Selzer comparing in the simile of the goblins in paragraph 1? What is the effect of this comparison?

3. What is metaphorical about the statement in paragraph 4 that the professor "has dwelt in that House of Intensive Care"? What does Selzer gain in connotative meaning through this metaphor?

4. What metaphor organizes paragraph 6, and how does Selzer develop or extend it?

5. Why does the husband remind Selzer of the gods of ancient Greece?

6. What similes and metaphors do you find in paragraphs 15 through 17? What feelings or ideas do these make vivid?

7. What central idea or thesis is Selzer developing through these lessons from the art of the surgery?

# WRITING ASSIGNMENTS

1. Write your lessons from another art you know how to perform — for example, the art of giving advice or the art of making friends. Use similes, metaphors, and personification where appropriate to make your ideas vivid to the reader.

2. In their selection of details, good writers often appeal to more than the visual sense. Concentrate on the other senses by writing a description of a playground or a busy city street as a blind person would perceive it.

# MARTIN AMIS

Martin Amis *was born in 1949 and educated at Oxford. He is one of the most talented novelists of his generation. Of his five books,* Money *(1984) has been recognized by the critics as one of the most important novels in recent times. He is also a prolific writer of book reviews which are themselves superb essays. In the following introduction to his recent collection of short stories,* Einstein's Monsters *(1987), he writes of the threat posed by nuclear weapons.*

# EINSTEIN'S MONSTERS

They squat on our spiritual lives. There may be a nuclear 'priesthood', but we are the supplicants, and we have no faith. The warheads are our godheads. Nuclear weapons could bring about the Book of Revelation in a matter of hours; they could do it today. Of course, no dead will rise; nothing will be revealed (*nothing* meaning two things, the absence of everything and a thing called *nothing*). Events that we call "acts of God" — floods, earthquakes, eruptions — are fleshwounds compared to the human act of nuclear war: a million Hiroshimas. Like God, nuclear weapons are free creations of the human mind. Unlike God, nuclear weapons are real. And they are here.

2    Revulsion at MAD [Mutually Assured Destruction] is understandable and necessary. I suggest, however, that MAD is not just a political creation but a creation of the weapons themselves. Always we keep coming back to the weapons as if they were actors rather than pieces of equipment; and they earn this status, by virtue of their cosmic power. They are actors and, considered on the human scale, insane actors. The weapons are insane, they are MAD: they can assume no other form. In one of those philosopher's throat-clearings Anthony Kenny says that "weapons considered merely as inert pieces of hardware are not, of course, objects of moral evaluation. It is the uses to which they are put . . ." This isn't so. Recent evidence strongly suggests that nuclear weapons, in their inert state, are responsible for a variety of cancers and leukaemias. What toxicity, what power, what range. They cause death even before they go off.

3    The A-bomb is a Z-bomb, and the arms race is a race between nuclear weapons and ourselves. It is them or us. What do nukes do? What are they for? Since when did we all want to kill each other? Nuclear weapons deter a nuclear holocaust by threatening a nuclear holocaust, and if things go wrong then that is what you get: a nuclear holocaust. If things don't go wrong, and continue not going wrong for the next millennium of millennia (the boasted forty years being no more than forty winks in cosmic time), you get . . . What do you get? What are we getting?

4    At the multiracial children's teaparty the guests have, perhaps, behaved slightly better since the Keepers were introduced. Little Ivan has stopped pulling Fetnab's hair, though he is still kicking her leg under the table. Bobby has returned the slice of cake that rightfully belonged to tiny Conchita, though he has his eye on that sandwich and will probably make a lunge for it sooner or later. Out on the lawn the Keepers maintain a kind of order, but standards of behaviour are pretty well as troglodytic as they ever were. At best the children seem strangely subdued or off-colour. Although they are aware of the Keepers, they don't want to look at them, they don't want to catch their eye. They don't want to think about them. For the Keepers are a thousand feet tall, and covered in gelignite and razor-blades, toting flamethrowers and machineguns, cleavers and skewers, and fizzing with rabies, anthrax, plague. Curiously enough, they are not looking at the children at all. With bleeding hellhound eyes, mouthing foul threats and shaking their fists, they are looking at each other. They want to take on someone their own size . . .

5    If they only knew it — no, if they only *believed* it — the children could simply ask the Keepers to leave. But it doesn't seem possible, does it? It seems — it seems unthinkable. A silence starts to fall across the lawn. The party has not been going for very long and must last until the end of time. Already the chldren are weepy and feverish. They all feel sick and want to go home.

## VOCABULARY

a. *paragraph 1:* supplicants

b. *paragraph 2:* inert, toxicity

c. *paragraph 3:* millennium

d. *paragraph 4:* troglodytic, gelignite, skewers, anthrax, hellhound

# QUESTIONS

1. In paragraph 2, Amis points out how important metaphor can be in our thinking about nuclear weapons. What metaphor does he use to inform the argument in the first paragraph? How effective is it?

2. The fourth paragraph develops the metaphor of the tea party at some length. How effective is it?

3. How do the rhetorical questions function in paragraph 3?

4. How is the figurative language generally used to create an effect? Is Amis's appeal to the reader primarily emotional?

5. Do you think that Amis's rapid-fire style might leave some readers behind? For instance, does his piling of image upon image and metaphor upon metaphor convince or befuddle the reader?

# WRITING ASSIGNMENT

1. Discuss another contemporary issue using an extended metaphor like Amis's tea party. Work at including detail to give the image specificity and depth.

# Faulty Diction

The word *diction* refers in general to choice of words in speaking and writing. The choice may simply be a matter of vocabulary — as in exposition, when you name a specific tool in performing a job, or in descriptive writing, when you choose concrete words or phrases and vivid images to create a mental picture. The choice may also be emotional — as in persuasive writing, when you choose words that are exact but that also move the reader to accept an idea or take action. In addition, diction concerns not only the nature and use of words but also their misuse. You must not only find words with appropriate connotations but also avoid words with misleading connotations.

We hear much today about the abuse of language — particularly about euphemism and equivocation, such as that cited by William Zinsser in his discussion of language included in "Writers on Writing":

> During the late 1960s the president of a major university wrote a letter to mollify the alumni after a spell of campus unrest. "You are probably aware," he began, "that we have been experiencing very considerable potentially explosive expressions of dissatisfaction on issues only partially related." He meant that the students had been hassling them about different things. — William Zinsser, "Simplicity"

We can guess what Zinsser would say about contemporary political language — about such phrases as "credibility gap" and "positive reference input" to describe the good and bad reputations of office holders and candidates, and in non-political discourse, "learning resource centres" and "interfaces between student and teacher" to describe libraries and conferences. Such vague and pretentious language can be comical, as Harry Bruce shows in "The Christmas Story Updated," but the abuses of language can lead to the kind of muddled thinking that ultimately threatens our freedom as individuals.

The three essays in this section offer an opportunity to consider many of these abuses and their possible causes. So does *Time* in its discussion of euphemism, earlier in this book.

The following suggestions will help you identify the faults in diction that John Leo, Harry Bruce, and Bob Blackburn satirize in this section:

1. Using the same word more than once in a sentence can be confusing if the senses are different:

   We were present for the presentation of the award.

   However, we need not avoid repeating a word if the senses are the same. Indeed, substituting can also be confusing.

   The person who entered was not the individual I was expecting.

   Though *individual* is a popular synonym for *person*, it has other meanings. The substitution could confuse the reader.

2. Needless repetition can make sentences hard to understand.

   There are necessary skills that writers need to make their ideas easy to understand and comprehensible.

3. Words that overlap in meaning can have the same effect:

   The result of the survey should produce a change in policy.

   The words *result* and *produce* mean the same thing in the sentence. The following sentence is satisfactory:

   The survey should produce a change in policy.

4. Euphemism — providing a mild or pleasant substitute for a blunt term — can be a source of ambiguity. The euphemism *delinquent* to describe a juvenile criminal or the words *slow* and *retarded* to describe children who have trouble learning or are crippled mentally help us avoid giving pain. What words should we use in speaking about children who have trouble learning or have broken the law? No easy answers exist: we know the price of speaking bluntly, but also the price of hiding facts.

5. Equivocal terms are also a source of ambiguity because they have double meanings. The word *exceptional* is widely used to describe bright children as well as crippled ones or children who have broken the law. We need to know which children we are talking about.

6. A cliché is a phrase or saying that has become trite through overuse: *sweet as sugar, conspicuous by his absence, more sinned against than sinning*. A bromide is a comforting platitude: *it's the effort that counts, not the winning*. Both rob prose of conviction and vigour.

7. Mixed metaphors cause confusion and can be unintentionally funny:

   Blows to one's pride stick in the craw.

8. Technical words or jargon can also have the same effect. The words *interface* (to describe the boundary between two independent machines) and *software* (to describe accessory equipment) are useful words in computer language. They become jargon in a different sense of the word — to quote H.W. Fowler, "talk that is considered both ugly-sounding and hard to understand" — when borrowed to describe other things. A conference is not an "interface," and referring to a book as "software" suggests something mechanical or perhaps dispensable.

9. Circumlocution means taking the long way around — in other words, saying something in inflated language: saying "he has difficulty distinguishing the real from the imagined" when we mean "he lies." Euphemisms often depend on inflation of this kind.

# JOHN LEO

*Having worked as a reporter for the* New York Times *and as an editor for* Commonweal *and* Time, *John Leo writes about the language of the journalist from first-hand experience. Leo does more than describe this language; like George Orwell, he discusses its causes. Leo focusses, however, on the day-to-day problems that encourage euphemism and other practices of the journalist.*

# JOURNALESE AS A SECOND LANGUAGE

1    As a cub reporter, Columnist Richard Cohen of the Washington *Post* rushed out one day to interview a lawyer described in many newspaper reports as "ruddy-faced." The man was woozily abusive and lurched about with such abandon that young Cohen instantly realized that the real meaning of ruddy-faced is drunk. This was his introduction to journalese, the fascinating second tongue acquired by most reporters as effortlessly as an Iranian toddler learns Farsi or a Marin County child learns psychobabble.

2    Fluency in journalese means knowing all about "the right stuff," "gender gap," "life in the fast lane" and the vexing dilemma of being caught "between a rock and a hard place," the current Scylla-Charybdis image. The Middle East is "strife-torn," except during those inexplicable moments when peace breaks out. Then it is always "much troubled." Kuwait is located just east of the adjective "oil-rich," and the Irish Republican Army always lurks right behind the word "outlawed." The hyphenated modifier is the meat and potatoes of journalese. Who can forget "the break-away province of Biafra," "the mop-top quartet" (the mandatory second reference to the Beatles) and the "ill-fated Korean jetliner," not to be confused with the "ill-fitting red wig" of Watergate fame. Murderers on death row are often saved by "eleventh-hour" reprieves, which would be somewhere between 10 and 11 p.m. in English but shortly before midnight in journalese.

3    Much of the difficulty in mastering journalese comes from its slight overlap with English. "Imposing," for instance, when used to describe a male, retains its customary English meaning, but when used in reference to a female, it always means battle-ax. "Feisty" refers to a person whom the journalist deems too short and too easily enraged, though many in the journalese-speaking fraternity believe it is simply the adjective of choice for any male under 5 ft. 6 in. who is not legally dead. This usage reflects the continual surprise among tall journalists that short people have any energy at all. Women are not often feisty, though they are usually short enough to qualify. No journalist in America has ever referred to a 6-ft. male as feisty. At that height, men are simply "outspoken" (*i.e.*, abusive).

4    In general, adjectives in journalese are as misleading as olive sizes. Most news consumers know enough to translate "developing nations" and "disadvantaged nations" back into English, but far smaller numbers know that "militant" means fanatic, and "steadfast" means pigheaded. "Controversial" introduces someone or something the writer finds appalling, as in "the controversial Miss Fonda," and "prestigious" heralds the imminent arrival of a noun nobody cares about as in "the prestigious Jean Hersholt Humanitarian Award."*

5    Television anchorpersons add interest to their monologues by accenting a few syllables chosen at random. Since print journalists cannot do this, except when reading aloud to spouse and children, they strive for a similar effect by using words like crisis and revolution. Crisis means any kind of trouble at all, and revolution means any kind of change at all, as in "the revolution in meat packing." "Street value" lends excitement to any drug-bust story, without bearing any financial relationship to the actual value of drugs being busted. Many meaningless adjectives, preferably hyphenated for proper rhythm, are permanently welded to certain nouns: blue-ribbon panel, fact-finding mission, devout Catholic, and rock-ribbed Republican. In journalese there are no devout Protestants or Jews, and no Democrats with strong or stony ribs.

6    Historians of journalese will agree that the first flowering of the language occurred in the sexist descriptions of women by splashy tabloids during the '30s and '40s. In contrast to Pentagonese, which favours oxymorons (Peacekeeper missiles, builddown), the

---

*An award given annually by the Academy of Motion Picture Arts and Sciences at the Oscar ceremonies. — Ed.

tabloids relied on synecdoche (leggy brunette, bosomy blonde, full-figured redhead). Full-figured, of course, meant fat, and "well-endowed" did not refer to Ford Foundation funding. "Statuesque" (too large, mooselike) and "petite" (too small, mouselike) were adjectives of last resort, meaning that the woman under discussion had no bodily parts that interested the writer. A plain, short woman was invariably "pert." For years, masters of this prose cast about for a nonlibelous euphemism for "mistress." The winning entry, "great and good friend," used to describe Marion Davies'* relationship to William Randolph Hearst, was pioneered, as it happens, by a non-Hearst publication, *TIME* magazine. "Constant companion" evolved later, and gave way to such clunking modernisms as "roommate" and "live-in lover." Nowadays, the only sexuality about which journalese is coy tends to be homosexuality, and that is adequately covered by "he has no close female friends" or "he is not about to settle down."

In political campaigns, underdogs fight uphill battles and hope for shifts of momentum   7
and coattail effects, all leading to rising tides that will enable the favorite to snatch defeat from the jaws of victory. A politician who has no idea about what is going on can be described as one who prefers "to leave details to subordinates." A gangster who runs a foreign country will be referred to as "strongman" until his death, and dictator thereafter. Strongman, like many terms in journalese, has no true correlative. "Nicaraguan Strongman Somoza" is not balanced with "Cambodian Weakman Prince Sihanouk."

What to say about a public figure who is clearly bonkers? Since it is unsporting and   8
possibly libelous to write: "Representative Forbush, the well-known raving psychopath," journalese has evolved the code words difficult, intense and driven. If an article says, "Like many of us, Forbush has his ups and downs," the writer is wigwagging a manic-depressive.

Political journalese, of course, requires a knowledge of sources. An unnamed analyst   9
or observer can often be presumed to be the writer of the article. The popular plural "observers," or "analysts," refers to the writer and his cronies. Insiders, unlike observer-analysts, sometimes exist in the real world outside the newsroom. This, however, is never true of quotable chestnut vendors in Paris, Greenwich Village bartenders and other colorful folk conjured up on deadline to lend dash to a story.

Almost all sources, like most trial balloonists, live in or around Washington. In order   10
of ascending rectitude, they are: informants, usually reliable sources, informed sources, authoritative sources, sources in high places and unimpeachable sources. Informants are low-level operatives, whose beans are normally spilled to police rather than to reporters. Informed sources, because of their informed nature, are consulted more often by savvy journalists. An unimpeachable source is almost always the President, with the obvious exception of Richard Nixon, who was not unimpeachable.

Journalese is controversial but prestigious, and observers are steadfast in averring that   11
it has the right stuff.

## VOCABULARY

a. *paragraph 1:* woozily

b. *paragraph 2:* fluency, Scylla-Charybdis

c. *paragraph 3:* deems, feisty

---

*Marion Davies was a popular film actress of the 1930s. — Ed.

d. *paragraph 4:* imminent

e. *paragraph 6:* sexist, oxymorons, synecdoche, pert

f. *paragraph 7:* correlative

g. *paragraph 8:* bonkers, psychopath

h. *paragraph 10:* unimpeachable, savvy

## QUESTIONS

1. What are the characteristics of journalese — the jargon or special language of reporters?

2. How does Leo illustrate the overlap of journalese with English? Why is this overlap essential to journalese?

3. What are the reasons or motives for using journalese? Does Leo state these reasons or imply them?

4. What is the purpose of the essay — to illustrate journalese, to warn the general reader about it, to discourage journalists from using it?

5. If a politician appears drunk in a public place, should a reporter state this fact and use the word *drunk*, use the phrase *ruddy-faced*, or omit the fact from the news story? Is journalese sometimes a necessity, or should journalists never use it?

## WRITING ASSIGNMENTS

1. Analyse the journalese you hear on a series of newscasts or read in newspaper editorials or columns. Discuss what seems to you to be the reasons or motives for these uses.

2. The term *psychobabble* has been defined as a "monotonous patois, this psychological patter, whose concern is to faithfully catalog the ego's condition" — for example, the expressions "Go with the feeling" and "You gotta be you 'cause you're you." Psychobabble takes its words and phrases from fashionable psychological theories that encourage easy talk about people and their behaviour. Give examples of psychobabble that you hear on television or at the movies or in talk with friends and relatives, or that you read in newspapers, magazines, and possibly textbooks. Use your analysis to make a point about communication or about the way people today see and talk about themselves.

## HARRY BRUCE

*In the following essay, Harry Bruce subjects that great model of English prose, the King James Version of the Bible, to parodic treatment by translating its account of the Nativity into the jargon of bureaucrats and social scientists.*

# THE CHRISTMAS STORY UPDATED

It's the season to send *social expression products* (greeting cards to you, madam), and as a   1
greeting to my readers, I've decided to clarify the Christmas story by translating into
current English the relevant verses from Chapter 2, St. Luke, in the King James author-
ized version of the Bible. Here we go:

And it came to pass in those days that there was distributed a systematized, incremental   2
projection in memorandum form from Caesar Augustus that the entirety of personnel with
globular parameters should be subject to revenue enhancement. And the aforesaid comprehensive complement of the human species subsequently adopted the non-stationary or
perambulatory mode in order to participate in the program of receipts strengthening, each
one employing a synchronized, transitional mobility in order to enter his or her own
urban-oriented megalopolis.

And Joseph, a practitioner in the medium of wood, also became a unit of the transpor-   3
tation function from the designated administrative division of Galilee, travelling from the
metropolitan matrix of Nazareth into the interactive sociometric structure of Judea, and
hence to the urban network zone of David, the terminology identification of which was
Bethlehem.

There, the previously mentioned Joseph would contribute to tax-base broadening, with   4
Mary, his espoused wife, the magnitude of whose abdominal region was substantive due
to the circumstance of her anticipating the impending arrival on the subject-area stage of
an infant human unit with whom she might experience a meaningful, interpersonal
relationship.

After considering her functional management options, she produced her initially   5
birthed male offspring, and in accordance with operational, interactive, parenting concepts, she enveloped the said client in swaddling garments, and installed Him in a supine
position within a trough-like receptacle from which, in the normal course of events, animals of the species of *Bos taurus*, *Bos indica* and *Equus Caballus* consumed fodder. The
creatures apparently uttered neither moo nor neigh. The nuclear family of household-head
Joseph temporarily resided in this single-purpose agricultural structure because the hospi-
tality industry was such that no dwelling modules were available at the inn.

And there were in the aforementioned designated region certain agricultural techni-   6
cians whose occupation involved the superintendence of domesticated ruminant mammals
of the genus Ovis of the Bovidae family, and these custodial engineers were observing, as
was their wont, their assemblages of ruminants under nocturnal conditions.

And, if you will kindly acknowledge an event of a supernatural nature, the chief agent   7
of the Supreme Being appeared to take on substance within their presence, and the transitional, hyperbolic illumination of the Supreme Being was in evidence even to the furthest
viable parameters, and the agricultural technicians responded with an emotion that was
almost involuntary and marked by several physical reactions prompted by an increased
flow of catecholamines, chemicals in the blood that include adrenalin or epinephrine and
which stimulate the sympathetic nervous system. Those fellows were sore afraid.

But the chief agent of the Supreme Being gave them a realistic, harmonious concept.   8
He advised them not to succumb to a primitive, violent, and usually crippling emotion,
marked by extensive bodily changes. He undertook to transmit to them, via a functional
communications policy, positive data of significant gratification, which would benefit the
aggregate of personages.

The data concerned the birth, in the urban conglomerate of David, of a Savior, whose   9
social security number was not yet recorded but whose identity had already been substantially confirmed as that of "Christ the Lord." The chief agent apprised the agricultural
technicians that — within an integrated, organizational time-phase and if they watched out

for the right signals and the bottom line — they would, in all probability, find the Savior lying in a supine position within a trough-like receptacle from which, in the normal course of events, large, domesticated, herbivorous animals consumed fodder.

10    At that particular point in time, a numerous representation of lesser agents joined the chief agent, emitting compliments of the Supreme Being, expressing in a choral mode their assertion of His transitional, hyperbolic illumination at the utmost altitude, and in addition advocating terrestrial conditions of a pacific nature, and optimal, positive feelings toward the human male population of the fifth largest planet in the solar system.

11    It subsequently occurred that the agents utilized their volitational skills to convey themselves in functional, airborne equilibrium up to an unlocationalized area that, according to qualified sources grants eternal life in a trouble-free environment to some of those who suffer negative patient outcome at earthbound treatment centres.

12    The agricultural technicians were left to compare their integrated, incremental capability with their balanced, monitored flexibility. Their decision was a matter of diverse, interpersonal awareness leading to profound, societal oneness. They did the right thing . . .

13    Now that I've explained the plot in language we all understand, allow me to revert, for old time's sake, to the stilted, archaic lingo of the King James Bible:

14    "And they came with haste, and found Mary, and Joseph, and the babe lying in a manger.

15    "And when they had seen it, they made known abroad the saying which was told them concerning this child . . ."

16    And, clearly, the trouble with the fellows who strung such stuff together for James I was that they just didn't know any big words.

## VOCABULARY

a. *paragraph   2:* incremental, parameters, perambulatory, synchronized, megalopolis

b. *paragraph   3:* matrix, sociometric

c. *paragraph   5:* swaddling, supine, modules

d. *paragraph   6:* ruminant

e. *paragraph   7:* viable, catecholamines, epinephrine

f. *paragraph   8:* succumb, functional, gratification, aggregate

g. *paragraph   9:* conglomerate, herbivorous

h. *paragraph 10:* hyperbolic, terrestrial

i. *paragraph 11:* volitational, unlocationalized

## QUESTIONS

1. The bureaucratic language Bruce parodies reflects bureaucratic ideas. Here is one example: ". . . there was distributed a systematized, incremental projection in memorandum form from Caesar Augustus that the entirety of personnel with globular para-

meters should be subject to revenue enhancement." What current attitude toward language is Bruce satirizing? How does the language he uses help him to satirize the idea?

2. The author of this Christmas story prefers the far-fetched to the simple, as in the expression "utilized their volitational skills." What other examples can you cite of euphemism, circumlocution, and other faults of diction?

3. What examples of repetitious phrasing and sentence padding do you find?

4. What kind of specialist jargon is Bruce satirizing toward the end of his version?

5. What other ideas is Bruce satirizing in the course of his telling of the story?

## WRITING ASSIGNMENT

Rewrite another well-known story in the modish language of advertising or other contemporary jargons and styles. Let your choice of jargon and style make a point — or several points — as Bruce's retelling of Christ's Nativity does.

## BOB BLACKBURN

Bob Blackburn *wrote a regular column on language for the review journal* Books In Canada. *A vigilant defender of good English, Blackburn is as entertaining as he is instructive, a claim which is nicely illustrated by the following essay on computerese.*

## FLUDGED AGAIN

Five years ago this month, I broke my oath never to use *access* as a verb. I bought a computer. Almost overnight, I stopped making derisive references to *computer jargon* and began respectfully calling it *terminology*, which, of course, is what it is. Jargon is what *others* speak.

Computer terminology is also called *computerese*, particularly by those who don't speak it, and that term will serve us here. Whatever you call it, it is a young and imperfect language. This is not surprising, considering that the generation that is developing it is also hell-bent on destroying English. Computer enthusiasts will tell you, rightly, that they must use computerese in order to understand one another. In view of this, it seems odd that many of them show no sign of having the same feeling about English. Few of them worry about whether *presently* means now or means soon. Few care that there is a distinction between *incredible* and *incredulous*. It is inevitable that a technical vocabulary created by people with no regard for precise diction in their use of the mother tongue will be a mess.

The computerese verb *access* is one of the least offensive neologisms. It simply means to gain access to. A computer user might ask you if he may access your bathroom (you should refuse), but he is unlikely to. When he is using his computer, however, he does so damn much *accessing* that a short verb is essential. *Access* serves the purpose well, and such use is harmless if it is not permitted to escape to the outside world.

Not so pardonable is the computerese corruption of *clone*. I have what is commonly (and unfortunately) called an IBM clone. This is a misnomer. In English, a clone is an organism that is genetically identical to its forebear, and the word is not a good choice to describe an imitation. Before *clone* gained currency in computerese, some manufacturers

1

2

3

4

used *workalike* for this purpose. That made more sense, but I suppose three syllables was a bit much for some people.

5    My new printer, the manual tells me, *emulates* two standard makes of printer. It may, indeed, do so, since *emulate* means rival, but for years writers of computerese have been misusing *emulate* to mean *simulate*, and I am certain the writer of this manual meant *simulate*.

6    One of the main *action* keys on a computer keyboard is labelled either ENTER or RETURN. What it does is *enter* what you've just typed into the innards of the beast. It doesn't *return* anything. Somewhere along the way, some bigbrain had the idea that, because in some circumstances the ENTER key does something that resembles the function performed by the carriage return key on an electric typewriter, people new to computers would find the keyboard friendlier if the key were labelled RETURN. Millions of computers, including the Apple, included that aberration, and the resultant confusion during conversations between users of different brands was terrible to behold. It almost destroyed one of my oldest friendships.

7    Computerese is as much abused as is English. Many, perhaps most, who try to speak it fail to grasp the distinction between *bug* and *glitch*, or between *upload* and *download*. Like English, it is graced by vigorous slang. I love *farkled* and *fludged* and *munged*.

8    I am not fluent in computerese. I came to it late in life, and am still too preoccupied with my effort to learn English (something I have been trying to do for more than 60 years) to do well with a second language, but I have observed that the people who speak it well are those who speak English well. The personal computer is only a decade old, and the lingo it spawned has made only minor inroads in English, but this will change. What it has done so far is surely less frightening than the fact that we now have a suffix — *gate* — that means scandal. Computerese, which is being created by people whose lack of regard for English is exceeded only by their ignorance of it, has, so far, done nothing as bloody awful as that to us, but it will, it will.

9    Now, if you will excuse me, I shall do what I usually do on completing a column: I shall go to the kitchen and access a cold beer.

## VOCABULARY

a. *paragraph 1:* derisive

b. *paragraph 2:* incredible, incredulous

c. *paragraph 3:* neologisms

d. *paragraph 5:* simulate

e. *paragraph 6:* aberration

f. *paragraph 7:* bug, glitch, upload, download, farkled, fludged, munged

## QUESTIONS

1. In what paragraph does Blackburn state his thesis? How does he develop it?

2. Do the examples in paragraphs 3 through 6 prove his main point?

3. How does paragraph 8 shift the argument? How plausible is the claim made in its last sentence?

4. What is the tone of the essay? Is Blackburn amused as well as irritated by computers?

## WRITING ASSIGNMENTS

1. Analyse three paragraphs from a current textbook in one of your courses to determine how much needless jargon is employed.

2. Analyse a published speech of a major political figure. How much jargon does he or she use? How much of it is avoidable?

# WRITERS ON WRITING

There is no single way to begin an essay. We each write for different reasons and for different audiences, and we each find our inspiration and our ideas and details in various ways. Nor is the act of writing always the same even for individual writers, as Jane Rule's and Mordecai Richler's essays on writing suggest. Richler made repeated false starts over a number of years on his best novel, *St. Urbain's Horsemen,* and he revises all his novels extensively in successive drafts. Rule discusses the patience required for learning the craft of writing, and explores questions of subject matter and aesthetic distance as well.

In his essay on simplicity, William Zinsser describes what happens in the course of writing and afterwards, as we rethink and revise initial drafts. Zinsser gives the same advice that Northrop Frye gives in his essay "Elementary Teaching." In his discussion of how to avoid ready-made words and phrases, Frye deplores the helpless banality of a speech by an authority at an educational conference, and suggests that the man writes badly because "he has never been trained to think rhetorically, to visualize his abstractions, . . . to realize that figures of speech are not the ornaments of language, but the elements of both language and thought." Zinsser shows how to deal with this problem of ready-made words and ideas. "The secret of good writing is to strip every sentence to its cleanest components," he states, and he illustrates how to do so.

These three essays by no means suggest all the ways writers proceed. They agree, however, on one point — that the act of writing is not aimless. Writers give attention to what they have written — to its clarity and effectiveness — at some stage in the act of writing and sometimes at all stages.

## WILLIAM ZINSSER

William Zinsser *has had a long and varied career as a journalist, critic, columnist, and teacher of writing. His numerous essays are collected in* The Lunacy Boom *(1970) and other books. In this essay from his book* On Writing Well *(1976), Zinsser discusses the clutter that infects so much American writing today, and he emphasizes the importance of revision and editing in the act of writing. In the sample extract that concludes the essay, Zinsser gives an example of his own revising and editing.*

## SIMPLICITY

1    Clutter is the disease of American writing. We are a society strangling in unnecessary words, circular constructions, pompous frills and meaningless jargon.

2    Who can understand the viscous language of everyday American commerce and enterprise: the business letter, the inter-office memo, the corporation report, the notice from the bank explaining its latest "simplified" statement? What member of an insurance or medical plan can decipher the brochure that tells him what his costs and benefits are? What father or mother can put together a child's toy — on Christmas eve or any other eve — from the instructions on the box? Our national tendency is to inflate and thereby sound important. The airline pilot who wakes us to announce that he is presently anticipating experiencing considerable weather wouldn't dream of saying that there's a storm ahead and it may get bumpy. The sentence is too simple — there must be something wrong with it.

But the secret of good writing is to strip every sentence to its cleanest components. **3** Every word that serves no function, every long word that could be a short word, every adverb which carries the same meaning that is already in the verb, every passive construction that leaves the reader unsure of who is doing what — these are the thousand and one adulterants that weaken the strength of a sentence. And they usually occur, ironically, in proportion to education and rank.

During the late 1960s the president of a major university wrote a letter to mollify the **4** alumni after a spell of campus unrest. "You are probably aware," he began, "that we have been experiencing very considerable potentially explosive expressions of dissatisfaction on issues only partially related." He meant that the students had been hassling them about different things. I was far more upset by the president's English than by the student's potentially explosive expressions of dissatisfaction. I would have preferred the presidential approach taken by Franklin D. Roosevelt when he tried to convert into English his own government's memos, such as this blackout order of 1942:

> Such preparations shall be made as will completely obscure all Federal buildings and non-Federal buildings occupied by the Federal government during an air raid for any period of time from visibility by reason of internal or external illumination.

"Tell them," Roosevelt said, "that in buildings where they have to keep the work going **5** to put something across the windows."

Simplify, simplify. Thoreau said it, as we are so often reminded, and no American **6** writer more consistently practiced what he preached. Open *Walden* to any page and you will find a man saying in a plain and orderly way what is on his mind.

> I love to be alone. I never found the companion that was so companionable as solitude. We are for the most part more lonely when we go abroad among men than when we stay in our chambers. A man thinking or working is always alone, let him be where he will. Solitude is not measured by the miles of space that intervene between a man and his fellows. The really diligent student in one of the crowded hives of Cambridge College is as solitary as a dervish in the desert.

How can the rest of us achieve such enviable freedom from clutter? The answer is to **7** clear our heads of clutter. Clear thinking becomes clear writing: one can't exist without the other. It is impossible for a muddy thinker to write good English. He may get away with it for a paragraph or two, but soon the reader will be lost, and there is no sin so grave, for he will not easily be lured back.

Who is this elusive creature the reader? He is a person with an attention span of about **8** twenty seconds. He is assailed on every side by forces competing for his time: by newspapers and magazines, by television and radio and stereo, by his wife and children and pets, by his house and his yard and all the gadgets that he has bought to keep them spruce, and by that most potent of competitors, sleep. The man snoozing in his chair with an unfinished magazine open on his lap is a man who was being given too much unnecessary trouble by the writer.

It won't do to say that the snoozing reader is too dumb or too lazy to keep pace with the **9** train of thought. My sympathies are with him. If the reader is lost, it is generally because the writer has not been careful enough to keep him on the path.

This carelessness can take any number of forms. Perhaps a sentence is so excessively **10** cluttered that the reader, hacking his way through the verbiage, simply doesn't know what it means. Perhaps a sentence has been so shoddily constructed that the reader could read it in any of several ways. Perhaps the writer has switched pronouns in mid-sentence, or has switched tenses, so the reader loses track of who is talking or when the action took place. Perhaps Sentence B is not a logical sequel to Sentence A — the writer, in whose head the connection is clear, has not bothered to provide the missing link. Perhaps the writer has used an important word incorrectly by not taking the trouble to look it up. He may think that "sanguine" and "sanguinary" mean the same thing, but the difference is a bloody big one. The reader can only infer (speaking of big differences) what the writer is trying to imply.

11    Faced with these obstacles, the reader is at first a remarkably tenacious bird. He blames himself — he obviously missed something, and he goes back over the mystifying sentence, or over the whole paragraph, piecing it out like an ancient rune, making guesses and moving on. But he won't do this for long. The writer is making him work too hard, and the reader will look for one who is better at his craft.

12    The writer must therefore constantly ask himself: What am I trying to say? Surprisingly often, he doesn't know. Then he must look at what he has written and ask: Have I said it? Is it clear to someone encountering the subject for the first time? If it's not, it is because some fuzz has worked its way into the machinery. The clear writer is a person clear-headed enough to see this stuff for what it is: fuzz.

13    I don't mean that some people are born clear-headed and are therefore natural writers, whereas others are naturally fuzzy and will never write well. Thinking clearly is a conscious act that the writer must force upon himself, just as if he were embarking on any other project that requires logic: adding up a laundry list or doing an algebra problem. Good writing doesn't come naturally, though most people obviously think it does. The professional writer is forever being bearded by strangers who say that they'd like to "try a little writing sometime" when they retire from their real profession. Good writing takes self-discipline and, very often, self-knowledge.

14    Many writers, for instance, can't stand to throw anything away. Their sentences are littered with words that mean essentially the same thing and with phrases which make a point that is implicit in what they have already said. When students give me these littered sentences I beg them to select from the surfeit of words the few that most precisely fit what they want to say. Choose one, I plead, from among the three almost identical adjectives. Get rid of the unnecessary adverbs. Eliminate "in a funny sort of way" and other such qualifiers — they do no useful work.

15    The students look stricken — I am taking all their wonderful words away. I am only taking their superfluous words away, leaving what is organic and strong.

16    "But," one of my worst offenders confessed, "I never can get rid of anything — you should see my room." (I didn't take him up on the offer.) "I have two lamps where I only need one, but I can't decide which one I like better, so I keep them both." He went on to enumerate his duplicated or unnecessary objects, and over the weeks ahead I went on throwing away his duplicated and unnecessary words. By the end of the term — a term that he found acutely painful — his sentences were clean.

17    "I've had to change my whole approach to writing," he told me. "Now I have to *think* before I start every sentence and I have to *think* about every word." The very idea amazed him. Whether his room also looked better I never found out.

18    Writing is hard work. A clear sentence is no accident. Very few sentences come out right the first time, or the third. Keep thinking and rewriting until you say what you want to say.

5 --

is too dumb or too lazy to keep pace with the ~~writer's~~ train of thought. My sympathies are ~~entirely~~ with him. ~~He's not so dumb.~~ If the reader is lost, it is generally because the writer ~~of the article~~ has not been careful enough to keep him on the ~~proper~~ path.

This carelessness can take any number of ~~different~~ forms. Perhaps a sentence is so excessively ~~long and~~ cluttered that the reader, hacking his way through ~~all~~ the verbiage, simply doesn't know what _it_ ~~the writer~~ means. Perhaps a sentence has been so shoddily constructed that the reader could read it in any of _several_ ~~two or three different~~ ways. ~~He thinks he knows what the writer is trying to say, but he's not sure.~~ Perhaps the writer has switched pronouns in mid-sentence, or ~~perhaps he~~ has switched tenses, so the reader loses track of who is talking ~~to whom~~ or ~~exactly~~ when the action took place. Perhaps $\underline{\text{Sentence}}$ $\underline{\underline{B}}$ is not a logical sequel to $\underline{\text{Sentence}}$ $\underline{\underline{A}}$ -- the writer, in whose head the connection is ~~perfectly~~ clear, has not _bothered to provide_ ~~given enough thought to providing~~ the missing link. Perhaps the writer has used an important word incorrectly by not taking the trouble to look it up, ~~and make sure.~~ He may think that "sanguine" and "sanguinary" mean the same thing, but ~~I can assure you that~~ the difference is a bloody big one, ~~to the reader.~~ _The reader_ ~~He~~ can only ~~try to~~ infer ~~when~~ (speaking of big differences) what the writer is trying to imply.

Faced with _these_ ~~such a variety of~~ obstacles, the reader is at first a remarkably tenacious bird. He ~~tends to~~ blame ^s himself. ~~H~~e obviously missed something, ~~he thinks,~~ and he goes

6 --)

back over the mystifying sentence, or over the whole paragraph,

piecing it out like an ancient rune, making guesses and moving

on. But he won't do this for long.) ~~He will soon run out of~~

~~patience.~~ (The writer is making him work too hard,) ~~harder~~

~~than he should have to work~~ -- (and the reader will look for

~~a writer~~ one who is better at his craft.

The writer must therefore constantly ask himself: What am

I trying to say? ~~in this sentence?~~ (Surprisingly often, he

doesn't know.) ~~And~~ Then he must look at what he has ~~just~~

written and ask: Have I said it? Is it clear to someone

encountering ~~who is coming upon~~ the subject for the first time? If it's

not, ~~clear,~~ it is because some fuzz has worked its way into the

machinery. The clear writer is a person ~~who is~~ clear-headed

enough to see this stuff for what it is: fuzz.

I don't mean ~~to suggest~~ that some people are born

clear-headed and are therefore natural writers, whereas

others ~~other people~~ are naturally fuzzy and will ~~therefore~~ never write

well. Thinking clearly is a ~~an entirely~~ conscious act that the

writer must force ~~keep forcing~~ upon himself, just as if he were

embarking ~~starting out~~ on any other ~~kind of~~ project that requires ~~calls for~~ logic:

adding up a laundry list or doing an algebra problem ~~or playing~~

~~chess.~~ Good writing doesn't ~~just~~ come naturally, though most

people obviously think it does. ~~it's as easy as walking.~~ The professional

Two pages of the final manuscript of this chapter. Although they look like a first draft, they had already been rewritten and retyped — like almost every other page — four or five times. With each rewrite I try to make what I have written tighter, stronger and more precise, eliminating every element that is not doing useful work, until at last I have a clean copy for the printer. Then I go over it once more, reading it aloud, and am always amazed at how much clutter can still be profitably cut.

# JANE RULE

Jane Rule *was born in New Jersey in 1931 and educated at Mills College, California, and University College, London, England. She moved to Vancouver in 1956 and lectured intermittently in English and Creative Writing at the University of British Columbia from 1958 to 1976. Her novels of social realism explore such themes as lesbianism, the relationship of art and the artist to society, and the materialism of contemporary society.*

## THE PRACTICE OF WRITING

Those questions about creative process which deal with the mechanics of writing have always bored me. Whether I use a pencil, pen, or typewriter is not determined by what is objectively effective but by left-handedness, a bad back, lack of funds, and anyway, who really cares? A far more interesting mechanical question than how each of us gets words onto the page might be why so many writers refuse to drive cars, but that investigation would lead away from the point, which is what aspects of the creative process might be usefully shared with other people. 1

Two of the most important problems for any writer are locating material and conceiving form. As a very young writer my passion for form served my need to learn the rudiments of my craft and also distracted me from what I felt — wrongly it now seems to me — was my lack of experience. What I really lacked was simply enough distance from my experience to know how to use it. Instead I invented material of a sort that can still make me blush. I wrote about ironically wise talking Minah birds who broke up marriages, black men with yellow hair and green eyes who raped sheep. (After that particular story was read aloud to a writing class, my fellow students burst into "We are little black sheep who have gone astray" every time they saw me.) The only way I can explain those choices is to suppose I was grafting my new sexual edginess onto such reading as *Lassie, Come Home* and *Black Beauty*. At sixteen I simply had no taste. But my appetite for every literary device, every theory of language was enormous. Questions about point of view, symbolism and time occupied me at my desk and away from it. The more complex the form of anything, the more I admired it whether in my own work or in Faulkner's, Joyce's or Virginia Woolf's. In fact, philosophy and aesthetics were more interesting than fiction because principles could be isolated, the human clutter evident in even the purest fiction done away with. There are very young writers who come to their own material guilelessly and learn their craft by simply serving more and more accurately what they have to say. Many more of us, influenced by the academy or not, practice ablative absolutes, archaic synonyms, periodic sentences, points of view entirely beyond us, symbolic structures to rival Dante before we make any attempt to come to terms with what is ours to say. In what can sometimes seem a discouragingly pretentious process, technique is learned. 2

Writing is, more than is often acknowledged, a craft that has to be practiced, like tennis or the flute. Just as an athlete or musician works long hours in solitary repetition of the hardest techniques of the craft before performing them in game or concert, so a writer needs to concentrate, particularly at first, on what is most difficult. The skill is so complex that a great many of its requirements must become, through dogged repetition, nearly automatic. Otherwise writing a novel would be impossible. In much the same way that any speaker of the language knows how to make subject and verb agree without thinking about it, a writer must develop higher and higher automatic skills so that a choice of sentence structure is rarely mistaken even the first time, so that the dozens of minor technical choices involved in each scene can be made almost without thought. The questions for the 3 beginning writer are often ones too mundane for any teacher of literature ever to raise: how do I stop my characters talking and get into the narrative voice again? How do I get through three months in a paragraph? How do I find words for a sexual experience which will illuminate rather than offend? How do I stop this skateboard of a story going down hill except by crashing into a light pole? These are questions answered not by fine theories but by practice, by being there over and over again until the solution occurs as simply as the familiar way home.

4      Because we all use language every day, there is an illusion that anyone with adequate intelligence and something to say ought to be able to sit down and write a book about it. But speakers of the language do not practice language as a writer must in order to be prepared to solve the problems that arise. That is why even a second-rate writer can, disappointingly, write a more engaging book than someone with a great deal more to say. That is also why a writer deprived of time to practice the craft continually will rarely emerge as a major voice late in life. We are not as bound to childhood opportunity as ballet dancers, nor as limited by our bodies as any of the performing artists, but we still share with all of them the need to be *practicing* artists. The creative process in any art takes time.

5      Time is, however, not enough. No matter how many hours of the day, years of a life, one practices language, there is still the question of what to write about. Though books can be a source of all kinds of technical help, they are rarely a place for discovering subject matter or insight. Those who find their subject matter early are usually autobiographical writers. Both the inventors of fantasy and the realists for whom social, political and moral questions are paramount may take longer. Whatever the choice, a certain detachment, aesthetic distance is necessary. Without it, the courage and ruthlessness of the autobiographical writer can become nothing more than vengeful self-indulgence. The clever inventions of fantasy must serve a deeper insight or be found empty tricks. The social realist can turn shallow propogandist. No matter is safe from mean use. None is beneath wonder. All choices are personal and justified only after they have been proven.

6      As a writer, I have discovered my subject matter in the world we share in common, that is, what we all may experience as distinct from what I experience either in my unique life (autobiography) or my unique imagination (fantasy), though there are certainly elements of both in my work. When I present a character, I neither take a real person I know nor invent a being out of an ideal concept; rather I take half a dozen people I've known who similarly have faced circumstances I want to write about — the loss of a parent, rivalry among siblings, political defeat — and draw even more widely than that on physical attributes, inheritance, social circumstances to make up the character I need for the experience I have designed. If that character slips easily into the slot I have made, I am suspicious, wonder if I have been superficial or glib. A character should, like a real human being, resist categorizing, resist simple-minded solutions. The characters I trust I have usually the hardest time with, for they are often conceived in enough complexity to foil my less interesting plots. I have fairly often written about characters I don't much like but never about characters I don't care about. A subjective quirk of mine is to give each of my characters something of my own. It may be a habit or fear, a cough or a favorite word, an old jacket or a childhood landscape. Whatever it is, however small, it is a kind of talisman against any petty or vindictive treatment. I don't like killing characters even when the structure of a story obviously requires it. I refuse to belittle them.

7      A circumstance and its resolution are harder for me to come upon than characters to inhabit the experience. Plot often seems to me over-judgmental. It caters to the righteous indignation in us to see characters punished by fate if not by law. I am more interested in insight than in judgment; therefore, I tend to work on circumstances with modest resolutions, which must not be as morally or psychologically simple as they might seem at first

glance. I write a fiction of reversed or at least reserved judgment. More and more I have found myself working with novels because I am interested in writing about groups of people and need that much room. The long tradition of fiction with a central character around whom all others must find their secondary place supports hierarchies I don't find interesting, promotes an egotism that is positively boring. Though it is a common enough fantasy, it is simply not true that any one of us is center of the world. Why should novels perpetuate a false view? In choosing the world we share as my subject matter, my authenticity is more exposed and my compassion more required than either would be in autobiography or fantasy. Those are safeguards important to me as a writer.

Where I live seems to me a question like how I get words on paper, not really relevant    **8**
to the question of creative process. We live as we can, hoping for that balance of nourishment and peace which will sustain us in our work. I live where I can be sure I am free to practice writing rather than being a writer.

## MORDECAI RICHLER

*The following brief account of why a writer works at his craft tells us much about what motivates Canada's finest comic novelist.* Mordecai Richler *engagingly discusses what compels him to put pen to paper, ingenuously revealing a range of reasons both intellectual and emotional.*

## WHY I WRITE

Why do you write?    **1**

Doctors are seldom asked why they practise, shoemakers how come they cobble, or    **2**
baseball players why they don't drive a coal truck instead, but again and again writers, like housebreakers, are asked why they do it.

Orwell, as might be expected, supplies the most honest answer in his essay, "Why    **3**
I Write."

"1. Sheer egoism. Desire to seem clever, to be talked about, to be remembered after    **4**
death, to get your own back on grownups who snubbed you in childhood, etc. etc." To this I would add egoism informed by imagination, style, and a desire to be known, yes, *but only on your own conditions.*

Nobody is more embittered than the neglected writer and, obviously, allowed a certain    **5**
recognition, I am a happier and more generous man than I would otherwise be. But nothing I have done to win this recognition appals me, has gone against my nature. I fervently believe that all a writer should send into the marketplace to be judged is his own work; the rest should remain private. I deplore the writer as a personality, however large and undoubted the talent, as is the case with Norman Mailer. I also do not believe in special licence for so-called artistic temperament. After all, my problems, as I grudgingly come within spitting distance of middle age, are the same as anybody else's. Easier maybe. I can bend my anxieties to subversive uses. Making stories of them. When I'm not writing, I'm a husband and a father of five. Worried about pollution. The population explosion. My sons' report cards.

"2. Aesthetic enthusiasm. Perception of beauty in the external world, or, on the other    **6**
hand, in words and their right arrangement." The agonies involved in creating a novel, the unsatisfying draft, the scenes you never get right, are redeemed by those rare and memorable days when, seemingly without reason, everything falls right. Bonus days. Blessed

days when, drawing on resources unsuspected, you pluck ideas and prose out of your skull that you never dreamt yourself capable of.

7    Such, such are the real joys.

8    Unfortunately, I don't feel that I've ever been able to sustain such flights for a novel's length. So the passages that flow are balanced with those which were forced in the hothouse. Of all the novels I've written, it is *The Apprenticeship of Duddy Kravitz* and *Cocksure* which come closest to my intentions and, therefore, give me the most pleasure. I should add that I'm still lumbered with the characters and ideas, the social concerns I first attempted in *The Acrobats*. Every serious writer has, I think, one theme, many variations to play on it.

9    Like any serious writer, I want to write one novel that will last, something that will make me remembered after death, and so I'm compelled to keep trying.

10   "3. Historical impulse. Desire to see things as they are. . . ."

11   No matter how long I continue to live abroad, I do feel forever rooted in Montreal's St. Urbain Street. That was my time, my place, and I have elected myself to get it right.

12   "4. Political purpose — using the word 'political' in the widest possible sense. Desire to push the world in a certain direction, to alter other people's idea of the kind of society that they should strive after."

13   Not an overlarge consideration in my work, though I would say that any serious writer is a moralist and only incidentally an entertainer.

# Writing Effective Sentences

This part of the section on style will show you how to make your sentences more effective as you draft and revise your paragraphs and essays. Unity and proper emphasis are just as important in sentences as they are in paragraphs. In fact, sentences can be loosely viewed as miniature paragraphs. For example, in the same way that the topic sentence of a paragraph states the core idea that the remainder of the paragraph develops, the main clause of a simple or complex sentence states the core idea that the rest of the sentence develops through its modifiers:

> *I heard* instead the shriek of brakes, the heavy throbbing of the once-a-day Braniff airliner into Minot, the shattering sirens born of war, the honk of a diesel locomotive which surely cannot call to faraway places the heart of a wakeful boy like the old steam whistle in the night. — Eric Sevareid, "Velva, North Dakota" [italics added]

The core subject and verb of this complex sentence (*I heard*) is completed by a series of modified objects — the final object further modified by a lengthy subordinate clause beginning with the word *which*.

Just as a series of main ideas combine in a single paragraph, so can simple and compound sentences join to form larger, single sentences:

> You can walk down the streets of my town now and hear from open windows the intimate voices of the Washington commentators in casual converse on the great affairs of state [*simple sentence: main clause with compound predicate*]; but you cannot hear on Sunday morning the singing in Norwegian of the Lutheran hymns [*simple sentence: main clause with simple predicate*]; the old country seems now part of a world left long behind and the old-country accents grow fainter in the speech of my Velva neighbors [*compound sentence: two main clauses with simple predicates*]. — Sevareid, "Velva, North Dakota" [italics added]

And so can main and subordinate ideas, expressed in main and subordinate clauses and their modifiers, combine to form larger sentences:

> Attic and screen porch are slowly vanishing [*main clause*] and lovely shades of pastel are painted upon new homes [*main clause*], tints that once would have embarrassed farmer and merchant alike [*subordinate clause modifying the appositive "tints"*]. — Sevareid, "Velva, North Dakota" [italics added]

Though the parallel between paragraphs and sentences suggested here is not exact (main clauses do not always contain the most important idea of a sentence), it does suggest that, like paragraphs, sentences build from cores to which subordinate ideas and details must relate. And sentences, like paragraphs, also can contain two or more core ideas.

We write as we speak — stressing the core idea of a simple sentence and joining several core ideas into compound ones. We also place modifying words, phrases, and clauses in different positions in writing, as in speech, to gain different kinds of emphasis. In addition, we frequently make special use of the beginning and ending of a simple sentence for emphasis. We can, however, achieve emphasis in other ways. The following sections illustrate these possibilities.

# Addition and Modification

As a paragraph usually begins with a topic sentence that states the subject or central idea, so a sentence may begin with a main clause that performs a similar job. Here is a sentence from Northrop Frye's account of how students learn:

> *I am certainly no expert on the teaching of children.*
>> *but it* seems obvious
>>> *that all* such teaching has to follow the child's own rhythm of thought and development,
>>> *and not* project on him some half-baked adult mystique,
>>> *whether that* mystique claims to derive from the anti-intellectual left or the anti-intellectual right. — Northrop Frye, "Elementary Teaching" [italics added]

The three subordinate clauses — beginning *that all, and not, whether that* — qualify the idea expressed in the first main clause: they tell us Frye's "non-expert" views on elementary teaching. Notice that these clauses are each as long as the main clause. Notice, too, that the third clause modifies an element in the second. English sentences can be modified endlessly. They are not, however, because the reader would soon lose sight of the central idea. The length of a sentence often depends on how many ideas and details a reader can grasp.

# Emphasis

In speaking, we vary our sentences without much, if any, thought, interrupting the flow of ideas to emphasize a word or phrase, or to repeat an idea. The speaker of the following sentence, a witness before a royal commission, repeats certain phrases and qualifies his ideas in a typical way:

> My experience is that we hold people sometimes in jail, young people in jail, for days at a time with a complete lack of concern of the parents, if they do live in homes where parents live together, a complete lack of concern in many instances on the part of the community or other agencies as to where these young people are or what they are doing.

Sentences as complex and disjointed as this one seems when transcribed are understood easily when spoken because the speaker is able to vary the vocal inflection to stress key words and phrases. Written punctuation sometimes clarifies the points of emphasis, but in a limited way. Because we cannot depend directly on vocal inflection for clarity and emphasis in writing, we instead suggest these inflections by shaping the sentence in accord with ordinary speech patterns. Clearly written sentences stay close to these patterns.

The core of English sentences, we saw, can be expanded, and at length, if each modifier is clearly connected to what precedes it. To achieve special emphasis the writer may vary the sentence even more, perhaps by making special use of the end of the sentence — the position that in Engish tends to be the most emphatic:

> The cold passed reluctantly from the earth, and the retiring fogs revealed an army stretched out on the hills, *resting*. — Stephen Crane, *The Red Badge of Courage* [italics added]

Or the writer may break up the sentence so that individual ideas and experiences receive separate emphasis:

> The youth stopped. He was transfixed by this terrific medley of all noises. It was as if worlds were being rended. There was the ripping sound of musketry and the breaking crash of the artillery. — Crane, *The Red Badge of Courage*

The relation of subordinate clauses to other elements in a sentence is controlled largely by the requirements of English word order. The position of subordinate clauses that serve as nouns or adjectives (sometimes called noun clauses and adjective clauses) is rather fixed; the position of subordinate clauses that serve as adverbs (sometimes called adverb clauses) is not. The position of the adverb clause depends on its importance as an idea and on its length:

> I majored in zoology *because I like working with animals*.
> *Because I like working with animals*, I majored in zoology.

The position of the subordinate clause determines what information is stressed. In the first sentence, the subordinate clause seems to express the more important idea because it follows the main clause. In the second sentence, the main clause receives the emphasis. But the end of the sentence will not take the thrust of meaning if ideas appearing toward the beginning are given special emphasis.

Our informal spoken sentences show the least variation and depend heavily on coordination. The *stringy sentence* in writing — a series of ideas joined loosely with *and* and other conjunctions — is a heavily coordinated sentence without the usual vocal markers. The sentence *fragment* — a detached phrase or clause, or a sentence missing either a subject or a verb — sometimes derives from the clipped sentences and phrases common in speech.

# LOOSE AND PERIODIC SENTENCES

Sentences are sometimes classified as loose or periodic to distinguish two important kinds of emphasis: the use made of the beginning or the end of the sentence. The loose sentence begins with the core idea, explanatory and qualifying phrases and clauses trailing behind:

> It was not a screeching noise, only an intermittent hump-hump as if the bird had to recall his grievance each time before he repeated it. — Flannery O'Connor, *The Violent Bear It Away*

If the ideas that follow the core are afterthoughts, or inessential details, the sentence will seem "loose" — easy and relaxed in its movement, a leisurely accretion of detail:

> It mingled with the smell of chalk dust and eraser crumbs, of crude ink splashed into inkwells by unsteady jug-bearers, of apples and pencil shavings and gum. — Fredelle Maynard, "The Windless World"

A subordinate element will not seem unemphatic or plodding, however, if it expresses a strong action or idea:

> The giggle rose to a laugh, then to a piercing *falsetto* peal. He began to dance about the lobby, skipping and cackling. — Cam Stirling, "The Fall, Rise, and Fall of Elevators"

Opening with subordinate elements or with a series of appositives, the periodic sentence ends with the core:

> If we had not felt that, after coming to this conclusion, we were bound to set aside our private opinions on matters of detail, if we had not felt ourselves bound to look at what was practicable, not obstinately rejecting the opinions of others nor adhering to our own; if we had not met, I say, in a spirit of conciliation, and with an anxious, overruling desire to form one people under one government, we never would have succeeded. — Sir John A. Macdonald, "Confederation"

The strongly periodic sentence is usually reserved for unusually strong emphasis:

> To believe your own thought, to believe that what is true for you in your private heart is true for all men — that is *genius*. — Ralph Waldo Emerson, "Self-Reliance"

Most contemporary English sentences fall between the extremely loose and the extremely periodic. Compound sentences seem loose when succeeding clauses serve as afterthoughts or qualifications rather than as ideas equal in importance to the opening idea:

> At that point, things got pretty hot and heavy — at least, I imagine they did. — Erika Ritter, "Mangiamania"

Periodic sentences are used sparingly, with a distribution of emphasis more often through the whole sentence, as in Macdonald's sentence above. Sometimes two moderately periodic sentences will be co-ordinated, with a corresponding distribution of emphasis:

> Though reliable narration is by no means the only way of conveying to the audience the facts on which dramatic irony is based, it is a useful way, and in some works, works in which no one but the author can conceivably know what needs to be known, it may be indispensable. — Wayne C. Booth, *The Rhetoric of Fiction*

# CLIMAX

Periodic sentences achieve climax by delaying the main idea or the completion of the main idea until the end of the sentence. Even in loose or co-ordinated sentences, modifying or qualifying phrases and classes following the main idea can be arranged in the order of rising importance — as in *I came, I saw, I conquered*. Here are sentences of Annie Dillard's that do the same:

> But shadows spread, and deepened, and stayed.

> I close my eyes and I see stars, deep stars giving way to deeper stars, deeper stars bowing to deepest stars at the crown of an infinite cone. — Annie Dillard, "At Tinker Creek"

A sense of anticipation, promoted through the ideas themselves, is necessary to climax. Anticlimax will result if the culminating idea is less significant than what has gone before. The resulting letdown may be deliberately comic:

> If once a man indulges himself in murder, very soon he comes to think little of robbery; and from robbing he next comes to drinking and Sabbath-breaking, and from that to incivility and procrastination. — Thomas De Quincey, *Supplementary Papers*

# PARALLELISM

The italicized words in the following sentence are parallel in structure; that is, they perform the same grammatical function in the sentence and, as infinitives, are the same in form:

> So long as I remain alive and well I shall continue *to feel* strongly about prose style, *to love* the surface of the earth, and *to take* a pleasure in solid objects and scraps of useless information. — George Orwell, *Why I Write* [italics added]

In speaking and writing, we make elements such as these infinitives parallel naturally. No matter how many words separate them, we continue the pattern we start. Indeed, our "sentence sense" tells us when a pattern has been interrupted. We know something is wrong when we read:

> I shall continue to feel strongly about prose style, to love the surface of the earth, and taking pleasure in solid objects and scraps of useless information. — Orwell, *Why I Write*

Parallelism is an important means to concision and focus in sentences. It also allows us to make additions to the sentence without loss of clarity. A special use of parallelism is the balancing of similar ideas in a sentence for special emphasis:

> The savage bows down to idols of wood and stone: the civilized man to idols of flesh and blood. — George Bernard Shaw, *Man and Superman.*

Notice that the parallel phrases here are of the same weight and length. Writers can balance clauses as Sir John A. Macdonald does in the following example from "Confederation":

> Ourselves already threatened, our trade interrupted, our intercourse, political and commercial, destroyed, if we do not take warning now when we have the opportunity, and while one avenue is threatened to be closed, open another by taking advantage of the present arrangement and the desire of the Lower Provinces to draw closer the alliance between us, we may suffer commercial and political disadvantages it may take long for us to overcome. — Macdonald, "Confederation"

The marked rhythm of this sentence creates a highly formal effect by slowing the tempo. Such exact balance interrupts the natural flow of the sentence, giving emphasis to most or all of its parts. For this reason it is exceptional to find sentences as studied and formal as this in modern writing. But we do find a moderate balance used to give a greater emphasis to similar ideas than ordinary parallelism provides.

# ANTITHESIS

When contrasting ideas are balanced in sentences and paragraphs, they are said to be in antithesis:

> History proves that dictatorships do not grow out of strong and successful governments, but out of weak and helpless ones. — Franklin D. Roosevelt

This moderate balancing to heighten the contrast of ideas is found often in modern writing, though usually in formal discussions. Like the exact balance of similar ideas, the balancing of sentences containing antithetical phrases is exceptional today. The following passage is the climax of a long book on the history of Roman society:

> Rome did not invent education, but she developed it on a scale unknown before, gave it state support, and formed the curriculum that persisted till our harassed youth. She did not invent the arch, the vault, or the dome, but she used them with such audacity and magnificence that in some fields her architecture has remained unequaled. — Will Durant, *Caesar and Christ*

# SENTENCE LENGTH

There is nothing inherently effective or ineffective, superior or inferior about short or long sentences, just as there is nothing inherently effective or ineffective in a single note of the scale. How effective a sentence is depends on what it does in a paragraph or essay. The very short, disconnected sentences in this passage by Guy Vanderhaeghe express the resignation that a man in his mid-thirties feels, having reconciled himself to a permanent estrangement from his wife:

> I'm tired. Waiting is tiring. And then because I don't want to see things I have to keep my eyes open. The rain makes this hard. It can lull you. I wonder how long it will keep up. It's a fine thing this smell of drenched, yielding earth. If I could only close my eyes without seeing things I could sleep. And if I could sleep I know I'd soon be as right as rain. Right, right as rain. — Guy Vanderhaeghe, *My Present Age*

A sentence, as we have seen, often starts with the main idea and develops it:

> The speech of a small child is full of chanting and singing, and it is clear that the child understands what many adults do not, that verse is a more direct and primitive way of conventionalizing speech than prose is. — Frye, "Elementary Teaching"

How much detail a writer can provide depends on how prominent the main ideas are — whether in a sentence consisting of a single core idea, followed by a series of modifiers, or in one consisting of a series of connected core ideas or main clauses, modified as in this sentence:

> At this moment, in consequence of the ill-feeling which has arisen between England and the United States — a feeling of which Canada was not the cause — in consequence of the irritation which now exists, owing to the unhappy state of affairs on this continent, the Reciprocity Treaty, it seems probable, is about to be brought to an end — our trade is hampered by the passport system, and at any moment we may be deprived of permission to carry our goods through United States channels — the bonded goods system may be done away with, and the winter trade through the United States put an end to. — Macdonald, "Confederation"

# GLOSSARY

**allusion:** An indirect reference to a presumably well-known literary work or a historical event or figure. The phrase "the Waterloo of his political career" is a reference to Napoleon's disastrous defeat at the Battle of Waterloo in 1815. The allusion implies that the career of the politician under discussion has come to a disastrous end.

**analogy:** A point-by-point comparison between two unlike things or activities (for example, comparing writing an essay to building a house) for the purpose of illustration or argument. Unlike a comparison (or contrast), in which the things compared are of equal importance, analogy exists for the purpose of illustrating or arguing the nature of one of the compared things, not both.

**antithesis:** The arrangement of contrasting ideas in grammatically similar phrases and clauses (*The world will little note, nor long remember, what we say here, but it can never forget what they did here.* — Lincoln, *Gettysburg Address*). See *parallelism*.

**argument:** Proving the truth or falseness of a statement. Arguments are traditionally classified as *inductive* or *deductive*. See *deductive argument* and *inductive argument*. Argument can be used for different purposes in writing. See *purpose*.

**autobiography:** Writing about one's own experiences, often those of growing up and making one's way in the world. The autobiographical writings of Stephen Leacock and Alice Munro describe their childhood experiences.

**balanced sentence:** A sentence containing parallel phrases and clauses of approximately the same length and wording (*You can fool all the people some of the time, and some of the people all of the time, but you cannot fool all the people all of the time.* — Lincoln).

**cause and effect:** Analysis of the conditions that must be present for an event to occur (*cause*) and of the results or consequences of the event (*effect*). An essay may deal with causes or with effects only.

**classification and division:** *Classification* arranges individual objects into groups or classes (GM cars, Chrysler cars, Ford cars). *Division* arranges a broad class into subclasses according to various principles (the broad class *GM cars* can be divided on the basis of their transmission or manufacturing unit).

**cliché:** A once-colourful expression made stale through overuse (*putting on the dog, mad as a wet hen*).

**coherence:** The sense, as we read, that the details and ideas of a work connect clearly. A paragraph or essay that does not hold together seems incoherent. Transitions are a means of coherence.

**colloquialism:** An everyday expression in speech and informal writing. Colloquialisms are not substandard or "illiterate" English. They are common in informal English and occur sometimes in formal English.

**comparison and contrast:** The analysis of similarities and differences between two or more persons, objects, or events (A and B) for the purpose of a relative estimate. The word *comparison* sometimes refers to the analysis of similarities and differences in both A and B. *Block comparison* presents each thing being compared as a whole (that is, if the comparison is between A and B, then features a, b, c of A are discussed as a block of information, then features a, b, c of B are compared to A in their own block of information). *Alternating comparison* presents the comparable features one by one (a, a, b, b, c, c).

**complex sentence:** A sentence consisting of one main or independent clause, and one or more subordinate or dependent clauses (*The rain began when she stepped outside*).

**compound sentence:** A sentence consisting of coordinated independent clauses (*She stepped outside and then the rain began*).

**compound-complex sentence:** A sentence consisting of two or more main or independent clauses and at least one subordinate or dependent clause (*She stepped outside as the rain began, but she did not return to the house*).

**concrete and abstract words:** Concrete words refer to particular objects, people, and events (Wayne Gretzky, the Olympics, the Rocky Mountains); abstract words refer to general shared qualities (cowardice, courage, beauty). Concrete writing makes abstract ideas perceptible to the senses through details and images.

**concreteness:** Making an idea exist through the senses. Writing can be concrete at all three levels — informal, general, and formal. See *concrete and abstract words*.

**connotation:** Feelings, images, and ideas associated with a word. Connotations change from reader to reader, though some words probably have the same associations for everybody.

**context:** The surrounding words or sentences that suggest the meaning of a word or phrase. Writers may dispense with formal definition if the context clarifies the meaning of a word.

**co-ordinate sentence:** A sentence that joins clauses of the same weight and importance through the conjunctions *and, but, for, or, nor,* or *yet,* or through conjunctive adverbs and adverbial phrases (*however, therefore, nevertheless, in fact*).

**deductive argument:** Reasoning from statements assumed to be true or well-established factually. These statements or assumptions are thought sufficient to guarantee the truth of the inferences or conclusions. In formal arguments they are called *premises*. A valid argument reasons correctly from the premises to the conclusion. A sound argument is true in its premises and valid in its reasoning. See *enthymeme, syllogism*.

**definition:** Explaining the current meaning of a word through its etymology or derivation, its denotation, or its connotations. Denotative or "real" definitions single out a word from all other words (or things) like it by giving *genus* and *specific difference*. Connotative definitions give the associations people make to the word. See *connotation*.

**description:** A picture in words of people, objects, and events. Description often combines with narration and it may serve exposition and persuasion.

**division:** See *classification and division*.

**enthymeme:** A deductive argument that does not state the conclusion or one of the premises directly. The following statement is an enthymeme: *Citizens in a democracy, who refuse to register for the draft, are not acting responsibly.* The implied premise is that the responsible citizen obeys all laws, even repugnant ones.

**essay:** A carefully organized composition that develops a single idea or impression or several related ideas or impressions. The word sometimes describes a beginning or trial attempt that explores the central idea or impression instead of developing it completely.

**example:** A picture or illustration of an idea, or one of many instances or occurrences that is typical of the rest.

**exposition:** An explanation or unfolding or setting forth of an idea, usually for the purpose of giving information. Exposition is usually an important part of persuasive writing. Example, process analysis, casual analysis, definition, classification and division, and comparison and contrast are forms of exposition.

**expressive writing:** Essays, diaries, journals, letters, and other kinds of writing that present personal feelings and beliefs for their own sake. The expressive writer is not primarily concerned with informing or persuading readers.

**figure of speech:** A word or phrase that departs from its usual meaning. Figures of speech make statements vivid and capture the attention of readers. The most common figures are based on similarity between things. See *metaphor, personification, simile.* Other figures are based on relationship. See *allusion. Metonymy* refers to a thing by one of its qualities (the sceptre for sovereignty). *Synecdoche* refers to a thing by one of its parts (*wheels* as a reference to racing cars). Other figures are based on contrast between statements and realities. See *irony.* Related to irony is *understatement,* or saying less than is appropriate (*Napoleon's career ended unhappily at Waterloo*). *Hyperbole* means deliberate exaggeration (*crazy about ice cream*). *Paradox* states an apparent contradiction (*All great truths begin as blasphemies* — G. B. Shaw). *Oxymoron,* a kind of paradox, joins opposite qualities into a single image (*lake of fire*).

**focus:** The limitation of subject in an essay. The focus can be broad, as in a panoramic view of the mountains, or it may be narrow, as in a view of a particular peak. For example, a writer may focus broadly on the contribution to scientific thought of scientists from various fields, or focus narrowly on the achievements of astronomers or chemists or medical researchers, or focus even more narrowly on the achievements of Albert Einstein as representative of twentieth-century science.

**formal English:** Spoken and written English, often abstract in content, with sentences tighter than spoken ones, and an abstract and sometimes technical vocabulary. See *general English* and *informal English.*

**general English:** A written standard that has features of informal and formal English. See *formal English* and *informal English.*

**image:** A picture in words of an object, a scene, or a person. Though visual images are common in writing, they are not the only kind. Images can also be auditory, tactile, gustatory, and olfactory. Keats's line *With beaded bubbles winking at the brim* appeals to our hearing and taste as well as to our sight. His phrase *coming musk-rose* appeals to our sense of smell. Images help to make feelings concrete.

**implied thesis:** The central idea of the essay, suggested by the details and discussion rather than stated directly. See *thesis.*

**inductive argument:** Inductive arguments reason from particulars of experience to general ideas — from observation, personal experience, and experimental testing to probable conclusions. Inductive arguments make predictions on the basis of past and present experience. An argumentative analogy is a form of inductive argument because it is based on limited observation and experience and therefore can claim probability only. Analysis of causes and effects is inductive when used in argument.

**"inductive leap":** Making the decision that sufficient inductive evidence (personal experience, observation, experimental testing) exists to draw a conclusion. Sometimes the writer of the argument makes the leap too quickly and bases his conclusions on insufficient evidence.

**informal English:** Written English, usually concrete in content, tighter than the loose sentences of spoken English, but looser in sentence construction than formal English. The word "informal" refers to the occasion of its use. A letter to a friend is usually informal; a letter of application is usually formal. See *formal English* and *general English.*

**irony:** A term generally descriptive of statements and events. An ironic statement says the opposite of what the speaker or writer means, or implies that something more is meant than is stated, or says the unexpected. (*He has a great future behind him*). An ironic event is unexpected or is so coincidental that it seems highly improbable (*The fireboat burned and sank*).

**jargon:** The technical words of a trade or profession (in computer jargon, the terms *input* and *word processor*). Unclear, clumsy, or repetitive words or phrasing, sometimes the result of misplaced technical words (*He gave his input into the decision process*).

**loose sentence:** A sentence that introduces the main idea close to the beginning and concludes with a series of modifiers (*The car left the expressway, slowing on the ramp and coming to a stop at the crossroad*). See *periodic sentence*.

**metaphor:** An implied comparison which attributes the qualities of one thing to another (the word *mainstream* to describe the opinions or activities of most people).

**mixed metaphor:** The incongruous use of two metaphors in the same context (*the roar of protest was stopped in its tracks*).

**narration:** The chronological presentation of events. Narration often combines with description and it may serve exposition or persuasion.

**order of ideas:** The presentation of ideas in a paragraph or an essay according to a plan. The order may be *spatial*, perhaps moving from background to foreground, or from top to bottom, or from side to side; or the order may be *temporal* or chronological (in the order of time). The presentation may be in the order of *importance*, or if the details build intensively, in the order of *climax*. The paragraph or essay may move from *problem* to *solution* or from the *specific* to the *general*. Some of these orders occur together — for example, a chronological presentation of details that build to a climax.

**parallelism:** Grammatically similar words, phrases, and clauses arranged to highlight similar ideas (*There are streets where, on January nights, fires burn on every floor of every house, sending fragrant smoke through the cold black trees. There are meadows and fields, long rows of old oaks, bridges that sparkle from afar, ships about to leave for Asia, lakes, horses and islands in the marsh* — Mark Helprin). See *antithesis*.

**paraphrase:** A rendering of a passage in different words that retain the sense, the tone, and the order of ideas.

**periodic sentence:** A sentence that builds to the main idea (*Building speed as it curved down the ramp, the car raced into the crowded expressway*). See *loose sentence*.

**personification:** Giving animate or human qualities to something inanimate or inhuman (The sun *smiled* at the earth).

**persuasion:** The use of argument or satire or some other means to change thinking and feeling about an issue.

**point of view:** The place or vantage point from which an event is seen and described. The term sometimes refers to the mental attitude of the viewer in narration. W. O. Mitchell's *Who Has Seen The Wind* narrates the adventures of a boy on the Canadian prairies from the point of view of the boy, not of an adult.

**premise:** See *syllogism*.

**process:** An activity or operation containing steps usually performed in the same order. The process may be mechanical (changing a tire), natural (the circulation of the blood), or historical (the rise and spread of a specific epidemic disease such as bubonic plague at various times in history).

**purpose:** The aim of the essay as distinguished from the means used to develop it. The purposes or aims of writing are many; they include expressing personal feelings or ideas, giving information, persuading readers to change their thinking about an issue, inspiring readers to take action, giving pleasure. These purposes may be achieved through description, narration, exposition, or argument. These means can be used alone or in combination, and an essay may contain more than one purpose.

**reflection:** An essay that explores ideas without necessarily bringing the exploration to completion. The reflective essay can take the form of a loosely organized series of musings or tightly organized arguments.

**satire:** Ridicule of foolish or vicious behaviour or ideas for the purpose of correcting them. *Social satire* concerns foolish but not dangerous behaviour and ideas — for example, coarse table manners, pretentious talk, harmless gossip. Robertson Davies's *Tempest-Tost* is a social satire. *Ethical satire* attacks vicious or dangerous behaviour or ideas — religious or racial bigotry, greed, political corruption. Stephen Leacock's *Arcadian Adventures with the Idle Rich* is an ethical satire.

**simile:** A direct comparison between two things (*A growing child is like a young tree*). See *figure of speech, metaphor.*

**simple sentence:** A sentence consisting of a single main or independent clause and no subordinate or dependent clauses (*The rain started at nightfall*).

**slang:** Colourful and sometimes short-lived expressions peculiar to a group of people, usually informal in usage and almost always unacceptable in formal usage (*nerd, goof off*).

**style:** A distinctive manner of speaking and writing. A writing style may be plain in its lack of metaphor and other figures of speech. Another may be highly colourful or ornate.

**subordinate clause:** A clause that completes a main clause or attaches to it as a modifier (She saw *that the rain had begun*. *When it rains*, it pours).

**syllogism:** The formal arrangement of premises and conclusions of a deductive argument. The premises are the general assumptions or truths (*All reptiles are cold-blooded vertebrates. All snakes are reptiles*) from which particular conclusions are drawn (*All snakes are cold-blooded vertebrates*). This formal arrangement helps to test the validity or correctness of the reasoning from premises to conclusion. See *deductive argument.*

**symbol:** An object that represents an abstract idea. The features of the symbol (the five joined rings of the Olympic flag) suggest characteristics of the object symbolized (the meeting of athletes from five continents for friendly competition). A *sign* need not have this representative quality: a green light signals "go" and red light "stop" by conventional agreement.

**thesis:** The central idea that organizes the many smaller ideas and details of the essay.

**tone:** The phrasing or words that express the attitude or feeling of the speaker or writer. The tone of a statement ranges from the angry, exasperated, and sarcastic, to the wondering or approving. An ironic tone suggests that the speaker or writer means more than the words actually state.

**topic sentence:** Usually the main or central idea of the paragraph that organizes details and subordinate ideas. Though it often opens the paragraph, the topic sentence can appear later — in the middle or at the end of the paragraph.

**transition:** A word or phrase (*however, thus, in fact*) that connects clauses and sentences. Parallel structure is an important means of transition.

**unity:** The connection of ideas and details to a central controlling idea of the essay. A unified essay deals with one idea at a time.

# COPYRIGHTS AND ACKNOWLEDGEMENTS

The editors wish to thank the publishers and copyright holders for permission to reprint the selections in this book, which are listed below in order of their appearance:

COUNTRY SUPERSTITIONS  From *Wandering Through Winter* by Edwin Way Teale (Dodd, Mead and Company, Inc., 1966). Reprinted by permission of the publisher. Selection title by editors.

THE OLD HOUSE  From *Obasan* by Joy Kogawa © 1981. Reprinted by permission of Lester and Orpen Dennys Publishers, Ltd., Canada. Selection title by editors.

SEPTEMBER CHRISTMAS  By Gary L. Saunders, reprinted from *The Atlantic Advocate*, December 1986. Reprinted by permission of the author.

THE VIKINGS  By Robert McGhee, reprinted from *Canadian Geographic*, August/September 1988, 12–21. Reprinted by permission of the author.

MAKING HISTORY  By George Galt, reprinted from *Saturday Night*, January 1987. Reprinted by permission of the author.

VELVA, NORTH DAKOTA  From *This Is Eric Sevareid* by Eric Sevareid. Copyright © 1964 by Eric Sevareid. Reprinted by permission of the Harold Matson Company, Inc. Selection title by editors.

THE WINDLESS WORLD  From *Raisins and Almonds* by Fredelle Bruser Maynard (Doubleday, 1972). Reprinted by permission of the author.

THE ETERNAL QUEST  By Debra Black, reprinted from *Equinox*, January/February 1987. Reprinted by permission of the author.

WALKER BROTHERS COWBOY  From *Dance of the Happy Shades* by Alice Munro. Copyright © 1968 by Alice Munro. Reprinted by permission of McGraw-Hill Ryerson Limited.

THE URBAN LIFE  From *The Scotch* by John Kenneth Galbraith. Copyright © 1964, 1985 by John Kenneth Galbraith. Reprinted by permission of Houghton Mifflin Company.

DONALD CREIGHTON  From "The Northern Empire: Donald Creighton" from *Radical Tories* by Charles Taylor (Toronto: House of Ananoi Press, 1982). Reprinted by permission of the publisher. Selection title by editors.

DRYDEN'S BACKYARD  From *The Game* by Ken Dryden © 1983. Reprinted by permission of Macmillan of Canada, A Division of Canada Publishing Corporation. Selection title by editors.

THE MORALS OF MODERN TECHNOLOGY  By George Grant, reprinted from *Canadian Forum*, 66, October 1986, 11–17. Reprinted by permission.

ELEMENTARY TEACHING  From *The Stubborn Structure* by Northrop Frye (Methuen, 1970). Reprinted by permission of Methuen & Co.

IN AN ELEVATOR  By E.B. White. Copyright 1938 by E. B. White. From *The Second Tree From the Corner* by E.B. White. Reprinted by permission of Harper & Row, Publishers, Inc.

MY FIRST INTRODUCTION TO THE CLASSICS  From *My Early Life* by Winston S. Churchill (Charles S. Scribner's Sons, 1930). © renewed 1958 by Winston Churchill. Reprinted by permission. Selection title by editors.

HOW THE WEST WAS LOST  By Robert Fulford, reprinted from *Saturday Night*, 100 (July, 1985), 5–8. Reprinted by permission of the author.

PEACE AND WAR  From *The Russian Album* by Michael Ignatieff (Viking, 1987). Reprinted by permission of the publisher. Selection title by editors.

BEING SANTA  By Mark L. Dembert, reprinted from *The New York Times*, December 22, 1985, Magazine. Copyright © 1985 by the New York Times Company. Reprinted by permission. Selection title by editors.

ON GOING HOME  From *Slouching Towards Bethlehem* by Joan Didion. Copyright © 1967, 1968 by Joan Didion. Reprinted by permission of Farrar, Straus and Giroux, Inc.

THE WATCHER  From *Man Descending* by Guy Vanderhaeghe © 1982. Reprinted by permission of Macmillan of Canada, A Division of Canada Publishing Corporation.

QUEEN VICTORIA AT THE END OF HER LIFE  From *Queen Victoria* by Lytton Strachey. Copyright © 1921 by Harcourt Brace Jovanovich, Inc.; renewed 1949 by James Strachey. Reprinted by permission of the publisher. Selection title by editors.

ODE TO A CAFÉ   By Danielle Crittenden. Published in *The Idler*, May/June 1987. Reprinted by permission of the author.

AT TINKER CREEK   From *Pilgrim at Tinker Creek* by Annie Dillard. Copyright © 1974 by Annie Dillard. Reprinted by permission of Harper & Row, Publishers, Inc. Selection title by editors.

CENTRAL PARK   Copyright © 1956 by John Updike. Reprinted from *Assorted Prose* by John Updike, by permission of Alfred A. Knopf, Inc.

MAIN STREET   From *The Street* by Mordecai Richler. Used by permission of the Canadian Publishers, McClelland and Stewart, Toronto.

THE DEATH OF BENNY PARET   From *The Presidential Papers* by Norman Mailer. Copyright © 1960, 1961, 1962, 1963 by Norman Mailer. Reprinted by permission of the author and the author's agents, Scott Meredith Literary Agency, Inc., 845 Third Ave., New York, NY 10022. Selection title by editors.

TOBOGGANING   From *With a Pinch of Sun* by Harry J. Boyle. Copyright © 1966 by Harry J. Boyle. Reprinted by permission of Doubleday & Company, Inc.

PARENTS NIGHT   From *There's a Lot of It Going Around* by Eric Nicol. Copyright Eric Nicol. Published by Doubleday Canada Ltd. Reprinted by permission of Doubleday Canada Ltd.

ONCE MORE TO THE LAKE   By E.B. White. Copyright © 1941 by E.B. White. From *Essays of E.B. White*. Reprinted by permission of Harper & Row, Publishers, Inc.

NEW YORK   By E.B. White. Copyright © 1949, 1977 by E.B. White. From *Essays of E.B. White* by E.B. White. Reprinted by permission of Harper & Row, Publishers, Inc. Selection title by editors.

WELFARE WEDNESDAY   By William Deverell, reprinted from *Saturday Night* (January 1987), excerpt. Reprinted by permission of the author.

MDS PLAY ROULETTE WITH WOMEN'S LIVES   By June Callwood. Published in *The Humanist in Canada* (Summer 1987). Reprinted by permission.

GOOD OLD US   From *But Not In Canada* by Walter Stewart © 1976. Reprinted by permission of Macmillan of Canada, A Division of Canada Publishing Corporation.

THE HISTORIAN AS ARTIST   Copyright © 1964 by Alma Tuchman, Lucy T. Eisenberg & Jessica Tuchman Matthews. Reprinted from *Practicing History* by Barbara Tuchman, by permission of Alfred A. Knopf, Inc.

A FEW KIND WORDS FOR SUPERSTITION   By Robertson Davies, reprinted from Newsweek, 1978. Reprinted by permission of the author.

NOTES ON PUNCTUATION   From *The Medusa and the Snail* by Lewis Thomas. Copyright © 1974, 1975, 1976, 1977, 1978, 1979 by Lewis Thomas. All rights reserved. Reprinted by permission of Viking Penguin Inc.

WHAT A LOVELY GENERALIZATION!   Copyright © 1953 James Thurber. Copyright © 1981 Helen Thurber and Rosemary A. Thurber. From *Thurber Country*, published by Simon & Schuster.

GALACTIC ENCOUNTERS   By Terence Dickinson. Published in *Equinox*, November/December 1986. Reprinted by permission of the author.

TERRITORIAL BEHAVIOUR   From *Manwatching: A Field Guide to Human Behaviour* by Desmond Morris. Copyright © 1977 by Desmond Morris. Reprinted by permission of the publisher, Harry N. Abrams, Inc., New York.

WHY THE SKY LOOKS BLUE   From *The Stars in their Courses* by Sir James Jeans (Cambridge University Press). Copyrighted by and reprinted with the permission of Cambridge University Press.

THE EXPANDING UNIVERSE   From *Other Worlds* by Paul Davies. Copyright © 1980 by Paul Davies. Reprinted by permission of Simon & Schuster, Inc. Selection title by editors.

A LIBERAL EDUCATION   From *Science and Education: The Collected Essays* by Thomas H. Huxley (Greenwood Press). Reprinted by permission of the publisher.

TEACHING AS MOUNTAINEERING   By Nancy K. Hill. Copyright 1980, *The Chronicle of Higher Education*. Reprinted by permission.

THE WARFARE IN THE FOREST IS NOT WANTON   By Brooks Atkinson. Copyright © 1968 by The New York Times Company. Reprinted by permission.

THE ATHLETE AND THE GAZELLE   From *The Ascent of Man* by Jacob Bronowski with the permission of BBC Enterprises Ltd.

SCOTLAND'S FATE, CANADA'S LESSON   By Hugh MacLennan, reprinted from *Maclean's*, 1973. Reprinted by permission.

THE OLD FARM AND THE NEW FRAME   From *My Remarkable Uncle* by Stephen Leacock (McClelland & Stewart, 1942), 20–24. Copyright © 1942; reprinted by McClelland and Stewart, 1965. Reprinted by permission of the Canadian Publishers, McClelland & Stewart, Toronto.

"MANLY" AND "WOMANLY"   From *Words and Women* by Casey Miller and Kate Swift. Copyright © 1976 by Casey Miller and Kate Swift. Reprinted by permission of Doubleday, a division of Bantam, Doubleday, Dell Publishing Group, Inc.

# Author Index

**To the owner of this book:**

We are interested in your reaction to **Prose Models: Canadian, American, and British Essays for Composition** by Levin, Lynch, and Rampton.

1. What was your reason for using this book?

—— university course      —— continuing education course

—— college course      —— personal interest

                         —— other (specify)

2. In which school are you enrolled? _____

3. Approximately how much of the book did you use?

—— ¼      —— ½      —— ¾      —— all

4. What is the best aspect of the book?

5. Have you any suggestions for improvement?

6. Is there anything that should be added?

**Fold here**

---